ISBN 978-1-332-34361-4
PIBN 10316664

1 MONTH OF
FREE
READING

at

www.ForgottenBooks.com

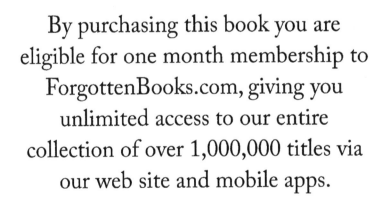

By purchasing this book you are eligible for one month membership to ForgottenBooks.com, giving you unlimited access to our entire collection of over 1,000,000 titles via our web site and mobile apps.

To claim your free month visit: www.forgottenbooks.com/free316664

English
Français
Deutsche
Italiano
Español
Português

www.forgottenbooks.com

Mythology Photography **Fiction**
Fishing Christianity **Art** Cooking
Essays Buddhism Freemasonry
Medicine **Biology** Music **Ancient**
Egypt Evolution Carpentry Physics
Dance Geology **Mathematics** Fitness
Shakespeare **Folklore** Yoga Marketing
Confidence Immortality Biographies
Poetry **Psychology** Witchcraft
Electronics Chemistry History **Law**
Accounting **Philosophy** Anthropology
Alchemy Drama Quantum Mechanics
Atheism Sexual Health **Ancient History**
Entrepreneurship Languages Sport
Paleontology Needlework Islam
Metaphysics Investment Archaeology
Parenting Statistics Criminology
Motivational

LONDON

SIMPKIN, MARSHALL, HAMILTON. KENT & CO., LMD.

PRINTED BY ALEXANDER GARDNER, PAISLEY

GALLOWAY AND THE COVENANTERS

OR

THE STRUGGLE FOR RELIGIOUS LIBERTY IN THE SOUTH-WEST OF SCOTLAND

BY

ALEX. S. MORTON

PAISLEY: ALEXANDER GARDNER
Publisher by Appointment to the late Queen Victoria

1914

"Your honourable ancestors, with the hazard of their lives, brought Christ to our hands; and it shall be cruelty to posterity if ye lose him to them."—Rutherfurd's letter to the Earl of Cassillis, Sept. 9, 1637.

PREFACE.

It is not surprising that comparatively little is known of the Covenanters of Galloway. Their story is not to be found in any single volume, but must be gleaned here and there from many scarce and curious books and other out-of-the-way sources. Believing the story worthy of telling, and of preserving, I have endeavoured to gather the threads of it together, and the following pages are the result. It has been a labour of love, carried on amidst many difficulties, and it has assumed proportions I little dreamed of when I began. No one is more conscious of its defects and short-comings than I am myself, but when it became a question of this or nothing, I preferred this.

I have freely availed myself of the works of others, and I have not hesitated to follow Wodrow closely, notwithstanding all that has been said against him.

The articles in the latter part of the volume, so placed to be less cumbersome, are not in chronological order.

" Many will be able to recognise the footprints of a remote ancestry, in situations, and under circumstances, of which they were previously ignorant. . . . ' Here, on this very spot where I now stand, centuries ago stood one whose blood I know, or believe, to be circling in my own veins. . . . His eye has rested on the same object upon which mine own rests ; and has wandered over the surrounding expanse under all the varied moods of mind which that exciting period would necessarily call forth ; and which I can yet sympathise with and appreciate. In yonder village he must certainly have signed the Covenant's " National and Solemn League " perhaps with that blood (many did so), a portion of which is the source of my own vitality. And it must have been under that time-scathed tree that his dwelling once stood— where he lived, worshipped, suffered (perhaps sinned), and died, for a cause which, if I think lightly of, I am not worthy of such a sire.' "—Preface to Minute Book of Stewartry War Committee.

CONTENTS.

PAGE

INTRODUCTION, - - - - - - 21

CHAPTER I., - - - - - - - 25

Early Scottish Covenants—Gordon of Airds, the pioneer of the Reformation in Galloway—Bishop Gordon of Galloway turns Protestant—Parliament abolishes the jurisdiction of the Pope, and ratifies the Confession of Faith—First General Assembly of the Church of Scotland—Alexander Stewart of Garlies a member.

CHAPTER II., - - - - - - - 32

Queen Mary in Scotland—Knox and the Ayr Covenant—Quentin Kennedy, prior of Whithorn—Rupture between Knox and the Master of Maxwell—The Friars Church of Kirkcudbright granted by Mary to the Magistrates—Mary's marriage to Darnley—Rising of Protestant lords—Cassillis, Maxwell, Douglas, and Gordon of Lochinvar support the Queen—Darnley murdered—Mary marries Bothwell: is defeated, taken prisoner, and resigns the crown to her son James—Galloway nobles sign Articles to oblige future Kings to defend the true religion—Mary escapes—Many Galloway families support her, but the Stewarts, Dunbars, and M'Kies declare for the Regent—Langside—Mary flees to Galloway—The Regent burns Kenmure Castle and issues a Proclamation to the Wigtownshire lairds—Plotting among the nobles—Stewart of Garlies killed—Episcopacy established—The Regent Morton executed.

CHAPTER III., - - - - - - 43

The National Covenant—Pilgrimages prohibited, and Whithorn suffers—Galloway lairds on the assize for the Ruthven conspiracy—The Black Acts—Ministers refusing to comply to quit the country—Lord Maxwell goes to Spain to urge an attack on England—Returns and musters his followers to act in concert with the Spanish Armada—The King marches against him—Maxwell's narrow escape—He flees and takes a boat at Kirkcudbright, but is captured by Sir William Stewart, brother of Garlies—Act of Annexation—Galloway Commissioners to enforce Acts against Jesuits, etc.—Galloway ministers to take subscriptions to National Covenant and

8   CONTENTS.

Confession of Faith—The King's panegyric on the Church—
The Charter of the Liberties of the Kirk—The Spanish
blanks.

CHAPTER IV.,   -   -   -   -   -   -   52
Bothwell's attempt on the Crown—Strained relations between
King and Kirk—A stormy meeting—The King's proclamation
against the ministers—He leaves Holyrood for Linlithgow—
The ministers prepare for the worst, and invite Lord
Hamilton to place himself at the head of those embracing
the cause of the Kirk—The King marches on Edinburgh, and
in the High Church justifies himself and blames the ministers.

CHAPTER V., -   -   -   -   -   -   -   55
James introduces Episcopacy—Death of Elizabeth—James goes
to England—Ministers assembled at Aberdeen apprehended—
John Welsh—The Parson of Penninghame constituted Archdeacon of Galloway—Gavin Hamilton made Bishop of
Galloway—The High Commission Court and Galloway Com-
missioners—The Glasgow Assembly of 1610—Parliament
rescinds the Act of 1592, the great Charter of Presbytery—
The Five Articles of Perth opposed by Galloway ministers,
being particularly obnoxious to Gallovidians—Death of James
—Charles visits Scotland—Distributes honours—High Commission Court established with Commissioners from Galloway
—Lord Galloway and Lord Kirkcudbright withdraw from the
Court on its showing bias against Presbyterians—Robert
Glendinning, minister of Kirkcudbright deprived of his living
—The Kirkcudbright magistrates ordered to be imprisoned
in Wigtown jail—William Dalgleish, minister of Kirkma-
breck, deposed—Samuel Rutherfurd banished to Aberdeen.

CHAPTER VI., -   -   -   -   -   -   -   64
The Laud Liturgy—Jenny Geddes in St. Giles—King appealed
to—People assemble in Edinburgh—Sydeserf Bishop of
Galloway attacked, and Earls of Wigtown and Troqueer
going to his assistance also put in danger—The National
Covenant prepared—Signed in Grey Friars Church, Edinburgh—Copies sent all over the country—Signed with
enthusiasm in Galloway—Livingston, minister in Stranraer,
takes copies to London—The King's threat against him—
The King submits—The General Assembly of 1638 makes a
clean sweep of the Bishops, and libels Sydeserf—Arranges
Presbyteries and Synods—Preparations for war—Galloway
commanders—Terms arranged—Presbyterians in Parliament
—Civil war—Battle of Newburn—Gallantry of the Galloway
troops—Son of Patrick M'Kie of Larg killed in the engagement.

CONTENTS.

CHAPTER VII., - - - - - - 74

Parliament confirms the overthrow of Episcopacy—Contest between Earl of Wigtown and Sir William Cowburn for office of hereditary usher—Galloway members of Parliament —Commissioners of Supply for Wigtownshire—The War Committee—The Galloway Commanders of horse and foot —The Solemn League and Covenant—Philiphaugh—Lord Kirkcudbright's regiment—James Agnew receives thanks of Parliament for his gallant conduct—Additional regiments raised in Galloway—New Parliament members for Galloway —List of War Committee for Wigtownshire, showing unanimity of baronage—Charles surrenders himself to the Scotch army—He is delivered to the English Commissioners, tried, and executed—The Scotch proclaim his son King— Commissioners sent to Hague to lay conditions before him— He ultimately accepts these and signs the National Covenant and the Solemn League, and is crowned—Act of Indemnity —Galloway Protesters and Resolutioners—Cromwell—The Galloway leaders divided—Cromwell's Ironsides disperse the Galloway levies—Kenmure Castle and the House of Freugh burned—Lord Galloway fined £4,000.

CHAPTER VIII., - - - - - - 85

Death of Cromwell—Restoration of Charles—Ministers arrested in Edinburgh—Cassillis refuses to sign Oath of Allegiance unless limited to civil affairs—Large sum voted to the King—List of Commissioners to collect in Wigtownshire and Stewartry—Parliament rescinds all Acts from 1640—Restoration of Bishops—Sharp made Archbishop of St. Andrews— Act of Supremacy—Synod of Galloway preparing a Petition against Episcopacy is dissolved by the Earl of Galloway— Whithorn complains to Parliament—Presbytery of Kirkcudbright appoint two of their members to present a Petition to the Privy Council—Reasonableness of the Petition— The Indemnity (so called)—Persons fined in Galloway.

CHAPTER IX., - - - - - - - 96

The Drunken Act—Nonconformist ministers in Galloway—Privy Council's Act against Galloway ministers—Certain Galloway ministers compear personally—Outed ministers—Origin of Conventicles—Induction of curates results in rioting at Kirkcudbright and Irongray—Commissioners proceed to Kirkcudbright—Lord Kirkcudbright and others sent prisoners to Edinburgh—Earlston refuses to introduce curate to his parish—Commissioners proceed to Irongray—Arnot of Littlepark sent prisoner to Edinburgh—Sympathetic visitors to the prison, and order by the Council—The Council's deliverance—Prisoners fined and banished.

CHAPTER X., - - - - - - - 106

Act against Presbyterian ministers from Ireland coming to Scotland—The Earl of Galloway and others appointed to examine
them—John Gordon of Stranraer prisoner for treasonable
speeches—Episcopal ministers' trying time—Register of the
Synod of Galloway—Complaints of parishioners absenting
themselves from preaching; of seditious ministers; of their
own hard necessitous condition; of conventicle keepers—
Bond to be tendered to disorderly parishioners—The state
of the Glenkens—Episcopalians get no support there—Kirkcowan Curate cannot get a Session—Patrick Vans of Sorbie
to be proceeded against for disorderly baptism.

CHAPTER XI., - - - - - - - 114

Proceedings against Welsh, Semple, Blackadder, Arnot, Peden,
and other ministers for keeping conventicles and baptising
—The people persecuted for hearing outed ministers—Sir
James Turner sent into Galloway to crush any opposition—
The rising at Dalry—The sufferings endured in Galloway—
Fines in Stewartry parishes—Quarterings and other aggrava-
tions.

CHAPTER XII., - - - - - - 121

Bitter persecution after Pentland—Sir William Bannatyne sent
into Galloway with large party of soldiers—Oppression of
the people—Roger Gordon of Holm, Earlston, David M'Gill
of Dalry, Gilbert Monry in Marbreck, Alexander Gordon of
Knockbrack—Bannatyne's horrible cruelty—List of persons
pursued for forfeiture—Numbers ordered to be executed
when taken—Change of King's advisers—King's Indemnity—
Long list of exceptions—Bond to keep public peace—Parties
appointed in Wigtownshire and the Stewartry to get it
signed—Differences of opinion as to its true intent and
meaning.

CHAPTER XIII., - - - - - - 128

Inquiry as to extortions by the military—Report showing what
Galloway had to suffer from Sir James Turner—Turner
dismissed—Bannatyne fined and removed from the Kingdom
—Those who have failed to take advantage of the Indemnity
to be seized—Lists of those in Carsphairn parish and Dalry
parish—Attempt on Archbishop Sharp—Pentland prisoners
dealt with—Another rising feared—Cockburn sent to the
Glenkens—Cannon of Mardrochat taken prisoner, and turns

CONTENTS. 11

informer—Indulgence—Withdrawal of troops from Galloway
—Dissensions among the Covenanters in Galloway over the
Indulgence—Mr. Park indulged to Stranraer, but Mr.
Naismith appointed by the Bishop.

CHAPTER XIV., - - - - - - 140

The parishioners of Balmaclellan and Urr fined for outrages
committed on their curates—Garthland ignores a letter from
the Privy Council to grant Row, curate of Balmaclellan, a
presentation to Stonykirk—Gilbert M'Adam of Waterhead
gets up two Bonds extorted from him—Parliament asserts
the King's supremacy over all persons and in all causes
ecclesiastical within the Kingdom—Galloway men present at
armed conventicle in Fife—The Black Act—Field preaching
a capital offence—Cassillis speaks fearlessly against it—
Anna, Countess of Wigtown, fined for attending conventicles
—Gordon of Dundeugh gets up a Bond extorted from him—
Another Indulgence to outed ministers—Parties sent out to
apprehend conventicle preachers—Reward of £400 offered
for arrest of Welsh or Semple—Galloway lairds denounced
for harbouring inter-communed persons—William M'Millan
allowed to go to Balmaclellan—Welsh betakes himself to
North of England.

CHAPTER XV., - - - - - - 147

Proclamation that all heritors to bind themselves, and be
responsible for their families and servants, not to attend
conventicles, or baptize or marry with outed ministers—
Galloway lairds protest—Murray of Broughton appointed for
Wigtown and Kirkcudbright to get the Bond signed—The
Highland Host—Their instructions—Sheriffs of Wigtown,
Kirkcudbright, and elsewhere get orders to convene heritors
to sign bonds for themselves, families, servants, tenants and
their families not to attend conventicles—Inhabitants to be
disarmed—The King takes lawburrows against his subjects
—The Highlanders ravage Ayrshire and Galloway—Lochnaw
and the House of Freugh suffer from them—Highlanders
return home laden with spoil as from a sacked city.

CHAPTER XVI., - - - - - - 153

Muir, Commissary Clerk at Kirkcudbright, libelled for attending
conventicles--M'Dowall of Garthland, Hay of Park, M'Dowall
of Freugh, Blair of Dunskey, and others cited for resetting
John Welsh—M'Dowall of Freugh tried for seditious speeches
at instigation of Row, the curate—Claverhouse quarters on
M'Meekan of Miltonise—M'Meekan's wife's capture, escape,
and re-capture—Bishop of Galloway gets dispensation to

reside in Glasgow or Edinburgh—Thomas Warner cited for
being at conventicles—Gordon of Earlston and many others
denounced and put to the horn for being at conventicles—
Proclamation for the arrest of Welsh, Semple, and Arnot.

CHAPTER XVII., - - - - - - 161

Troops quartered in Galloway—William Kyle, Galloway minister,
captured—Sheriff's Depute appointed for Wigtownshire and
the Stewartry to enforce laws against non-conformists—
Galloway Presbyterians join others for self preservation—
Drumclog—Many flock to the Covenanters—Divided counsels
—Galloway horse exercise near Bothwell Bridge—Earl
Nithsdale ordered to call out the whole gentlemen, heritors,
and freeholders in Wigtownshire and the Stewartry, and
march to Edinburgh—The Covenanters differ about the Indulgence—Bitter feeling between them—They preach against
each other—Supplication to Monmouth—The Covenanters
cannot agree on anything, and are attacked by Livingstone
—Gallant conduct of Galloway men who are ordered to retire
from Bothwell Bridge—Defeat and rout of the Covenanters
—Gordon of Earlston killed—Proclamation against rebels—
Claverhouse follows the fugitives to Galloway, and harasses
the country—Andrew Sword tried and executed.

CHAPTER XVIII., - - - - - - 169

The Scottish nobility petition the King against Lauderdale in
"Some Particular Matters of Fact"—What Presbyterians
admittedly had to suffer—Forfeitures against those at Bothwell—Galloway gentlemen the first sacrifices—M'Dowall of
Freugh forfeited, and his estate granted to Claverhouse—
Other Galloway lairds forfeited—Bishop Aitken allowed to
reside in Edinburgh—Commission to get lists of those at
Bothwell—Instructions for regulating the Indulgence, with
special reference to Galloway—Garrisons placed at Kenmure
and Freugh.

CHAPTER XIX., - - - - - - 178

Graham has commission to uplift the moveables of fugitives in
Galloway—Court at New Galloway—The Societies—The
Sanquhar Declaration supported by Galloway men—Proclamation against Cameron and others—All persons over
sixteen years of age to be cited in Minnigaff, Penninghame,
Carsphairn, Balmaclellan, Dalry, Kells, Irongray, and other
parishes to declare what they know of the traitors—The
oath sworn by the King.

CONTENTS.

CHAPTER XX., - - - - - - 184

Seven troops of horse and a regiment of foot sent into Galloway—
The country harassed—Incredible losses inflicted in Galloway
parishes—Ayrsmoss—John Malcolm, Dalry, captured and
executed—The Sheriff of Galloway ordered to sentence
tradesmen and others refusing to work for the orthodox
clergy—Courts at New Galloway, Dalry, and Kirkcudbright
—Proceedings ordered against those in Wigtown and Kirkcudbright in the late rebellion—The Test Act—Garrisons at
Dumfries and the House of Freugh—Persons forfeited for
Bothwell to be pursued to the death—List of those in
Galloway—Sir James Dalrymple refuses the Test—The
Steward of the Stewartry, Sir Andrew Agnew, Viscount
Kenmure, and the Earl of Galloway refuse the Test, and
are deprived of their heritable jurisdictions—Wigtown Burgh
takes the Test.

CHAPTER XXI., - - - - - - 193

Claverhouse sent into Galloway with troops—He is granted a
Sheriff's commission for Kirkcudbright, Wigtownshire, and
Dumfries—Letters from Claverhouse referring to the Gordons
and to Sir James Dalrymple of Stair—Claverhouse captures
M'Clurg, the Minnigaff smith—A trooper in trouble—Soldiers
ordered to Kirkcudbright to secure Lord Livingstone in the
Estates forfeited to him—Claverhouse writes Viscount Ken-
mure to prepare his house for a garrison—His persecutions
—He seizes John Archibald, Anthony M'Bride, John
Cleanochan, and John Wallace, imprisons them in Stranraer,
and quarters horses at their houses—A troop of the horse in
Anwoth.

CHAPTER XXII., - - - - - - 203

Major Learmond, Barscobe, and others captured, and ordered to
be hanged—Execution not carried out—Letter showing how
soldiers quartered in Galloway—Andrew Heron of Kirroughtree dealt with for harbouring his son—Fined 5,000 merks,
and imprisoned till it is paid—Claverhouse forces Sir John
Dalrymple to appear before the Council—Dalrymple fined
£500, and committed to Edinburgh Castle till it is paid.

CHAPTER XXIII., - - - - - - 208

William Martin of Dullarg indicted for treason—He produces a
renunciation, and the diet is deserted—William M'Clelland of
Auchenguil, Hugh Maxwell of Cuill, and William M'Culloch
of Cleichred libelled—Edward Atkin, Earlston's servant,
sentenced to be hanged—Proclamation appointing persons

to see the Test is taken in Galloway—John Cochrane of
Waterside, tried at Ayr Circuit, and forfeited—William
Thorburn of Stranraer forfeited—His sufferings—Cornet
Graham holds Courts at Balmaghie—Courts at the Clachan
of Penninghame—William M'Ewmont refusing the Test, is
banished, and dies at sea—Thomas Lidderdale's persecutions
in Twynholm—Report by Claverhouse on his work in
Galloway.

CHAPTER XXIV., - - - - - - 215

Coltrane, Provost of Wigtown, David Graham, and Sir Godfrey
M'Culloch of Mertoun tender the Test in Wigtownshire—
List of Wigtownshire lairds refusing the Test—Wigtown
Burgh grants Bond to the King—The Commissioners hold
Courts at Wigtown—Examples of their dealings—Accused
parties committed to irons, fined, banished to the plantations,
and others sent for trial before the Lords of Justiciary.

CHAPTER XXV., - - - - - - 221

Commission to try "divers desperate rebels" in Kirkcudbright,
Wigtown, and Dumfries—James M'Gachan in Dalry and
others transported—Garrisons at Kenmure, Machermore,
Minnigaff, and Carsphairn—The Cochranes of Ochiltree and
Waterside denounced rebels—The fugitive roll applicable
to Galloway—"A list of very good people persecuted for
conscience's sake"—Nearly 220 Galloway people to be
apprehended.

CHAPTER XXVI., - - - - - - 232

New Justiciary Courts—Appointments for Wigtownshire, the
Stewartry, and Dumfries—Instructions to seize all preachers,
to turn out wives and children of forfeited persons, to impose fines and quarter on the stubborn, to suffer no man to
travel with arms except gentlemen of known loyalty who
have taken the Test; to allow no yeoman to travel three
miles from his house without a pass—Hay of Park sent
prisoner to Blackness—Liberated a year later on Bond for
£1,000—Courts at Dumfries, Kirkcudbright, and Wigtown—
A "Cheerful" offer to his Majesty of twenty months' cess—
William Martin and James Martin of Dullarg fined at Kirkcudbright—Their sufferings—James Martin dies in prison—
The Society's "Apologetical Declaration"—Proclamation
against it—Cruel persecutions—James Graham, Crossmichael,
executed, and William Auchenleck, Buittle, shot dead without any reason—The Laird of Lagg at Dalry—Courts at
Twynholm and Kirkcudbright.

CHAPTER XXVII., - - - - - - 240

Women as well as men cited and examined on oath—Gavin M'Clymont, Carsphairn, has seven cows taken away—John Corson, Borgue, imprisoned and fined 6,000 merks—Intention to sentence his wife to be drowned at Kirkcudbright—Lagg holds Courts at Carsphairn—Peter Pearson, curate of Carsphairn, sits in Court and informs against the inhabitants —The Glenkens has one visitation after another—Mrs. M'Dowall of Gillespie forced to retire to Ireland—Charles Stewart of Knock apprehended by Claverhouse, and imprisoned in Stranraer—Auchencloy—The troops' oppressions in Galloway—John Hallam executed.

CHAPTER XXVIII., - - - - - - 244

Death of Charles—General Election, and members for Galloway —James grants an Indemnity—Sir James Dalrymple and others put to the horn—Edward Kyan, from Water of Minnock, shot dead—Dunbar of Baldoon, M'Culloch of Myreton, and others, to assist Colonel Douglas to put down rebels —Five men shot at Ingleston cave—M'Kie of Larg with the rebels—Andrew M'Quhan shot dead—Second Sanquhar Declaration—David Halliday and George Short shot dead —Machermore garrison strengthened—Ochiltree, Earlston, Craighlaw, and other estates annexed to the Crown.

CHAPTER XXIX., - - - - - - 251

Major Wynram stationed at Wigtown—Barnkirk house stripped —Tenant's wife imprisoned in Wigtown for eleven weeks with infant—John Wallace of Knockiebay has his house and stock despoiled—Remission to Sir James Dalrymple—His son made King's Advocate—James' Indulgences—The Cameronians hold out—Renwick seized and executed—Invitation to the Prince of Orange—His Declaration for Scotland—He lands at Torbay, accompanied by Sir James Dalrymple— Report of 10,000 Irish Papists burning Kirkcudbright—The Privy Council's proclamation for the defence of religion— The Galloway Commanders—The Cameronians in arms— Grierson of Lagg—William orders a meeting of Scotch Estates at Edinburgh—The Galloway representatives—The Convention guarded by the Cameronians—Sir John Dalrymple refutes the claim of Divine Right put forward for James—The Crown settled on William and Mary—Parliament abolishes Prelacy—Synod of Galloway—General Assembly meets.

CHAPTER XXX., - - - - - - 262

DALRY RISING.

Sir James Turner sent into Galloway to collect fines—John M'Clelland of Barscobe, John Maxwell of Monreith, Colonel Wallace, and another rescue Grier from soldiers near Dairy, and induce others to join them—Encounter with soldiers at Balmaclellan—The Covenanters' Rising—March on Dumfries and seize it, Sir James Turner being taken prisoner—They return to Dalry, and proceed north—Welsh, Veitch, and M'Kail join them at Bridge of Doon—Invitation from Clydesdale—March to Muirkirk—Renew the Covenants at Lanark, and issue Declaration—March to Bathgate—Their forlorn appearance—At Rullion Green—The Royal troops come up to them (28th November, 1666) and put them to flight— Proclamation by the Government—John Maxwell's narrow escape—Excerpt from Glasserton Session Records—Document showing William Maxwell had no accession to the Rebellion —Eleven prisoners sentenced to be executed, including M'Culloch of Barholm, Captain Arnot, and the Gordons of Knockbrex--Neilson of Corsock executed, though Turner tries to save him—John Grierson and William Welsh hanged at Dumfries—Memorial stones and inscriptions—The Martyrs' monument and inscription—James Kirk's martyrdom— William Welsh, John M'Call, James Muirhead, and others sent to Ayr to be executed.

CHAPTER XXXI., - - - - - - 286

SAMUEL RUTHERFURD.

A native of Roxburghshire—Professor of Humanity, 1623— Resigns owing to unfounded rumours—Called to Anwoth, 1627, through influence of Viscount Kenmure--His earnest life and great enthusiasm—Rutherfurd's witnesses on Mossrobin farm—Tragic death of dyker—Visit of Archbishop Ussher and traditions—The eleventh commandment—Rutherfurd summoned before High Commission Court, 1630—Publishes his famous work against Jesuits and Arminians, 1636— Summoned before the High Commission Court at Wigtown— Lord Lorne, afterwards Marquis of Argyle, befriends him, but he is deposed and ordered to confine himself in Aberdeen —Letters to his parishioners—Returns to Anwoth, 1638— Attends General Assembly of 1638 at Glasgow—Professor of Divinity at St. Andrews—Letters to people of Anwoth— Refuses professorship at Utrecht and Harderwick—Appointed one of the commission to Westminster Assembly—Publishes Lex Rex—Indicted for high treason—His answer to the summons—Died 19th March, 1661—Inscription on tombstone —Monument near Gatehouse and inscription.

CONTENTS.

CHAPTER XXXII., - - - - - - 300

ANWOTH CHURCHYARD.

Burial place of Galloway families—Martyr's tombstone and inscription—Bell of Whiteside, his thrilling adventures and hairsbreadth escapes—David Halliday of Mayfield, Robert Lennox of Irelandton, Andrew M'Robert, Beoch, James Clement, and Bell surrender on promise of quarter, but are immediately shot—Viscount Kenmure challenges Lagg for his barbarities—Tombstone in Balmaghie churchyard to Halliday and inscription—Tombstone in Twynholm churchyard to M'Robert and inscription—Tombstone in Girthon churchyard to Lennox and inscription—Tombstone to James Clement and inscription—Monument and inscription.

CHAPTER XXXIII., - - - - - - 311

Kirkwood of Sanquhar helps two Galloway Covenanters to escape —Pierson of Carsphairn a zealous persecutor—Some of the Covenanters go to reason with him—A scuffle—Pierson is shot by M'Michael—M'Michael responsible for a previous tragedy, having inflicted a mortal wound on Roan near Dalry —Engaged in Enterkin Pass rescue—M'Michael killed on Auchencloy Hill—Robert Ferguson, Robert Stuart, and John Grier shot—Martyrs' tombstone in Dalry churchyard and inscription—Tombstone to Ferguson and inscription—Martyrs' monument and inscription—Tombstone in Kirkcudbright churchyard to William Hunter and Robert Smith.

CHAPTER XXXIV., - - - - - - 319

ALEXANDER PEDEN.

Born in Ayrshire about 1626—Minister of New Luce, 1659— Ejected by the Drunken Act, 1662—Farewell services—A wanderer among the wilds of the South-west of Scotland— Charged with conventicle keeping—Joined Dalry rising but left them at Lanark—Forfeited by Act, 1669—Miraculous escapes—Arrested by Major Cowburn and sent to Bass Rock—Transferred to Edinburgh Tolbooth—Sentenced to be transported to Virginia—Sails from Leith with sixty others banished—Foretells their delivery—Liberated—Returns to Scotland—Foretells the Covenanters' defeat at Bothwell— Preaching in Galloway—Predicts his own death, and that his body will be raised from the grave—His prophecy of the death of John Brown fulfilled—His last illness, death, and burial—His body raised from the grave, and re-interred by the soldiers at Cumnock—Tombstone and inscription— Monument and inscription.

CHAPTER XXXV., - - - - - - 329

Martyrs' tombstone to John Wallace, William Heron, John Gordon, and William Stuart—Monument and inscription—Story of their martyrdom—Edward Gordon and Alexander M'Cubbin hanged at Irongray—Tombstone and inscription—Robert Grierson banished to West Indies, and returns after the Revolution.

CHAPTER XXXVI., - - - - - - 335

Earlston Castle—Disciples of Wickliffe welcomed to Earlston—Religious meetings in Wood of Airds—Alexander Gordon, refusing to receive curate at Dalry, is fined and banished to Montrose—Member of General Assembly of 1638—The Bishop unsuccessfully objects to him—Some of Rutherfurd's letters addressed to his son William—William refuses to assist Commission to settle curate at Irongray, and himself claims the right of patronage—Indicted for conventicle keeping and banished—Returns to Scotland—Prepares to join the Covenanters at Bothwell, but, being delayed, sends his son and follows later—Not knowing of the Covenanters' defeat, he encounters a body of English dragoons at Crookitstone, and refusing to submit is killed—Buried in Glassford churchyard—Monument to his memory and inscription—His son's narrow escapes—Alexander Gordon elected by the Societies to advocate their cause abroad—He is apprehended while setting sail at Newcastle, and casts his papers overboard—He is taken to London, sent to Scotland, and condemned to be beheaded—Intention to torture him to get confessions and implicate others—Thrice reprieved, and then sent to Bass Rock—The Revolution sets him free—*Lady Earlston's Soliloquies*—Earlston a member of the Convention which settled the Crown on William and Mary.

CHAPTER XXXVII., - - - - - 347

William M'Millan of Caldow persecuted and becomes fugitive—Goes to Ireland—Licensed to preach—Arrested in Galloway—Extract from Kirkcudbright Burgh Records, showing an order for his removal to Edinburgh Tolbooth—Imprisoned at Dumfries for thirty-five months without any charge—Liberated—Failing to appear is denounced rebel—Arrested and taken to Wigtown—Sent to Kirkcudbright and then to Dumfries Castle—Imprisoned in Edinburgh and afterwards at Dunottar.

CHAPTER XXXVIII., - - - - - 354

STEWARTRY WAR COMMITTEE.

Names of Committee and of those who received their instructions
—Commissioners—Gold and silver plate surrendered for the
cause—List of those delivering up silver work with details—
Assessment imposed, and crops valued—Valuers—Definition
of " cold covenanter "—Reports by members of Committee
of cold covenanters in their respective parishes.

CHAPTER XXXIX., - - - - - - 361

ANDREW FORSYTH.

Blames his father for harbouring Covenanters—Meets Renwick—
Throws in his lot with the Covenanters—Father's opposition
—Leaves home—Adventures and escapes—Returns to Kirk-
cowan after the Revolution.

CHAPTER XL., - - - - - - 364

Patrick Laing—John Ferguson of Weewoodhead—John Clark—
Escape from Edinburgh prison—Samuel Clark—John Fraser
—John Clement — John Dempster — Retribution — David
M'Briar—Bailie Muirhead of Dumfries—M'Roy of Half Mark
—The Gordons of Largmore—Renwick in Galloway—His
adventures and escapes—M'Lurg shoots a spy and wields
the Galloway Flail—Kirkcudbright Burgh Records—Robert
M'Whae—The Kirkandrews Martyr—Alexander Linn—Craig-
moddie, Kirkcowan.

CHAPTER XLI., - - - - - - 389

IRONGRAY COMMUNION.

Awe inspiring circumstances—Congregation of 3,000 to 6,000—
Natural surroundings—Sentinels posted—The memorials of
the communion—Samuel Arnot preached in the morning—
Welsh preached " the action sermon," and Blackadder and
John Dickson of Rutherglen took part—Blackadder's simple
and impressive eloquence—" The enemy are coming, make
ready for the attack "—The Clydesdale men form in battle
array—The men of Galloway and Nithsdale follow their
example—Rumours that the enemy are about, but no trace
of them can be got—The assembly disperses, guarded to
different points by horse and foot—Torrential rainfall—Huge
conventicle next day with horse and foot on guard—Monument and inscription—Communion cups amissing—The Old
Jail at Scaur and its tradition—Escape of Welsh of Scaur—
Similar story about John Clark of Drumcloyer—The Rev.
John Blackadder, minister of Troqueer.

CONTENTS.

20 CONTENTS.

CHAPTER XLII., - - - - - - 399

Tombstone at Caldons Wood and inscription—The first erected by Old Mortality—James and Robert Dun, Thomas and John Stevenson, James M'Clive, and Andrew M'Call—Tradition of their martyrdom—Captain Urquhart's dream and death—Letter from privy council—A romantic story—Narrow escape —The Duns of Benwhat.

CHAPTER XLIII., - - - - - - 406

THE WIGTOWN MARTYRS.

Wodrow's narrative—The execution on 11th May, 1685—Scenes at the Bladnoch—Buried in Wigtown churchyard—Tombstones and inscriptions—Napier's *Case for the Crown in re. the Wigtown Martyrs proved to be Myths*—Petition by Margaret M'Lauchlan for recall of sentence of death—A reprieve granted, but not given effect to—Procedure in another case showing pardon granted—Wigtown case had no such ending —Proof of martyrdom shown by (1) Tradition, (2) Early pamphlets, (3) Earlier Histories, (4) Minutes of local Church Courts, Kirkinner, Penninghame, and Wigtown, (5) Monumental evidence—Miscellaneous—Singular dream of Margaret M'Lauchlan's daughter re. Provost Coltrain of Drummorral —The Stirling monument—The Wigtown monument.

CHAPTER XLIV., - - - - - - 441

William Johnstone—John Milroy—George Walker—Peden's prophecy—The Milroys of Kirkcalla, captured and tortured, mutilated and banished—Gilbert Milroy survives the Revolution and returns to Kirkcowan.

CHAPTER XLV., - - - - - - 446

The sufferings in Penninghame—The sufferings in Kirkinner—William Graham, the Crossmichael Martyr—Grierson of Balmaclellan—The M'Cartneys of Blaikit—John Gordon, Viscount Kenmure, and Lady Kenmure—Gabriel Semple—John Livingstone, minister of Stranraer—Knox in Galloway —The Coves of Barholm—The Galloway Covenants of 1638 —Borgue Covenant and signatures—Minnigaff Covenants and signatures.

INDEX, - - - - - - - - 479

INTRODUCTION.

Nothing stirs the enthusiasm of Scotsmen more than the story of the trials and triumphs of the Covenanters, and yet we are apt to forget that the civil and religious liberties which we now enjoy and take too much as a matter of course have been secured to us only by the noble stand and heroic sacrifices of our covenanting forefathers.

No part of Scotland figured more prominently in the struggle for religious liberty than the south-west corner called Galloway. From the dawn of the Scottish Reformation in the beginning of the sixteenth century to that wonderful Revolution in the end of the seventeenth, Galloway was the theatre of many of the vital events of that most critical time. The principal actors might play their parts elsewhere, but to Galloway they came too, and the stage is crowded with men and women of all creeds and of all characters. Here we meet with the stern and unrelenting Knox; the beautiful but ill-fated Mary; Gordon of Airds, Cassillis, and Garlics, our early reformers; Anna, Countess of Wigtown, fined for conventicle keeping; the Earl of Wigtown, ever foremost in the Privy Council against Presbyterians; Claverhouse, the heartless persecutor; Lagg, the notorious; Sir James Turner and Sir William Bannatyne sent to crush the Covenanters, the former captured by a handful of Galloway

men and the latter banished for his misdeeds; the
Earls of Linlithgow, Galloway, Annandale, Queens-
berry, Drumlanrig, and Kenmure; the Dalrymples of
Stair; Dunbars of Mochrum; Agnews of Lochnaw;
Macdoualls of Logan; Murrays of Broughton; Herons
of Kirroughtree; Dunbars of Machermore; M'Cullochs
of Barholm; Gordons of Earlston—and in fact all the
Galloway nobility and baronage and families of note;
Peden the Prophet; Rutherfurd of Anwoth; John
Welsh; Samuel Arnot, Gabriel Semple, and many
other outed ministers; Margaret M'Lachlan and
Margaret Wilson, the martyrs drowned in Bladnoch;
Neilson of Corsock; Cameron, Cargill, and Renwick,
the last of the martyrs; and a host of others whose
names will be found in the pages that follow.

Here the Covenanters first took to arms and marched
against their oppressors, and ever afterwards, where-
ever a Declaration or Claim of Right was to be made
or a blow struck for freedom, the men of Galloway
were foremost in the fray. Pentland, Drumclog,
Bothwell, Ayrsmoss, and the Sanquhar Declarations
all testify that the men of Galloway never shirked
their duty, however dangerous it might be. The Privy
Council might thunder against them the most terrible
denunciations, might send upon them vast forces of
horse and foot, let loose the Highland Host, and
subject them to the bitterest persecution that the most
cruel heart could imagine, yet in their principles they
remained firm and immovable as the granite rocks of
their beloved Galloway.

Words cannot picture the sufferings that they endured. Age or sex was no protection. Women were imprisoned, fined, and tortured for speaking to their husbands, and not revealing their hiding places, so that they might be captured and shot. Parents were similarly treated for their children, and children for their parents. History affords scarce any parallel to the atrocities committed. The country was devoured with fire and sword. The people were hunted and shot down on the moors and mountains like vermin, their bodies refused burial, and even when interred by friends raised again and hung on a gibbet. For a time the land was literally soaked with the blood of the martyrs, and there is scarcely a churchyard in Galloway but has its monument to the memory of the men and women who endured to the death rather than betray those principles which they held so dear. Others were imprisoned, fined of all they possessed, soldiers quartered on them till everything was eaten up, their crops deliberately wasted, their horses, cattle, and sheep driven away, their houses burned down, and the very plenishing destroyed or carried off. Women were outraged, and, as well as men, were tortured, mutilated, and banished from the country, many of them being ship-wrecked and lost. Their cattle and sheep were seized, and brought into the churches, and cooked at fires made from the pews and seats. The very plantations were burned, and the whole country left desolate. Trade and agriculture were at a standstill, and famine was in sight when the dawn broke.

We can to-day scarcely realise that all this was done simply because the people claimed the liberty to read the Bible, and to worship God according to their conscience; yet even the most prejudiced will admit that these were the objects, pure and disinterested, of the early Scottish Reformers, whatever motives they may ascribe to some who joined the Presbyterians towards the end of the struggle. If some who did not truly share the views of the Covenanters joined with them in the hope of gaining a material advantage, the Covenanters were not to blame, and if individuals of the Covenanters in their desperation were led to commit deeds of which we cannot approve, let us not forget that they were driven to it by the terrible persecutions and sufferings they endured; let us not judge the whole by these isolated actions, which were as soundly condemned by the Covenanters generally as they can possibly be by us. Let us not linger over the mistakes of the movement, but look to the glorious victory which the Covenanters achieved, the fruits of which the world is now enjoying.

GALLOWAY
AND THE COVENANTERS.

CHAPTER I.

Early Scottish Covenants—Gordon of Airds, the pioneer of the
Reformation in Galloway—Bishop Gordon of Galloway turns
Protestant—Parliament abolishes the jurisdiction of the
Pope, and ratifies the Confession of Faith—First General
Assembly of the Church of Scotland—Alexander Stewart of
Garlies a member.

THE story of the Scottish Covenants goes back to the
time of Knox. In the beginning of the sixteenth
century, Scotland, in common with the rest of Europe,
was under the sway of the Pope. Already reformers
had been active on the Continent, and some of them
had paid the penalty with their lives, but a glimmer
of light from the martyrs' fires had pierced even to
Scotland, so true it is that no good work is done in
vain. Knox tells us that in 1556 most of the gentlemen of Mearns vowed to refuse all society with
idolatry, and bound themselves to the utmost of their
power to maintain the true preaching of the Evangel

3

of Jesus Christ. It is not certain whether this was a written Bond or a verbal undertaking. The following year, however, a written Bond was entered into at Edinburgh, by which the subscribers vowed that " we, by His Grace, shall, with all diligence, continually apply our whole power, substance, and our very lives to maintain, set forward, and establish the most blessed word of God." Many copies of this Bond were sent out for signature, and a copy in the National Museum of Antiquities in Edinburgh has the signatures of Argyl, Glencairn, Morton, Lorne, and John Erskine.

Galloway was not behind in the great work of Reformation. Early in the sixteenth century, Alexander Gordon of Airds, in the Stewartry, entertained some of the followers of Wycliffe, and had a New Testament in the Vulgar Tongue, which he read to his neighbours, in a wood near his house, at a time when severe pains and penalties were enacted against all who did so. Among those who held the same views and attended these secret devotional meetings was Alexander Stewart, the eldest son of Stewart of Garlies. He was sent to England as a hostage for his father, who had been taken prisoner at Solway Moss, and, on his return, he preached the reformed religion in Dumfries. He was zealous for the Reformation, and was a Commissioner from the Kirks of Nithsdale to the General Assembly in 1560.

In the Scots Parliament of 1543, the first legislative step to the final overthrow of the Roman Catholic religion had been taken. The Solway Moss prisoners had been thrown into company in England which confirmed their Protestant leanings. Cassillis had lived chiefly with Cranmer and Latimer, and Garlies with followers of Wycliffe. Thus it came about that a motion was made by Lord Maxwell, a Catholic, that the Bible should be allowed to be read in the vulgar tongue. This was bitterly opposed by Archbishop Dunbar, a native of Galloway, and many others, but, after much discussion, it was carried, and, for the first time in Parliamentary strife, the prelates found themselves in a minority in the Estates.

The Archbishop had been Prior of Whithorn, and was a son of David Dunbar of Mochrum, and Janet, daughter of Sir Alexander Stewart of Garlies. He conducted the education of the young King, and discharged this important trust with much satisfaction to the rulers of the kingdom, and James took many opportunities of showing his gratitude to his early benefactor. When Beaton was appointed to the primacy of Scotland, Dunbar became Archbishop of Glasgow.

Dunbar and Bishop Wemyss of Galloway afterwards took part in the proceedings against George Wishart. When banished from St. Andrews, Wishart came to South Ayrshire and Galloway. He was supported by Lord Cassillis, Lord Glencairn, and his son, Lord Kilmaurs, and more especially by the young Laird of Garlies. William Harlow, in Dumfries, on 23rd October, 1558, denounced the Mass as rank idolatry, and proclaimed the pure Gospel of Salvation in Christ. He had begun his mission at Garlies, no doubt with the warm approval of Alexander Stewart. When the

Dean sent a legal emissary to Harlow to ask by whose authority he preached, being a layman, Garlies, who had been threatened with proceedings for encouraging heretical preachers and doctrines, boldly answered, " I do avow them, and will maintain and defend such against any or all kirkmen that may be put at them."

In Wigtownshire the good work had otherwise made a beginning. John M'Briar, Canon of Glenluce, renounced his vows in 1548, and preached the reformed religion. He was apprehended, and imprisoned in Hamilton Castle, whence he was rescued by John Lockhart of Barr, and escaped to England.

In 1558, an enraged crowd in Edinburgh attacked the procession in honour of St. Giles, the patron saint of the city, smashed the image of the saint, and maltreated those taking a principal part in the proceedings. Andrew Durie, the Bishop of Galloway, received such a fright on this occasion that he died shortly afterwards. He was succeeded by Alexander Gordon, son of John Gordon, Master of Huntly, and Jane Stewart, natural daughter of James IV. Gordon, however, had not long succeeded till he embraced the Protestant faith, and has the distinction of being the first prelate in Scotland to do so.

The leaders in the reform movement banded themselves together in an association called " The Congregation," which quickly grew in numbers and influence. " The Congregation," in 1559, summoned to Edinburgh a Parliamentary Convention, which suspended the Queen Regent, and elected a Council for the management of public affairs, four ministers being appointed to assist in the consideration of religious matters. These were Knox, Willock, Goodman, and Gordon.

In 1559, the Reformers entered into three Covenants, the first at Perth on 31st May, " to put away all things that dishonour His name, that God may be truly and purely worshipped." The second in July, at Edinburgh, was afterwards adopted at St. Andrews as " The Letteris of Junctioun to the Congregatioun," and, as such, was taken by more than three hundred persons. The third Covenant was entered into at Stirling on 1st August—all having as their general object the advancement of the Reformation. Another Covenant was entered into at Edinburgh on 27th April, 1560, and in this Bond reference is made to the oppression by the French and the help expected from the English. These were changed days from the time when Scotland and France were great allies, but the religious struggle in which Scotland as well as England was engaged, was breaking up old compacts, forming new friendships, and making many great changes. This Covenant, Knox tells us, was signed by all the nobility, barons, and gentlemen professing Christ Jesus in Scotland.

These Covenants led to the Confession of Faith, prepared by Knox, Winram, Spottiswoode, Willock, Douglas, and Row.

Parliament met at Edinburgh in August, 1560, and, as the Reformers were in the majority, the state of religion was naturally the foremost subject of consideration. Among the members were Alexander

Gordon, Bishop of Galloway; Gilbert Brown,* Abbot of New Abbey; Edward Maxwell, Abbot of Dundrennan; Robert Richardson, Commendator of St. Mary's Isle; the Earls of Cassillis and Morton; the Master of Maxwell; the Barons of Lochinvar and Garlies. This Parliament repealed the Acts favouring the Church of Rome, abolished the jurisdiction of the Pope in Scotland, prohibited the celebration of Mass under pain of death for the third conviction, and ratified the Confession of Faith, which continued from 1560 to 1647 the recognised standard of the Church of Scotland.

The first Book of Discipline was prepared for the future government of the Church. It gave rise to considerable discussion, was bitterly opposed, and many of the nobles absolutely refused to sign it. The clergy, however, approved of it. Two of its points may be noted. It provided for the institution of parish schools, and it committed the election of ministers to the people. The Book of Discipline and the Confession of Faith were both approved of by Alexander Gordon,

---

* Brown was descended from the ancient family of Carsluith in Kirkmabreck parish. Over the armorial bearings above the door of Carsluith is the date 1364, and under that, 1581. About the year 1600 this Gilbert was engaged in a controversy with the celebrated John Welsh who was sometime minister at Kirkcudbright and afterwards at Ayr. Welsh attacked the principles of the Roman Catholic faith, and Brown wrote an answer. Welsh, in replying, proposed a public disputation, which Brown declined. Brown was apprehended about 1607, and sent to Blackness. A few days afterwards he was removed to Edinburgh Castle. Shortly after that, he was allowed to leave the kingdom, and died in France in 1612.

the Earl of Morton, the Master of Maxwell, and the Barons of Garlies and Lochinvar.

One Act ever to be regretted passed by this Parliament was that which provided for demolishing Abbey Churches. Spottiswoode tells us that a pitiful devastation ensued. The churches were either defaced or pulled to the ground, the vessels employed for religious uses were destroyed or sold, and—greatest loss of all, the libraries and Church manuscripts were cast into the fire. The monasteries of Galloway suffered less than those of other places, thanks to the good offices of Lord Maxwell and other powerful proprietors. Thus the Abbey of Luce sustained no injury, and Dundrennan Abbey remained intact for the present, though it was afterwards burned down.

It may be noted that the first General Assembly of the Church of Scotland was held in December, 1560, in the Church of St. Mary Magdelene in the Cowgate of Edinburgh. There were only forty-two members, and only six of these are named as ministers. As already mentioned, Garlies represented the Kirks of Nithsdale.

CHAPTER II.

Queen Mary in Scotland—Knox and the Ayr Covenant—Quentin
Kennedy, prior of Whithorn—Rupture between Knox and
the Master of Maxwell—The Friars Church of Kirkcudbright
granted by Mary to the Magistrates—Mary's marriage to
Darnley—Rising of Protestant lords—Cassillis, Maxwell,
Douglas, and Gordon of Lochinvar support the Queen—
Darnley murdered—Mary marries Bothwell: is defeated,
taken prisoner, and resigns the crown to her son James—
Galloway nobles sign Articles to oblige future Kings to
defend the true religion—Mary escapes—Many Galloway
families support her, but the Stewarts, Dunbars, and M'Kies
declare for the Regent—Langside—Mary flees to Galloway
—The Regent burns Kenmure Castle and issues a Proclama-
tion to the Wigtownshire lairds—Plotting among the nobles
—Stewart of Garlies killed—Episcopacy established—The
Regent Morton executed.

MARY QUEEN OF SCOTS returned to Scotland from
France in 1561, her husband, Francis II., having died
at Orleans on 6th December, 1560. In 1562, she proceeded North as far as Inverness, winning many to
her side as she went. The following year, Mary came
to Galloway. She visited the Stewarts at Clary and
at Garlics, and she was entertained for two days,
13th and 14th August, 1563, by Sir John Gordon of
Kenmure. Considerable apprehension arose among
some of the Reformers as the result of her progress,
and Knox, alarmed by the rumours, prevailed on many
of the gentlemen of Ayr to enter into another Covenant

at Ayr on 4th September, 1562, in support of the true
religion.

This Covenant was in the following terms:—

" WE, whose names are under-written, do promise,
in the presence of God, and of his Son our Lord
Jesus Christ, that we, and every one of us, shall
and will maintain and assist the preaching of his
Holy Evangel, now of his mere mercy offered unto
this realm, and also will maintain the ministers of
the same against all persons, power, and authority
that will oppose the doctrine proposed, and by us
received. And further, with the same solemnity,
we protest and promise that every one of us shall
assist others, yea, and the whole body of Pro-
testants within this realm, in all lawful and just
actions against all persons; so that whosoever shall
hurt, molest, or trouble any of our body shall be
reputed enemy to the whole, except the offender
will be content to submit himself to the judgment
of the Kirk now established among us. And this
we do, as we desire to be accepted and favoured
of the Lord Jesus, and re-accounted worthy of
credit and honesty in the presence of the Godly.
At the borough of Ayr, the ferd * day of September, the year of God, MDLXII."

Knox was appointed by the General Assembly of
1562 to visit the churches in Kyle, Galloway, and
Dumfries.

* Fourth.

At Dumfries he carried through the election of
Mr. Robert Pont as Moderator for the congregations
in Dumfries and Galloway. Pont was entrusted with
the payment of parish ministers, the visitation of kirks,
and generally the duties hitherto devolving upon the
bishop. Knox had conferences with many individuals
of note on his way, and Quentin Kennedy of the House
of Cassillis, prior of Whithorn and Abbot of Crossraguel, challenged the Reformer to a public discussion,
which afterwards took place at Maybole. In May,
1563, this same Quentin was tried for having the
previous month celebrated Mass in defiance of " an
Act and Proclamation," and was adjudged to be put
in ward within the Castle of Dumbarton. He seems,
however, to have kept out of the way, and could not
be apprehended. It is interesting to note that among
those on the Assize were Lochinvar, Sir John Maxwell
of Terregles, John Dunbar of Mochrum, and Gavin
Dunbar of Baldoon. At this time, Malcolm Fleming,
Commendator of Whithorn, was also proceeded against
for celebrating Mass, and was ordered to be put in
ward in Stirling Castle, there to remain during the
pleasure of the Queen.

Mary's first Parliament in 1563 passed an Act of
Indemnity since March, 1558, and the Earl of Morton
and the Commendator of St. Mary's Isle were among
the Commissioners appointed to consider who were to
get this privilege.

When Mary was on a visit to Stirling, Mass was
celebrated in the Royal Chapel at Holyrood, and two
Presbyterian ministers forced their way into the chapel

and denounced the proceedings. Mary ordered them to be put on trial for forethought felony, and Knox at once summoned the brethren to meet him in Edinburgh to make common cause with the two ministers. This led to a rupture between Knox and the Master of Maxwell. Knox insisted that in spiritual matters he owed no allegiance to any earthly sovereign. Maxwell listened respectfully, and then replied, " Well, you will find men will not bear with you in time to come as they have in the past." He then withdrew in company with Gordon of Lochinvar, and the old familiarity between them was never renewed. Knox was afterwards tried for treason, but unanimously acquitted.

In 1564, the General Assembly besought the Queen to grant the Friars' Church of Kirkcudbright to the Magistrates to be used as a parish church. She did so, and it became the place of worship for a Protestant congregation.

Mary's marriage to Darnley in 1565 led to the rising of the Protestant lords, who were joined by Maxwell and Douglas of Drumlanrig. The Earl of Cassillis and Lord Fleming approved of the marriage. Maxwell wrote to the Queen that he had advised his friends to disband, and that they were going to Dumfries to consider the position. They refused to take Maxwell's advice. Three thousand troops speedily assembled under Mary's banner, and marched to Dumfries. As they approached, the Protestant lords withdrew to Carlisle, but Maxwell, Douglas, and Gordon of Lochinvar waited the arrival of the royal army, their loyalty on this occasion proving stronger than their love for the reformed religion. These formed a powerful trio, and still more powerful and equally devoted to the cause of the Queen was the Earl of Cassillis, whose influence in the South-west was proverbial.

> " Frae Wigtoun to the toon o' Ayr,
>   Portpatrick to the Cruives o' Cree,
> Nae man need think for to bide there
>   Unless he ride wi' Kennedy."

On 9th February, 1567, Darnley was murdered. Bothwell was the chief conspirator, and there can be no doubt but Mary was cognisant of the whole plot. On 15th May following, Mary married Bothwell. This proved her undoing. Few had heart to support her cause, and a month later she was taken prisoner by the Earl of Morton, and lodged in Lochleven Castle, and there Mary, on 24th July, 1567, was prevailed upon to resign the Crown to her infant son, James, and to constitute the Earl of Moray Regent of the realm. The following day the nobles, barons, and commissioners of towns signed certain Articles—in fact, another Covenant—in which they bound themselves, among other things, to punish crimes, especially the murder of Darnley, to defend the young prince, and bring him up in the fear of God, and to oblige future Kings and rulers to promise before their Coronation to maintain, defend, and set forward the true religion. Among those who subscribed this were the following:—The Earl of Morton, Alexander Gordon, Bishop of Galloway, Kennedy of Blairwham,

Dunbar of Mochrum, Douglas of Drumlanrig, James Dalrymple of Stair, predecessor of the Earl of Stair, Stewart of Garlies, Thomas MacDowall, Charles Murray of Cockpool, afterwards Viscount of Annan and Earl of Annandale, Gordon of Lochinvar, Maclellan of Bombie, James Rig, Provost of Dumfries, James Wallace in Dumfries, M'Culloch of Cardoness, John Gordon, younger, of Craighlaw, John Cathcart of Carleton, the Laird of Myretoun, Murray of Broughton, Alexander Crichton of Newhall, Patrick M'Kie of Larg, Roger Grierson of Lag, Vaus or Vans of Barnbarroch, and William Kirkpatrick of Kirkmichael.

On 2nd May, 1568, Mary escaped from Loch Leven Castle, and many powerful nobles ranged themselves on her side. These included the Lords Herries and Maxwell, the Abbot of Dundrennan, Gordon of Lochinvar, Maclellan of Bombie, Douglas of Drumlanrig, Sheriff Agnew of Galloway, Bishop Gordon of Galloway, the Commendators of Dundrennan, Soul-seat, and Glenluce, the Kennedys headed by the M'Cullochs, Gordons of Craighlaw, the Baillies of Dunragit, all of whom put their forces in the field. The Stewarts of Garlies, the Dunbars, and the M'Kies declared for the Regent. The close connection of the Stewarts with Darnley accounts for them having remained unsoftened to Mary during her subsequent troubles. Six thousand men gathered under Mary's banners, but Langside, 13th May, 1568, proved fatal to her cause. Among her supporters taken prisoners were the eldest sons of the Earls of Eglinton and Cassillis, and the

Sheriff of Ayr. Mary herself watched the engagement
from an eminence half a mile distant, and when she
saw that all was lost, she sought safety in flight. She
was accompanied by the Master of Maxwell and his
followers of Galloway men, who were accused of
seizing the horses of their companions in arms to make
greater speed. A tradition has come down that, when
they were passing through the Glenkens, Earlston
Castle, which had been built by and was occasionally
the residence of Bothwell, was pointed out to Mary,
and that she became much agitated and burst into
tears. There is, however, good reason to doubt whether
Mary came this way. The result of careful historical
research is rather in favour of the Dumfriesshire route.
Mary waited a night or two in Galloway, and then
crossed to England, never to see Scotland again. She
left Galloway at a place called Port Mary, and her
landing place in England is now called Mary Port.

One result of this effort on behalf of Mary was
that the Regent brought an army into Galloway to
punish those who had befriended her. He reached
St. John's town of Dalry on 15th June, where he expected to receive the submission of Sir John Gordon
of Lochinvar. As the latter did not appear, the Regent
marched to Kenmuir Castle, burned it, and then destroyed the houses of others in the neighbourhood who
had supported Mary. He issued a proclamation to
the lairds of Wigtounshire, calling on them to answer
before him at Ayr on 20th March to such things as
might be laid to their charge. It was in these terms:—

"JAMES, by the grace of God, with advice and consent of our dearest cousin, our Regent—We charge straitly Patrick Agnew, Sheriff of Galloway; Hugh Kennedy of Chappell, Master Patrick Vaux of Barnbarroch, Thomas Baillie of Little Dunraggit, Andrew Bailzie of Dunraggit, Alexander Gordon of Craighlaw, Thomas Hay, Abbot of Glenluce; Archibald Kennedy of Sinnyness, William Kennedy, M'Culloch of Ardwell, M'Culloch of Kelleser, to compeer personally before our dearest goodsir and Regent, upon the 20th of March inst., at Ayr, to answer such things as shall be laid to their charge, under the pain of tresson; with certification to any of them gif they failzie, ye said day being by-past, they shall be repute, halden, esteemit, demesnit, and pursuit with fire and sword, as traitors and enemies to God, us their sovereign, and their native countrie."

It was about this time that Cassillis was negotiating for a lease of the Abbey lands of Glenluce, when the Abbot died before the bargain was completed. Cassillis, however, was not the man to let a trifle like this stand in his way. He got a monk to forge the dead man's signature to a deed purporting to convey. the lands to him. Then, fearing the monk might betray him, he employed a man, Carnochan, to murder the monk, and then, afraid that Carnochan might reveal too much, he induced his kinsman, Hew Kennedy of Bargany, to accuse Carnochan of theft and hang him in Crossraguel. "And sa the landis of Glenluce was conqueist."

During the minority of the King, there was plotting and counter-plotting among the nobles. The Regent Moray was murdered in 1570. He had given the first sanction of the Crown to the Reformation, and had secured a short period of rest to the struggling Church, and thus earned the title of "The Good Regent." For some time after his death, the country was in a deplorable state. There were two contending factions —one in support of the young King, and the other in favour of Mary—but each more intent on gaining its own private ends than anything else. No man's property or life was safe, industry was at a standstill, and the nation was rapidly sinking into a state of barbarism and bankruptcy. At last, on 12th July, 1570, the Earl of Lennox, who, as the father of Darnley, naturally belonged to the King's party, was appointed Regent with the approval of Elizabeth, but the Queen's supporters avowed their resolution never to acknowledge him, and both parties prepared for war. Lennox was fatally wounded in an attack on Stirling in September, 1571, and at the same time the gallant Alexander Stewart of Garlies fell while bravely supporting his kinsman. The Earl of Mar was then chosen Regent. He died on 28th October, 1572, and his death was not free from the suspicion of poison. The Earl of Morton was the most able and powerful of the nobility. He was supported by the great majority of the nobles, by the influential party of the Church, and by Elizabeth, and he was accordingly chosen Regent on 24th November, 1572.

The same day died Knox, in his sixty-seventh year.

In this year also, the representatives of the Privy Council and a committee of ministers came to an arrangement which amounted to nothing less than the establishing of Episcopacy in the Church of Scotland. It was agreed " (1) That the names and titles of the archbishops and bishops be not altered, or the bounds of the dioceses confounded, but that they continue in time coming, as they did before the reformation of religion, at least till the king's majesty's majority or consent of Parliament; (2) that the archbishoprics and bishoprics vacant should be conferred on men endowed, as far as may be, with the qualities specified in the Epistles of Paul to Timothy and Titus; (3) that to all archbishoprics and bishoprics that should become vacant, qualified persons should be presented within a year and a day after the vacancy took place, and those nominated to be thirty years of age at the least; (4) that the spiritual jurisdiction should be exercised by the bishops in their dioceses; (5) that abbots, priors, and inferior prelates, presented to benefices, should be tried as to their qualification and their aptness to give voice in Parliament, by the bishop or superintendent of the bounds, and upon their collation should be admitted to the benefice, but not otherwise; (6) that the elections of persons presented to bishoprics should be made by the chapters of the cathedral churches; and because the chapters of divers churches were possessed by men provided before his

Majesty's coronation, who bore no office in the Church, that a particular nomination of ministers should be made in every diocese, to supply their rooms until the benefice should fall void; (7) that all benefices, with cure under prelacies, should be conferred on actual ministers, and on no others; (8) that ministers should receive ordination from the bishops of the diocese, and where no bishop was as yet placed, from the superintendent of the bounds; (9) that the bishops and superintendents, at the ordination of ministers, should exact of them an oath for acknowledging his Majesty's authority, and for obedience to their ordinary in all things."

In 1578, Parliament approved of the demission of the Regency by Morton, and of the King taking the government upon himself, but Morton still retained the real power. The day came, however, when he too found the intrigues against him too much. He was ultimately accused of Darnley's murder, condemned, and executed, though great efforts were made to save him by Elizabeth's representative. The barony of Prestoun, in the Stewartry which belonged to Morton, with the Castle of Wreaths which he frequently occupied, was, upon his forfeiture, granted to the family of Nithsdale.

CHAPTER III.

The National Covenant—Pilgrimages prohibited, and Whithorn suffers—Galloway lairds on the assize for the Ruthven conspiracy—The Black Acts—Ministers refusing to comply to quit the country—Lord Maxwell goes to Spain to urge an attack on England—Returns and musters his followers to act in concert with the Spanish Armada—The King marches against him—Maxwell's narrow escape—He flees and takes a boat at Kirkcudbright, but is captured by Sir William Stewart, brother of Garlies—Act of Annexation—Galloway Commissioners to enforce Acts against Jesuits, etc.—Galloway ministers to take subscriptions to National Covenant and Confession of Faith—The King's panegyric on the Church—The Charter of the Liberties of the Kirk—The Spanish blanks.

In spite of the Covenants that had been signed, matters did not go altogether smooth for the Reformers. The King, who had now arrived at years of discretion, was far from favourable to them, but was afraid to risk too much, yet, notwithstanding the vacillating policy of both King and Parliament, and their frequent efforts to impose the order of Bishops on the Church, the Reformers persevered in their noble work, and all previous Covenants were eclipsed in interest and importance by the National Covenant, or the second Confession of Faith, prepared by John Craig, minister of Holyrood House. Its original title was " Ane Short and General Confession of the True Christiane Faith and Religione, according to God's verde, and Actis of our Parliamentis, subscryved by the Kingis Majestie and his household with sindrie otheris to the glorie of God and good example of all men at Edinburghe the 28th day of Januare, 1580, and 14th yeare of his Majestie's reigne." In it the subscribers " protest, that, after long and due examination of our own consciences . . . we are now thoroughly resolved in the truth by the spirit and Word of God, and therefore we believe . . . and constantly affirm before God and the whole world, that this only is the true Christian faith and religion, pleasing God and bringing salvation to man, which now is, by the mercy of God revealed to the world by the preaching of the blessed evangel." The Confession of Faith is upheld, and then it proceeds: "And therefore we abhor and detest all contrary religion and doctrine; but chiefly all kind of Papistry in general and particular heads, even as they are now damned and confuted by the Word of God and Kirk of Scotland." This Covenant is now preserved in the Advocate's Library, Edinburgh. The immediate occasion of it was the discovery of a secret dispensation from Rome agreeing to the profession of the reformed religion by Roman Catholics, but instructing them at the same time to promote to the best of their ability "the ancient faith." It was well enough known in many quarters that the King was in sympathy with the policy of Rome, but he durst not resist the indignation of the people against the Romish intrigues, and so he and his household signed the Covenant. It was afterwards subscribed by all ranks throughout the kingdom, and the ministers of

Galloway were particularly zealous in getting it signed throughout their respective parishes.

The Act of 1581 (7 James VI., Cap. 104), prohibiting the observance of Saints' Days, and suppressing pilgrimages, must have told severely on Wigtownshire. Royal and other pilgrims to the Shrine of St. Ninian at Whithorn had spent lavishly as they passed to and fro, but now this was all at an end.

In 1582, some of the Protestant lords, alarmed by learning that the King had consented to arraign them for conspiracy against his person, seized the King at Ruthven Castle, and kept him prisoner for nearly a year. He then escaped, punished some of the conspirators, and pardoned others. Among those on the Assize were the Master of Cassillis, Patrick Agnew, Sheriff of Galloway; John Gordon of Lochinvar, and William M'Culloch of Myrtoun. Parliament met in May, 1584, and set about the overthrowing of the Presbyterian policy. Only these from whom no opposition was apprehended were summoned to the meeting, and they were sworn to secrecy at the opening of each sitting. When some of the ministers got a hint of what was going on, and sent representatives to protest, they found the doors so closely guarded that they could not obtain admission. The Rev. David Lindsay was selected to carry a protest to the King, but he was arrested and sent a prisoner to Blackness. These Acts thus passed became known as the Black Acts, and by them " (1) The ancient jurisdiction of the three estates was ratified (one of the three being the bishops), and to speak evil of any one of them is treason. (2) The King was supreme in all causes and over all persons, and to decline his judgment is treason. (3) All convocations not specially licensed by the King are unlawful (Church Courts are thus made to depend on the King's will). (4) The chief jurisdiction of the Church lies with the bishops (who thus take the place of Assemblies and Presbyteries). (5) None shall presume, privately or publicly, in sermons, declamations, or familiar conferences, to utter any false, untrue, or slanderous speeches, to the reproach of his Majesty or council, or meddle with the affairs of his highness and estate, under the pains contained in the Acts of Parliament made against the makers and reporters of lies."

Three months afterwards, a further Act was passed —that all ministers must, within forty days, subscribe the Acts concerning the King's jurisdiction over all estates, temporal and spiritual, and promise to submit themselves to the bishops, their ordinaries, under pain of being deprived of their stipends. As was to be expected, many of the ministers refused, and were commanded to quit the country within twenty days. Some of them fled, but others remained and preached openly, and disturbances took place in several parts of the country.

The General Assembly met with the Royal sanction in May, 1586, and James seemed desirous for a better understanding between the two parties. David Lindsay was elected Moderator, the King himself voting for him. It was decided that "bishops" should mean only such as are described by St. Paul; that they

might visit certain bounds assigned to them, subject
to the advice of the Synod; and that in receiving pre-
sentations and giving collation to benefices, they must
act according to the direction of the Presbytery, and
they were to be answerable for their whole conduct to
the General Assembly. It was also agreed to have
annual meetings of the Assembly.

In April, 1587, Lord Maxwell went abroad, giving
surety that he would attempt nothing prejudicial to
the reformed religion. He kept faith by going straight
to Spain where the Invincible Armada was being fitted
out, and he urged that England should be attacked
through Scotland, and in pursuance of this scheme he
landed at Kirkcudbright the following year, and
mustered his kinsmen and adherents to act in concert
with the Armada on its arrival. Maxwell was at once
summoned before the King, but replied by arming the
royal castles of Lochmaben, Dumfries, Threave, and
Langholm, and his own castle of Caerlaverock. The
King at once marched to Dumfries, and Maxwell
narrowly escaped being captured. While the royal
troops were at the gate, he jumped on a horse, and
galloped to Kirkcudbright, where he embarked with
some others on a small boat, and set out in the hope of
falling in with the Armada. He was followed in
another boat by Sir William Stewart, brother of the
Laird of Garlies, and captured on the Carrick coast,
and sent prisoner to Edinburgh. All those who were
in the boat with him were condemned to the gallows.
Maxwell himself, however, was liberated the following
year, and he was afterwards appointed one of the

Commissioners to assist Lord Hamilton as Lord Lieutenant while the King was in Norway.

Parliament, in July, 1587, passed an Act of Annexation, by which the temporal possessions of bishoprics, abbacies, and priories went to the Crown, and this meant practically the uprooting of Episcopacy, as the bishops, deprived of their baronial possessions, could not exert the same influence. The measure was afterwards regretted by the King when the nature of its operation became apparent, but the lands that thus fell to him had passed out of his hands to needy, and greedy courtiers, and no remedy was left.

In 1588, the King signed "The General Bond," to protect "the said true religion," and at Aberdeen, on 30th April, 1589, he and many others subscribed still another Bond "for the defence and suretie of the said trew religioun," and for the pursuit of "Jesuitis Papistis of all sortis, their assisteris and pairttakaris."

Certain Acts having been passed against "Jesuits, Seminarie Priests, and ex-communicated persons," Commissioners were appointed to see these enforced. In Wigtownshire this duty was entrusted to Alexander Stewart of Garlics; Uthred M'Dowell of Garthland, and Patrick Vaux of Barnbarroch, and in the Stewartry to John Gordon of Lochinvar, Thomas M'Clelland of Bombie, and James Lidderdale of St. Mary's Isle.

The Lords of Privy Council also authorised certain ministers to take the subscriptions of the inhabitants to the National Covenant and the Confession of Faith, Mr. James Hamilton and Mr. David Blythe being appointed for the Stewartry of Kirkcudbright, and

Mr. Ninian M'Clenachan and Mr. John Young for Wigtownshire.

James personally attended the General Assembly of 1590, and delivered a panegyric upon the Church of Scotland which has often been quoted. He praised God that he had been born " in such a time as that of the light of the Gospel, and in such a place as to be King in such a Kirk, the purest Kirk in the world. The Kirk of Geneva keepeth Pasche and Yule.* What have they for them? They have no institution, and as for our neighbour Kirk in England their service is an evil-said mass in English, wanting nothing but the liftings.† I charge you, my good people, ministers, doctors, elders, nobles, gentlemen, and barons, to stand to your purity, and exhort the people to do the same, and I, forsooth, so long as I brook my life and crown, shall maintain the same against all deadly."

Finding himself faced by certain difficulties, and anxious to secure the aid of the Kirk, he began to flatter it by unwonted concessions. The General Assembly was not slow to notice this, and resolved to take full advantage of it, so when Parliament met in June, 1592, the Assembly presented the following requests:—(1) That the Acts of Parliament made in the year 1584 against the discipline and liberty of the Kirk should be repealed, and the present discipline ratified. (2) That the Act of Annexation should be abolished, and the patrimony of the Church restored; (3) That the abbots, priors, and other prelates pre-

---

* Easter and Christmas.   † Raising the host.

tending to ecclesiastical authority and giving their vote in matters without any delegated power from the Kirk should not be hereafter permitted to vote in Parliament or other convention.

The King felt it politic to consent, and an Act was passed which is still regarded as the Charter of the Liberties of the Kirk. It confirmed the system of Church government by General Assemblies, Synods, Presbyteries, and Sessions, declared that the Acts passed in 1584 were not to be prejudicial to the privileges of the office-bearers in regard to matters of heresy, questions of excommunication, appointment and deposition of ministers, and it rescinded the Act giving commissions to bishops to receive the royal presentation of bishoprics, etc.

The discovery, in December, 1592, of the Spanish Blanks,* and the refusal of the Lords implicated to surrender, led to an expedition to the North early in

---

* A Roman Catholic named George Kerr was arrested on board a vessel when setting out on a secret mission to Spain. Among his papers were found letters from Jesuits and seminary priests in Scotland with blank sheets having affixed the signatures and seals of the Earls of Huntley, Errol, and Angus, the Lairds of Auchindoun, Fintry, and other zealous Roman Catholics. Kerr, under torture, revealed the conspiracy. The King of Spain was to land an army of 30,000 on the west of Scotland, where the Roman Catholic Lords, with all the supporters they could muster, would join him. 15,000 were to march across the border while the remainder were to secure the overthrow of the Protestant Church. The sheets were to be filled up by William Crichton, a Jesuit, according to instructions which Kerr had received, and were then to be delivered to the King of Spain. Hence the plot received the name of The Spanish Blanks.

1593, and in Aberdeen the King and many nobles
entered into still another Bond for the maintenance
and defence of religion.

But as the dangers and difficulties that beset his
path disappeared or were overcome, he began to show
his leaning towards the Roman Catholics.

CHAPTER IV.

Bothwell's attempt on the Crown—Strained relations between
King and Kirk—A stormy meeting—The King's proclamation
against the ministers—He leaves Holyrood for Linlithgow—
The ministers prepare for the worst, and invite Lord
Hamilton to place himself at the head of those embracing
the cause of the Kirk—The King marches on Edinburgh, and
in the High Church justifies himself and blames the ministers.

BOTHWELL, encouraged by the Queen of England,
resolved to make an attempt on the King and Crown,
but the King got secret information of the plot, and
in the High Church of Edinburgh, after the sermon,
he informed the people of what he knew, and declared
his determination to lead his whole forces in person
against Bothwell, and then raising his hand to heaven,
he took a solemn vow to God that, if they would
instantly arm and advance with him, he would never
rest till, in return for such service, he had thoroughly
suppressed and banished the Catholic Lords from his
dominions.

Bothwell soon realised the hopelessness of his
adventure, dispersed his company, and became a
refugee in England.

But in spite of all these solemn Covenants, James
still hankered after Prelacy, and the relations between
him and the Kirk became strained to breaking point.
The ministers were in genuine alarm for their religion,
and certain of the Protestant Lords, with two ministers

—Bruce and Watson—were sent to interview the King in the Upper Tolbooth, Edinburgh, on 17th December, 1596. Bruce said they were come from the nobles, barons, and ministers, assembled to bemoan and avert the dangers threatened to religion. "What dangers?" asked James, "and who dares convene contrary to my proclamation?" "Dares!" retorted Lord Lindsay, "We dare more than that; and shall not suffer the truth to be overthrown, and stand tamely by." A large crowd had followed them to the building. A tumult arose between the factions, the King's person was in danger, and matters looked black enough for a time, but quietness was restored, and he returned to Holyrood. Next day, however, he and his Court left for Linlithgow, and the same morning a Proclamation was made at the Cross of Edinburgh, in which reference was made to the treasonable uproar of the previous day raised by the factious ministers, who, it stated, after having uttered most seditious speeches in the pulpit, had assembled with the noblemen, barons, and others, had sent an irreverent message to the King, persuaded the citizens to take arms and put his Majesty's life in jeopardy. This treasonable conduct had convinced his Majesty that the capital was no longer a fit place for his residence or the ministration of justice. He had, therefore, left it, and he now commanded the Lords of Session, Sheriffs, and all other officers of justice to remove themselves furth of the city of Edinburgh, and repair to such other places as should be appointed. All noblemen and barons were ordered to depart to their own houses, and not to assemble again till they had received the Royal permission.

The ministers were not dismayed. They resolved to prepare for the worst, and secretly invited Lord Hamilton to place himself at the head of the nobles and barons who had embraced the cause of the Kirk. Hamilton, however, took the invitation to the King. James summoned his followers from north and south, and marched on Edinburgh. The Provost and Magistrates delivered the keys of the city on their knees to the King, and professed their deep sorrow for the recent tumult, of which they declared they were guiltless. James in the High Church, after sermon by Mr. David Lindsay, made an oration to the people, in which he justified himself, cleared his councillors, and greatly blamed the ministers.

CHAPTER V.

James introduces Episcopacy—Death of Elizabeth—James goes to England—Ministers assembled at Aberdeen apprehended— John Welsh—The Parson of Penninghame constituted Archdeacon of Galloway—Gavin Hamilton made Bishop of Galloway—The High Commission Court and Galloway Commissioners—The Glasgow Assembly of 1610—Parliament rescinds the Act of 1592, the great Charter of Presbytery— The Five Articles of Perth opposed by Galloway ministers, being particularly obnoxious to Gallovidians—Death of James —Charles visits Scotland—Distributes honours—High Commission Court established with Commissioners from Galloway —Lord Galloway and Lord Kirkcudbright withdraw from the Court on its showing bias against Presbyterians—Robert Glendinning, minister of Kirkcudbright deprived of his living —The Kirkcudbright magistrates ordered to be imprisoned in Wigtown jail—William Dalgleish, minister of Kirkmabreck, deposed—Samuel Rutherfurd banished to Aberdeen.

JAMES now began to bring about the establishment of Episcopacy. Like all the Stuarts, he believed firmly in the Divine Right of Kings, especially of himself, and determined to assert his authority.

In March, 1598, at Dundee, the General Assembly, in which the King had secured a majority, adopted a proposal for certain of their number as Bishops or Commissioners to sit in Parliament, but the proposal had given rise to bitter opposition and was keenly debated, James himself taking a leading part in the discussion in its favour. It was carried by a majority of ten. The election of Commissioners was to belong partly to the King and partly to the Kirk. "Thus," says Calderwood, "the Trojan horse of Episcopacy was brought in covered with caveats that the danger might not be seen; which, notwithstanding, was seen by many and opponed unto; considering it to be better to hold thieves at the door than to have an eye unto them in the house that they steal not; and indeed the event declared that their fear was not without just cause, for those Commissioners, voters in Parliament, afterwards Bishops, did violate their caveats as easily as Samson did the cords wherewith he was bound."

The death of Elizabeth, on 24th March, 1602, led to James being declared heir and successor, and on 5th April, 1603, he left Scotland, accompanied by many noblemen, prelates, and others, among whom were Gavin Hamilton and Andrew Lamb, both afterwards Bishop of Galloway. A month later he entered London, accompanied by a large body of both Scotch and English nobility, guarded and ushered by the Lord Mayor and five hundred citizens on horse-back, and welcomed by the deafening shouts of an immense multitude of his new subjects.

In England, James was freer to promote Prelacy, and he steadily persevered in his purpose. He ignored repeated requests of the Scotch ministers that they should be allowed to meet in the General Assembly, and when some of them, in 1605, ventured to assemble at Aberdeen without the royal authority, they were apprehended. Their trial was a farce, as is shown by a letter written by Sir Thomas Hamilton to the King on the day sentence was passed. Lord Hailes, in publishing the letter, says: "We here see the Prime Minister, in order to obtain sentence agreeable to the King, address the Judges with promises and threats, pack the Jury, and then deal with them without scruple and ceremony." Six of the ministers were thus found guilty of treason and sentenced to death, but were afterwards ordered to be banished. Among them was John Welsh, minister of Kirkcudbright, son-in-law of John Knox. He went to France, where Louis XIII. allowed him to preach. In 1622, James gave him permission to return to England, but on no account to cross the Scottish border, for he felt it would be fatal to Episcopacy in Scotland if Welsh were allowed to resume his ministration there. Neither was he allowed to preach in London till he was near his end. Then he was given permission. He preached with great fervour, and died two hours afterwards.

Parliament assembled at Perth in 1606, and ordained that the bishops should be restored to their formal Episcopal estates, to their ancient honours, dignities, privileges, and rights, including their seats in Parliament. Chapters which had been abolished were again erected. The parson of Penninghame was constituted archdeacon of Galloway and first member of the Bishop's Chapter. In the Chapter were likewise the parsons of Crossmichael, Twynholm, Kirkcudbright, Dalry, and Borgue. The church of the priory at Whithorn was the Cathedral and Chapter House.

Gavin Hamilton was now promoted to the bishopric of Galloway, which had been vacant for thirty years. Its revenue was "so depleted that it scarcely was remembered to have been." James, anxious for the dignity of the bishops, conferred upon Hamilton the Abbey of Dundrennan, the Abbey of Tongland, the Priory of Whithorn, and the Monastery of Glenluce, which the King had acquired by the General Annexation Act of 1587. This made it the richest bishopric in Scotland, being inferior in revenue only to the two primacies of St. Andrews and Glasgow. In Chalmers' *Caledonia*, the net rental of the bishopric at the Revolution, when Episcopacy in Scotland was suppressed, is given at £5,634 15s., Scots, besides the patronage of more than twenty churches, all then vested in the Crown.

Shortly afterwards, the King instituted the two Courts of High Commission,* composed of bishops and their friends, with an archbishop as president. Among the Commissioners for the South Division of Scotland were the Earls of Cassillis and of Wigtown; the Bishop of Galloway, James Halliday, Commissary of Dumfries, and Thomas Ramsay, minister there. The two Courts were afterwards united, and Cowper, Bishop of Galloway was appointed a Commissioner. James was very astute in the steps he took to secure the establishment of Episcopacy in Scotland, and, while doing everything to bring it about, he at the same time openly encouraged the execution of enactments against Papacy in the hope of allaying the alarm of

---

* The King's letter for the appointment of these Courts is dated May 1608. Their jurisdiction extended over persons of all ranks, whether churchmen or laymen, and there was no appeal from their decisions.

the Presbyterians. Reference is made elsewhere to the great loss sustained through Abbeys being burned and libraries consigned to the flames. In 1609, Archbishop Spottiswoode of Glasgow proceeded to New Abbey, and took possession of the house of Gilbert Brown, the abbot, who was suspected of Popish practices. A great number of Popish books, pictures, images, vestments, and other articles were seized, taken to Dumfries, and burned in the High Street on market day.

A packed General Assembly met at Glasgow in 1610, conferred additional powers on bishops, and declared the King to be the supreme governor and head of the Church. The Earl of Wigtown, the Bishop of Galloway, the Barons of Drumlanrig and Bombie, with the following ministers from the Stewartry:— John Aitken, William Hamilton, Robert Glendinning, and James Donaldson; and from Wigtownshire:— James Adamson, John Watson, and George Kinnaird, sat in this Assembly. Its Acts were ratified by Parliament, with some omissions suggested by the King. Thus the restoration of the Episcopal Government and the civil rights of the bishop had been secured, but "there was yet wanting that, without which, so far as the Church was concerned, all the rest was comparatively unimportant." Accordingly, the Archbishop of Glasgow, Lamb, the Bishop of Brechin, and Hamilton, Bishop of Galloway, were summoned to the English Court, and consecrated according to the form in the English Ordinal, and this qualified them to give valid ordination to the other bishops. In 1612,

Parliament formally rescinded the Act of 1592—the Great Charter of Presbytery.

Bishop Hamilton died in 1614, and was succeeded by William Cowper, minister of Perth, who had been for many years a zealous Presbyterian, but who, like many others, had yielded to temptation in the shape of promises and preferment. The Cowper Cairn, near Glen Trool, is said to be named after him from his habit of retiring to the hills for meditation.

The Assembly of 1616 decided to prepare a Liturgy and a new Confession of Faith, and for this important work, several learned divines were selected, the chief of whom was the Bishop of Galloway.

James visited Scotland in 1617, and Cowper preached before him at Dumfries. The King gave orders for the repair of the Royal Chapel at Holyrood, and for the erection of gilt statues of the Apostles. The people, viewing these acts as the first step towards Popery, became alarmed, and Cowper, as Dean of the Royal Chapel, thought it well for the peace of the community to dissuade the King from his purpose.

The General Assembly of 1618, at Perth, carried by a majority what have since become known as The Five Articles of Perth. They were bitterly opposed by some, and James Simpson, minister of Tongland, David Pollock, minister of Glenluce, and Thomas Provan, minister of Leswalt, incurred the wrath of the Bishop of Galloway for voting against them according to the dictates of their conscience. The Articles were ratified by Parliament in August, 1621, by a majority of twenty-seven. The Earls of Wig-

town and of Nithsdale, Lords Garlies and Sanquhar,
John Carson, Commissioner for Dumfries, and John
Turner, Commissioner for Wigtown, voted in support
of the Articles. David Arnot of Barcaple, Com-
missioner for Kirkcudbright, voted against them.
The Articles were particularly obnoxious to the
Gallovidians. By them—

(1) Kneeling at the Lord's Supper was approved.

(2) Ministers were to dispense that sacrament in
private houses to those suffering from infirmity or from
long or deadly sickness.

(3) Ministers were to baptise children in private
houses in case of great need.

(4) Ministers were, under pain of the bishop's
censure, to catechise all children of eight years of age,
and the children were to be presented to the bishop
for his blessing.

(5) Ministers were ordered to commemorate Christ's
birth, passion, resurrection, ascension, and sending
down of the Holy Ghost.

While all this was going on, the Reformers were
neither idle nor silent. They did what they could,
though it had little effect at the time, for those opposed
to them would brook no opposition in the course they
had determined to follow.

James died on 29th March, 1625, and was succeeded
by Charles, from whom much was looked for by the
Presbyterians. Charles, however, had other views.
It is doubtful whether his projects would ever have
succeeded, though many believe that, with time and
greater caution, he might have got his own way.

Certain it is that, with Laud as his adviser, and a nature impatient of delay, and believing blindly in his Divine Right, he never would have succeeded.

Charles visited Scotland in 1633, and distributed honours with lavish hand, in the hope of conciliating his northern subjects. He made Sir John Gordon Viscount Kenmure and Lord of Lochinvar, Sir Robert M'Clelland Lord Kirkcudbright, and advanced Viscount Drumlanrig to the Earldom of Queensberry. Charles, however, had to return to England a disappointed man, for he had failed to bring the Scottish Church into conformity with the English Church, and his conduct in the Scots Parliament in conniving at the false declaration of a vote cost him the confidence and affection of his Scottish subjects. He, however, persevered with his purpose. Every new appointment to the Scottish Church was made with the view of exalting Episcopacy and degrading Presbytery. The High Commission Court was established by warrant, dated the 21st October, 1643. The Court had power to deal with "All that are either scandalous in life, doctrine, or religion, resetters of seminary priests, hearers of mass, adulterers, contemners of church discipline, blasphemers, cursers, or swearers." Those appointed Commissioners for Galloway were the Earl of Galloway, the Sheriff of Galloway, the Bishop of Galloway, Lord Kirkcudbright, Sir John M'Dowall of Garthland, the Provosts of Wigtown and Kirkcudbright, Mr. Abraham Henderson, minister of Whithorn, Mr. Alexander Hamilton, Mr. David Leach at Dundrennan. The Court soon showed bias against

Presbyterians, and Lord Galloway and Lord Kirk-cudbright declined to have anything to do with it. This, however, only gave greater freedom to the clerical party who proceeded to prosecute avowed Presbyterians. Robert Glendinning, minister of Kirkcudbright, was deprived of his living by this Court because he would not conform to a recent innovation, and would not admit into his pulpit one of the bishop's minions. The magistrates of the burgh continued to attend his church, and listened to his sermons, so the bishop * issued a warrant for his arrest, but his own son, who was one of the bailies of Kirkcudbright, refused to imprison his venerable father, who had reached the advanced age of seventy-nine years. Accordingly, he and the rest of the magistrates were ordered to be imprisoned in Wigtown jail.

William Dalgliesh, minister of Kirkmabreck, was next deposed for nonconformity. The same year, Samuel Rutherfurd was summoned before the High Court of Commission, and banished to Aberdeen, as we shall see later.

---

* A bishop and four others formed a quorum of the Court. It acted in the most arbitrary manner, especially against the non-conformists in Galloway, often without accusation, probation or defence, when and where the bishop liked.

CHAPTER VI.

The Laud Liturgy—Jenny Geddes in St. Giles—King appealed
to—People assemble in Edinburgh—Sydeserf Bishop of
Galloway attacked, and Earls of Wigtown and Troqueer
going to his assistance also put in danger—The National
Covenant prepared—Signed in Grey Friars Church, Edinburgh—Copies sent all over the country—Signed with
enthusiasm in Galloway—Lindsay, minister in Stranraer,
takes copies to London—The King's threat against him—
The King submits—The General Assembly of 1638 makes a
clean sweep of the Bishops, and libels Sydeserf—Arranges
Presbyteries and Synods—Preparations for war—Galloway
commanders—Terms arranged—Presbyterians in Parliament
—Civil war—Battle of Newburn—Gallantry of the Galloway
troops—Son of Patrick M'Kie of Larg killed in the engagement.

IN spite of many warnings, the King persisted in his
course of conforming the religion of Scotland to that
of England. The new Service Book was to be the
instrument of this. In an earlier draft it was mainly
the work of Bishop Wedderburn, Bishop Maxwell of
Ross, and Bishop Sydeserf of Galloway. The King
asked Laud to consider the alterations proposed by
the Scottish bishops on the English Prayer Book,
which had been taken as a basis. He seems to have
altered it considerably, and the book became known
as "Laud's Liturgy."

The King issued a Proclamation requiring every
parish to have two copies of it before Easter. This

aroused great opposition, for many looked on the new service as nothing but Popery in disguise. The bishops took steps to enforce the Proclamation, but the opposition grew greater every day. This attempt to impose the Liturgy on the people precipitated the crisis. Everybody knows the story of how, on 23rd July, 1637, when Dean Hanna started to read the Liturgy in St. Giles Cathedral, Jenny Geddes flung a stool at his head, and, as the tablet recently erected to her memory sets forth, "struck the first blow in the great struggle for freedom of conscience."

The King was appealed to, but he had evidently made up his mind, and ordered that the Liturgy was not to be withdrawn. He also commanded that no persons were to be elected magistrates of burghs who would not strictly conform to the prescribed mode of worship. Notwithstanding this, another application was made to the King, whose answer was expected on 18th October, and on this date deputations of gentlemen, ministers, and burghers assembled in Edinburgh in great numbers from all the southern counties. The Edinburgh magistrates were forced to join in a petition against the Service Book. Then the crowd, meeting with Sydeserf, Bishop of Galloway, and, remembering his unrelenting severity, attacked him with shouts of "Papist loon! Jesuit loon! betrayer of religion!" and were tearing off his coat to discover a golden crucifix which he was said to wear under his vest, when he was rescued, and sought refuge in the Privy Council Chamber. The crowd surrounded it, and demanded that he should be delivered up. The

Earls of Wigtown and of Troqueer, with their followers, went to his relief, but they, too, found themselves in a perilous position, for the crowd increased and became more clamorous. Troqueer was thrown down on the street, and his hat, cloak, and white staff of office as Lord Treasurer taken from him. It was only when some of the nobles opposed to the Service Book earnestly requested the people to desist that order was restored, and Sydeserf managed to escape to Dalkeith.

No satisfaction was granted by the King, and the Presbyterians decided to resort to the Covenant once more. The National Covenant of 1580 was chosen, and additions made to it in two parts—the part known as "the legal warrant," summarising the Acts of Parliament condemning Papacy, and ratifying the Confessions of the Church was drafted by Archibald Johnston of Warriston, the other part with special religious articles for the time, and Bond suiting it to the occasion, was drawn by Alexander Henderson Luchars—and with these additions it became known more than ever as the National Covenant. It was written on a sheet of parchment, four feet long by three feet eight inches broad. The spot chosen for the solemnities of the first subscription was Grey Friars Church, Edinburgh. "The selection," writes the Historiographer Royal for Scotland, "showed a sound taste for the picturesque. The graveyard in which their ancestors have been laid from time immemorial stirs the hearts of men. The old Gothic church of the Friary was then existing; and landscape art in Edinburgh has by repeated efforts established the opinion that from that spot we have the grandest view of the precipices of the Castle and the National fortress crowning them. Here the Reformers gathered 'the legitimate charters' of their nation into one document, and presented them before Heaven. Henderson began the solemnities of the day with a never-to-be-forgotten prayer. Louden followed with a fearless and inspiring address, and about four o'clock in the afternoon Johnston unrolled the parchment in which these Scottish charters were inscribed, and read them in a clear, calm voice. When he had finished, all was still as the grave. But the silence was soon broken. An aged man of noble air was seen advancing. He came forward slowly, and deep emotion was visible in his venerable features. He took up the pen with a trembling hand, and signed the document. This was the Earl of Sutherland, and he was immediately followed by Sir Andrew Murray. A general movement now took place. All the Presbyterians in the church pressed forward to the Covenant, and subscribed their names. But this was not enough; a whole nation was waiting. The immense parchment was carried into the churchyard, and spread out on a huge tombstone to receive on this expressive tablet the signature of the Church. Scotland had never beheld a day like that. Both sides were crowded with names. No place was left even on the margin for another signature. So eager were the people to sign it that, when little room remained, they shortened their signatures, some writing only their initials so close that it is difficult to ascertain how many have signed it. Many signed it with their blood, whilst tears bedewed their cheeks. This was the 28th of February, 1638, and when Charles learned what had taken place, he exclaimed, 'I have no more power in Scotland than a Doge of Venice.' "

Hundreds of copies of the Covenant were made, and were carried through all the country for signature, and nowhere was the Covenant welcomed with greater enthusiasm than in the Wilds of Galloway. John Livingston, afterwards minister of Stranraer, a man of address and talent, was sent to London with several copies. He was not long in London till the Marquis of Hamilton sent him word that the King had said that Livingston was come, but he would "put a pair of fetters about his feet." Livingston took the hint, bought two horses, and, avoiding the main thorough-fares, hastened back to Galloway. The King tried an astute move by introducing a rival Covenant. He, too, took the Covenant of 1580, and added to it the General Bond of 1588, but this attempt to divide the Covenanters came too late, and entirely failed. He soon realised that he must submit to the Covenanters, so he abolished Courts, Canons, Liturgies, and Articles, and consented to the calling of a General Assembly. This was the first free General Assembly of the Church of Scotland for forty-two years—the famous Assembly of 1638, which met at Glasgow on 21st November. It was dissolved after a few days by the Royal Com-missioner when he saw the work it intended to do, but Henderson, the Moderator, pointed to the Royal

Commissioner's zeal for an earthly King as an incentive to the members to show their zeal for their Heavenly King, and, in spite of the Commissioner's order to dissolve, the Assembly continued to sit. The losses of the Assembly by the withdrawal of the Commissioner and five members were compensated by fresh accessions, namely:—Argyle, Wigtown, Kinghorn, Galloway, Mar, Napier, Almond, and Blackhall. It made a clean sweep of the bishops, their jurisdiction, and their ceremonies. The Articles of Perth were also expunged. The Assembly then took up a complaint against Sydeserf, Bishop of Galloway. He was called by an officer, but failed to answer. His Procurator, John Hamilton, was also called, but likewise failed to appear, and the libel was then read:—" That he had taught Arminian tenets; that he kept a crucifix in his closet, and defended the use of it by his own example; that he, at his own hand, had indicted two anniversary fasts in his diocesan Synod; that he had compelled the ministers to receive the sacrament of the Lord's Supper kneeling; that he had deposed and procured the banishment of some of the most eminent of the ministry for nonconformity; that he had fined and confined several gentlemen for no better reason; that he had embraced excommunicated Papists, and preferred more love to them than to Puritans; that he had condemned the exercise of family prayer; and that he was an open profaner of the Sabbath, by buying horses on that day, and doing other secular affairs. All which having been proved against him, he was deposed, and excommunicated."

Maxwell, Bishop of Ross, a Galloway man, was also deposed and excommunicated.

Commissions for trying clerical delinquents were appointed to sit at specified dates at Kirkcudbright and half a dozen other places.

This Assembly made a new arrangement of Presbyteries and Synods. The river Urr became the division between the Presbyteries of Kirkcudbright and Dumfries, and the Synods of Galloway and Dumfries. The eight parishes in the east of Wigtownshire with the two parishes of Minnigaff and Kirkmabreck in the Stewartry of Kirkcudbright were formed into the Presbytery of Wigtown. The nine parishes in the west of Wigtownshire with the parishes of Colmonell and Ballantrae in Ayrshire were formed into the Presbytery of Stranraer.

Having effaced almost every vestige of Episcopacy and brought about the second Reformation, this famous Assembly dissolved. Among those from Galloway who had attended it were Samuel Rutherfurd, minister of Anwoth; William Dalgliesh, minister of Kirkmabreck; John M'Clelland, minister of Kirkcudbright; Alexander Gordon of Earlston, elder; William Glendinning, Provost of Kirkcudbright; Robert Gordon of Knockbrex, burgess, New Galloway; Andrew Anderson, minister of Kirkinner; Andrew Lauder, minister of Whithorn; Andrew Agnew of Lochnaw, elder; Alexander Macghie, burgess of Wigtown; John Livingston, minister of Stranraer; James Blair, minister of Port Montgomery (Portpatrick); Alexander Turnbull, minister of Kirkmaiden; Sir Robert Adair, elder; and James Glover, Clerk of Stranraer. The Earls of Galloway, Wigtown, Cassillis, Eglinton, and Dumfries also sat in the Assembly.

After these steps nothing but war remained, and both sides at once got ready. Lords Cassillis and Kirkcudbright raised regiments, in which the younger members of the baronage eagerly enrolled themselves as captains, thoroughly trained officers from foreign services accepted lieutenancies, and the people flocked in hundreds to their standards. James Agnew, Alexander Agnew, sons of the Sheriff, and James Dalrymple of Stair were among the first named as captains in these local corps. The great bulk of the proprietary of Galloway identified themselves with the movement, and the Galloway contingent was everywhere noted for its good appearance and discipline.

Twenty-five thousand men were enrolled under Leslie, and encamped on Dunse-law ready to intercept the King's forces when they advanced. Fortunately, both sides were wanting in confidence, and negotiations were entered into. Charles agreed that a General Assembly should be held in August, and that a Parliament would be called later to ratify its proceedings. The Assembly met (the Earl of Traquair being the King's Commissioner), rejected the Service Book, the Book of Canons, the High Commission, Prelacy, and the ceremonies. Parliament met on 31st August, 1639, as arranged. Traquair presided as the representative of the King, and among those present were the Earls of Wigtown, Galloway, Cassillis,

Queensberry, and Annandale; the Lords Kirkcudbright and Johnstone; the Lairds of Larg and Kilhilt,
as representatives of Wigtownshire. William Glendinning, Commissioner of the Burgh of Kirkcudbright; Robert Gordon, Commissioner of New
Galloway; Patrick Hannay, Commissioner of Wigtown; and John Irving, Commissioner of Dumfries.
The Presbyterians had a large majority, and it was
easily seen that Parliament would go much further
than the King desired. The Royal Commissioner,
therefore, adjourned it from time to time, and then
prorogued it till June, 1640.

The King tried to prevent it meeting then, but it
assembled on 2nd June, without the King's Commissioner, and ratified the proceedings of the General
Assembly of 1639.

Once more civil war seemed inevitable, and the
Presbyterians were soon in arms. Colonel Munro
collected forces in Wigtownshire, Kirkcudbright, and
Dumfries, and joined the army which had assembled
at Dunse. They entered England, gained the battle of
Newburn, and took Newcastle, 28th August, 1640, and
then Charles agreed to the terms proposed by the
Covenanters. In this battle, a handful of Galloway
knights under Patrick M'Kie of Larg, whose son was
killed in the action, gave a splendid example of
gallantry, for with their long spears they threw the
dense body of the enemy into such confusion as to
secure an easy victory. They pursued the English,
and captured every man who tried to stand his ground.
Sir Patrick's son was standard-bearer to Colonel

Leslie's troop. He was a brave young man, and having seized the English General's colours, was flourishing with them when he was mistaken for one of the foe and slain. He was the only person of note who fell on the side of the Covenanters, and was much lamented by the whole party. Zachary Boyd, in a long poem, entitled "Newburn Brook," thus laments his death:—

> " In this conflict, which was a great pitie,
> We lost the son of Sir Patrick McGhie."

Mr. Livingston, minister of Stranraer, officiated as Chaplain, and was present at Newburn.

Note.—Several copies of the 1638 Covenant, signed in different parts of the country, are still extant. One signed at Borgue, Kirkcudbright (22nd April, 1638), is preserved in the Register House, Edinburgh. Dr. King Hewison, in his admirable work on *The Covenanters,* states that the tradition of the Covenant being carried out of Grey Friars' church to the people in the churchyard, and there signed on a tombstone amid scenes of religious fervour, rests on an unsatisfactory basis. Probably some of the details have been overcoloured, but, even so, we have, as he says, "a picture unique in Scots history."

CHAPTER VII.

Parliament confirms the overthrow of Episcopacy—Contest
between Earl of Wigtown and Sir William Cowburn for
office of hereditary usher—Galloway members of Parliament
—Commissioners of Supply for Wigtownshire—The War
Committee—The Galloway Commanders of horse and foot
—The Solemn League and Covenant—Philiphaugh—Lord
Kirkcudbright's regiment—James Agnew receives thanks of
Parliament for his gallant conduct—Additional regiments
raised in Galloway—New Parliament members for Galloway
—List of War Committee for Wigtownshire, showing
unanimity of baronage—Charles surrenders himself to the
Scotch army—He is delivered to the English Commissioners,
tried, and executed—The Scotch proclaim his son King—
Commissioners sent to Hague to lay conditions before him—
He ultimately accepts these and signs the National Covenant
and the Solemn League, and is crowned—Act of Indemnity
—Galloway Protesters and Resolutioners—Cromwell—The
Galloway leaders divided—Cromwell's Ironsides disperse the
Galloway levies—Kenmure Castle and the House of Freugh
burned—Lord Galloway fined £4,000.

PARLIAMENT met at Edinburgh on 17th August, 1641,
Charles himself being present, and confirmed the Acts
of Parliament of June, 1640, overthrowing Episcopacy
and establishing Presbytery.

A curious incident occurred at the King's entrance
to Parliament. A contest having arisen between the
Earl of Wigtown and Sir William Cowburn of Lang-
ton regarding the office of hereditary usher to the
Parliament, Cowburn forcibly seized the mace, and

carried it before the King at his entrance to the House.
A complaint having been made, the King without
investigation issued a warrant to apprehend Cowburn,
and confined him in the Castle, but the King afterwards apologised and declared before Parliament that
he was not aware when he issued the warrant that
Cowburn was a member of the House.

The Earls of Galloway, Wigtown, and Cassillis,
Viscount Kenmuir, and Lord Kirkcudbright, with
Gordon, Laird of Earlston, from the Stewartry of
Kirkcudbright, the Lairds of Kilhilt and Merton from
Wigtownshire, and Sir Robert Grier of Lagg and Sir
John Charters of Amisfield from Dumfries, attended
this Parliament, with Commissioners from Kirkcudbright, Wigtown, Whithorn, and New Galloway. The
King submitted to the Estates a list of those whom he
had nominated to be Privy Councillors. Parliament
approved of the names of the Earls of Cassillis and
Wigtown, but expunged the names of the Earls of
Galloway and Dumfries. The Presbyterians had now
secured all that they wanted, but in the midst of the
gratification that this gave them, there was not
wanting the fear that, should favourable opportunity
ever occur, the King would take back all that he had
given them.

The rebellion in Ireland had its influence in
Galloway. Ten thousand men were ordered to be
embodied, and Commissioners of Supply were named
for the respective counties:—The Sheriff of Galloway
and the Laird of Garthland for Wigtownshire, and the
War Committee was composed of Sir Andrew Agnew,

apparent of Lochnaw; Sir Robert Adair of Kilhilt; James M'Dowall of Garthland; Alexander M'Dowall of Logan; Gordon of Craighlaw; John Murray of Broughton; John Vaus of Barnbarroch; Uthred M'Dowall of Freugh; James Ross of Balneil; Thomas Hay of Park; Fergus Kennedy of Stranraer; Patrick Hannay for Wigtown. Lord Kirkcudbright was appointed to the horse of Kirkcudbright, the Laird of Garthland to the horse of Wigtown, and the Earl of Cassillis and Lord Garlies to command the foot.

Charles, however, had more than enough to attend to in England.

The English Commissioners from the Long Parliament desired help from the Convention of Estates and the General Assembly, and proposed that the two nations should enter into a strict Union and League with the object of bringing them closer together in Church matters, and of extirpating Popery and Prelacy from the land. Henderson suggested that the League should be religious as well as civil, and this was agreed to, and he thereupon drafted the famous Solemn League and Covenant. It was accepted by the Convention of Estates and by the General Assembly, and by both Houses of the English Parliament. It breathed the spirit of the National Covenant, condemned the Papal and Prelatic system, pled for a constitutional monarchy, and outlined a comprehensive programme for future efforts in extending the principles of the Reformation. On September 25th, 1643, it was subscribed in St. Margaret's Church, Westminster. The members of Parliament in England and the Westminster Assembly of Divines stood with uplifted hands, and as article after article was read, they took the Oath to God. The Commissioners from Scotland (among whom were Rutherfurd and Lord Cassillis) to the Westminster Assembly united with the people of England in the solemnity of the day. The Covenant was signed throughout Scotland, England, and Ireland.

Charles somewhat reluctantly empowered the Earl of Montrose to proceed against the Scottish Covenanters, and he secured victory after victory till at Philiphaugh, on 13th September, 1645, Leslie gained a decisive triumph over him. In this battle, John, third Lord Kirkcudbright, commanded a regiment which he had raised at his own expense, chiefly among his Galloway tenants. James Agnew was Lieutenant Colonel, and received the thanks of Parliament for his gallant conduct, and Sir Andrew Agnew afterwards was awarded 3,750 merks as his brother's share of 15,000 merks awarded to Lord Kirkcudbright's regiment for their bravery.

A new corps was raised in the valley of the Nith, styled the South Regiment, and another in the west, styled Lord Galloway's Regiment, of whom the first Colonel was Alexander Agnew, the Sheriff's fourth son.

Then besides Lord Kirkcudbright's Regiment, commanded by his third son, a second was raised in the Stewartry by Lord Kenmure, which he commanded in person. As to this corps, we find it mentioned in the Parliamentary Journals, 15th December (1646):

"Orders to Viscount Kenmure's Regiment to march to Montrose."

Towards the close of the year, there was a General Election, when Sir Andrew Agnew, Knight, and Sir Robert Adair, Knight, of Kilhilt, were chosen for Wigtownshire, and William Grierson of Bargatten for the Stewartry, and William Glendinning for the Borough of Kirkcudbright.

This Parliament sat continuously until 1651.

The new Parliament named War Committees on the 18th April, 1648, that for Wigtownshire proving the unanimity of the Galloway baronage at this period of the struggle:—

Earl of Cassilis, Viscount Ardes, Lord Garlies, Sir Patrick Agnew, Sheriff of Galloway; Sir Andrew Agnew, younger, of Lochnaw, Knight; Sir Robert Adair of Kinhilt; Lairds of Park (Hay), Freuch (M'Dowall), Craigcaffie (Neilson), Balneill (Ross), Ardwell (M'Culloch), Achrocher (Colonel Agnew), Synniness (Kennedy), Gillespie (Kennedy), Knockglass (M'Dowall), Killeser, elder and younger (M'Culloch); Andrew M'Dowall of Lefnoll, Patrick Agnew of Sheuchan, James Kerr, Factor to the Earl of Cassilis; Lairds of Dunragit (Baillie), Larg (Linne), Little Dunragit, Garnock (Cathcart), the Provost of Stranraer, the Lairds of Barnbarroch (Vaus), Craichlaw (Gordon), Mertoun (M'Culloch), Mochrum (Dunbar), Brochtoun (Murray), Kilcreache (Cascreugh, Dalrymple), Baldoon (Dunbar), Grange (Gordon), Glasnock, Fontalloch (Stewart), Wig (Agnew), Dalregle (M'Dowall), Drummorell (M'Culloch), Monreith (Maxwell), Drummastoun, elder and younger (Houstoun); Houstoun of Cutreoch, the Provost of Wigtoune, the Provost of Whithorne, Stewart of Tonderghie, Francis Hay of Ariolland, Dunbar, younger, of Mochrum, Gordon of Balmeg, Hew Kennedy of Arieheming, Patrick M'Kie of Cairn, Agnew of Galdenoch, William Gordon of Penningham, the Laird of Garthland, and Mr. James Blair (minister of Portpatrick).

The position of Charles became hopeless, and he resolved to place himself in the hands of the Scottish army. He came, disguised as a postillion (May, 1646), and was received with every respect, and many were of opinion that had he accepted the Solemn League and Covenant, all Scotland would even then have espoused his cause. This, however, he could not do. Among the Commissioners sent to treat with him were the Earl of Cassillis and the Laird of Garthland. The Scottish forces had a huge sum due by the English, and, as they received £400,000 shortly before Charles was delivered up to the Commissioners of the English Parliament, they have been unjustly accused of selling their King. The English army next resolved to gain possession of the King's person, and this being effected, Charles made great promises to the officers. To Cromwell he offered the Garter, a Peerage, and chief command of the army, and to others different commands. But concessions and promises came too late. He was accused of treason, found guilty, and executed in front of his own palace on 30th of January, 1649.

The Scotch Commissioners in London used their influence to prevent the execution of Charles, but they failed, and on 5th February, 1649—six days after the execution—the Parliament of Scotland had his son proclaimed at the Market Cross of Edinburgh as King of Great Britain, Ireland, and France. They were eagerly anxious that he should be their King, but they were equally determined he should not over-ride their General Assembly or their Parliament. The Estates resolved to put the country in a posture of defence, and nominated colonels and commanders of horse and foot for the various counties, those for Wigtownshire being the Earl of Cassillis, the Sheriff of Galloway, Sir Robert Adair, and William Stewart. Commissioners, among whom were the Earl of Cassillis and Livingstone, were sent to the Hague to lay before the youthful Charles the conditions upon which he would be received as King. He would not accept their conditions, and negotiations failed. Ultimately, Charles came to see that his only chance of obtaining the Crown was to accept the terms proposed. In March, 1650, the Estates again sent the Earl of Cassillis, Livingstone, and others to Breda to treat with the King. An arrangement was come to, and he subscribed the National Covenant and the Solemn League and Covenant before landing in Scotland on 16th June, 1650. On 16th August, he agreed to the Dunfermline Declaration that he would have no enemies but the enemies of the Covenant, and that he would have no friends but the friends of the Covenant, and expressing his detestation of all Popery, superstition, and idolatry, together with Prelacy, and all errors, heresy, schism, and profaneness which he was resolved not to tolerate in any part of his kingdom. He was accordingly crowned at Scone on 1st January, 1651, when he again swore to and subscribed the National Covenant and the Solemn League and Covenant. The King was anxious that his own friends should be allowed to serve in the army, and urged that the Act which disqualified " malignants " from defending their country should be repealed, and ultimately an Act of Indemnity was passed. The Commission of the General Assembly agreed that all who showed evidence of repentance might be employed. The Assembly confirmed the resolution, and a protest was then taken against the lawfulness of the Assembly, the five south-western counties, Renfrew, Ayr, Wigtown, Kirkcudbright, and Dumfries, taking the most prominent part in these proceedings. Those who took up this position were called Protesters, and the others who adhered to the resolution were called Resolutioners. Among the Protesters were Lord Kirkcudbright, Samuel Rutherfurd, John Livingstone, John M'Clellan, Adam Kae (Borgue), Thomas Wyllie (Kirkcudbright), John Semple, Quentin M'Adam, Alexander Gordon of Knockgray, Captain Andrew Arnot. The people of Galloway warmly concurred in the protest, and Samuel Rutherfurd, John Livingstone, Thomas Wyllie, and Lord Kirkcudbright and Alexander Gordon of Knockbrex were among these appointed to present it.   Meanwhile, Cromwell had obtained his first great victory, and proceeded to follow it up.

The Galloway leaders unfortunately were divided. Lords Cassillis and Kirkcudbright and the Laird of Garthland declared for the King against Cromwell, but sided with the Protesters. Sir Andrew Agnew, Sir Robert Adair, and other lairds indignantly opposed the Protesters, and declared for the King and the Estates. Sir Patrick Agnew, Lords Galloway and Kenmure, disgusted by the weakness of Parliament, proposed to support the King independently of the Estates, and were termed " Cavaliers."

Kenmure displayed great activity in enlisting recruits, and had a large cask of brandy carried at the head of his regiment which was known as " Kenmure's drum."

Cromwell's Ironsides dispersed the Galloway levies * near Dumfries, and then took Kenmure Castle, following this up by a raid on Kirkcudbright, where the victors took " 60 muskets and firelocks, 8 great barrels of powder, each containing near three ordinary barrels, match and ball proportionable, and great store of meal and beef."

---

* It is not clear whether the older Galloway regiments kept distinct from the new levies and followed Charles in a body when he crossed the Borders, returning afterwards. In the Journals of Parliament, 2nd December, 1650, it is "ordered by the House that the Western Forces with the three regiments of Kirkcudbright, Galloway, and Dumfries, be joined with Robert Montgomery and be under his command."

The King's cause went from bad to worse. Dunbar and Worcester left him hopeless, and after many escapes, he deemed it prudent to leave the country, and betook himself to the Continent.

Cromwell was now at the head of affairs, and encouraged the ministers in the discharge of their sacred duties, but he refused to let them interfere with State business, and he prohibited General Assemblies. None was allowed to interfere with the people in the performance of their religious service.

In Ireland, also, Cromwell gained the ascendency, and ordered the removal of "all popular Scots out of Ulster." Among those were Lord Ardes—Sir Robert Adair; Captain John Agnew; Patrick Agnew; William Agnew; Francis Agnew; James Shaw; John Blair; Andrew Adair; Alexander Adair; Alexander Stewart; James Stewart; John M'Dowall; John Dunbar; John Hannah; all having a Galloway connection. Lands were to be found for them south of the Shannon in place of their lands in Ulster, which were to be confiscated. Mr. Livingstone, minister of Stranraer, obtained access to Cromwell, and succeeded in bringing about a better understanding.

Galloway suffered severely from Cromwell. Kenmure Castle and the House of Freugh were burned to the ground, and Lord Galloway was fined £4,000 merely for being an adherent of Charles I. He afterwards petitioned to be compensated for this fine, but instead of being relieved from the fines imposed "for the relief of the King's good subjects who had suffered in the late troubles," the Estates passed an Act ordaining the Commissioners of Excise within the Stewartry to give intimation to the heritors to meet, that they might lay on the proportion of the levy thus imposed, that the petitioner might have repetition of what he had paid and given out more than his just proportion. It is very doubtful whether he got satisfaction.

CHAPTER VIII.

Death of Cromwell—Restoration of Charles—Ministers arrested in Edinburgh—Cassillis refuses to sign Oath of Allegiance unless limited to civil affairs—Large sum voted to the King—List of Commissioners to collect in Wigtownshire and Stewartry—Parliament rescinds all Acts from 1640—Restoration of Bishops—Sharp made Archbishop of St. Andrews—Act of Supremacy—Synod of Galloway preparing a Petition against Episcopacy is dissolved by the Earl of Galloway—Whithorn complains to Parliament—Presbytery of Kirkcudbright appoint two of their members to present a Petition to the Privy Council—Reasonableness of the Petition—The Indemnity (so called)—Persons fined in Galloway.

CROMWELL died in 1658, and steps were at once taken for the restoration of Charles. James Sharp, minister of Craill, was sent to London to look after the interests of the Church of Scotland, but when too late, it was discovered that he had betrayed his trust. The intention of the Government soon became apparent. Certain monumental inscriptions (*e.g.*, those on the tombs of Alexander Henderson and George Gillespie) were ordered to be effaced, and *Lex Rex*, Rutherfurd's famous treatise, was burned by the hands of the common executioner. On 23rd August, 1660, some of the leading Presbyterians, among whom was John Semple, minister of Carsphairn, fearing the overthrow of Presbytery, met in a private house in Edinburgh to draw up a Supplication to the King. They were arrested by the Committee of Estates and imprisoned in the Castle. A few days afterwards, Sharp brought a letter from his Majesty, in which he said, "We do also resolve to protect and preserve the Government of the Church of Scotland *as it is settled by law.*" A suggestion that this might be understood in two ways was condemned as an intolerable reflection on the King. Parliament met in January, 1661, M'Dowall of Freuch and Murray of Broughton representing Wigtownshire, and M'Briar of Newark the Stewartry. The oath of allegiance administered to the members declared the King's supremacy over "all persons and in all causes." The Earl of Cassillis and the Laird of Kilbirnie alone refused to sign it until they were allowed to limit the King's supremacy to civil affairs, and this being refused, they withdrew from the House.

Parliament voted £40,000 to the King. The proportion to be paid by the Sheriffdom of Wigtown was £204 12s., and by the Stewartry of Kirkcudbright, £348. The Commissioners appointed to collect it were for Wigtownshire:—James, Earl of Galloway; Alexander, Lord Garlies; Andrew Agnew, appearand of Lochnaw; Thomas Dunbar of Mochrum; Patrick MacDowall of Logan; Wm. Stewart of Castlestewart; Uchtred Macdowall of Freuch; William Gordon of Craighlaw; Sir Jas. Dalrymple of Stair; David Dunbar of Baldoon; Alexander Maculloch of Ardwell; John Murray of Broughton; John Houston of Drummaston; William Stewart of Myrton; William M'Guffock of Alticry; Thomas Stewart of Glenturk; Richard Murray of Broughton, Junior.

For the Stewartry of Kirkcudbright:—Robert, Earl of Nithsdale; James, Earl of Galloway; Robert, Viscount Kenmure; Alexander, Lord Garlies; John, Lord Herries; Robert, Master of Herries; John, Lord Kirkcudbright; Sir James Murray of Barberton; David M'Briar of Newark; James Maxwell of Brackenside; Mr. Thomas Hay of Lands; Richard Murray of Broughton; John Herries of Maybie; William Maxwell of Kirkhouse; Alexander Spotswood of Sweetheart; Roger Gordon of Traquair; William Gordon of Shirmers; William Gordon, Earlston; Robert Maxwell of Orchardton; William Maclelland of Colin; George Maxwell of Munches; Alexander Macghie of Balmaghie; William Grierson of Bargatton; John Carson of Sennick; Gilbert Brown of Kempleton; John Dunbar of Machirmore; John Muir, tutor, of Cassincarie; Andrew Herron of Kirrouchtrie; John Ewart of Mulloch; and the Provost and Bailies of Kirkcudbright, and the Provost of New Galloway, for the time being.

Parliament, in March, 1661, rescinded all the Acts passed from and including 1640, and thus at one stroke swept away all the civil sanction which had been given to the Second Reformation. The Solemn League and Covenant was burned with much parade at Linlithgow on 29th May, 1661, the King's birthday, while a fountain in the town ran plentifully with French and Spanish wines, to the great joy of the inhabitants.

Sharp went back to London, and returned in the end of August with a letter indicating the King's determination to interpose his authority for restoring the Church of Scotland "to its right Government of Bishops *as it was by law established* before the late troubles," and justifying his action by his promise of the previous year. The Privy Council approved of the King's determination, and Proclamation was immediately issued announcing the restoration of bishops. Sydeserf was the only one of the old bishops who remained, and he was appointed to Orkney. Sharp went to England in October, and the following month he was appointed Archbishop of St. Andrews and Primate of Scotland, and in December he was consecrated in Westminster Abbey after being privately ordained as a deacon and a priest. At the same time, Hamilton was consecrated Bishop of Galloway. Parliament became the puppet of the King, and passed the Act of Supremacy, giving all he claimed. The Acts Rescissory declared the Covenants unlawful and seditious deeds. No one was to be admitted to any public trust or office unless he acknowledged that they were unlawful. Ministers were to receive patrons' presentation and Archbishops' collation or quit their parishes. In April, 1661, the Synod of Galloway met to prepare a Petition to Parliament against Episcopacy and in favour of the liberty of the Church, but the Earl of Galloway appeared and, in the name of the King, dissolved the meeting. The Moderator, Mr. John Park, minister of Stranraer, protested against this encroachment as illegal, and would not disperse the meeting till he had prayed and regularly dissolved it.

The people of Whithorn complained to this Parliament that their town had been "altogether *depauperated* by the quarterings of three troops of English horse," and an Act was passed authorising the magistrates to raise voluntary contributions within the Sheriffdoms of Galloway, Nithsdale, Teviotdale, and Lanark, "to relieve them from the burden which had been thus imposed." In May, Parliament proceeded to the trial of the Marquis of Argyle, who had been a great friend of the Covenanters. Among the witnesses were John, Lord Kirkcudbright; John Carson, Provost of Kirkcudbright, and William Grierson of Bargatton. He was sentenced to death, but escaped for the present.

Mr. Guthrie, a minister, was accused of framing the "Western Remonstrance," and the "Cause of God's Wrath," and he, too, was ordered to be executed. These proceedings showed the people of Galloway what they had to expect from the new Government.

The Court of High Commission was again established for the peace and order of the Church, and on behalf of the government thereof by archbishops and bishops. In consequence of the encroachments upon the rights of the Church and the prohibitions issued by the Privy Council against the assembling of Synods or petitioning for the redress of grievances, the Presbytery of Kirkcudbright, in January, 1662, appointed Mr. John Duncan, minister of Rerrick, and James Buglass, minister of Crossmichael, to proceed to Edinburgh to present a Petition to the Privy Council, but their request was disregarded, and though they asked nothing but a fair hearing, this was denied.

The nature and reasonableness of the Petition may be seen from the closing paragraphs:—

"And particularly we humbly beg, that we may have liberty, with freedom and safety, to express our minds against the re-introduction of Prelacy upon this church and kingdom; in doing whereof we resolve in the Lord to walk (according to the measure we have received) close by the rules of scripture, of Christian prudence, sobriety, and moderation; in all our actions testifying our real affection, faithfulness, and loyalty to the king's most excellent majesty; the preservation of whose royal person, and whose long flourishing reign in righteousness, is the thing in this world that is and ever shall be dearest unto us, next unto the flourishing of the Kingdom of Jesus Christ.

"His Majesty's gracious condescending unto those our just and humble desires, will yet more engage our already most deeply engaged hearts and affections unto his majesty's person and government, under whom it is the firm resolution of our hearts, to live in all dutiful obedience, praying that the Lord may long preserve his royal person under the droppings of his grace, and abundant loadenings of his best blessings, and special mercies: and your honours' favourable acceptance of this our humble petition off our hands, and transmitting of the same to his sacred majesty, seconded with your lordship's inter-cessions for his majesty's grant of these our just desires, will make the present generation bless you, and the generation to come call you happy, and shall add to our former obligations to supplicate at the throne of grace for the Spirit of counsel and government, in the fear of the Lord, unto your lordships, and that your persons and government may be richly blessed of the Lord. Thus we rest, expecting your honours' favourable answer."

The Presbytery had also under consideration the form of an address to Parliament written by the Rev. Mr. Wylie, minister of Kirkcudbright, but no opportunity was given for presenting it.

An Act of Indemnity was passed (1662), but several hundreds had to pay fines " for the relief of the King's good subjects who had suffered in the late troubles." The Act was headed " The King's Free Pardon," and narrated that the King, being desirous that all animosities and differences should be buried in oblivion, had resolved to grant a general Act of Indemnity and Pardon, but had thought to burden this pardon to some whose guiltiness had rendered them obnoxious to the laws and placed their lives and fortunes at his Majesty's disposal, with the payment of some small sums. What these " small sums " were may be understood when it is stated that they amounted to over £84,000. In Galloway alone, an immense sum was raised, and the following persons were fined:—Colonel William Stuart, £600; Sir Andrew Agnew, Sheriff of Galloway, £600; —— Gordon of Grange, £1,800; —— M'Culloch, younger of Ardwall, £1,200; John Cathcart of Gennock, £2,000; Francis Hay of Hareholm, £1,000; Patrick Agnew of Sewchan, £1,200; Patrick Agnew of Whig, £2,000; Gilbert Neilson of Catchcathie, £1,300; Patrick M'Ghie of Largie, £260; William M'Kieffock, collector of Wigtownshire, £3,600; George Campbell, captain-lieutenant to Sir Robert Adair, £600; Alexander Kennedy of Gillespie, £480; James Johnston in Stranrewart, £600; John Bailie of Litledoneraclet, £360; Alexander Bailie of Meikleton, £360; —— M'Donald of Crachen, £360; John M'Dougal of Creesein, £600; Alexander Agnew of Crach, £600; Martin M'Ghie of Penningham, £600. William M'Kuffock, £3,600; —— Stuart, bailie of Wigtown, £360; —— Cantrair, late provost of Wigtown, £1,200; William M'Ghie of Magdallen, £360; —— Ramsay of Boghouse, £400; John M'Culloch in Glen, £400; Patrick Agnew of Galdnoth, £1,000; Thomas Boyd of Kirkland, £360; Alexander Martin in Stranrewart, £600; Patrick Kennedy there, £360; John Machans, tanner, there, £600; Gilbert Adair there, £360; David Dunbar of Calden, £4,800; John Gordon, merchant in Stranrewart, £240; John M'Dougal there, £240; William M'Culling there, £240; John Adair of Littlegennock, £600; Alexander Crawford, tutor of Herymen, £360; William Gordon of Barnfallie, £360; John Hannah in Granane, £480; William M'Dougal in Kilroe, £1,000; —— Frissel, burgess of Wigton, £360; Adam M'Kie, late provost of Wigton, £1,000; —— Stuart of Fintilloch, £1,000; James Mackitrick in Kirkmaiden, £360; Michael Malrae in Stonykirk,

£600; James Macnaught in Portpatrick, £360; Nevin Agnew in Clod-house, £240; —— Agnew in Kilconquhar, £240; John Macmaister in Kirkcum, £360; John Macguieston in the Inch, £360; Andrew Agnew of Park, £360; Patrick Hannah in Gas, £360; —— Mackinlenie in Darmenew, £300; Gilbert M'Cricker in Knockedbay, £360; John Macilvain in Milboch, £360; —— Mackinnen of Glenhill, £360; —— Mackinnen of Glenbitten, £360; —— Kennedy of Barthangan, £240; Edward Lawrie in Derward, £240; Mr. William Cleland in Sheland, £240; Thomas Macmoran there, £360; John Paterson there, £360; —— Mackinnen in Polpindoir, £240.

KIRKCUDBRIGHTSHIRE.

Major M'Culloch of Barhome, £800; Robert Kirk of Kildane, £360; Robert Howison, sub-collector, £240; Alexander Gordon of Knockgray, elder and younger, £120; William Whitehead of Milhouse, £360; John Corcadi of Senwick, £1,200; David Arnot in Barnkapel, £360; Mr. William Gordon of Earlston, £3,500; John Gordon of Rusco, £2,400; John Turner in Adwell, £360; —— Gordon of Traquair, £2,400; John Fullarton of Carleton, £1,000; John Macart in Blaikit, £600; John Gordon in Waterside, £600; —— Gordon of Ballechston, £300; James Logan of Hills, £1,000; —— Logan of Bogrie, £480; Patrick Ewing of Anchescioch, £1,000; John Maxwell of Milton, £800; —— of Dendeoch, £600; William Gordon of Midton, £240; Robert Stuart of Mungohill, £1,000;

Archibald Stuart of Killyreuse, £1,000; John Thomson of Harriedholm, £240; John Brown of Muirheadston, £360; —— Brown of Lochill, £360; Alexander Gordon of Culvennan, £600; John Lindsay of Fargirth, £600; John Aitken of Auchinlaw, £360; William Gordon of Chirmers, £600; James Chalmers of Waterside, £600; —— Heron of Kerrochiltree, £600; William Gordon of Robertson, £360; William Corsan there, £240; John Logan in Edrick, £240; William Glendoning of Curroch, £360; William M'Culloch of Ardwall, £600; Robert M'Lellan of Bargatan, £360; Alexander Mackie, merchant in Kirkcudbright, £200; Alexander M'Lellan, merchant there, £200; Alexander M'Lelland, maltman there, £280; William Telfer in Dunroe, £300; —— Gibson of Brockloch, £360; John Stuart of Shambellie, £600; David Gordon of Glenladie, £600; Alexander Gordon of Auchincairn, £200; Laird Mertine, £240; William Gordon of Menibue, £280; John Wilson of Corsock, £600; Robert M'Culloch of Auchillarie, £240; Cornet Alexander M'Ghie of Balgown, £480; Edward Cairns of Tore, £240; —— Corsan in Dundrennan, £200; James Logan of Boge, £600; John M'Michan of Airds, £360; John M'Millan of Brackloch, £360; John Cannor of Murdochwood, £360; Robert Gordon of Grange, £2,400; John Grierson there, £600; Robert Gibson in the parish of Kells, £360; Edward Gordon of Barmart, £480; Alexander Cairns of Dulliparish, £480; James Glendonning of Mochrum, £480; James Neilson of Ervie, £360; —— Grierson, son of Bargatan, £600; —— Martin in Dullard, £360; William

Glendonning of Logan, £360; Robert Ga there, £360; James Wilson in Clierbrane, £240; Alexander Livingstone of Countinspie, £360; Robert Corsan in Netherrerick, £360; James Black of Parborest, £240; Patrick Corsan of Cudoe, £600; John Harris of Logan, £360; —— Telfer of Harecleugh, £1,800; James Thomson of Inglistoun, £1,000; Robert M'Lellan of Balnagoun, £240; Captain Robert Gordon of Barharro, £240; —— Gordon of Gedgill, £300; —— Bugbie in Comrie, £240; Edward Clauchane in Casselzowere, £240; John M'Gill in Gall, £240; John Cannan in Guffockland, £240; John Hamilton in the Muir of Kirkpatrick, £240; Thomas Neilson of Knockwhawock, £240; William Gordon of Mackartnie, £240; James Gordon of Killnelnarie, £240; John Welsh of Skair, £240; James Smith of Drumlaw, £240; Robert Greill in Kinharvie, £240; William Maxwell in Nether-rait, £600.

CHAPTER IX.

The Drunken Act—Nonconformist ministers in Galloway—Privy
   Council's Act against Galloway ministers—Certain Galloway
   ministers compear personally—Outed ministers—Origin of
   Conventicles—Induction of curates results in rioting at
   Kirkcudbright and Irongray—Commissioners proceed to
   Kirkcudbright—Lord Kirkcudbright and others sent prisoners
   to Edinburgh—Earlston refuses to introduce curate to his
   parish—Commissioners proceed to Irongray—Arnot of Little-
   park sent prisoner to Edinburgh—Sympathetic visitors to
   the prison, and order by the Council—The Council's deliverance—Prisoners fined and banished.

STEPS were now being taken to enforce the Act against
ministers who would not obtain presentation from the
patron and collation from the bishop, and almost every
minister in Galloway refused to comply. The Act was
passed at what is known as the Drunken Meeting at
Glasgow, because only one member of the Privy
Council, Sir James Lockhart of Lee, was sober during
the proceedings. The following is a list of the nonconformist ministers of Galloway at this time:—

Those marked with R were alive at the revolution;
those marked with G were outed by the Act of Council
at Glasgow, 1662; those marked with C were confined
to their parishes; those marked with P were outed by
particular sentences of Parliament or Council; and
those marked with S were outed by the Diocesan
Synod.

Synod of Dumfries.

MINISTERS IN GALLOWAY.

Messrs. John Welsh of Irongray, G; Robert Paton of Terregles, G R; John Blackadder of Traquair, G; Anthony Murray of Kirkbean, G; William Mean of Lochrutton, G R; Alexander Smith of Colvend, G; Gabriel Semple of Kirkpatrick Durham, G R; George Gladstone of Urr, C; James Maxwell of Kirkgunzeon, C (some lists make this Thomas Maxwell).

Synod of Galloway.

PRESBYTERY OF KIRKCUDBRIGHT.

Messrs. Thomas Wylie of Kirkcudbright, P; Thomas Warner of Balmaclellan, G R; Adam Kay of Borgue; John Semple of Carsphairn; John Macmichan of Dalry; John Cant of Kells, R; John Duncan of Rerick and Dundrennan; John Wilkie of Twynam; Adam Alison of Balmaghie; John Mean of Anwoth; James Fergusson of Keltoun; James Bugloss of Corsmichael; William Erskine of Girton, R; Thomas Thomson of Partan; Samuel Arnot of Tongland; Robert Fergusson of Buittle.

PRESBYTERY OF WIGTOWN.

Messrs. Archibald Hamilton of Wigtown, R; George Waugh of Kirkinner, R; Alexander Ross of Kirkcowan; William Maitland of Whithorn; Alexander Fergusson of Mochrum; William Maxwell of Monygaff; Patrick Peacock of Kirkmabreck, R. (One list adds Robert Ritchie of Sorbie).

PRESBYTERY OF STRANRAER.

Messrs. James Lawrie of Stonykirk, R; John Park of Stranraer; James Bell of Kirkholm, R; Thomas Kennedy of Kirkmaiden, R (another list makes this Lisward); John Macbroom of Portpatrick; James Wilson of Inch (another list makes it Kirkmaiden); Alexander Peden of New Glenluce. (One list adds John Dick of Old Luce).

In February, 1663, the Privy Council passed the following Act against some of the Galloway ministers:—

" THE lords of his majesty's privy council being informed that there are several ministers in the diocese of Galloway, who, not only contrary to the order of council dated at Glasgow, October 1st last, do continue at their former residence and churches, but in manifest contempt thereof, and contrary to the indulgence granted them by the late Act, dated December 23rd last, do yet persist in their wicked practices, still labouring to keep the hearts of the people from the present government in church and state, by their pernicious doctrine; and more particularly that Messrs. Archibald Hamilton, minister at Wigton, William Maitland at Whithorn, Robert Richardson at Mochrum, George Wauch at Kirkindair, Alexander Ross at Kirkcowan, Alexander Hutcheson (it ought to be Fergusson) at Sorbie, ministers in the presbytery of Wigtown; Messrs. Alexander

Pedin at the Muirchurch, Glenluce, John Park
at the Shappel, Thomas Kennedy at Lisward,
James Lawrie at Stainkirk, James Wilson at
Kirkmaiden, John M'Broom at Portpatrick,
ministers within the presbytery of Stranraer.
Messrs. Patrick Peacock at Kirkmabreck, William
Erskine, minister at Garston, Adam Kay, mini-
ster at Borg, Robert Ferguson at Boittil, Samuel
Arnot at Tongland, John Wilkie at Twinam,
James Buglos, minister at Crossmichael, Thomas
Warner at Balmaclelland, John Cant at Kells,
Adam Alison at Balmagie, John M'Michan at
Dalry, John Duncan at Dundrennan and Rerick,
and Thomas Thomson, minister at Parton,
ministers in the presbytery of Kirkcudbright, and
Mr. Alexander Smith at Cowend and Siddock,
are the chief instruments in carrying on that
wicked course: have therefore ordained letters to
be directed against the forenamed persons,
charging and commanding them, and every one
of them, to remove themselves, wives, bairns,
servants, goods, and gear, forth and from their
respective dwelling places and manses, and out
of the bounds of the presbytery where now they
live, betwixt and the 20th day of March next; and
that they do not take upon them to exercise any
part of the ministerial function; and also charging
them to appear before the council, the 24th of
March next to come, to answer for their former
disobedience with certification as above specified."

A month later, Messrs. Maitland, Kay, Wilkie, Waugh, Lawrie, Cant, Alison, M'Michan, and Smith, "being called, compeared personally, and being severely examined upon their obedience to the late acts of parliament and council, anent their obedience and submission to the government of the church, as the same is presently established by law, declared they were not yet clear to give obedience thereunto; but they were ready and willing like as they then judicially promised to obey the said acts, for removing from their manses and parishes, and desisting from preaching, conform to the same in every point. In consideration whereof, the lords declare that they do continue (*i.e.*, delay) to insist against them for their former carriages, while they be of new cited." The others did not appear, and were obliged to leave their kirks and manses.

The outed ministers were not silent, nor did they desert their flocks. They became, if possible, more faithful and zealous in their work, and showed a firmness of principle and a contempt of suffering which greatly endeared them to their people.

They preached in the fields, moors, and on the hillsides, and this was the origin of conventicles. When Gabriel Semple, minister of Kirkpatrick-Durham, was outed from his parish, he took up his abode with Neilson of Corsock. He preached in Corsock Castle till the place would not hold his audience. Then he took to the garden. It, too, became too small, and he went to the open field, and so we have the beginning of the field preaching that became so characteristic of the times of persecution. There were between three and four hundred ministers outed, and they were replaced by "the poorest creatures ever known as ministers in Scotland, illiterate, juvenile, drunken, and openly vicious,"—little wonder that the people refused to hear them.

The induction of curates resulted in rioting in several places, and at Kirkcudbright and Irongray the women took a prominent part in the proceedings. The Chancellor wrote the magistrates of Kirkcudbright, commanding them to discover the individuals who had been engaged in the riot, and to order their appearance before the Privy Council, with the husbands, fathers, and masters of such women as had been concerned in the tumult. In consequence of this injunction, there appeared before the Council Adam Gumquhen, John Halliday, John M'Staffen, Alexander M'Lean, —— Renthoun, John Carson, and Alexander M'Kay, inhabitants of Kirkcudbright, who denied that they had taken any part in the tumult. M'Staffen and M'Lean were ordered to find caution for the production of their wives, and the rest were sent to prison until their wives appeared before the Council. James Hunter, cited and not compearing, was ordained to be denounced. But the Council, finding there were no acting magistrates in Kirkcudbright, appointed a Committee to proceed to the South to make the most searching enquiry into the particulars of this contempt of authority. These Commissioners were the Earls of Linlithgow, Galloway, and Annandale, Lord Drumlenrig, and Sir John Wauchope of Nidrie, and they were accompanied by military force. They met at Kirkcudbright in May, 1663, and called before them all those who were supposed to have been engaged in the riot, including over thirty women. After taking evidence, they found that Lord Kirkcudbright, even from his own confession, had opposed the introduction of the curate, and had refused to give any assistance in quelling the disturbance. They ordered him to be sent a prisoner to Edinburgh. John Carson, late Provost of Kirkcudbright, was dealt with in the same way, and John Ewart, who had been chosen Provost at the last election but refused to accept office, was declared to be the chief cause of the disorganisation of the magistracy, and had declined to give his advice as to dealing with the tumult on the ground that he was no Councillor, so he too was taken prisoner to Edinburgh. A new election of magistrates was then ordered. William Ewart was chosen Provost; John Newall and Robert Glendinning, Bailies; and John Livingstone, Treasurer. They all accepted office, and signed a Bond for the faithful discharge of their duties. After taking further evidence, the Commissioners found that Agnes Maxwell, Christina M'Cavers, Jean Rome, Marion Brown, and Janet Biglam had been most active in the outrage, and they were ordered to be carried prisoners to Edinburgh to answer before the Privy Council. A dozen others were ordered to be imprisoned till they found caution under the penalty of £100 sterling to appear before the Privy Council. Ellen Cracken and others were ordered to be apprehended by the Sheriff of Wigtown, and imprisoned by the magistrates of Kirkcudbright.

From Kirkcudbright the Lords addressed a letter to Gordon of Earlston, requiring him to introduce the curate of his parish, but he refused, as will be seen in the article dealing with Earlston.

The Commissioners then proceeded to Irongray, and called before them William Arnot of Littlepark, George Rennie of Beoch, and several others. They, found that Arnot had held several meetings before the tumult for the purpose of opposing the admission of Mr. Bernard Sanderson to the Church, and that, when requested by the Rev. John Wishart and those who went to serve the edict, to hold the women off them, he declared he neither could nor would do it, and that he afterwards drew his sword, and putting his back against the church door, said, "Let me see who will, place a minister here this day." Arnot was ordered to be taken prisoner to Edinburgh. Rennie was declared an accomplice because he had been present and not assisted to overcome the opposition. He was ordered to find security to a large amount to appear before the Council when called. The whole of the military were ordered to live on the inhabitants at free quarters till the following Monday.

The Commissioners having given in their reports, dated 25th and 30th May, 1663, to the Privy Council, the men from Kirkcudbright who had appeared for their wives, after finding caution for their good behaviour, were set at liberty. Those still detained

seem to have had many sympathetic visitors, for the following curious order was issued, 23rd June, 1663:—
" The Lords of council being informed that ministers and other persons visit the prisoners for the riot at Kirkcudbright, now in the tolbooth of Edinburgh, and not only exhort, but pray for the said persons to persist in their wicked practices, affirming that they are suffering for righteousness' sake, and assure them God will give them an outgate, recommend it to the keeper to notice who visits them, and what their discourse and carriage is when with them."

On the 13th August, the Privy Council gave the following deliverance on the report of the Commissioners:—

" The Lords having considered several petitions of the prisoners from Kirkcudbright and Irongray, and the report of the commissioners sent to that country, do find John Carson of Sennick, John Euart, late provost of Kirkcudbright, and William Arnot of Littlepark in Irongray, to have been most guilty of the abuses and disorders there, and fine John Carson in the sum of eight thousand merks, and the said William Arnot in the sum of five thousand merks: and order them to find caution before they depart from prison, to pay the said sums to his majesty's exchequer betwixt and Martinmas next, with certification if they fail, they shall be banished out of the kingdom: and ordain and command the said William Arnot, betwixt and the 25th of October next to come, to make public acknowledgment of his offences two several Sabbaths at the kirk of Irongray before that congregation. Like as the said lords do banish the said John Euart forth of this realm for his offence, and ordain and command him forth of the same betwixt and this day twenty days, not to be seen therein at any time hereafter, without license from his majesty or the council, at his highest peril.

"And the said lords finding Agnes Maxwell, Marion Brown, Jean Rome, Christian M'Cavers, and Janet Biglam, to have been most active in the said tumult, do ordain them, betwixt and the 15th day of September next to come, to stand two several market days at the market-cross at Kirkcudbright, ilk day for the space of two hours, with a paper on their face, bearing their fault to be for contempt of his majesty's authority, and raising a tumult in the said town; and ordain them before they depart out of prison, to enact themselves in the books of council, to give obedience to this; and the magistrates of Kirkcudbright to execute this sentence; and if they fail or delay so to do, that they cause whip them through the said town, and banish them forth of the same, and the liberties thereof."

CHAPTER X.

Act against Presbyterian ministers from Ireland coming to Scotland—The Earl of Galloway and others appointed to examine them—John Gordon of Stranraer prisoner for treasonable speeches—Episcopal ministers' trying time—Register of the Synod of Galloway—Complaints of parishioners absenting themselves from preaching; of seditious ministers; of their own hard necessitous condition; of conventicle keepers—Bond to be tendered to disorderly parishioners—The state of the Glenkens—Episcopalians get no support there—Kirkcowan Curate cannot get a Session—Patrick Vans of Sorbie to be proceeded against for disorderly baptism.

On 7th October, 1663, the Privy Council passed an Act to prevent Presbyterian ministers from Ireland getting a shelter in Scotland, and also against those who would not attend the parish church to hear the curates. Among those appointed to call before them persons coming from Ireland for examination were the Earl of Galloway, the Provost of Ayr for the time, Maxwell of Munches, the Provost of Wigtown for the time, and Stewart of Tonderghie.

In January, 1664, the Chancellor wrote Sir James Turner, as follows:—" Sir,—Upon information given to his majesty's privy council of some treasonable speeches uttered by one John Gordon burgess in Stranraer, for which he is now prisoner in that Burgh, they order you to send him in prisoner, with as many soldiers as may be sufficient for that purpose, that the council may take such course with him, as they shall think fit."

No more appears about him.

Although supported by the Government, the Episcopal ministers who were sent to Galloway had a very trying time.

In the Register of the Synod of Galloway we get frequent glimpses of the difficulties they had to contend with. On October 26th, 1664, it is complained that many of the parishioners wilfully absent themselves from the preaching of the Word and other divine ordinances, and refuse to bring their children to the church to be baptised by them, but either keep them unbaptised or take them to outed ministers of their own principles to be baptised privately by them.

On November 1st, 1665, it is represented to the Bishop of the Synod that their bounds were much pestered and troubled with seditious ministers who kept conventicles and unlawful meetings to the great hindrance of the work of the ministry in those parts, and the Presbytery of Kirkcudbright was instructed to get detailed information and represent the same to the Lords of His Majesty's High Commission. The Presbytery further declared that one of the chief causes, as they supposed, why their bounds were in such an unsettled condition was that they had not, like other shires, Justices of the Peace who might concur with them for the settlement of the same.

At a meeting at Kirkcudbright, on 26th April, 1666, the ministers represented their hard, necessitous, and singular condition as that they (being all and everyone of them newly planted within this said diocese of Galloway, as also come from the several places of this kingdom) had vast expense and charge in accommodating themselves for transporting themselves to, and settling themselves in this then so unruly and unsettled country. As also that they being now come do find that their respective stipends, though mean, yet are altogether unsettled. As also that these unsettled stipends are very ill and unthankfully paid, partly by reason of the backwardness of diverse disaffected and mal-contented persons and partly by and through the present deadness of trade, the principal nerves and sinews of that country. They accordingly ask to be relieved of an annuity imposed on them by Acts of Parliament.

At the same meeting, representatives were appointed to give the names of ministers who kept conventicles within the presbytery, to Sir James Turner, who was then in the town, desiring him to take such course as may remedy the same. These ministers' names were as follows, viz.:—Mr. Adam Allison, Mr. John Wilkie, Mr. Samuel Arnot, Master James Buglass, Mr. Alexander Robertson, Mr. William Hay, Master John Cant, Mr. Thomas Vernor, and Master John Blaicater.

The several ministers within the diocese were commanded to give in an exact and impartial list of all wilful and ordinary withdrawers, conventicle keepers, and abettors of the same within their respective congregations.

At this meeting a committee was appointed to advise with Sir James Turner as to the terms of a Bond to be tendered by every minister to their disorderly parishioners. The draft Bond was submitted and approved by the Bishop and Synod as follows, and the ministers were ordained to have it observed:—

" I ——— Forasmickle as Sir James Turner commander of his Majesty's forces of foot in Galloway having full and ample Commission to take up ye fines imposed by act of Parliament upon such as willfully absent themselves from the church, the hearing of ye word and other divine ordinances, and to punish such as frequent Conventicles forbidden by the law, and resetts such outed ministers as do preach at these Conventicles, And I being one of that number that have transgressed in all or some one or other of ye premises, And yet being most civilie discreetly and gentilly delt with in ye matter of my fines for my bygane faults of that kind by ye said Sir James Turner, in hopes of and upon my promise to keep ye church duly and to frequent all divine ordinances for ye future and to dishaunt all Private Conventicles and to disown and discountenance all Conventicle preachers, Therefore wit ye me to be bound and oblig'd like as by thir presents I bind and oblige me to keep and observe this my promise in all ye particulars above rehearsed, As likewise in case it shall happen me at any time hereafter to dishaunt ye church, hearing of ye word or other divine ordinances for two Lords days together, unlesse I be hindered by sicknesse or by permission of the minister of the Parish, And in case I shall be found to be present at any private Conventicle or meeting forbidden by ye law, or shall countenance or reset in my house, or contribute for the supply of any Conventicle preachers, In these cases and every one of them I bind and oblige me by my heirs and executers to content and pay to ———— his heirs and executers the summe of ———— Scots money, and that within six days next after my committing any of the said failings in any particular of the premises the samen being proven as accords in law, or, in case I shall refuse to clear myselfe by the oath, before ye minister of the Parish where I live or before the Presbytery of the place, And for the more securitie etc."

At the same meeting, ministers who had not already given in a list of wilful with-drawers and conventicle keepers did so, and reference is made to a conventicle at Glenvogie, within the parish of Penninghame, on the last day of December, 1665, " but Mr. James Garshore, minister of the parish, being not now in the country," they could not get full information about it. The Presbytery of Stranraer being interrogated anent their wilful with-drawers, declared that they had none except the Earl of Cassillis, the late ministers, some chaplains (which chaplains the Synod ordained them to proceed against conform to former Acts), and one James Johnstone, a fugitive.

The state of the Glenkens seems to have given the Synod considerable trouble, and they agreed to write certain gentlemen there:—in the parish of Carsphairn, Gilbert Macadam of Waterhead, William Gordon of Dundeugh, and Alexander Gordon of Knockgray; in the parish of Dalry, Robert Stewart of Ardoch, James Logan of Bogue, and Robert Grier of Millmark; in the parish of Balmaclellan, William Gordon, Shirmers, Gordon of Holm, and Robert Gordon, Trochqueen; in the parish of Kells, the Provost of New Galloway; James Chalmers of Waterside, and John Grier of Dalton, desiring them to meet with some of the ministers to confer anent settling of their respective parishes. Many of these gentlemen were devoted Covenanters. The Synod appointed their well beloved brethren, Mr. James Colquhoun, minister of Penninghame, Mr. Andrew Simpson, minister of Kirkinner, Mr. Alexander Cowper, minister of Sorbie, and Mr. Alexander Irving, minister of Parton, to go to meet them. These ministers afterwards reported that they had proceeded to New Galloway as arranged, "but, although they stayed there a considerable time, yet none of the gentlemen that were written to and desired to be present came except one of them—Shirmers—so that nothing was done in the matter." Some of the ministers were appointed to go there and preach, but they one and all had some excuse, because we find the following:—Reported by Mr. James Hutcheson "That he could not keep the diet appointed the last Synod by reason of the greatness of the waters."

Reported by Mr. Thomas Ireland, " That he was lying very sick of a fever." Reported by Mr. Alexander Cowper " That he went not, being unwell." Reported by Mr. James Colquhoun " That he went to Carsphairn according to appointment, but he got not an auditory." Reported by Mr. Alexander Irving " That he was going, but——(a very significant blank, excuses having apparently run short). Reported by Mr. James Shaw " That he went not, conceiving that he would get not auditory." Nothing further is required to show how determined the Glenkens folk were to have no dealings with Episcopacy.

At Kirkcudbright, on 29th April, 1669, the Bishop and Synod having heard that within the Presbytery of Stranraer there are several disorders, as some baptising their children by outed ministers, and hearing also that it hath been the study of some gentlemen within the bounds to break the discipline of the Church, especially within the parish of Kirkmaiden, obstructing so far as they could Church censure against known delinquents, illegally opposing the minister, and weakening his hands in order to the exercise of discipline in that part, ordained the Presbytery of Stranraer to begin their visitations at Kirkmaiden Church, and to cite before them such persons as are guilty of said dismeanours, and if they get no satisfaction, to represent the matter to the Privy Council.

The Bishop and the Synod appointed the several Presbyteries to write or speak to the late ministers who kept conventicles and baptised children of other men's congregations, that they would desist from so doing, or else application would be made to the Privy Council thereanent.

At a meeting at Wigtown, 28th April, 1670, the minister of Kirkcowan complains that he cannot get a Session to concur with him in the exercise of discipline, and the Presbytery of Wigtown is recommended to appoint some of their number to meet with him to supply the place with a Session.

The proceedings contain reference to Patrick Vans in the parish of Sorbie, for disorderly baptising of his child, and the Presbytery of Wigtown is ordained to proceed against him.

CHAPTER XI.

Proceedings against Welsh, Semple, Blackadder, Arnot, Peden,
   and other ministers for keeping conventicles and baptising
   —The people persecuted for hearing outed ministers—Sir
   James Turner sent into Galloway to crush any opposition—
   The rising at Dalry—The sufferings endured in Galloway—
   Fines in Stewartry parishes—Quarterings and other aggrava-
   tions.

TOWARDS the end of January, 1666, at the instigation
probably of the bishop of Galloway, the Council
direct proceedings to be taken against "Mr. John
Welsh, late minister of Irongray; Mr. Gilbert Semple,
late minister of Kirkpatrick of the Muir; Mr. John
Blackadder, late minister of Troqueer; Mr. Robert
Archibald, late minister of Dunscore; Mr. Samuel
Arnot, late minister at Kirkpatrick-durham; Mr.
John Douglas, late minister at   ; Mr. Alexander Peden, late minister at   ; Mr. William
Reid, late minister at   ; Mr. John Wilkie, late
minister at   ; Mr. John Crookshanks, and John
Osborne in Keir, on the ground that they do still
presume to keep conventicles and private meetings and
presume to preach, and in their sermons and conference
traduce, reflect upon, and declare against authority,
and the government civil and ecclesiastical, as it is
established by law in Church and State, and do not
only withdraw from the ordinary and public meetings

for divine worship, but do most seditiously by their
practice and example and by their speeches and dis-
courses seduce and endeavour to withdraw others from
the same, and particularly the said Mr. John Welsh
does presume frequently at least once every week to
preach in the parish of Irongray in the Presbytery
of Dumfries, and himself and these who frequent his
conventicles do convene together armed with swords
and pistols, at the which meetings he also baptises
children that are brought to him by disaffected
persons." Other charges of a similar nature are
narrated against the others, and of Alexander Peden
it is said that the conventicles were "kept under
cloud of night with a great deal of confusion, as also
the said Mr. Alexander rides up and down the country
with sword and pistol in grey clothes." Osborne's
crime is giving notice to the people of these unlawful
meetings. Accordingly, they are to be charged at the
Market Cross of Edinburgh, Dumfries, Kirkcudbright, Pier and Shore of Leith, to appear personally
before the Lords of Council at Edinburgh, to answer
to the premises under pain of rebellion and putting
to the horn.

Not only were conventicles forbidden, but all who
attended them were liable to severe pains and penalties.
The people met in the moors and fields to hear their
outed ministers, and were persecuted for so doing and
for refusing to hear the Episcopal curates. They were
hunted like criminals, and Sir James Turner was sent
into Galloway with troops to enforce compliance and

to crush any opposition. This led to the outbreak at
Dalry, followed by the defeat of the Covenanters at
Rullion Green. The facts and circumstances connected
with the Rising will be dealt with separately.

In a letter from a gentleman in Galloway, published
in Wodrow, it is stated that the first of these
sufferings was in 1663, about mid May, when the
forces came into Dumfries and Kirkcudbright. The
second was in 1665, when the horse and foot came in
under Sir James Turner. "The third was in this
present year—1666—when about the month of March
or beginning of April the Party came in under the
command of Sir James Turner." After narrating the
hardships endured, the letter continues—

"These people are weakened in their estates
indeed, but confirmed in their opinion. It is
palpable that the extended conformity cannot be
gained by such extreme dealing, but rather
marred; and will not the report of this rigid
dealing (which cannot be hid) have influence upon
all those of their judgment to alienate them the
more from the course? I confess this consideration is like to have little weight with some
covetous soldiers (employed here) assuming to
themselves an arbitrary power to pray upon a
desolate people for their own private gain, but
I expect that judicious and unbiassed men who
tender the good of the country and his Majesty's
interest therein, will lay this to heart and take

their best way to represent it to our rulers for remedy in the matter and moving their compassion towards a poor people that have few to speak for them.

" Follows that brief relation of this country's sufferings, which I promised you in my letter, wherein this is enclosed, in which you have set down, 1. The enumerate sums of money; 2. Some general aggravations—

1. The Parish of Carsphairn, forty-nine families in that called kirk fines, has suffered the loss of - - - - £4,864 17 4
2. In the Parish of Dalry, forty-three families,   9,577 6 8
3. In Balmaclellan, forty-nine families, - 6,430 10 4
4. In the Parish of Balmaghie, nine families,   425 11 8
5. In Tungland Parish, out of two or three poor families, - - - - - - 166 12 8
6. In Twynam Parish, from some poor persons, - - - - - - - 81 4 0
7. In Borg Parish, out of twenty families, - 2,062 17 4
8. In Girton Parish, out of nine poor families,   525 10 4
9. In Anworth Parish, from some poor families, - - - - - - - 773 6 4
10. In Kirkpatrick-durham Parish, out of thirty-four inconsiderable families, - 2,235 16 0
11. In Kirkmabreck Parish, some few families,   563 6 0
12. In Monygaff, three families, - - - 600 0 0
13. In Kirkcudbright, eighteen families, - 2,580 0 0
14. In Lochrutton Parish, out of thirty-seven poor families, notwithstanding they want a minister, - - - - - - 2,080 0 0
15. In Troqueer Parish, twelve poor families,   756 10 0
16. In Kells Parish, - - - - - 466 13 4
17. In Corsmichael Parish, - - - - 1,666 13 4
18. In Parton Parish, from twenty-four families, 2,838 9 4
19. In Irongray Parish, forty-two families, - 3,362 18 8

"In the Sheriffdom of Nithsdale
or Dumfriesshire—

1. In the town and parish of Dumfries, from fifty-one families, was exacted the sum of	4,617	15	4
2. In the parish of Kirkmaho, from twenty poor families, - - - - - -	1,341	6	8
3. In Dunscore parish, from fourteen families,	1,411	13	4
4. In Glencairn parish, from families, - -	2,146	14	8
The total of these sums extend to - -	£51,575	13	4

"Besides the sums above named, it is to be considered that the great expense of quartering is
not received in most parts of the parishes above-
named, which would make a great addition to
the former sums, but it cannot well be counted.

. . . .

"That all these forementioned sums are by and
attour all the fines imposed by the State which,
within the Stewartry of Galloway upon ninety-
one persons, extend to the sum of £47,860, and
in the Sheriffdom of Nithsdale upon forty-one
persons, extend to £29,260: which being laid together the Parliament fines within the Stewartry
of Galloway, and Sheriffdom of Nithsdale, extend
to £77,120: and that besides the expense of cess
and quarter for the fines themselves for several
persons, was put to pay near as much more cess
as their fines came to besides quarter.

"That by and attour all the foresaid losses,
there are many families (whose sums are not here

reckoned) in probability totally ruined, and many others scattered already: for instance in Lochrutton, a little parish, I find to be reckoned to be above sixteen families utterly broken. In Irongray parish the most part of the families put from house keeping already, the soldiers having violently taken away both there and elsewhere from several families the thing they should have lived on, even to the leading away of their haystacks. I forbear to set down the rest of the broken and ruined families until I can give you a more distinct account: only I can tell you in the general that utter ruin to the most part of the families in this country is like to be the consequence of these grievous and intolerable impositions: and also to my certain knowledge, there are several gentlemen who formerly were well to live, that are now put from house keeping, and forced to wander: yea, ofttime to be beholden to others for a night's lodging, the soldiers having possessed themselves in their houses, cattle, plenishing, barns, etc.

"Ordinarily, wherever they came to quarter, they do not rest content with sufficiency, but set themselves to waste needlessly; at some times send for sheep off the hill, and cast whole bulks of them to their hounds and ratches: also by treading and scattering corn and straw, they and their pedies at their pleasure, and usually saying, We came to destroy, and we shall destroy you.

"It is specially to be considered, that besides all which the country hath suffered hitherto, the soldiers are sent forth through the country again, and fine, cess, and quarter is imposed of new upon the same persons and families who were fined before, yea, upon some it is doubled and trebled. I have lately heard that some yeomen are fined in five hundred merks, besides, the gentlemen in six or seven hundred pounds. I cannot see what shall be the fruit of these things, except utter ruin to their worldly estates.

.   .   .   .

"Notwithstanding all these impositions upon that people and aggravation of their sufferings above mentioned, yet the people are commanded to take a Bond, wherein (besides all the particular obligations required in that Bond) is contained an acknowledgment that the commander of the party has dealt civilly and discreetly with them."

CHAPTER XII.

Bitter persecution after Pentland—Sir William Bannatyne sent
into Galloway with large party of soldiers—Oppression of
the people—Roger Gordon of Holm, Earlston, David M'Gill
of Dalry, Gilbert Monry in Marbreck, Alexander Gordon of
Knockbrack—Bannatyne's horrible cruelty—List of persons
pursued for forfeiture—Numbers ordered to be executed
when taken—Change of King's advisers—King's Indemnity—
Long list of exceptions—Bond to keep public peace—Parties
appointed in Wigtownshire and the Stewartry to get it
signed—Differences of opinion as to its true intent and
meaning.

AFTER the overthrow of the Covenanters at Pentland,
many of the outed ministers crossed to Holland, but
others continued to preach to the people at conventicles. Bitter persecution followed immediately
on Pentland, and then there was a lull, during which
the preachers became bolder, and multitudes flocked
to hear them. Sir William Bannatyne was sent into
Galloway with a large party of soldiers. He brought
four hundred foot and a troop of horses to Roger
Gordon's of Holm, in the parish of Dalry, and
quartered them there. They ate up everything about
the place, and when all was consumed they forced the
neighbours to carry to them. They then proceeded to
the house of Earlston, which they turned into a
garrison, and sent out parties to harass the whole
district. David M'Gill of Dalry was being searched

for, but he disguised himself in a woman's clothes, and got away. The soldiers, asserting that his wife had been privy to his escape, seized her and bound her and tortured her by putting lighted matches between her fingers. She suffered terribly, lost one of her hands, and in a few days she died. Heavy fines were imposed without any reason, and where they could not all be paid at once, bonds were exacted for the balance.

Gilbert Monry of Marbreck in Carsphairn was fined fifty merks without any alleged fault. When he asked Sir William Bannatyne why he was fined, the other answered, " Because you have gear, and I must have a part of it." And indeed a similar answer might have been given in regard to all his exactions.

Alexander Gordon of Knockbrack, for his sons being at Pentland, was made to suffer a great deal, and John Gordon in Carneval had everything taken from him, his loss being 16,000 merks.

In the parish of Balmaghie, Bannatyne went into a public house, and after getting some liquor, attempted to take advantage of the mistress of the house. Her husband went to protect her, and Bannatyne struck him dead on the spot. " Bannatyne and his party drank in the house most of the Lord's Day; and when they could drink no more, let what remained run upon the ground, and rifled the house of all in it. In short, it was known in this country that Bannatyne never refused to let his men rob and plunder wherever they pleased. His oppressions, murders, robberies, rapes, adulteries, etc., were so many and atrocious that the managers themselves were ashamed of them, and we shall afterwards hear that he was called to some account for them, and forced to flee the nation."

Many were imprisoned upon mere suspicion. James Grierson of Dargoner was imprisoned in Ayr without any fault, although he earnestly craved trial. At length he was let out upon giving caution for his appearance when called. In August, 1667, a Justice Court was held at Edinburgh, when the Lord Advocate produced a commission to pursue the following persons for forfeiture before the Court as having been in the late Rebellion in the west:—

"Colonel James Wallace, Major Joseph Learmont, William Maxwell of Monreif younger, John M'Clellan of Barscob, John Gordon of Knockbrex, Robert M'Clellan of Barmageichan, James Cannon of Barnshalloch younger, Robert Cannon of Mardrochat younger, John Welsh of Scar, —— Welsh of Cornley, —— Gordon of Garry in Kells, Robert Chalmers brother to Gadgirth, Henry Grier in Balmaclellan, David Scott in Irongray, John Gordon in Middleton of Dalry, William Gordon there, John M'Naught there, Robert and Gilbert Cannons there, Andrew Dempster of Carradow, James Grierson of Dargoner (who was delayed), James Kirk of Sundaywell, —— Ramsay in Mains of Arnistoun, John Hutchison in Newbottle, —— Row, Chaplain to Scotstarbet, Patrick Listoun in Calder, Patrick Listoun his son, James Wilkie in Mains of Cliftounhall, William Muir of Caldwell, the goodman of Caldwell, Mr. John Cuningham of Bedland, William Porterfield of Quarreltoun, Alexander Porterfield his brother, Robert Ker of Kers-

land, William Lockhart of Wicketshaw, David Poe
in Pokelly, Mr. Gabriel Semple, Mr. John Semple,
Mr. John Guthrie, Mr. John Welsh, Mr. Samuel
Arnot, Mr. James Smith, Mr. Alexander Pedin, Mr.
—— Orr, Mr. William Veitch, Mr. —— Paton, Mr.
John Cruickshanks, Mr. Gabriel Maxwell, Mr. John
Carstairs, Mr. James Mitchell, and Mr. William
Forsyth."

The Court, upon their non-appearance, decerned
them to be denounced rebels and their lands to fall
to his Majesty's use. A simple forfeiture was not
reckoned a good enough claim for the estates to be
disposed of, and the advocate urged to have the sentence
of death passed upon as many of them as he saw fit
to insist against. This was utterly illegal, but the
persecutors let nothing stand in the way to gain their
end, and accordingly proceedings were taken against
Colonel James Wallace of Auchanes; Major Joseph
Learmont; John M'Clellan, Barscob; Mr. John
Welsh; Mr. James Smith; Patrick Listoun of Calder;
William Listoun, his son; William Porterfield of
Quarreltoun. They were, as a matter of course,
ordered to be executed when taken, and their estates
forfeited. A few days afterwards, 16th August, 1667,
the same farce was gone through against William Muir
of Caldwell; John Caldwell of Caldwell younger;
Robert Ker of Kersland; Mr. John Cuningham of
Bedland; Alexander Porterfield, brother to Quarreltoun; Maxwell, son of Monreif; Robert M'Clellan
of Barmageichan; Robert Cannon of Mardrochat,
younger; Robert Chalmers, brother to Gadgirth;

Mr. Gabriel Semple; Mr. John Guthrie; Mr. Alex. Peden; Mr. William Veitch; Mr. John Crookshanks; and Patrick M'Naught in Cummock. They also were ordered to be executed when taken, and their estates forfeited. Robert Chalmers was afterwards (1669) pardoned.

During this year, many changes took place among the King's Councillors, and there was a disposition to relax the proceedings against the Presbyterians, and to disband the army. Sir Robert Murray was sent to Scotland to learn how matters stood, and on 23rd August, 1667, the King's command was made known— that the army was to be forthwith disbanded. On 1st October, 1667, the King's Indemnity was given to those in the Rebellion, excepting always from his pardon the persons and fortunes of Colonel James Wallace; Major Learmont; —— Maxwell of Monreif, younger; —— M'Clellan of Barscob; —— Gordon of Barbreck; —— M'Clellan of Barmageichan; —— Cannon of Barnshalloch, younger; —— Cannon of Barley younger; —— Cannon of Mardrochat, younger; —— Welsh of Scar; ——Welsh of Cornley; —— Gordon of Garrery in Kells; Robert Chalmers, brother to Gadgirth; Henry Grier in Balmaclellan; David Scott in Irongray; John Gordon in Midtoun of Dalry; William Gordon there; John M'Naught there; Robert and Gilbert Cannons there; —— Gordon of Bar, elder, in Kirkpatrick-durham; Patrick M'Naught in Cumnock; John M'Naught, his son; Gordon of Holm, younger; —— Dempster of Carridow; —— of Dargoner; —— of Sundaywell; —— Ramsay in the

Mains of Arnistoun; John Hutchison in Newbottle; Patrick Listoun in Calder; William Listoun, his son; James Wilkie in the Mains of Cliftonhall; the laird of Caldwell, the goodman of Caldwell, younger; the laird of Kersland, younger; the laird of Bedland Cuningham; —— Porterfield of Quarrelton; Alexander Porterfield, his brother; —— Lockhart of Wicketshaw; Mr. —— Trail, son to Mr. Robert Trail, sometime chaplain to Scotstarbet; David Poe in Pokelly; Mr. Gabriel Semple; John Semple; Mr. John Guthrie; Mr. John Welsh; Mr. Samuel Arnot; Mr. James Smith; Mr. Alexander Peden; Mr. —— Orr; Mr. William Veitch; Mr. —— Paton, preacher; Mr. —— Crookshanks; Mr. Gabriel Maxwell; Mr. John Carstairs; Mr. James Mitchell; Mr. William Forsyth; and of all others who were forfeited, or under process of forfeiture, as also excepting all such who, since the late rebellion, had been accessory to the robbing of ministers' houses and committing violence upon the persons of ministers, and processed for the same, and found guilty thereof.

The pardon was only to extend to those who before 1st January gave Bond for keeping the public peace, and among those appointed to take this Bond were the Master of Herries, the Sheriff of Galloway, the Laird of Baldoon, —— Maxwell of Munches, and —— Maxwell of Woodhead for the Sheriffdom of Wigtown and Stewartry of Kirkcudbright.

A Bond was also prepared to be signed by noblemen, gentlemen, heritors, and feuars for themselves, tenants, and servants, that they would keep the public peace

(*i.e.*, abstain from conventicles) under the penalty of
the heritor's yearly rent, the tenant's rent, and the
servant's fee. The Earls of Linlithgow, Annandale,
Galloway, and Lord Drumlanrig were appointed for
the Shire of Wigtown, the Stewartry of Kirkcudbright
and Shire of Dumfries, and Stewartry of Annandale,
to convene these parties at the heads of the different
districts on 7th November to sign this Bond.

There was considerable difference of opinion as to
the true intent and meaning of the words, " Keep the
public peace." Some accepted the Bond without
demur as containing nothing contrary to the principles
of Presbyterianism, some absolutely refused it as
homologating the Government both in Church and
State, and others took a middle course and signed along
with it a protestation against any supposed unlawful
meaning of the Bond, declaring that if it was intended
to oblige the subject to approve of and submit to
Prelatic government, or to restrict anything for
extirpation of the same, contrary to that great
indissoluble standing Bond—The Solemn League and
Covenant—it was most sinful and perfidious, and
utterly to be refused.

CHAPTER XIII.

Inquiry as to extortions by the military—Report showing what
Galloway had to suffer from Sir James Turner—Turner
dismissed—Bannatyne fined and removed from the Kingdom
—Those who have failed to take advantage of the Indemnity
to be seized—Lists of those in Carsphairn parish and Dalry
parish—Attempt on Archbishop Sharp—Pentland prisoners
dealt with—Another rising feared—Cockburn sent to the
Glenkens—Cannon of Mardrochat taken prisoner, and turns
informer—Indulgence—Withdrawal of troops from Galloway
—Dissensions among the Covenanters in Galloway over the
Indulgence—Mr. Park indulged to Stranraer, but Mr.
Naismith appointed by the Bishop.

ABOUT the end of 1667, Sheriff Agnew, Lords
Galloway and Kenmuir made representation to the
Government as to the extortions of the military, and
a commission was granted to Lords Nithsdale and
Kenmuir and the Laird of Craigdarroch (Ferguson)
to enquire into the conduct of Sir James Turner and
Sir William Bannatyne. The report anent Sir James
Turner shows how much the people of Galloway had
to suffer at his hands:—

"The Committee appointed for trial of Sir
James Turner's carriage, having given in their
report, bearing that, according to order, they
having met upon the 28th of November last, drew
up fit queries and instructions concerning it, and
orders to some gentlemen in the west, to take

information of all sums of money exacted by Sir James, or his order, for fines, cess, or otherwise, and of all his deportments: and to be sure of a speedy return, sent Thomas Buntine with letters and orders above-mentioned, appointing him to attend the prosecution of them, and bring back the reports, which he accordingly did, before the 10th of January.

"The Committee did thereafter deliver to Sir James a paper containing some grievances drawn out from the Stewartry of Kirkcudbright only, those in the other shires not being so clear and full. They allowed Sir James to see all the reports in the Clerk's hands, and enjoined him to give in his answers in writing, the 17th instant, which he did. And the Committee having read and considered all, and examined Sir James upon every point that occurred, after a full debate, agreed to offer to the council their humble opinion, that the council do, in obedience to his majesty's commands, transmit to the secretary the following report to be communicated to his majesty:—

"The lords of his majesty's privy council did no sooner receive his command in his gracious letter, of the 21st of November last, for taking exact information of Sir James Turner's deportment in the west, but they ordered and empowered a committee of their number to enquire diligently thereinto: and by their report it appears that upon information from the Stewartry of Kirkcudbright, given in upon oath of parties, or their masters or neighbours, many illegal exactions have been made, and disorders committed, such as—

"1mo, Quartering of soldiers, for levying of fines and impositions. 2nd, exacting cess, or quartering money, for more soldiers than were actually present, sometimes for double the number, or more, and that besides free quarters for those present, sometimes eightpence, sometimes twelvepence, sometimes sixteenpence, and sometimes more for each man. 3tio, Cess exacted for divers days, sometimes eight, ten, or more, before the party did actually appear. 4to, Imposing of fines, and quartering, before any previous citation or hearing of parties. 5to, Fining without due information from ministers. 6to, Fining such as lived orderly, as appears by minister's certification. 7mo, Fining and cessing for causes for which there are no warrants from acts of Parliament or council; as, 1mo, Baptising of children by outed ministers. 2do, Baptising by neighbouring ministers when the parish church was vacant. 3tio, Marrying by outed ministers. 4to, For keeping of conventicles. 8vo, Fining for whole years preceding his coming to the country, and that after they had begun to live orderly. 9no, Fining fathers for their daughters baptising their children by outed ministers, though forisfamiliate six months before, and living in another parish. 10mo, Fining without proportioning the sum with the fault. 11mo, Fining the whole parishes, promiscuously, as well those that lived orderly, as those that did not. Fining the whole parishes, where there was no incumbent minister. 13mo, Fining one that lay a year bed fast. 14mo, Forcing Bonds from the innocent. 15mo, Cessing people who were not fined. 16mo, Taking away cattle. All those actings were illegal.

"Misdemeanours of other kinds were. 17mo, Agreeing for fine and cess both in one sum, whereby accounts are confounded. 18mo, Not admitting of complainers, who were cessed, to come to his presence, alleged to be his constant practice. 19mo, Permitting his servants to take money for admitting people to him, and yet access denied. 20mo, Increasing the number of quartering soldiers after complaints. 21mo, Exacting money for removing soldiers after cess and fines were paid. Everyone of the foregoing articles was made out by information upon oath, which yet doth not amount to a legal proof, which in most of these cases will be difficult, if not impossible to obtain, in regard that no witnesses can be had, that are not liable to exception, unless by examining officers, soldiers, and servants, which would take up much time and labour.

"Sir James Turner's defences, as to such of the foregoing articles as he acknowledged, are commission and instructions from the then lord commissioner for quartering to raise fines, for fining those who forbore going to church, or married, or baptised by outed ministers, or kept conventicles, and that upon the delations of credible persons and to prefer them to those of ministers, but he does affirm, that all the commissions and instructions were taken from him by the rebels, when he was made prisoner, and so had nothing to show for his vindication: And for all the other heads above written, he either denies matter of fact, ascribes the transactions to others, or pleads ignorance.

"The sums of money received for fines and cess, and bonds taken, he acknowledged to have amounted to thirty thousand pounds Scots. The sums charged upon him by the country, besides quartering, came to about thirty-eight thousand pounds Scots: wherein is not reckoned what was exacted from any of those who rose in rebellion, and some parishes whence no information was returned."

Turner was dismissed the service.

In regard to Bannatyne, the Council, on 4th August, 1668, passed the following Act:—

"The lords of Council, considering the complaints given in against Sir William Bannelden, and the answers given thereto, do fine the said Sir William in the sum of two hundred pounds sterling, allowing him a precept drawn by the lords of the treasury for one thousand three hundred merks which he answered; and in respect the said Sir William hath exhibited all the bonds and papers taken by him in Galloway, and given sufficient caution to remove off the kingdom betwixt and the first of September next, and not to return without special order, under the penalty of five hundred pounds sterling, do assoilie the said Sir William from all other pains and punishments that might have followed upon the said complaint."

He went over to the Low Countries, and was killed by a cannon ball at the siege of Grave.

A Report being called for of how many had signed the Bond to keep the public peace, it is stated that "in the Stewartry of Kirkcudbright 14 have taken the Bond and 128 have not." On May 9th, 1668, a Proclamation is made ordering magistrates and officers to seize those who had failed to take advantage of the so-called Indemnity. A huge list is given, among the names being the following:—

In Carsphairn Parish.

Nathanael Cannon in Formator.
James Macmitchel in Knockinreoch.
John Macmillan in Strong-gashel.
Robert Macmillan in Kiltarsen.
William Macmillan in Bradinoch.
James Mackilney in Polmidow.
John Logan in Loch Head.
John Crawford in Drumjohn.
John Cunninghame in Longford.
——— Macadam in Waterhead.
John Hannah there.

John Macmillan, younger, in Brockloch.

George Macadam in Bow.

George Ferguson in Woodhead.

David Cubbison in Moss.

James Macadam in Knockgray.

Alexander Macmillan in Bank.

William Smith at Bridge of Geuch.

John Wylie in Smiton.

Roger Macolm in Netherholm.

Robert Macolm in Netherglen.

In Dalry Parish.

David Cannon, brother to Morgrie.

Edward Crichton in Knockstring.

James Ferguson in Trostan.

Robert Crichton in Fingland.

Andrew Crichton there.

John Machutcheon in Clachan of Dalry.

James Welsh, his brother.

John Welsh in Skeoch.

Robert Wallat in Scar.

Herbert Biggar, son to Herbert Biggar of Barbuie.

Thomas Smith, son to James Smith of Drumlyre.

Robert Sinclair, son to Robert Sinclair in Lag.

William Welsh in Ingliston.

James Biggar in Margloby.

John Currier in Newark.

Robert Currier in Dalquhairn.

David Currier in Ruchtree.

Robert Colvin in Ingliston.

John Hunter in Barncleugh.

John Wallat in Holhill.

John Welsh in Knachston.

John Wright in Larbreck.

John Whitehead in Cludden.

James Macbirnie in Crobmor.

John Wilson in Traquair.

Andrew Haining, servant to John Neilson of Corsock.

John Gaw, son to Robert Gaw in Airncrogue.

The King's disposition at this time to allow Presbyterians more liberty was checked by the attempt of James Mitchell to shoot the archbishop of St. Andrews at the head of Black Friar's Wynd, Edinburgh, on 11th July, 1668.

Following on a letter of 23rd July, 1668, the King allowed the Council to do with those concerned in Pentland as they saw fit. Some were banished to Virginia, and others were admitted to take the Bond, while William Welsh and James Welsh in Irongray, whose names had been erroneously inserted in the Proclamation of 9th May last, appeared before the Council and satisfied them that they were not at Pentland, and, on signing a Bond, were allowed to go.

On August 12th, the Council, understanding that some of the late rebels were gathering together, granted power to the Earl of Linlithgow to dissipate them, and ordered all where he came to assist him. There was nothing like any stir among the Presbyterians at this time, and it is difficult to say why this alarm arose unless as a pretext for something else. However, Lieutenant Mungo Murray was ordered, September 3rd, to search with sixty horse in the heads of Kyle and Nithsdale, and apprehend any rebels in arms, and another party, under William Cockburn, was sent to search in the Glenkens of Galloway.

It was probably at this time that Robert Cannon, younger, of Mardrochat, contrived to be taken prisoner, for in November the Council ordered Sir James Turner, Chalmers of Waterside, and Mardrochat, elder to come to Edinburgh to be witnesses against him. On 7th January, 1669, he was liberated, and eight months later was pardoned. He proved worthy of it, for he became a spy and informer, and sought every opportunity of betraying the Covenanters, some of whom had been his boon companions from his earliest years.

On March 4th, 1669, the Council prohibited the baptism of children by any but the parish minister established by the Government. For default, every heritor was to forfeit a fourth part of his yearly valued rent, each tenant £100 Scots, and suffer six weeks' imprisonment, each cottar £20 and six weeks' imprisonment.

In April, 1669, the Council published another Act against conventicles, specially applicable to the shires of Lanark, Renfrew, Ayr, and the Stewartry of Kirkcudbright, certifying that each heritor in whose lands a conventicle was held was to be fined £50 *toties quoties.*

For some time the feeling in the country had been growing steadily in favour of greater liberty to dissenters, and Lord Tweeddale prevailed upon some of the Presbyterian ministers to send a letter to London containing full expression of their affection for the King, and disclamation of some positions alleged to be treasonable, charged upon some Presbyterians. Tweeddale undoubtedly used his influence in favour of greater liberty, and on 15th July, 1669, the Council received a letter from the King authorising them to appoint so many of the outed ministers " as have lived peaceably and orderly in the places where they have resided, to return and preach and exercise other functions of their ministry in the parish churches where they formerly resided and served (provided they be vacant) and to allow patrons to present to other vacant churches such others of them as you shall approve of; and that such ministers as shall take collation from the Bishop of the diocese and keep presbyteries and synods may be warranted to lift their stipends as other ministers of the kingdom'." Those who would not be collated were only to possess the manse and glebe, and get a yearly maintenance. Those of the outed ministers who had behaved peaceably and orderly and were not re-entered were to be allowed four hundred merks out of the vacant churches for their maintenance, and instructions were given that, as there were now no pretences for conventicles, if any should preach without authority or keep conventicles, they were to be proceeded against with all severity, both preachers and hearers.

The quarterings of the soldiers upon private persons was ordered to cease, and finally instructions were given for the withdrawal of the troops in Galloway. It is a well known story that, when the Council decided on this step, the archbishop of Glasgow exclaimed in dismay, "O, my Lords, if the army is disbanded, the Gospel will go clean out of the diocese."

The Indulgence gave rise to serious dissensions in the ranks of the Covenanters. Many of them held that it was sinful to accept it, as involving recognition of the royal supremacy in ecclesiastical matters. These were in the majority in Galloway, and refused to hear the indulged ministers, while some of them even went so far that they would have nothing to do with those non-indulged who would not denounce the indulged. These were named "the irreconcilables," the "hill folk," and afterwards "the Cameronians." The banished ministers in Holland strongly condemned the Indulgence, and this greatly strengthened the Hill folk at home. The differences that now arose among the Covenanters were never afterwards healed. Under the Indulgence, the Rev. John Cant was re-appointed to Kells, John M'Michan at Dalry, and William Maitland, who had been minister at Whithorn, was appointed to Beith. Mr. Park was re-appointed to Stranraer, but to defeat this the bishop admitted one Naismith to the church three days after Mr. Park was indulged. The town and parish would not give any countenance to Mr. Naismith, and, as one man, adhered to their former minister. The bishop caused the parties to be summoned to Edinburgh that the Council might determine the competition. When Mr. Park appeared before the Council, instead of going into the question of precedency between Mr. Naismith's admission and his act of indulgence, which was the point upon which he was cited, Mr. Naismith libelled Mr. Park for causing the church doors to be locked against him after his admission by the bishop, the falsity of which was made apparent by many of the people of Stranraer cited for their adherence to Mr. Park. He also accused Mr. Park of seditious doctrine. Notwithstanding very mean and base methods used to secure a conviction, the libel was brought in "Not Proven." When the Council came to the competition, it was alleged for Mr. Naismith that his presentation was prior to Mr. Park, and answered by Mr. Park that it was *a non habente potestatem,* the King being patron, and the bishop having most illegally taken upon him to present, and, although Mr. Park's act was prior to Mr. Naismith's admission, yet the Council without even hearing Mr. Park decided in favour of Mr. Naismith.

Mr. Park was a man of great learning, author of a treatise on patronages. This book was considerably enlarged by his son, Robert Park, Clerk to the General Assembly after the Revolution, and Town Clerk of Glasgow.

CHAPTER XIV.

The parishioners of Balmaclellan and Urr fined for outrages
committed on their curates—Garthland ignores a letter from
the Privy Council to grant Row, curate of Balmaclellan, a
presentation to Stonykirk—Gilbert M'Adam of Waterhead
gets up two Bonds extorted from him—Parliament asserts
the King's supremacy over all persons and in all causes
ecclesiastical within the Kingdom—Galloway men present at
armed conventicle in Fife—The Black Act—Field preaching
a capital offence—Cassillis speaks fearlessly against it—
Anna, Countess of Wigtown, fined for attending conventicles
—Gordon of Dundeugh gets up a Bond extorted from him—
Another Indulgence to outed ministers—Parties sent out to
apprehend conventicle preachers—Reward of £400 offered
for arrest of Welsh or Semple—Galloway lairds denounced
for harbouring inter-communed persons—William M'Millan
allowed to go to Balmaclellan—Welsh betakes himself to
North of England.

THE English curates were not looked on with any
favour by the parishioners among whom they settled in
Galloway, and there are one or two instances recorded
of violence against them. On 30th September, 1669,
a party of three individuals dressed as females broke
into the house of Mr. Row, the curate at Balmaclellan,
during the night, dragged him out of bed, assaulted
him, and helped themselves to whatever they wanted.
Mr. Thomas Warner, James Grier of Millmark, his
father-in-law, Gordon of Holm, Gordon of Gordonston, John Carsan, and James Chalmers, heritors there,
were charged as "actors, committers, at least con-

trivers and assisters, at least have since supplied or reset them." Failing to appear, the heritors and life-renters of Balmaclellan were decerned to pay Mr. Row £1,200 Scots. As soon as they could, they proceeded to Edinburgh, and offered to stand their trial. Nothing could be proved against them, but they were ordered to pay their shares of the fine imposed. Row was afterwards transferred to Stonykirk, Wigtownshire, and the Council wrote a letter to the Laird of Garthland, patron there, to grant him a presentation. Garthland, however, seems to have had other matters to attend to, for in March, 1673, a complaint was made to the Council that, when Row went to Stonykirk, the kirk locks were spoiled, and he could not get access, and was likewise hindered from possessing the manse and glebe.

The Council ordered an inquiry, but nothing seems to have followed on it. Row, however, got possession, and he subsequently became a Roman Catholic.

Three men in disguise broke into the house of Mr. Lyon, curate of Urr, in November, helped themselves to what they wanted, and, not finding him, carried off his wife as hostage, but soon let her go. The Council decerned the parish to pay Mr. Lyon £600 Scots, and ordered out letters against one John Smith, alleged to be concerned in the affair. After the Revolution, Mr. Lyon applied for admission as a Presbyterian minister, and his application was favourably received.

On 8th July, 1669, Gilbert M'Adam, Waterhead, was allowed to get from the Clerk of the Privy Council his Bond for 600 merks and another for 700 merks, extorted from him by violence by Sir William Bannatyne.

Parliament met in October, 1669, and almost the first thing they did was to pass that remarkable Act asserting his Majesty's supremacy over all persons and in all causes ecclesiastical within this his kingdom.

During 1670, further proclamations were made against conventicles.

The first armed conventicle since the Restoration was held at Beeth Hill in Fife by Mr. John Blackadder and Mr. John Dickson about the middle of June, 1670. There were some Galloway men present, including Barscobe and nine or ten others. While the preaching was going on, a lieutenant of the Government forces came on the scene, and afterwards wanted to get away, apparently to bring the troops, so some of the watch desired that he would stay till the preaching was ended, telling him his abrupt departure would offend and alarm the people. He refused, and began to threaten, drawing his staff, but they held him by force as he was putting his foot on the stirrup. Upon this, Barscobe and another young man who were upon the opposite side, seeing him drawing his staff, which they thought was a sword, ran with pistols, and cried, "Rogue, are you drawing?" Though they raised a little commotion on that side, the bulk of the people were very composed. The minister, seeing Barscobe and the other hastening to be at him, fearing they might kill him, immediately broke off to intervene, desiring the people to sit still till he returned. Eventually the lieutenant was allowed to go, and the minister returned, preaching for about three-quarters of an hour. All the time there were several horsemen riding at the foot of the hill in view of the people, but none offered to come near, for a terror had seized them, as was heard afterwards, and confessed by some of themselves. This conventicle gave new life to the friends of religion, and was the means of multiplying and enlarging their meetings throughout the United Kingdom, and was publicly given thanks for in the Scottish congregations abroad.

On 11th August, 1670, Mr. John Blackadder, for holding conventicles, was denounced and put to the horn.

The Black Act was passed on 13th August, 1670. It made field preaching a capital offence, attendance at conventicles treason, and those who would not volunteer information were to be held equally guilty. Lord Cassillis, to his immortal honour, spoke fearlessly against it, but he was not supported, and stood alone. When Leighton heard of it, he remonstrated with the Earl of Tweeddale on the inhumanity of it, and Tweeddale excused it on the pretext that it was not intended to enforce it, and indeed religious matters in Galloway were for a time allowed by the Government to drift so that conventicles became an institution, the bulk of the people attending the preaching of their favourite ministers without fear of molestation.

On 2nd March, 1671, Sir Charles Erskine, Lord Lyon, had commission to deal with the estates, goods, and gear of those forfeited for the rebellion of 1666 within the shires of Dumfries, Wigtown, and Kirkcudbright, for the year and crop 1670 and 1671, and to call intromitters before that time to account. The estates concerned were those of M'Clelland of Barsscobe, M'Clelland of Barmageichan, Canon younger of Mardrochat, John Neilson of Corsock, John Gordon of Knockbrex, Robert Gordon his brother, Major John MacCulloch of Barholm, Mr. Alexander Robertson, George M'Cartney of Blackit, Gordon in Porpreck, Cannon of Barshalloch, Welsh of Cornley, Gordon of Holm, —— of Scar. It appears that the name of M'Cartney of Blackit should not have been in the Commission at all. The sufferings of this family are dealt with separately.

On 27th July, 1672, Anna, Countess of Wigtown, was fined four thousand merks for attending two conventicles, while in most of the proceedings against the Covenanters at this time it is noticed that the Earl of Wigtown subscribed as a member of the Privy Council. On 25th January, 1672, Gordon of Dundeugh got up a Bond of six hundred merks, extorted from him by Sir William Bannatyne. A new Act was passed for observing the 29th of May, 1762, as the anniversary of the Restoration of the King, and instructing bells to be rung all day, bonfires at night, and the ministers were to preach yearly on that day, and give thanks to God Almighty for his so signal goodness to these kingdoms. On 3rd September, 1672, another Indulgence was granted to the ministers outed since 1667, and they were appointed to retire to the parishes named, and allowed to preach and exercise the other parts of their ministerial functions therein. In Carsphairn there were John Semple and Mr. William Erskine; in Kells, Mr. Cant and Mr. George Waugh; Dalry, Mr. John M'Michan and Mr. Thomas Thomson; in Balmaclelland, Mr. James Lawrie and Thomas Vernor in place of John Ross, who was going to Stonykirk. This Indulgence, like all the others, caused trouble amongst the ministers as to whether it was right to accept it. On 2nd April, 1673, there was another proclamation against conventicles. None of the indulged ministers observed the 29th May, and on June 12th letters were directed against those indulged in Kirkcudbrightshire for not keeping it. On July 12th, Messrs. John M'Michan in Dalry, John Semple at Carsphairn, and John Cant at Kells, were fined and lost the half of their stipend.

In 1674, parties were sent out to apprehend conventicle preachers, and any of the guard who should apprehend Mr. John Welsh or Mr. Gabriel Semple were promised a reward of £400 sterling. On August 3rd, 1676, Alexander Gordon of Knockbrack, Henry M'Culloch of Barholm, —— Hay of Arrowland, old Lady Monteith, Robert M'Clelland of Barmageichan, Robert Vans of Drumblair, all in Galloway, were ordered to be denounced for harbouring, resetting, and speaking with inter-communed persons.

On May 3rd, the Earl of Dumfries represented to the Council that Mr. William M'Millian had been for some time imprisoned in Dumfries for nonconformity, and that he should be let out and confined to Bal-

maclellan parish. This was agreed to. On February
13th, 1677, Lord Maxwell got authority to apprehend
Presbyterian ministers and preachers and substantial
heritors found at conventicles in the shires of Dumfries, Wigtown, and Stewartry of Kirkcudbright, and
was empowered to uplift five thousand merks, a fine
imposed on the parish of Dunscore for riots.

John Welsh went to the North of England, but in
the spring of 1677 returned to Galloway, and conventicles became numerous. On August 4th, 1677, a
number of the indulged ministers appeared before the
Council, among them Mr. John Park of Stranraer,
and on 11th August, Mr. John Blackadder and
Mr. John Semple, Carsphairn. There is nothing to
show why they were brought, but doubtless it was in
connection with conventicle keeping. Then the records
bear that Mr. —— Gilchrist had been inducted by
Mr. John Welsh into the kirk of Carsphairn upon the
indulged minister's death, and that he now possesses
the kirk, manse, and glebe, so they ordained Mr.
Gilchrist to be dispossessed and brought prisoner to
Edinburgh. It is, therefore, likely that Mr. John
Semple, Carsphairn, died about that time.

CHAPTER XV.

Proclamation that all heritors to bind themselves, and be
responsible for their families and servants, not to attend
conventicles, or baptize or marry with outed ministers—
Galloway lairds protest—Murray of Broughton appointed for
Wigtown and Kirkcudbright to get the Bond signed—The
Highland Host—Their instructions—Sheriffs of Wigtown,
Kirkcudbright, and elsewhere get orders to convene heritors
to sign bonds for themselves, families, servants, tenants and
their families not to attend conventicles—Inhabitants to be
disarmed—The King takes lawburrows against his subjects
—The Highlanders ravage Ayrshire and Galloway—Lochnaw
and the House of Freugh suffer from them—Highlanders
return home laden with spoil as from a sacked city.

On August 2nd, 1677, Proclamation was made that
all heritors, wadsetters,* life-renters, had to engage
themselves by a Bond, not only for themselves and
families, but for all who lived under them, not to
attend any conventicles or baptise or marry with outed
ministers, under the highest penalties. Against this
the Lairds of Cassillis and Galloway, the latter's
brothers, the Lairds of Ravenstoun and Castle Stewart,
all the Gordons, the M'Dowells of Freugh, and Sheriff
Agnew strongly. protested. This had no effect, and
Richard Murray of Broughton was appointed for
Wigtown and Kirkcudbright to get the Bond signed.

* Lenders in possession of the security subjects.

The Presbyterians, of course, rejected the Bond, and then the Government, on the pretext that the Western shires were in a state of rebellion, decided to overrun them with a host of Highlanders in order to force compliance with their wishes. The King in a letter to the Privy Council, dated 11th December, 1677, says:—

"We have been very much concerned at the accounts we have had, not only out of Scotland, but from several other hands, of the great and insufferable insolencies lately committed by the fanatics, especially in the shires of Ayr, Renfrew, Stewartry of Kirkcudbright, and other adjacent places, and also in Teviotdale, and even in Fife, where numerous conventicles, which by Act of Parliament are declared 'rendezvouses of rebellion,' have been kept, with solemn communions of many hundreds of people, and seditious and treasonable doctrine preached against our person, and all under us, inciting the subjects to open rebellion, and to rise in arms against us and our authority and laws, unlawful oaths imposed, the churches and pulpits of the regular clergy usurped, by force invaded, and their persons still threatened with assassination and murder, and what they have not formerly attempted, preaching houses have been lately built, and unlawful meetings of the pretended synods and presbyteries kept; thereby designing to prosecute their rebellious intentions, and to perpetuate the schism."

The Commission for raising the Highlanders is dated 26th December, 1677. It proceeds on the narrative that, as the Government has been of late much affronted, and "the peace of this our ancient kingdom much disquieted by irregular flocking to field conventicles, nurseries of rebellion, by withdrawing from public ordinances, invading the persons and pulpits of the orthodox clergy, building of meeting houses, the killing, wounding, and invading of some that were commanded in our name to repress the said insolencies, we have thought fit in maintenance of our laws and out of the tender care which we have always had of this our ancient kingdom, to require and empower the lords of our Privy Council to call together not only our standing forces and militia, but we did likewise warrant them to commissionate and empower such noblemen and others as did offer to bring any of their vassals, tenants, or adherents to the assistance of our forces." They are authorised to take free quarter, to seize all horses for carrying their sick men, ammunition, and other provisions, and are indemnified against all pursuits civil and criminal for anything they do, whether killing, wounding, apprehending, or imprisoning such as shall make opposition to authority; and all whom they please to put upon must rise and march with them, act, and say as they shall be commanded upon their highest peril.

On 28th January, 1678, the Council's Committee at Glasgow had the Sheriffs of Wigtown, Dumfries, Kirkcudbright, and other counties before them to receive their orders. They were instructed to convene the heritors, liferenters, conjunct flars, and others within the shire to subscribe a Bond binding not only themselves, but their wives, bairns, and servants, their whole tenants and cottars, that they would no wise be present at any conventicles or disorderly meetings in time coming. They were instructed to disarm the inhabitants, except Privy Councillors and soldiers in the King's pay, noblemen and gentlemen of quality having license to wear swords only, and to send in the arms and ammunition within the shire, and they were to report diligence before 7th February.

Few were prepared to take such a Bond, and before 7th February, six thousand Highlanders were scattered all over Ayrshire living at free quarters, plundering and destroying and behaving generally as if in an enemy's country.

On 14th February, the Council passed an Act for securing the public peace by taking lawburrows. This narrated that the previous Bond not having been accepted, his Majesty had just reason to suspect the designs of those who refused or delayed to take the Bona as tending to overthrow his Majesty's authority, to subvert the established order of the Church, and the peace of his Majesty's good subjects. Accordingly all who refused the Bond were to enact themselves in the books of the secret Council that they, their wives, bairns, men, tenants, and servants, would keep his Majesty's peace, and particularly that they would not go to field conventicles, nor harbour, nor commune with rebels or persons intercommuned, etc. The Council had in fact decided that the Bond must be taken, or those who refused must be exterminated. The Highlanders continued to the utmost ravaging throughout Ayrshire and overspreading into Galloway, wasted the country wherever they went, and left behind them despair and devestation. They lived at free quarters, robbed and pillaged everywhere, killed cattle far beyond what they had any use for, drove away vast multitudes of valuable horses, tortured and outraged the inhabitants, and seemed intent on the destruction of everything they came across.

Tradition has it that Lochnaw suffered severely from the Highland Host. When they came to Lochnaw, the Laird sent the ladies of the family away, and he and his son sought refuge in a cave on the sea shore near the Sea King's Camp at Larbrax Bay. The Highlanders not only lived at free quarters, but seem to have delighted in destroying everything of value about the place, for all the pictures, furnishings, and heirlooms accumulated during generations of occupation up to this time have entirely disappeared.

The House of Freugh was also practically dismantled by the Highlanders, and M'Dowall fled from the scene vowing vengeance on those who had thus wrecked his home.

The Highlanders were sent home in the spring of 1678. Wodrow says: "When the Highlanders went back, one would have thought they had been at the sacking of some besieged town, by their baggage and luggage. They were loaded with spoil; they carried away a great many horses and no small quantity of goods out of merchants' shops, whole webs of linen

and woollen cloth, some silver plate bearing the names
and arms of gentlemen. You would have seen them
with loads of bedclothes, carpets, men and women's
wearing clothes, pots, pans, gridirons, shoes, and other
furniture whereof they had pillaged the country."

Note.—One of the most famous of the preaching
houses, referred to in the King's letter on page 148,
was on the west side of the Nith, opposite Dumfries.
Claverhouse describes it as a good large house, about
sixty feet in length. When he came to Dumfries, he
found conventicles being held here "at his nose,"
but he soon put an end to it, not without some regret,
perhaps, for his Report to the Privy Council on its
demolition concludes thus:—"So perished the charity
of many ladies."

CHAPTER XVI.

Muir, Commissary Clerk at Kirkcudbright, libelled for attending
conventicles--M'Dowall of Garthland, Hay of Park, M'Dowall
of Freugh, Blair of Dunskey, and others cited for resetting
John Welsh—M'Dowall of Freugh tried for seditious speeches
at instigation of Row, the curate—Claverhouse quarters on
M'Meekan of Miltonise—M'Meekan's wife's capture, escape,
and re-capture—Bishop of Galloway gets dispensation to
reside in Glasgow or Edinburgh—Thomas Warner cited for
being at conventicles—Gordon of Earlston and many others
denounced and put to the horn for being at conventicles—
Proclamation for the arrest of Welsh, Semple, and Arnot.

ON 7th March, 1678, Henry Muir, Commissary Clerk
at Kirkcudbright, was libelled for being present at
house and field conventicles where Mr. John Welsh,
Mr. Gabriel Semple, and Mr. Samuel Arnot were. He
acknowledged he had once heard Mr. Samuel Arnot at
a field conventicle, and through bishop Paterson of
Galloway he was dismissed without further trouble.

On August 1st, 1678, M'Dowall of Garthland,
Thomas Hay of Park, M'Dowall of Freugh, John
Blair of Dunskey, and Mr. James Lawrie at Freugh,
had a process commenced against them for resetting
John Welsh and others, declared rebels. On 11th
September, 1678, the Council called before them
Patrick M'Dowall of Freugh, Thomas Hay of Park,
John Blair of Dunskey, Andrew Agnew of Sheuchan,
and Mr. James Lawrie of Freugh, charged with house

and field conventicles and resetting Mr. John Welsh and Mr. Arnot. Andrew Agnew and John Blair compeared and denied the charge upon oath, and were assoilzied. The Council superseded the extracting of letters against the other three being absent. The same date the diet against M'Dowall of Garthland for certain seditious speeches was deserted upon absence of witnesses, who were outlawed. The process was resumed against Garthland, November 4th, charging him with having on July 14th said that the King and Lauderdale were establishing arbitrary government contrary to the fundamental laws of the land, and that every true-hearted Scotsman was concerned to oppose them, and with having on July 21st, when Mr. John Row preached in Stonykirk Church, where M'Dowall is heritor, against the National and Solemn League and Covenants, declared the said Mr. Row unworthy to be heard by the people.

The hand of Row is plainly seen in this prosecution. He, it will be remembered, had scant courtesy shown him by his parishioners in Balmaclellan.

Garthland appeared to stand his trial. Nothing was proved against him, and the process dropped.

James Graham of Claverhouse, with a numerous party of soldiers, quartered upon Gilbert M'Meekan of Miltonise and Gass in New Luce Parish. M'Meekan and his wife fled on their approach, and the troopers, after thoroughly searching the house, started to use whatever they wanted, killed the stock, and destroyed what they could not consume. After waiting for several days, they went off taking their valuable horses.

Some of the party, suddenly returning, surprised M'Meekan's wife, and bound her hand and foot and mounted her behind a trooper. She contrived to escape, and made up Glenwhilly. The officer in charge of the party reported the matter to Sir Charles Hay, who had accepted from the Government the bailiery of the Regality of Glenluce. He reluctantly gave his aid, and the lady was apprehended and lodged in jail. She was sent to Edinburgh, and is said to have been confined in Greyfriar's Churchyard, all the prisons being full. She was afterwards released on bail. The laird himself weathered the persecution, and died in 1731, at the age of eighty-four. John Arrol, who commanded the dragoons at Miltonise, was killed the next year at Drumclog. About this time, the bishop of Galloway got a dispensation to enable him to reside in Glasgow. This was a most unheard of proceeding, and the terms of the dispensation may be interesting:—

"Whereas none of our Archbishops or Bishops may lawfully keep their ordinary residence without the bounds of their diocese respective unless they have our royal dispensation, warrant, and license for that effect: those are, that in regard to John, Bishop of Galloway, is not provided in a competent manse or dwelling house in the diocese of Galloway, and for the better promoting of our service in the church, do allow and authorise the said bishop to live in or near the cities of Edinburgh or Glasgow, or in any other convenient place where he may be able to attend the public affairs of the church. With whose residence in the diocese of Galloway, we, by virtue of our royal supremacy in causes ecclesiastical, do by these presents dispense, as well with the time past preceding the date hereof as for the time to come, during our royal pleasure, any canon of the church or acts of parliaments, enjoining residence, notwithstanding. And we strictly require all our subjects, church-officers, and others, never to quarrel or call in question the said John, Bishop of Galloway, during the continuance of this our royal dispensation and license, as they will answer to us at their peril. Given at our Court at Whitehall, May 28th, 1678, and of our reign the 30th year.

" By his majesty's command,

" LAUDERDALE."

On 16th January, 1679, Thomas Warner was cited before the Council on a libel that having been indulged to the parish of Balmaclellan, he had broken his confinement, being present at house and field conventicles, and conversed with inter-communed persons. Not appearing, he was denounced and put to the horn, and a month later the parishioners were discharged from paying him any stipend. The same day Gordon of Earlston, Gordon of Holm, Gordon of Overbar, Neilson of Corsock, George M'Cartney of Blackit,

Maxwell of Hills, Hay of Park, M'Dowall of Freugh, M'Dougall of Corrochtree, James Johnstone late provost of Stranraer, William Spittle of Port, —— Johnstone, Collector there, Mr. William Cathcart and John Inglis, Commissary of Kirkcudbright, failing to appear on a charge of being at house and field conventicles since 1674 were denounced and· put to the horn. Inglis' office was declared vacant, and the bishop of Galloway was recommended to have it filled. On March 11th, a Petition was presented on behalf of Inglis, that he was unable to travel, and engaging to live properly in future. The matter was remitted to the bishop, and seems to have been amicably arranged. On 2nd April, 1679, Gordon of Craighlaw younger, and his spouse, Gordon of Culvennan, MacGhie of Drumbuy, Ramsay of Boghouse, Dame Stuart, Lady Castle Stuart, MacGhie, Laird of Larg, Heron of Littlepark, Dunbar younger of Machiermore, Archibald Stuart of Causeweyend, Anthony Heron in Wigg, and his spouse, Stuart of Tonderghie, MacGhie in Penningham, MacMillan in Craigwel, —— Stuart of Ravenstoun, brother to the Earl of Galloway, and Dame —— Dunbar, his lady, and ——, Provost of Wigtown, were charged with withdrawing from ordinances and being present at conventicles. Failing to appear, they were denounced and put to the horn.

On February 6th, the Council issued a Proclamation for the arrest of Messrs. John Welsh, Gabriel Semple, and Samuel Arnot. It is rather an interesting document, and is in the following terms:—

"Charles, by the grace of God, King of Great Britain, France, and Ireland, Defender of the faith, to our lovits.

macers of our council, messengers at arms, our sheriffs in that part, conjunctly and severally, specially constitute, greeting. Forasmuch as, by sentence of our justice court, Mr. John Welsh, Mr. Gabriel Semple, and Mr. Samuel Arnot are declared traitors for being in open rebellion against us, in the year 1666. And they having for divers years past, made it their work to prevent and abuse our people from their duty and allegiance at their field meetings, these rendevouzes of rebellion; and by their example and impunity, several others inter-communed and vagrant preachers having also followed that same method and way, whereby our people by not frequenting the public ordinances, and being exposed to hear jesuits or any other irregular persons, who dare take upon them the sacred office of the ministry are debauched to atheism and popery. We, therefore, with advice of our privy council, have thought fit, for the encouragement of our good subjects, in apprehending and discovering these persons, hereby do declare and give assurance to any person or persons, who shall apprehend and secure Mr. John Welsh (or so discover him, as he may be apprehended) shall have instantly paid to him or them, upon delivery of his person, to any of our privy council or com-

mitment of him to prison, nine thousand merks
Scots money, out of the first and readiest of our
cash, as a reward; and to any person who shall
apprehend and secure the said Mr. Gabriel Semple
and Mr. Samuel Arnot, also declared traitors, or
so discover them, as they may be apprehended,
three thousand merks for each of them, and to any
person or persons who shall apprehend and secure
any of these field preachers, who are declared
fugitives, or are intercommuned, for each of them
two thousand merks, and for each one of these
vagrant preachers in the fields that shall be
apprehended, the sum of nine hundred merks.
And which rewards we declare shall be instantly
paid to the person or persons who shall perform
the said service without any manner of delay or
defalcation. And further we declare that, if in
pursuit of the said persons, they or any of their
complices shall make resistance, and that thereupon they or any of them shall be hurt, mutilate,
or slain, the said persons, apprehenders of them
or any assisting them, shall never be called in
question for the same, criminally nor civilly in
all time coming, but shall be repute and esteemed
persons, who have done us and their country good
and acceptable service. Our will is herefore, and
we charge you strictly and command that incon-
tinent these our letters seen, ye pass to the market
cross of Edinburgh and other places needful, and
thereat, in our name and authority, by open

proclamation, make publication of the premises, that all our good subjects may have notice thereof: and ordain these presents to be printed. Given under our signet at Edinburgh, the 6th day of February, 1679, and of our reign the one and thirtieth year.

"THO. HAY, Cl. Secr. Concilii.

"GOD SAVE THE KING."

CHAPTER XVII.

Troops quartered in Galloway—William Kyle, Galloway minister, captured—Sheriff's Depute appointed for Wigtownshire and the Stewartry to enforce laws against non-conformists—Galloway Presbyterians join others for self preservation—Drumclog—Many flock to the Covenanters—Divided counsels—Galloway horse exercise neár Bothwell Bridge—Earl Nithsdale ordered to call out the whole gentlemen, heritors, and freeholders in Wigtownshire and the Stewartry, and march to Edinburgh—The Covenanters differ about the Indulgence—Bitter feeling between them—They preach against each other—Supplication to Monmouth—The Covenanters cannot agree on anything, and are attacked by Livingstone—Gallant conduct of Galloway men who are ordered to retire from Bothwell Bridge—Defeat and rout of the Covenanters—Gordon of Earlston killed—Proclamation against rebels—Claverhouse follows the fugitives to Galloway, and harasses the country—Andrew Sword tried and executed.

On 13th February, 1679, one company of foot was ordered to be quartered in Galloway, one troop of His Majesty's Guards, and one company of dragoons. They arrived in March, and immediately began their search for the Covenanters. Many had narrow escapes, and Mr. William Kyle, one of the Galloway ministers, was captured.

Garrisons were placed at Ayr, Kirkcudbright, and Dumfries. Murray of Broughton had been appointed Commissioner to execute the laws against nonconformists in August, 1677. The Laird of Lagg,

Claverhouse, and Earlshall were now appointed
Sheriffs Depute for Wigtownshire, of which Sir
Andrew Agnew was Sheriff, and Captain John
Paterson, Claverhouse, and Earlshall were appointed
Sheriffs Depute of the Stewartry, of which the Earl
of Nithsdale was Steward, and special instructions
were issued to these Deputes to put the laws against
nonconformists in force.

Archbishop Sharp was murdered in May, 1679, but
the Galloway fugitives were not implicated.

Driven from their homes by the fierce persecution,
the Galloway men joined with other Presbyterians,
and, knowing that their lives were sought, they carried
weapons for self defence. Claverhouse came upon an
armed conventicle on Sunday 1st June, 1679, at
Drumclog, but was defeated and driven from the field.
The news of this victory was received with the greatest
jubilation in Galloway, and resulted in many flocking
to the Covenanters; but divided counsels prevailed and
golden opportunities were lost.

On 6th June, the Earl of Linlithgow acquainted the
Chancellor that there was information from Glasgow
that the rebels were about Bothwell Bridge and
Hamilton, where they exercised the previous day; that
two troops of horse from Galloway, Newmills, and
Galston, and a company of foot with colours and drums
had joined them, and that the country was gathering
to them. The Earl of Nithsdale was written to the
following day to call together the whole gentlemen,
heritors, and freeholders in Wigtownshire and the

Stewartry of Kirkcudbright, and to march straight to
Edinburgh. The Covenanters rapidly increased in
numbers at Bothwell, but serious differences arose
among them, chiefly as to the Indulgence and as to
the exact cause of their taking arms. The one side,
known as the Moderates, sought freedom of conscience,
and, allowed that, were prepared to acknowledge the
King's government in other matters. John Welsh was
the leader of this section. The other side would have
no dealings whatever with those who tolerated Prelacy
in any form, or compromised the Presbyterian cause
by supporting indulged ministers. Donald Cargill
was the most prominent of the leaders on this side.
Bitter feeling prevailed, and these reverend champions
inveighed against each other in their respective congregations, and voted on different sides in their councils
of war. At a meeting to choose officers, these differences got to such a height that some of them withdrew,
and those who remained actually sent a supplication
—Welsh being one of those who went with it—to the
Duke of Monmouth, who was in command of the
Government forces, in which they represented the intolerable grievances under which they had suffered,
and offered, instead of deciding the dispute by arms,
to leave the whole subject of controversy to be settled
by a free Parliament and a free General Assembly.
They received back certain proposals, but they could
not agree among themselves upon anything, and no
answer was returned, so Lord Livingstone, at the head
of the royal foot guards, came up on 22nd June to

force the bridge. He was opposed by the Galloway men, who defended the bridge with great bravery. They killed several soldiers, and stood their ground till ammunition failed. They sent to Hamilton, their commander in chief, for more ammunition or fresh soldiers, and word came back to retire from the bridge. With sore hearts they did so, and the royal army passed the bridge and attacked the Covenanters. When the King's forces got over the bridge, the Galloway troop, commanded by Captain M'Culloch, joined with Captain Thomas Weir of Greenridge, and was riding down to attack them when Hamilton came up to him and said, "What mean you, Captain? Will you murder these men?" Mr. Weir answered he hoped that there was no hazard, and that he might give a good account of all the horses yet come along the bridge, especially when but forming. When Hamilton found the Captain's troop resolute, he dealt with the Galloway troop, and magnified the difficulties so that they shrank, and the Captain was obliged to retire with them. Hamilton took to his heels with the horse, and then the foot followed. Twelve hundred surrendered without a stroke of a sword. Gordon of Earlston was killed on his way to Bothwell, not knowing that the day had been lost.

The Privy Council issued the following Proclamation, discharging all persons from assisting, resetting, or corresponding with any of the rebels under pain of treason.

PROCLAMATION AGAINST REBELS, JUNE 26TH, 1679.

" Charles, by the Grace of God, King of Great
Britain, France, and Ireland, defender of the
faith: to all and sundry our lieges and subjects,
whom these presents do or may concern, greeting.

" Forasmuch as, upon the first notice given to
our Privy Council of the rising and gathering of
these disloyal and seditious persons in the west,
who have of late appeared in arms in a desperate
and avowed rebellion against us, our government
and laws, we did declare them to be traitors, and
discharged all our subjects to assist, reset, supply,
or correspond with any of them under the pain of
treason: and the said rebels and traitors, being
now (by the blessing of God upon our forces)
subdued, dissipated, and scattered; and such of
them as were not either killed or taken in the
field, being either retired secretly to their own
homes and houses, expecting shelter and protection
from the respective heritors in whose lands they
dwell, or lurking in the country; and we being
unwilling any of our good subjects should be
ensnared or brought into trouble by them, have
therefore, with advice of our privy council,
thought fit, again to discharge and prohibit all
our subjects, men or women, that none of them
offer or presume to harbour, reset, supply, correspond with, hide, or conceal the persons of
M'Clellan of Barscob, Gordons of Earlston, elder
and younger, M'Douall of Freugh, the laird of

Ravenstone, brother to the Earl of Galloway, the laird of Castle-Stewart, brother to the said Earl, Cannon of Mardrogat, Mr. Samuel Arnot, Mr. Gabriel Semple, Mr. John Welsh, Gordon of Craichley, etc., or any others who concurred or joined in the late rebellion, or who, upon the account thereof, have appeared in arms in any part of this our kingdom. And to the end all our good subjects may have timeous notice hereof, We do ordain these presents to be forthwith printed and published at the market crosses of Edinburgh, Linlithgow, Stirling, Lanark, Ayr, Rutherglen, Glasgow, Irvine, Wigton, Kirkcudbright, Dumfries, Cowpar in Fife, Jedburgh, Perth, etc.

"ALEX. GIBSON, Cl. Secr. Concilii.

"GOD SAVE THE KING."

The Earl of Galloway's two brothers subsequently made it appear to the satisfaction of the Council that they had not been engaged in the rebellion.

Claverhouse came to Galloway with some English dragoons, several troops of horse, and some companies of foot. In Carsphairn, he took abundance of horses, and those of any use he drove away, one man in Craigencallie having three taken from him. In the same parish they took £50 from a poor widow because they alleged a servant had been at Bothwell. In Balmaclellan they pursued the same course, and committed outrages upon some of the women.

On 15th August, 1679, the King wrote the Council to proceed against certain persons implicated at Bothwell, among them being Andrew Sword in the parish of Borgue, refusing to acknowledge the rebellion to be a rebellion, or the archbishop's murder a murder.

On November 10th, Andrew Sword, now designed as "weaver in the Stewartry of Kirkcudbright," and a great many others were brought before the Justiciary. Sword confessed he had taken arms and refused the Bond. He was ordered with four others to be taken to the Muir of Magus and hanged on 18th November, his body to be hung in chains until it rotted, and his estates forfeited.

On the scaffold he declared that he was entirely innocent of the death of Sharpe, having never to his knowledge even seen a bishop. After singing the 34th Psalm, he blessed God for preserving him from signing the "ensnaring bond." The bodies of the whole five were at first suspended in chains in accordance with the sentence, but afterwards interred in a field near Magus Muir, and in October, 1728, a stone with the following inscription was erected over their remains:—

> " 'Cause we at Bothwell did appear,
> Perjurious oaths refused to swear ;
> 'Cause we Christ's cause would not condemn,
> We were sentenced to death by men,
> Who raged against us in such fury,
> Our dead bodies they did not bury ;
> But upon poles did hing us high,
> Triumph of Bebal's victory.
> Our lives we fear'd not to the death,
> But constant proved to the last breath.

When the gravestone was set up, in 1728, the chains were taken out of their graves, and some of their bones and clothes were found undecayed—forty-nine years after their death. The stone fared badly at the hands of relic hunters, and has disappeared.

CHAPTER XVIII.

The Scottish nobility petition the King against Lauderdale in "Some Particular Matters of Fact"—What Presbyterians admittedly had to suffer—Forfeitures against those at Bothwell—Galloway gentlemen the first sacrifices—M'Dowall of Freugh forfeited, and his estate granted to Claverhouse—Other Galloway lairds forfeited—Bishop Aitken allowed to reside in Edinburgh—Commission to get lists of those at Bothwell—Instructions for regulating the Indulgence, with special reference to Galloway—Garrisons placed at Kenmure and Freugh.

MANY of the Scottish nobility had suffered through Lauderdale's actings though supporting the Government, and waited a favourable opportunity to table their grievances to the King. Accordingly, a Petition was framed, known as "Some particular matters of fact." It is interesting as showing what the Presbyterians admittedly did suffer during this period:—

"Some particular matters of fact relating to the administration of affairs in Scotland, under the Duke of Lauderdale, humbly offered to your majesty's consideration, in obedience to your royal command.

"The Duke of Lauderdale did grossly misrepresent to your majesty the condition of the western counties, as if they had been in a state of rebellion, though there had been never any opposition made to your majesty's authority, nor any resistance offered to your forces, nor to the execution of the law. But he, purposing to abuse your majesty, that so he might carry on his sinistrous designs by your authority, advised your majesty to raise an army against your peaceable subjects; at least did frame a letter which was sent to your majesty to be signed by your royal hand to that effect; which being sent down to the council, orders were thereupon given out for raising an army of eight or nine thousand men; the greatest part whereof were Highlanders. And notwithstanding, to avert this threatening, the nobility and gentry of that country did send to Edinburgh, and for the security of the peace, did offer to engage, that whosoever should be sent to put the laws in execution, should meet with no affront, and that they would become hostages for their safety. Yet this army was marched and led into a peaceful country, and did take free quarters, according to their commissions: and in most places levied great sums of money under the notion of dry quarters; and did plunder and rob your subjects, of which no redress could be obtained, though complaints were frequently made. All which was expressly contrary to the laws of the Kingdom. In these quarterings it was apparent, that regard was only had to that Duke's private animosities: for the greatest part of these places that were most quartered in, and destroyed, had been guilty of none of the field conventicles complained of: and many of the places that were most guilty were spared upon private considerations. The subjects were at that time required to subscribe an exhorbitant and illegal bond which was impossible to be performed by them, 'That their wives, children, and servants, their tenants, and their wives, children, and servants, should live orderly, according to the law, not to go to conventicles, nor entertain vagrant preachers,' with several other particulars: by which bond those who signed it were made liable for every man's fault that lived upon their ground. Your majesty's subjects were charged with lawburrows, denounced rebels; and captions were issued out for seizing their persons, upon their refusing to sign the foresaid bond; and the nobility and gentry there who had ever been faithful to your majesty, and had appeared in arms for suppressing the last rebellion, were disarmed upon oath, a proclamation was also issued forth, forbidding them, under great penalties, to keep any horse above four pounds ten groats price. The nobility and gentry in the shire of Ayr were also indicted at the instance of your majesty's advocate, of very high crimes and misdemeanors, whereof some did import treason. Their indictments were delivered them in the evening to be answered by them next morning upon oath. And when they did demand two or three days' time to consider their indictments, and craved the benefit of lawyers to advise with in matters of so high concernment, and also excepted against their being put to swear against themselves in matters that were capital, which was contrary to law and justice; all those their desires were rejected, though the like had never been done to the greatest malefactors in the kingdom. And it was told them that they must either swear instantly or they would repute them guilty, and proceed accordingly. The noblemen and gentlemen, knowing themselves innocent of all that had been surmised against them, did purge themselves by oath of all the particulars that were objected to them, and were thereupon acquitted. And though the Committee of Council used the severest way of inquiry to discover any sedition or treasonable designs which were pretended as the grounds of leading in that army to these countries, yet nothing could ever be proved. So false was that suggestion concerning the rebellion then designed, that was offered to your majesty, and prevailed with you for sending the forementioned letter. The oppression and quartering still continuing, the noblemen and gentlemen of these countries went to Edinburgh, to represent to your council the heavy pressures that they and their people lay under, and were ready to offer to them all that law and reason could require of them for securing the peace. The council did immediately, upon their appearance there, set forth a proclamation, requiring them to depart the town in three days, upon the highest pains.

And when the Duke of Hamilton did petition to
stay two or three days longer upon urgent affairs,
it was refused. When some persons of quality
had declared to the Duke of Lauderdale that they
would go and represent their condition to your
majesty; if they could not have justice from your
ministers, for preventing that, a proclamation was
set out, forbidding all the subjects to depart the
kingdom without license, so that your majesty
might not be acquainted with the sad condition
of your subjects; a thing without all precedent
law, to cut off your subjects from making
application to your majesty; not less contrary to
your majesty's true interest (who must be always
the refuge of your people) than to the natural
right of the subjects."

Particulars of the sufferings of individuals followed.
The Complaint failed, but there was some hope that,
as a result of it, matters would improve, and the Duke
of Monmouth was expected to get some favours for the
Presbyterians.

In 1680, forfeitures were passed in great numbers
against those alleged to be at Bothwell. The Galloway
gentlemen were the first sacrifices. On February 18th,
Patrick M'Dowall of Freugh was called, having been
cited before. His name is in the proclamation excepting persons from the Indemnity. In absence,
evidence was produced against him and others,
generally speaking by soldiers and spies, who had
been hired to traffic up and down the country. Some

deponed they saw Freugh at Sanquhar a commander of a body of four or five hundred men in arms, as they came to Bothwell. Two witnesses deponed they saw him at Hamilton Muir among the rebels. He was sentenced to be executed and demeaned as a traitor, and his heritage, goods, and gear to be forfeited to his majesty's use. His estate of Freugh was afterwards granted by the King to John Graham of Claverhouse. Mr. William Ferguson of Caitloch, Alexander Gordon, elder, and also the younger of Earlston, James Gordon, younger of Craichlaw, William Gordon of Culvennan, Patrick Dunbar of Machrimor, and —— M'Ghie of Larg, were called. Earlston, elder, had been killed after Bothwell. The prepared witnesses deponed as to their accession to the rebellion, and they were all forfeited, except M'Ghie of Larg, whose case was continued until the second Monday of June.

The lands of Caitloch, Earlston, and Craichlaw, were given to Colonel Maine, Major Ogilthorp, and Captain Henry Cornwall, but they did not hold them long.

Another process of forfeiture was commenced on the 2nd of June, and ended July 6th, against the following persons:—John Bell of Whiteside, John Gibson of Auchinchyne, —— Gibson, younger, of Ingliston, Gordon of Dundeugh, —— Grier of Dargoner, —— Smith of Kilroy, —— M'Clellan of Barmageichan, Thomas Bogle of Bogles-hole, —— Baird, younger, of Dungeonhill, —— Gordon of Craig, —— Lennox of Irelandton, —— Gordon of Bar-harrow, John

Fullarton of Auchinhae, David M'Culloch, son to Ardwel, William Whitehead of Millhouse, John Welsh of Cornley, —— Neilson of Corsack, Robert M'Clellan of Barscob, Samuel M'Clellan, his brother, —— Fullarton of Nether-mill, George M'Cartney of Blaikit, —— Gordon of Garrerie, —— Gordon of Knockgrey, ——Heron of Little park, ——Gordon of Holm, —— Gordon of Overbar, John M'Naught of Colquhad, Murdock, *alias* Laird Murdock, and John Binning of Dulvennan. The libel and indictment against these persons, is in the common form, murdering the archbishop, though probably none of them knew anything about it, burning the King's laws, accession to the rebellion. All of them were absent. Thomas Bogle and Baird of Dungeon-hill were libelled as the rest, and likewise for attacking major Johnstone, of which they were entirely free. No probation was adduced on this. Cannon of Mardrochat was witness against the Galloway gentlemen. The judges were not very exacting as to probation. The assize was not particular in the verdict, but found the pannels, in the general, guilty of the crimes libelled, and they were all forfeited.

Alexander Hunter of Colquhassen, Old Luce, who had been at Bothwell, was forfeited, and his estates given to the Countess of Nithsdale, and she possessed them till 1689. Alexander Hay of Arieollan, a neighbour, was treated in the same way. His mother, a pious old lady, about eighty years old, was imprisoned for mere nonconformity, and kept in Dumfries Prison to the danger of her life. She was

likewise forfeited for her annuity and life-rent out
of the estate, so that it might be given to a papist.

In January, a commission was given to the Earl
of Queensberry, Sir Robert Dalziel of Glenae, and
Claverhouse, or any two, or such as they should
appoint, to get exact lists of heritors who had been at
Bothwell from the shires of Dumfries and Wigtown
and the Stewartry of Kirkcudbright and Annandale.

Bishop Aitken was translated from Moray to
Galloway, 6th February, 1680, with dispensation to
reside in Edinburgh, as he was advanced in years and
the people of his diocese were rebellious and turbulent.
He kept himself in touch with the ministers, presbyteries, and synod, and by letters to them and a journey
thither secured as good order and discipline as if he
had been residing among them.   He opposed James in
taking off the penal laws against Roman Catholics.

On 6th May, 1680, a garrison was stationed at
Balgreggan.

Instructions were then given for regulating the
Indulgence (14th May).   The last of these directions
is worthy of notice, being specially applicable to
Galloway.

"9hly.   And seeing that we are informed that
the regular ministers in Galloway and some other
western places are exposed to great danger, from
the fury of some blind zealots among whom they
serve, and that even the necessaries of life, and
the help of servants and mechanics are denied
unto them for their money, you are, in a most
particular manner to consider their present case,

and to consult their protection, and the security of their persons in the best manner, and to see that the sheriffs, justices, and other magistrates be careful to have them defended and secured in their persons and goods, and the necessaries for living furnished and supplied unto them at the usual and ordinary rates of the country, to the end they may be effectually relieved and that our ancient kingdom may be vindicated from any just imputation of so great and barbarous inhumanity. Given at our Court at Windsor Castle, the 14th day of May, 1680, and of our reign the 32d year.

" By his majesty's command,

" LAUDERDALE."

On 10th August, further efforts were made to discover who were at Bothwell, and letters were sent to the Sheriffs of Fife, Lanark, Ayr, Wigtown, and Stirling:—" The Council, understanding there are divers persons lurking in your shire who were in the Rebellion and are reset, do require you to inquire thereinto and appoint persons in the several parishes, and do everything for that effect, and to send a list of them, their resetters, and witnesses to the Advocate betwixt and October."

On December 10th a garrison of thirty horse was ordered to be placed at Kenmure and another at the House of Freugh in Wigtownshire. Garrisons were thus placed at particular houses for the double purpose of punishing proprietors suspect of disaffection and overawing the surrounding population.

CHAPTER XIX.

Graham has commission to uplift the moveables of fugitives in Galloway—Court at New Galloway—The Societies—The Sanquhar Declaration supported by Galloway men—Proclamation against Cameron and others—All persons over sixteen years of age to be cited in Minnigaff, Penninghame, Carsphairn, Balmaclellan, Dalry, Kells, Irongray, and other parishes to declare what they know of the traitors—The oath sworn by the King.

GRAHAM had a commission to uplift the moveables of those in Galloway who had been at Bothwell or were fugitives. His brother, Cornet Graham, and he or some depute by him went through the several parishes. At New Galloway, there was a Court, at which all between sixteen and sixty were charged to appear under severe penalties, and declare upon oath how many conventicles they had been at, who preached, who were present, what children were baptised, etc. Every Court day numbers were forfeited and fined, and the money gifted to the soldiers, informers, etc.

After Bothwell, some of the sterner Presbyterians went off to Holland, but, in 1680, a number returned, following Mr. Donald Cargill, Richard Cameron, etc. Next year they began to meet in Societies, and termed themselves " The Societies United in Correspondence." They separated from all the rest of the Presbyterian ministers and others throughout the kingdom who would not reject the King's authority, and came to state their sufferings and testimony upon that head, and herein they stood by themselves, striving against Prelacy on the one hand, and as bitterly against their former friends on the other.

On June 22nd, 1680, the first anniversary of Bothwell, there was the famous Sanquhar Declaration.

Richard Cameron and his brother Michael and about a score of others, among them being some Galloway men, rode into Sanquhar, and drew up at the ancient Market Cross. The two Camerons dismounted, a psalm was sung, prayer was offered, and then Michael Cameron read the famous Declaration, and fixed a copy of it to the Cross while the inhabitants looked on in wonder and amazement. This document was headed " The Declaration and Testimony of the true Presbyterian, anti-prelatic, anti-erastian, persecuted party in Scotland. Published at Sanquhar, June 22nd, 1680." It had the warm approval of the great majority of the Galloway Covenanters, and was not a frenzied outburst, but a deliberate statement made after fully counting the cost. As has been well said, what was treason that day became only eight years afterwards the Revolution Settlement. Its import may be seen from the following excerpt:—" Therefore, although we be for Government and Governors such as the Word of our God and our Covenant allows, yet we for ourselves and all that will adhere to us as the representatives of the true Presbyterian Kirk and Covenanted nation of Scotland, . . . do by thir presents disown Charles Stuart that has been reigning

(or rather tyrannizing as we may say) on the throne of
Britain these years bygone, as having any right, title
to, or interest in the said Crown of Scotland for
Government, as forfeited several years since, by his
perjury and breach of covenant both to God and His
Kirk and usurpation of His Crown and Royal prerogative therein, and many other breaches in matters
ecclesiastic, and by his tyranny and breach of the very
leges regnandi in matters civil, For which reason we
declare, that several years since he should have been
denuded of being King, Ruler, or Magistrate, or of
having any power to act, or to be obeyed as such. As
also, we, being under the standard of the Lord Jesus
Christ, Captain of Salvation, do declare a war with
such a tyrant and usurper, and all the men of his
practices as enemies to our Lord Jesus Christ and
His cause and covenants, and against all such as have
strengthened him, sided with, or any wise acknowledged him in his tyranny, civil or ecclesiastic." It
disclaimed the Declaration at Hamilton, June 1679,
"chiefly because it takes in the King's interest," and
it disowned the Duke of York, "that professed papist,"
and protested against his succeeding to the Crown.

This was followed by a Proclamation against
Cameron and others, which set forth that Mr. Richard
Cameron and his brother, and Mr. Thomas Douglas,
accompanied by several ruffians and particularly John
Vallange, brother-in-law to Robert Park, one of the
Bailies of Sanquhar; Daniel M'Mitchell in Lorgfoot;
Thomas Campbell, son of —— Campbell, late of Dal-
blair in Auchenleck parish; John Moodie, brother to

the miller at Cubsmill, in the same parish; John Fowler, sometime servant to the deceased Lindsay of Covington; Patrick Gamil, son-in-law to Charles Logan, messenger at Cumnock Mains; James Stewart, son to Archibald Stewart at Causewayend, near to the Earl of Galloway's house; Alexander Gordon, called of Kilstuare; Francis Johnstone, merchant in Clydesdale; —— Crichton, son to Robert Crichton of Auchentitinch, now in Waterhead, and others to the number of twenty-one persons, did, upon 22nd June, enter within the Burgh of Sanquhar with drawn swords and pistols in their hands, and after a solemn procession through the town, did draw up at the Cross, and published and affixed upon the Cross and other public places thereof a most treasonable and unparalleled paper "disowning us to be their King and defaming us with the very same names and designations used by the usurpers in their greatest rage after they had murdered the King, our royal and blessed father of eternal memory." Accordingly, they were declared " open and notorious traitors and rebels," and all good subjects were required to do their utmost diligence to discover them.

"And to the effect that harbourers and resetters, or those who neglect to discover them, may be known and punished, we do require the haill heritors, or their bailiffs, or chamberlains in case of the heritors' absence, to cause call, and cite before them in a court, all persons living upon their respective lands, men, or women, above the age of sixteen years, in all the parishes underwritten, viz.:—Carsphairn, Balmaclel-

lan, Dalry, Kells, Bar in Carrick, the Moor kirk of
Kyle, Galston, Loudon, Tindergarth, Strathaven,
Lesmahago, Sanquhar, Irongray, Glencairn, Cumnock,
Monigaff, and Penninghame, upon the second and last
Tuesdays of July and August next; and to take the
oaths of all the said persons living upon their respective
lands, whether any of these traitors foresaid were in
that parish, and where and when; And lest they may
pretend not to know the said traitors, that they discover
upon oath any skulking or lurking persons, which they
have known to have been in that parish, after the
publication hereof in the respective shires and the
heritors or their bailiffs, and chamberlains in their
absence, to give an account of their diligence in
writing, within eight days after each diet foresaid,
to the sheriffs, stewarts, bailies of regalities, magistrates of burghs, and shall adjoin thereto the following
declaration upon oath. I, ——, do solemnly swear
by the eternal God, that I have truly and faithfully
examined upon oath the whole persons, men and
women, living upon my lands, who compeared, who
are above the age of sixteen years, whereof I am
heritor, bailiff, or chamberlain, within the parish of
——, and that I, ——, caused my officer give execution
upon oath, that he did cite all the said persons to the
aforesaid diets, and have given an account of the
persons who compeared not, or, compearing, refused
to give oath."

Those who may be inclined to take the view of this
Proclamation, and to think that Cameron and his party
were grossly to blame, should remember at the same

time that the King to whom they owed allegiance was
the King who had sworn the following oath, and who,
by his breach of it, had forced Cameron and the other
Covenanters to take the stand they did:—

"I, Charles, King of Great Britain, France,
and Ireland, do assure and declare, by my solemn
oath, in the presence of Almighty God, the
searcher of hearts, my allowance and approbation
of the National Covenant, and of the Solemn
League and Covenant above written, and faithfully oblige myself to prosecute the ends thereof in
my station and calling; and that I, for myself and
successors, shall consent and agree to all Acts of
Parliament enjoining the National Covenant and
Solemn League and Covenant, and fully establishing Presbyterial Government, the directory of
Worship, the Confession of Faith and Catechisms
in the Kingdom of Scotland, as they are approved
by the General Assembly of this Kirk and Parliament of this Kingdom. And that I shall give
my royal assent to the Acts and Ordinances of
Parliament passed or to be passed, enjoining the
same in the rest of my dominions, and that I shall
observe them in my own practice and family, and
shall never make opposition to any of these, or
endeavour any change thereof."

That was the King's solemn oath sworn to more than
once, and it was his deliberate and determined breach
of it that brought desolation to Scotland and disaster
to himself.

CHAPTER XX.

Seven troops of horse and a regiment of foot sent into Galloway—
The country harassed—Incredible losses inflicted in Galloway
parishes—Ayrsmoss—John Malcolm, Dalry, captured and
executed—The Sheriff of Galloway ordered to sentence
tradesmen and others refusing to work for the orthodox
clergy—Courts at New Galloway, Dalry, and Kirkcudbright
—Proceedings ordered against those in Wigtown and Kirkcudbright in the late rebellion—The Test Act—Garrisons at
Dumfries and the House of Freugh—Persons forfeited for
Bothwell to be pursued to the death—List of those in
Galloway—Sir James Dalrymple refuses the Test—The
Steward of the Stewartry, Sir Andrew Agnew, Viscount
Kenmure, and the Earl of Galloway refuse the Test, and
are deprived of their heritable jurisdictions—Wigtown Burgh
takes the Test.

On 30th June, 1680, seven troops of horse and a
regiment of foot were sent into Galloway. The
command was given to Linlithgow, Major Cockburn,
Strachan, Claverhouse, and others. Their avowed
object was to secure Richard Cameron, but all non-
conformists were harassed, and fearful severities
committed. Dreadful ravages were made by the
soldiers on the Sabbath Day, and incredible losses
were inflicted on Presbyterians in the parishes of
Carsphairn, Dalry, Balmaclellan, Crossmichael, and
many others.

At Ayrsmoss, 22nd July, 1680, both of the
Camerons fell. Many prisoners were taken, among

them John Malcolm from the parish of Dalry. They were sentenced to be hanged on 11th August, and were executed at the Grass-market at Edinburgh.

In September, 1680, Captain Inglis was persecuting violently in Carsphairn and in Dalry. He was particularly anxious to secure John Fraser and John Clark. Robert Cannon of Mardrochat, Commissioner to the persecutors, was made collector of cess and excise in Carsphairn and neighbourhood, and Inglis, Livingstone, and other commanders, who were hunting up and down the country, went by his instructions. The soldiers herded the whole countryside together, and Cannon was sent for to inform against them. During the harvest, courts were held at New Galloway, and grievous injuries inflicted.

In October, 1680, the Council, alleging that some of the orthodox clergy in Galloway were being defrauded of their stipends, and indirect methods taken to force them to leave, by tradesmen and others refusing to work for them, ordained the Sheriff to give sentences against such, and to call for soldiers to execute his sentences. This kind of process obliging tradesmen to work was something novel even in those days.

On 23rd December, 1680, the Council wrote to the Earl of Murray, to procure a remission to William Gordon of Culvennan who had been in the Rebellion. He resigned part of his lands in favour of some of the managers, as others did, in order to escape the sentences passed on them. In the beginning of 1681, Cornet Graham held a court at Dalry, when all men and women above sixteen years were cited to appear and made declare upon oath whether they had ever been at field meetings, or were married, or had children baptised with those who preached at them. They were also questioned on oath about their neighbours. Grierson of Lagg, and Thomas Lidderdale of St. Mary's Isle held similar courts at Kirkcudbright. On 21st June, 1681, it was represented to the Council that many persons in Kirkcudbright, Wigtown, and Dumfries who were in the late Rebellion continued to reside in their houses and intromit with their estates. The Sheriffs and other magistrates were ordained to proceed against them, and secure their rents and lands for his Majesty's use.

On 31st August, 1681, the famous Act known as the Test became law, under which all who held an office had to take an oath that they judged it unlawful for subjects, upon pretence of reformation or any other pretence, to enter into covenants or leagues, or to convocate, convene, or assemble in any councils, conventions, or assemblies, to treat, consult, or determine in any matter of state, civil or ecclesiastic, without his Majesty's special command or express license had thereunto, or to take up arms against the King or those commissionate by him, and that " I shall never so rise in arms or enter into such covenants or assemblies, and that there lies no obligation upon me from the National Covenant or the Solemn League and Covenant (so commonly called) or any other manner of way whatsomever to endeavour any change or alteration in the government either in Church or State as it is now established by the laws of this kingdom, and I promise and swear that I shall with my utmost power, defend, assist, and maintain his Majesty's Jurisdiction foresaid against all deadly, and I shall never decline his Majesty's power and jurisdiction, as I shall answer to God."

This Act, as we shall see, led to great tribulation in Galloway.

It would seem that former orders as to placing garrisons in Galloway had not been fulfilled, and on 6th October, the Council appointed the houses previously named, with the Castle of Dumfries, and the house of Freugh, instantly to be made patent to receive garrisons.

On 8th October, 1681, special proclamation was made that certain persons, having forfeited their lives, lands, and goods for treasonable rising in arms at Bothwell, did, notwithstanding, live at or near their dwelling places, and by themselves or others enjoyed their lands, rents, and goods, as if they were free and peaceable subjects. Authority was, therefore, given to the Sheriffs of Lanark, Ayr, Dumfries, the Steward of the Stewartry of Kirkcudbright, Sir Andrew Agnew of Lochnaw, Sheriff Principal of Wigtown, and their deputes, to apprehend the said rebels and traitors, and to pursue them to the death by force of arms or drive them forth of the bounds of their jurisdiction. Among those named in the Proclamation are Patrick M'Douall of Freugh; Mr. William and Alexander Gordons of Earlston; Mr. William Ferguson of Caitloch; —— Dunbar, younger of Machermore; John Bell of Whiteside; John Gibson of

Auchinchero; —— Gibson, younger of Ingleston;
—— Gordon of Dundeuch; —— Grier of Dargonar;
—— Smith of Kilroch; —— M'Clelland of Barma-
geichan; —— Gordon of Craigie; —— Lennox of
Irelandton; —— Gordon of Barharrow; John Fowler-
ton of Auchincrie; David M'Culloch, son of Ardwall;
William Whitehead of Milnhouse; John Welsh of
Cornley; —— Neilson of Corsock; Robert M'Clelland
of Barscobe; Samuel M'Clelland, his brother; ——
Fullerton of Nethermill; George M'Cartney of
Blackit; —— Gordon of Garrarie; —— Gordon of
Knockgray; —— Heron of Littlepark; —— Gordon
of Holm; —— Gordon of Overbar; John M'Knaught
of Culgnad; —— Murdock, *alias* Laird Murdock;
Andrew Sword in Galloway; John Malcolm in Dalry
in Galloway. Some of these had already suffered the
full penalty, but the present proceedings were intended
to secure their estates. Sir James Dalrymple, president of the Court of Session, sought to add to the
Test a clause regarding the Covenant, that the recipient
professed "the true protestant religion as set forth
in the Confession of Faith of 1567," but this was
refused, and he felt himself unable to subscribe the
oath. On 21st October, 1681, the Council wrote his
Majesty's Secretary to get Sir James Dalrymple of
Stair, as heritable Bailie of the Regality of Glenluce,
to take the Test before his Grace the Duke of Lauderdale, and on 18th December, there is a letter from the
Secretary to the Council in which it is stated that
Sir James Dalrymple of Stair had informed him that,

having quitted his public employment to his son, there was no obligation on him by law to take the Test. He removed to Galloway, and in October, 1682, went privately to Leyden.

On November 10th, the Council wrote the Laird of Lochnaw for the shire of Wigtown, and the Earl of Nithsdale for the Stewartry of Kirkcudbright, to send an account against 1st December whether they had taken the Test, that they may know and upon refusal appoint persons for these jurisdictions.

Owing to the holders not taking the Test, the following jurisdictions fell into His Majesty's hands. The Stewartship of Kirkcudbright, held by the Earl of Nithsdale, recommended to be given to Lord Livingstone and Sir Robert Maxwell. The Sheriffship of Wigtown, held by Sir Andrew Agnew, recommended to be given to the Laird of Claverhouse. The regality of Tongeland, held by Viscount Kenmure, recommended to be given to the Laird of Claverhouse. The regality of Whithorn, held by the Earl of Galloway, recommended to be given to the Earl of Queensberry. On January 26th 1682, the King approved of new commissions to these gentlemen. Others, however, were more compliant. Wigtown Town Council took the Test on the last day of December, 1681, as appears from their records:—

" Wigtoune, the threttie first day of December, 1681 zeirs. Wee, the magistrats, and Councell of the burgh of Wigtoune under-subscribed, solemnlie sweare in presence of the Eternall God, whom we invocat as judge and witnes of our sincere intentione of this our oath. That wee owne and sincerelie profess the trew protestant religione contained in the Confessione of Faith recordit in the first parliat, of King James the Sixt, and that wee beleive the same to be foundit on and agreeable to the Word of God. And Wee promise and sueir that Wee shall adheare yrto dureing all the dayes of our Lyftymes, and shall endeavore to educat our childrine yrin, and shall never consent to any change or alteratione con-traire yrto; And that Wee Disoune and renunce all such principles, doctrines, or practises, whither popish or prauaticall, which are contraire unto, and inconsistent with the said protestant religione and Confessione of Faith. And for testification of our obedience to our most gracious Soveraigne CHAIRLES the Second, Wee doe affirme and sueare by this our solemne oath that the King's Majestie is the only suppreame governour of this realme, over all persones and in all causes als weill ecclesiasticall as civile: and that noe forraigne prince, persone, pope, prelat, state, or potentat, hath or ought to have any jurisdictione, power, superiortie, preheminencie, or autoritie, Ecclisi-asticall or civile, within this realme. And their-foir Wee doe vterlie renunce and forsaik all forraigne jurisdictione, pouers, superiorities, and autorities: And doe promise that hencefurth Wee

shall beare faith and trew aledgeance to the
King's Majestie, his aires and Laull Successors:
And Wee farder afferme and suere by this our
solemn oath that Wee judge it unlaull (unlawful)
for subjects vpon pretence of reformatione or any
vyr pretence qtsover, to enter into Covenants or
Leagues, or to convocat, convein, or assemble in
any councels, conventions, or assemblies, to treat,
consult, or Determine in any maitter of state,
civill or ecclesiastick, without his Majestie's
special command or express Licence yrto; Or to
taik up airmes agt the King or those commis-
sionated by him: And that Wee shall never so
rise in airmes, or enter into such covenants or
assemblies. And that ther Lyes noe obligatione
one Us from the Nationall Covenant, or the
Solemne League and Covenant (so commonlie
called) or any vyr mainer of Way qtsoever to
endevore any chainge or alternatione in the
governement aither in church or state, as it is
now established be the Laws of this Kingdom,
And Wee promise and sueare that Wee shall with
our utmost pouer defend, assist, and maintaine
his Majesties jurisdictione forsd agt all Deidlie:
And we shall never decline his Majesties pouer
and jurisdictione, As Wee shall ansr. to God.
And finalie, Wee afferme and sueare this our
solumn oath is given in the plaine genuine sence
and meaning of the words, without any equivoca-
tione, mentall reservatione, or any mainer of

evasione qtsoever: And that Wee shall not accept or use any Dispensatione from any creature qtsoever. So help us God.

" (Signed)
1. WILL. COLTRANE, provost.
2. G. STEWART, baiellie.
4. WILL. CLUGSTOUNE.
13. ARCHIBALD RAMSAY, Clerk as
3. mandatory for MICHAEL SHANK, Treasurer.
5. JOHNNE M'KEAND.
8. A. (ADAM) M'KIE.
6. ADAM KYNEIR.
9. A. (ANTHONY) DALZELL.
7. WILL. GORDOUN.
12. PATT. BLAINE.
10. PATRICK M'KIE.
11. JOHNE KYNNIER.
ANDREW M'GUFFOCK.
JOHN M'CRACKEN.
ALEXR. STEWART.
JAMES BROUNE.
GEORGE KINCAID.
PATT. GARROCK."

CHAPTER XXI.

Claverhouse sent into Galloway with troops—He is granted a Sheriff's commission for Kirkcudbright, Wigtownshire, and Dumfries—Letters from Claverhouse referring to the Gordons and to Sir James Dalrymple of Stair—Claverhouse captures M'Clurg, the Minnigaff smith—A trooper in trouble—Soldiers ordered to Kirkcudbright to secure Lord Livingstone in the Estates forfeited to him—Claverhouse writes Viscount Kenmure to prepare his house for a garrison—His persecutions —He seizes John Archibald, Anthony M'Bride, John Cleanochan, and John Wallace, imprisons them in Stranraer, and quarters horses at their houses—A troop of the horse in Anwoth.

On 27th January, 1682, Claverhouse was sent into Galloway with a troop of guards, and was allowed to make use of the house or chapel belonging to Sir John Dalrymple to keep guard in, and of the house at Kirkcudbright belonging to Sir Robert Maxwell.

He was granted a Sheriff's commission to arrange all disorders, disturbances of the peace, and church irregularities in Kirkcudbright, Annandale, Wigtown, and Dumfries. The following are its terms —:

" Charles, by the grace of God, etc., greeting. Forasmuch as we have already thought fit to give and grant to John Graham of Claverhouse, a commission to be sheriff of the shire of Wigton, fallen in our hands, with the haill powers, privileges, and casualties belonging to the said office, during our pleasure, and considering that several persons of disaffected and seditious principles, in the shires of Wigton and Dumfries, and the stewartries of Kirkcudbright and Annandale, have for disquiet and disturbance of the peace, for divers years past, not only deserted the public ordinances in their parish churches, haunted and frequented rebellious field conventicles, and committed divers other disorders of that nature, to the great scandal of religion, and contempt of our government, but lately did break forth into, and joined in an open and most treasonable rebellion, and notwithstanding of the many reiterated offers of our gracious indemnity to them they continue in their former wicked and rebellious practices, being encouraged therein by the not due execution of our laws, and hopes of impunity, by their skulking from one place to another, when they are cited before our judicatories, and pursued and sought for by our forces, and we being fully resolved that our laws shall be put to due and vigorous execution against these delinquents, and these rebels brought to public punishment and example, in the places where they have been guilty thereof, do, with advice of our privy council, require and command the said John Graham of Claverhouse to call before him his deputes and substitutes, the persons frequenting and residing in the said shire of Wigton, guilty of withdrawing from the public ordinances in their parish churches, since our late act of indemnity, as also

the persons guilty of conventicles, disorderly
baptisms and marriages, harbouring and resetting
of rebels, during the said space, and to impose and
exact the fines conform to the acts of parliament,
and to do and perform everything requisite and
necessary, for putting the same to due and
vigorous execution; and considering that the
persons guilty of these disorders, do remove from
one jurisdiction to another, when they are called
in question and pursued, and that we find it
necessary for our service, in this exigent, that the
persons guilty of these disorders, in the places
adjacent, within the said shire of Dumfries, and
the Stewartries of Kirkcudbright and Annandale,
be brought to justice in order to the reducing
that country to the due obedience of our laws and
the securing the peace of our government, we,
with advice foresaid, do hereby nominate and
appoint the said John Graham to be our depute
within the said jurisdictions, for putting in
execution our laws, against transgressors and
delinquents in the cases foresaid, and to uplift
and exact the penalties incurred by them thereby.
It is hereby declared that this commission is no
ways to be prejudicial to the right of jurisdiction,
belonging to the sheriff of Dumfries, and Stewards
of the Stewartries of Kirkcudbright and Annandale, and that the said John Graham is only to
proceed and do justice in the cases foresaid, when
he is the first attacker. And further we with the
advice foresaid, have thought fit to give and grant,

and do hereby give and grant to the said John
Graham of Claverhouse our full pover, authority,
and commission, as justice in that part, to call
before him any person, not being heritor, who
shall be apprehended for being in the late
rebellion, and have not in due time taken the
benefit of our gracious act of indemnity, and for
that effect, to fence and hold courts, create clerks,
sergeants, dempsters, and other members of court
needful, and to call assizes and witnesses as often
as need be, absents to amerciate, unlaws and
amerciaments to uplift and exact, and, in the said
courts, to put the said persons to knowledge and
trial of an assize, and, according as they shall be
found innocent or guilty, that he shall cause
justice to be administrate on them according to
the laws and acts of parliament of this realm:
PROMITTEN to hold firm and stable whatsoever
things he shall lawfully do in the premises.
Given under our signet at Edinburgh, the last
day of January, 1682, and of our reign the
thirty-fourth year."

Claverhouse, in February, 1682, was passing up and
down through Galloway. In a letter to Queensberry,
dated from Newton of Galloway, 16th February, 1682,
he says:—"As to the Treasury Commission, I fear
I shall not be able to do what I would wish because
of the season. For of their corn and straw there is not
much left, and their beasts this time of the year is

not worth the driving." On 1st March, 1662, from Newton of Galloway, he writes:—" I wish the Gordons here were translated to the North and exchanged with any other branch of that family who are so very loyal there and disaffected here. I desire leave to draw out of the two regiments one hundred of the best musketeers who had served abroad, and I should take the horses here amongst the suffering sinners."

On 5th March, he wrote from Wigtown:—" Here in this shire I find the lairds all following the example of a late great man and considerable heritor * among them, which is to live regularly themselves, but have their houses constant haunts of rebels and inter-communed persons, and have their children baptised by the same and then lay the blame on their wives. But I am resolved this jest shall pass no longer here, for it (is) laughing and fooling the Government." He held his first court at Wigtown in March, and then proceeded to Stranraer. In a letter from Stranraer, dated 13th March, 1682, he mentions the capture of M'Clurg, the smith at Minnigaff, and his resolve to hang him.

" I am just beginning to send out many parties, finding the rebels become secure, and the country so quiet in all appearance. I sent out a party with my brother Dave three nights ago. The first night he took Drumbui † and one M'Lellan, and that great villain M'Clurg, the smith at Minnigaff that made

---

* This was Sir James Dalrymple of Stair.
† M'Kie of Drumbuie.

all the clikys,* and after whom the forces have trotted
so often. It cost me both pains and money to know
how to find him. I am resolved to hang him; for it
is necessary I make some example of severity, lest
rebellion be thought cheap here. There cannot be alive
a more wicked fellow." †

On one of his visits to Wigtown, one at least of
his troopers got into trouble with the citizens and
seems to have been severely handled by no less an
individual than the burgh treasurer. The Burgh
Records contain the following reference to the incident:—

"Wigtoune, Junu sevinth, 1682 zeirs.

"In presence of William Coltrane, provest,
Compeared personalie Patrick M'Kie, burges of
Wigt. who becam inacted bind and obliest as
cationer and surtie for William Gordoune, Lait
Thessrer, burges of the sd burgh, and Elizabeth
Stewart, his spouse, that they shall compeir befoir
the toun Court of Wigtoune vpon advertisement
to vnderly the Law for the alleged blood and
battrie, and vyr abusess committed by the sd
Elizabeth vpon William Meinzies, ane of the
gentlemen of Claverhous troup, and that vnder
the paine of Ane hundreth punds Scots money of
penaltie in caice of failzie attour preformance:
And the sds Wm. Gordoune and Elizabeth

---

* Cleiks, hooked knives on staves for cutting the cavalry bridles.
† M'Clurg seems to have escaped. At any rate, his name
appears in the list of fugitives.

Stewart obleiss them to relieve their sd. cationer of his cationrie for them in the premises, as also compeired personalie Alexr., Mure, Chirurgiane, burges of Wigt. Who becam inacted bund and obleist as cationer and surtie for James M'Crobine and Helen Stewart, his spouse that they shall compeir befoir the toun court of Wigt. vpon advertisement to vnderly the Law for the alleged blood and battrie committed be them vpon the sd. Wm. Meinzies, and for vyr abuses done to him; and that vnder the paine of Ane hundreth punds money foresaid, in caice of failzie attour performance and the sds James M'Crobine and Helen Stewart obleiss them to releive their sd. cationer of his cationrie in the premises. In Witness qrof their presents are subt. vpon day, zeir, and place, forsd. befoir thir witnesses, Thomas Stewart, laull sone to George Stewart, bailzie of Wigt. and Ard. Ramsey, toun clerk."

On September 2nd, 1682, the Council ordered a company of soldiers to go to Kirkcudbright to secure Lord Livingstone in the Estates forfeited to him. Claverhouse's troops came in and kept garrison at Kenmure this year.

The following letter from Claverhouse to Viscount Kenmure is interesting as showing that the Viscount had a week to prepare for his unwelcome visitors.

"My Lord:—It is a good tyme since the last Chancelor wrot to your Lordship, by order of Councell to make raid and void your house of

Kenmur, for to receive a garrison: and when I
cam into this contry som moneths agoe, it was
then in debeat wither or not the garison should
enter, but it was put af at my Lord's treasurer's
deseir, and my undertaking to secur the contry.
from rebelles without it; but this sumer the
councell thought fit to give me new orders about
it. Wherefor, my Lord, I expect your Lordship
will remove what you think not fit to leave there,
for the garison must be in by the first of
November. I expect your Lords's .answer, and
am,

"My Lord,
Your most humble
Servant,
J. GRAHAM.

" Newton,
the 21 of October
1682.
" For the Viscount Kenmure."

Each horse had three pecks corn, and eight stone
of straw or hay weekly. The troops settled at Kirkcudbright had for each horse two pecks corn and seven
stone of hay or straw. David Graham held Courts
at Twynholm, getting his information from the curate.
He imprisoned several women with children at their
breasts because they would not give bond to keep the
church and hear their persecuting incumbent.

In August, Claverhouse attacked multitudes of non-
conformists who were not so much as alleged to have

been in any rising. At New Luce he seized John Archibald, Anthony MacBryde, John Macleanochan and John Wallace for not hearing the incumbent. They were brought to Stranraer and put in prison for twelve weeks, and soldiers were sent to quarter at their houses. Twelve horses were quartered in one, seven in another, and so on in proportion as their stock would bear. The seven soldiers at MacBryde's had plenty of victuals, but they would have his wife go out one Sabbath Day and bring in two sheep and kill them. This she refused, and one of them attempted to throw her into a large fire, but was prevented by the rest of the family. After being in prison twelve weeks, Claverhouse ordered them to be tied two and two together and set upon bare-backed horses to be carried to Edinburgh to be tried. When they had gone a day's journey, they were liberated on signing a bond to pay one thousand merks each on demand, and, although they paid the money, this did not prevent their oppression afterwards.

A troop of horse came to Anwoth. Seven quartered on one gentleman, where they wanted for nothing but ale, and had milk in abundance. One of the soldiers ordered the gentleman to provide ale. He answered there was none about them to be had till the waters, then very large, had fallen. The soldier answered he would have to get ale though he should have to go to hell to seek it. The gentleman replied, " If once you were there, you will not come back to tell the news." The soldier set on him with a thorn staff, but the gentleman closed in and held his own and the other soldiers separated them. The soldier then went to the commanding officer with false charges and got him arrested. The matter was not considered for some time, and meanwhile the gentleman's horses were taken away, and the whole stock, etc., destroyed. When the officer came to consider the complaint by the soldier, he found it groundless, and liberated the gentleman, but gave him no satisfaction, and did not punish the soldier.

CHAPTER XXII.

Major Learmond, Barscobe, and others captured, and ordered to be hanged—Execution not carried out—Letter showing how soldiers quartered in Galloway—Andrew Heron of Kirroughtree dealt with for harbouring his son—Fined 5,000 merks, and imprisoned till it is paid—Claverhouse forces Sir John Dalrymple to appear before the Council—Dalrymple fined £500, and committed to Edinburgh Castle till it is paid.

WHEN any of the forfeited persons were captured, the old sentence in absence was put into force. Thus we find on 7th April, 1682, the Lords Commissioners, having considered the dooms of forfeiture already passed on Robert Fleming of Auchenfin, Hugh Macklewraith of Auchenfloor, Major Joseph Learmond and Robert M'Clelland of Barscobe for the crimes of treason and rebellion, ordain them to be hanged on dates specified, the Magistrates of Edinburgh to see the execution carried out. However, other influences came to bear, and the execution was not carried out.

As showing the way in which the soldiers were ordered to quarter on the inhabitants, the following letter by Lidderdale of St. Mary's Isle is given:—

"Sergeant Persie, in obedience to my Lord Livingstone's commands to me, you are hereby ordered to go with your fifteen dragoons, presently under your command, and quarter them proportionally, as you think convenient, upon the pretended heritors of Macartney and tenants thereof, the pretended heritors and possessors of the lands of Bar (and glaisters pertaining thereunto), ay and while they come into Kirkcudbright to me, and take tacks of the haill forementioned lands from me, in name of George Lord Livingstone, donatar of the same, and not only find caution for the yearly rent thereof in time coming, but also make payment of all bygones, preceding the term of Whitsunday last from Bothwell. You are to exact free quarter during your abode, and, if need be, to take what you stand in need of for your provision, from them, without prejudice to any other. You are also to dispossess and remove the lady Holm younger forth of the lands of Macartney, and to cause some of your party to possess the same till forther orders. And you are not to remove from any of your quarters till such time as you receive my order of new for that effect. Subscribed for warrant at Kirkcudbright, the 23rd day of October, 1682.

"Tho. Lidderdale."

In January, 1683, the Council had the case of Andrew Heron of Kirroughtree before them, and the following letter was written to the Secretary:—

" My Lord,

" There being one Andrew Herron of Kerrochtree, pursued before his Majesty's privy council,
for harbouring, resetting, entertaining, and in-
tercomunning with Patrick Herron his second
son, Anthony M'Ghie late of Glencard, and other
rebels: and the said Andrew having come volun-
tarily to the lord high treasurer before any,
citation given, how soon he understood the hazard
he was liable to by law, and confessed that out
of ignorance of the laws of the kingdom, and on
account of his near relation to his said son, and
his wife's nephew, he had sometimes seen and
conversed with them, and palliate a small trade
of cattle, which his son brought from England:
having confessed his crime humbly, and begged
his Majesty and the council's mercy: the council
having considered the specialities in his case, do
recommend to your lordship to interpose for a
remission both as to his life and estate. But
that others may be deterred from harbouring and
resetting rebels though never so nearly related,
the council desire that your lordship may procure a
letter under his majesty's royal hand, empowering
and authorizing them in this case (even though
the crime be capital in itself) to impose such a
fine as they think fit and just. This, in the
council's name, is signified by

Your lordship's etc.,

" ABERDEEN, CANCEL, I.P.D."

When intercession had been made for a remission
as to his life and estate, the managers wanted a fine
from him before he was dismissed. Accordingly,
on March 8th, "Andrew Heron of Kerrochtree in
Galloway, compears, and is libelled, for being at house
and field conventicles, and intercommuning with, and
resetting his son Patrick Heron a ring leader at
Bothwell Bridge, and his son in law who had been
likewise there. The lords of his majesty's privy
council fine him in 5,000 merks and appointed him to
lie in prison till he pay it." On March 17th, 1683,
the cash-keeper reports he has paid his fine.

Claverhouse had shown great bitterness against
Sir John Dalrymple, whom he forced to appear before
the Council in February, 1683, and charged him with
" weakening the command of Government in the shire
of Galloway, with opposing the Commission, and with
himself adjudging on charges made against his own
tenants, purposely to give them too low for their
attendance at conventicles," also that he did insolently
laugh at Claverhouse's proclamations. To this Sir
John retorted that he was the person aggrieved, and
that he had occasion to complain against both Claverhouse and his subordinates; that he had presented
himself at the Sheriff Court, and Claverhouse caused
his officers and soldiers to take the complainant by,
the shoulders and attack him, and that as to the fines
they had proved sufficient, and the people of Galloway
were becoming more orderly. "Orderly!" ejaculated
Claverhouse. "There are as many elephants and
crocodiles in Galloway as orderly persons." Dalrymple

was deprived of his bailliery of the regality of Glen-luce, and was fined £500 sterling, and committed to the Castle of Edinburgh till he paid.

He then sought safety in Holland, where his father and other exiles were quietly working for the over-throw of the oppressor at home.

CHAPTER XXIII.

William Martin of Dullarg indicted for treason—He produces a renunciation, and the diet is deserted—William M'Clelland of Auchenguil, Hugh Maxwell of Cuill, and William M'Culloch of Cleichred libelled—Edward Atkin, Earlston's servant, sentenced to be hanged—Proclamation appointing persons to see the Test is taken in Galloway—John Cochrane of Waterside, tried at Ayr Circuit, and forfeited—William Thorburn of Stranraer forfeited—His sufferings—Cornet Graham holds Courts at Balmaghie—Courts at the Clachan of Penninghame—William M'Ewmont refusing the Test, is banished, and dies at sea—Thomas Lidderdale's persecutions in Twynholm—Report by Claverhouse on his work in Galloway.

In January, 1683, William Martin, younger, of Dullarg, was indicted for treason and rebellion. The matter had been compromised, as in the case of some others, by a renunciation of part of his lands. When the libel was read, he declared himself ready to stand his trial as altogether innocent, and dissented from all further continuation of it, and produced a renunciation as follows:—" Be it kend to all men, me William Martin, eldest son of James Martin of Dullarg, for as much as I am pursued before the - Lords of Justiciary, for alleged being in the Rebellion 1679, and seeing I am neither heritor nor guilty of the said crime, therefore in their presence I renounce and resign in favour of the King's Most Excellent Majesty, Lord

High Treasurer, and Treasurer Depute, all lands and heritages befallen to me wherein I was infefted or had a right before the said Rebellion or His Majesty's Gracious Indemnity, and oblige me, my heirs, and successors to denude myself hereof *omni habili modo* at sight of the Lord Treasurer or Treasurer Depute and consent these presents be registrated, etc." The Lords, in respect of this, and his offering to abide trial, deserted the diet simpliciter, and ordained him to enact himself to compear when cited, whereupon he took instruments.

On January 15th, William M'Clelland of Auchenguil, and Hugh Maxwell of Cuill, were dealt with in the same way, and William M'Culloch of Cleichred renounced as above, took the Bond of Peace and the Test, and was set at liberty.

On July 12th, 1683, the process of Edward Atkin was before the Justiciary. He lived in the Abbeytown of Crawfordjohn. He went out of Scotland with Earlston as a servant and his guide, and was taken prisoner with him at Newcastle. He was found guilty of converse with Alexander Gordon and doing favours to him, though he knew him to be a forfeited and condemned traitor, and was sentenced to be hanged at the Grassmarket on Friday, 20th July.

On 13th April, 1683, Proclamation was made for Circuit Courts and for taking the Test, the Proclamation appointing persons for this purpose, and naming among others the following:—Sir Robert Grierson of Lagg, Robert Ferguson of Craigdarroch, Sir David Dunbar of Baldoon, Hugh M'Guffog of Ruscoe, Sir

Godfrey M'Culloch of Myreton; Robert Lawrie of Maxwellton.

On April 23rd, 1683, Grierson was continued the Stewart Depute of Kirkcudbright till the justice airs be over.

At the Circuit of Ayr, John Cochrane of Waterside was charged with being with a party of country-men who came from Galloway to Bothwell. He was indeed at the town of Cumnock on business when they passed on their road to Hamilton, and his acquaint-ances in Galloway, hearing he was there, called for him and he came out of a house and spoke to them. He thought it safer to withdraw and leave the country. In absence, witnesses were examined against him. None of them would swear he had arms, but with some difficulty they prevailed upon two to depone, *in terminis*, that they saw him converse with rebels when coming from Galloway to Hamilton. Upon this he was forfeited. We shall meet with him later.

It was at this same Circuit that William Torbran, ex-Provost of Stranraer, was cited, and afterwards forfeited. In March, 1679, for mere nonconformity, he was forced by a party of soldiers to leave his family and retire to Ireland. Meantime, his house was rifled, and the soldiers for some days helped themselves to what they wanted, and went not off without a con-siderable sum of money. In November the same year, he was again forced to retire for three months. He no sooner returned, than Claverhouse sent a party of seven dragoons to quarter on him, and he had to pay, a large sum before he was rid of them, besides the

hurt they did to his business, and all this without
any sentence against him or crime laid to his charge,
save his non-compliance with Prelacy. A citation
was left at his house, May, 1683, to appear before
the circuit of Ayr, though one of the Bailies and
another person of credit in the town deponed that they
saw him some time before go off to Ireland. All his
lawyers could get done was to have sixty days allowed
to cite him as one furth of the Kingdom. When these
were out, he was forfeited and sentence of death passed
on him, and that upon no crime proven against him
but his non-compearance. The Lords' sentence was
intimated at his dwelling house at Stranraer. He was
at great expense in transporting his goods and family
to Ireland before the expiration of the sixty days.
During the four years, as he himself expressed it,
he was obliged to live in a strange land upon what
the locusts had left, and when he returned in the year
1687, he found his loss far greater than he imagined,
for his debtors would pay him nothing of what was
owing, whether having taken occasion to transact his
bonds with those who had the gift of his forfeiture, or
for what reason, is not said. One gentleman was
owing him 3,000 merks, another £60 sterling, two
others 1,000 merks each, of which he never got a
farthing. And for some time after his return, his
trade and business was quite stopped. It was but
few would venture to deal with him till he got his
forfeiture removed.

Cornet Graham held his Courts at Balmaghie, and
the people of that parish and neighbouring parishes

were cited to the Kirk, and were rudely enough dealt with. When they came before him, they were welcomed with, "You dog, hold up your hand and swear." Then it was asked, "How many conventicles have you been at since Bothwell, who preached at them, who had their children baptised?" and the like, and it was really thought, by their rudeness and indiscretion in many places, they designed to affright some whom they could not otherwise reach, to noncompearance. If anything was extorted by this examination they were fined, and if they saw fit to suspect, and had not full probation, the Test was offered, and if refused they were suspect persons.

In the parish of Penninghame and neighbouring places, multitudes were brought to trouble by these Courts who never carried arms at Bothwell, Ayrsmoss, or anywhere else, and upon mere suspicion the Test was put to them, though none but heritors were named in the letters about it. In these remote corners, the persons entrusted by the Courts did what they pleased. William M'Ewmont, weaver in Myreton's land, who had never been in any rising was pressed to take the Test, and, refusing, was sent prisoner to Edinburgh, banished, and died at sea. The laird of Lagg is named in the Proclamation for these Circuits, and he exercised his power with the greatest virulence. He kept Court at the Old Clachan of Penninghame, and forced multitudes to take the Test, and in a very little time he returned and obliged many of the same persons to take it over again.

Thomas Lidderdale of St. Mary's Isle was likewise

named, and in the parish of Twynholm he carried on the persecution most violently. There was an old man confined to his house, and Lidderdale came to him, charged him with irregularities, and required to purge himself by taking the Test. He refused. The soldiers took away his cow, which was all he lived by, and threatened to carry him to prison,—thus he was prevailed on to take the Test. In a little, he was cited to another court for alleged reset and converse with his son, and there he was obliged never to reset or converse with him. The like courts were held at Kirkcudbright and Dumfries, and the same procedure adopted.

In a report on his work in Galloway by Claverhouse to the Privy Council in 1683, he seems to glory in the cruel methods he adopted. He says:—

"The churches were quyte desert: no honest man, no minister in saifty. The first work he did was to provyd magasins of corn and strawe in evry pairt of the contry that he might with conveniency goe with the wholl pairty wherever the King's service requyred, and runing from on place to ane other, nobody could knou wher to surpryse him: and in the mean tyme quartered on the rebelles, and indevoured to distroy them by eating up their provisions: but that they quikly perceived the dessein, and soued their corns on untilled ground. After which he fell in search of the rebelles, played them hotly with pairtys, so that there were severall taken, many fleid the

country, and all wer dung from their hants; and
then rifled so their houses, ruined their goods, and
imprisoned their servants, that their wyfes and
childring were broght to sterving; which forced
them to have recours to the saif conduct, and maid
them glaid to renounce their principles. . . .
He ordered the colecttors of evry parish to bring
in exact rolls, upon oath, and atested by the
minister, and caused read them every Sonday after
the first sermon, and marque the absents, who wer
severly punished if obstinat. And wherever he
heard of a parish that was considerably behynd,
he went thither on Saturday, having acquainted
them to meet, and asseured them he would be
present at sermon, and whoever was absent on
Sonday, was punished on Monday, and who would
not apear either at church or court, he caused
arest there goods, and then offer them saif conduct,
which brought in many, and will bring in all,
and actually broght in tuo outed disorderly
ministers.''

Such then were the methods the Government
emissaries admittedly adopted to compel compliance,
but often greater cruelties and more heinous outrages
were committed by these heartless persecutors without
the slightest justification.

CHAPTER XXIV.

Coltrane, Provost of Wigtown, David Graham, and Sir Godfrey
M'Culloch of Mertoun tender the Test in Wigtownshire—
List of Wigtownshire lairds refusing the Test—Wigtown
Burgh grants Bond to the King—The Commissioners hold
Courts at Wigtown—Examples of their dealings—Accused
parties committed to irons, fined, banished to the plantations,
and others sent for trial before the Lords of Justiciary.

In 1683, William Coltrane, Provost of Wigtown, was
appointed with David Graham, Claverhouse's brother,
and Sir Godfrey M'Culloch of Mertoun to tender the
Test to the inhabitants of Wigtownshire.

By the autumn, they had reported "that the haill
gentlemen and heritors" had taken the Test excepting
"Sir Andrew Agnew of Lochnaw, James Agnew, his
son, William M'Dowall of Garthland, William Gordon of Craighlaw, and William and David, the said
William's sons, Stewart of Tonderghie, Mr. Kennedy,
minister in Ireland, Mr. James Laurie, who lives at
Ayr."

By October, 1684, pressure had been brought to bear
on all who had not taken the Test in Wigtownshire.
The Royal Commissioners were then at Wigtown, and
the knowledge that the houses of those who did not
obey would be immediately burned was not without
its effect, so that they are able to report that all had
complied except six or seven who were prisoners.

It is rather significant that just at this time the Wigtown Burgh Records contain the following:—

"Bond to the King.

"Wigtoune, Octor., 15th, 1684.

"The qlk day the Provost, bailzies, and councell, for themselves and their successors in office, for the tym being have subscribed ane voluntar bond and offer to His Majestie, as a dew mark of their loyaltie and aledgeance to his Majestie and the preservan of themselves and posteritie and for the advancement of His sacred Majestie's royal power, authoritie, and greatness, and toward the advancement of his Majestie's fources, and ane just abhorence of all rebellion, have subscribed ane voluntar bond and offer to His Majestie of Fyve monthes cess yeirlie, for the space of four zeirs, beginning the first termes peyment at Mertinmas nixt, and soe freily to be vplyfted duering the sd. space in the same manner as the present supplie is collected and vplyfted, and which offer is by and attour the present supplie as also the Magistrates have bund and obleist themselves and yr successors in office that the haill inhabitants and communitie of the Burgh shall leive regularlie and peaceably in all tym coming, vyrwayes to extirpat and remove them out of the Burgh. In witness qrof, ther presents are subscribed day and dait forsd.

"William Coltrane, Provest.
"Patrick Stuart, Bailzie."

Coltrane was a noted persecutor, and Stuart, as we shall see, was the betrayer of the Wigtown Martyrs.

Excerpts from the proceedings of the Commissioners at Wigtown show how relentlessly the Presbyterians were harassed at this time. At a court at Wigtown, on 16th October, 1684, John Stewart in Glenlukok, refusing to take the Test, was committed to irons; Andrew Sloan in Glenlukok confessed accidental converse with William Kennedy, rebel, took the Test; Walter Hunter in Linloskin confessed that Kennedy, rebel, was at his house and drank there within these last twelve months, took the Test; John M'Ghie in Barnkirk agreed to take the Test, committed to prison; William M'Cammon in Culbratton refused the Test, confessed he took the Covenant at Risk about five years past when Mr. John Welsh preached, and had a child baptised by him then, committed to irons; Alexander Carson, servitor to Sir Godfrey M'Culloch, deponed that he met with Gilbert M'Ghie, rebel, and had drunken with him, that the rebel called him Cousin Carson, and that he knew him to be at Bothwell, but considered him a free man in respect he was Broughton's gunner. All this was within five or six weeks by past, committed to prison. John Kincaid, Chilcarroch, confessed he had heard Mr. Samuel Arnot and Mr. George Barclay preach in the house of Airyolland and Little Airies, and had a child baptised by Mr. Thomas Kennedy, minister in Ireland, confessed he was at the communion in Penninghame about the time of the Rebellion, when Mr. John Welsh preached, further confessed that he was at the breaking of the house of Mr. James Cowper, minister at Methvin, Mochrum, immediately before the Rebellion '79, committed to prison. John Henderson, being interrogate against setting fire to the thief's hole door at Wigtown, deponed—that that night the prison was burned, he met Margaret Doual at Bladnoch Water, who told him that the prisoner expected furth that night and that he spoke with the prisoner that night before the escape, committed to the irons. Margaret Milligan, spouse to James Martison, and Sarah Stewart, spouse to William Kennedy, and Margaret M'Lurg, spouse to Alexander M'Clingan, rebels; Milligan and M'Lurg confessed harbouring their husbands within a year and a half, but refused to depone if they were there since. Sarah Stewart confessed harbouring her husband within the past quarter of a year, and having a child a year old unbaptised, agreed that Mr. James Cahoun baptise the child, she holding the child up herself. Milligan and M'Lurg committed to prison. Sarah Stewart enacted. Next day the Court resumed, and the following judgments were pronounced:—John Stewart in Glenlukok, William M'Cammon in Culbratton, William Sproat in Clontarf, John M'Caffie in Gargrie, to be banished to the plantations and to remain in prison till a fit occasion for transporting them. John M'Kie in Barnkirk found egregiously guilty of converse, yet willing to take the Test—to remain prisoner in the meantime. John Kincaid in Chilcarroch and John Henderson, whose crimes are extraordinary, sent for trial before the Justice-General and Lords of Justiciary at Edinburgh. Margaret Gordon, Margaret Milligan, and Margaret M'Lurg ordained to be banished to the plantations and to remain prisoners in the meantime.

Andrew Adair of Genoch declined to attend the Episcopal service. The curate of Inch bided his time and informed against him for having a child baptised by a Presbyterian minister. " For this and for Genoch's other nonconformity he was fined by Sheriff Graham 15,000 merks." This was afterwards reduced to 5,000 merks, which he was obliged to pay. John M'Neill, a member of the Kirk Session of Glasserton parish, paid 50 dollars to Mr. David Graham for having had a child baptised with the Presbyterian minister, and Michael Hannay, another member, probably as in the former case a farmer, paid £40 to. Claverhouse's brother, and got a receipt for it, because he had a child baptised by Mr. Alexander Ferguson, a Presbyterian minister.

At the Sheriff Court, " Wigtown, August 19th, 1684, Catherine Lauder, spouse to Patrick M'Kie of Auchlean, confessed that she had withdrawn from the Church these two years bygone; Therefore the Judge fines the said Auchlean in £250 Scots." In this case, the husband deponed on oath that for three years she was so unwell she was not able to go out. Sheriff Graham, however, was not satisfied. On the 20th of August, John M'Gachie in Bordland deponed:—that he had been seldom in church these two years bygone, through want of health. However, he acknowledged he made a journey to Edinburgh, and went up and down the country about his affairs, and he was fined in £100 Scots for withdrawing.

On 19th September, 1684, Wigtown Town Council again took the Test, as the Minutes show :—" The qlk Day, the haill Magistrats councell and clerk have taiken the test vpon their kneyes, conform to acts of parliat. and councell maid yranent except only provest Clugstoun and Antony M'Clure, who are not present, and are to taik the same befoir they officiate."

CHAPTER XXV.

Commission to try "divers desperate rebels" in Kirkcudbright, Wigtown, and Dumfries—James M'Gachan in Dalry and others transported—Garrisons at Kenmure, Machermore, Minnigaff, and Carsphairn—The Cochranes of Ochiltree and Waterside denounced rebels—The fugitive roll applicable to Galloway—"A list of very good people persecuted for conscience's sake"—Nearly 220 Galloway people to be apprehended.

IN the beginning of 1684, a Commission was granted to James Alexander, Sheriff Depute of Dumfries, the eldest bailie for the time there, James Johnston of Westeraw, Stewart-depute of Annandale, Thomas Lidderdale of Isle, Stewart-depute of Kirkcudbright, David Graham, brother to Claverhouse, —— Bruce of Abbotshall, Captain Strachan, William Graham, Cornet to Claverhouse, or any three of them to try and judge "divers desperate rebels" in Dumfries, Kirkcudbright, Wigtown, and Annandale, to hold Courts, create members, call before them the persons foresaid not being heritors, put them to the trial of an Assize, and pass sentence and see justice done accordingly.

On June 19th, at Edinburgh, the Lords sentenced James M'Gachan in Dalry, John Criechton in Kirkpatrick, John Mathieson in Closeburn, John M'Chisholm in Spittal, libelled for reset and converse with rebels, and found guilty by their confession judicially adhered to, to be transported to the plantations.

On April 22nd, Colonel Graham was ordered to post his own troop at Dumfries or where he thought most convenient in that country, and to post the two troops of dragoons in the garrisons of Caitloch, Ballagan, Kenmure, Machermore, or Minnigaff.

May 5th, the Council " appoint a garrison at Kenmure and because the Lady is to lie in, the soldiers are for the time dispersed to Barscobe, Waterhead, Knockgray, and Caitloch." The garrisons in the south were increased as if it had been a country conquered by an enemy. Two were set up in the parish of Carsphairn. Parties from these garrisons were the great instruments of many of the murders in cold blood which now were becoming frequent.

An Act anent the army, August 1st, 1684, enacted that the General's troops of dragoons and Captain Strachan's lie at garrisons in Galloway and Nithsdale, and Colonel Graham of Claverhouse, Lieutenant Colonel Buchan or any of them or such as they shall think fit to appoint in their absence were authorised to call for and examine upon oath all who could give any information as to rebels in arms, and such as had been present at field conventicles or upon whose lands these conventicles had been kept.

December 22nd, Mr. John M'Michan, Mr. Cant, and Mr. Archibald M'Gachan were indicted before the Justiciary for reset of rebels. They appeared and offered to abide trial. The diet was deserted simpliciter, and the last enacted himself under five thousand merks to appear when called, and on January, 17th Mr. M'Michan and Mr. Cant were brought before the Council, and their bond taken that they would live peaceably and not preach.

April 8th, John Cochrane of Waterside was charged with having in June, 1679, joined the Laird of Barscobe and a party of rebels of five or six hundred, mounted his horse and rode with them and supplied them with wine and other provisions. Sir John Cochrane and his son were ordered to be denounced fugitives, and yet on April 9th, the Lords continued the Process of forfeiture against Sir John Cochrane of Ochiltree till the second Monday of July. There appears nothing more about him that year. The Indictment against his son, John Cochrane of Waterside, was taken up and witnesses adduced. One deponed he saw Waterside with the rebels at Cumnock at the Barrhill when rendevousing, but was at some distance, and did not hear him speak with Earlston and Barscobe. Another deponed that he saw Waterside walking among the rebels as he thought with a small sword. Another deponed that Waterside spake for him to the rebels, and got him leave to go home that he might return to them again. He was found guilty of treason, and ordained to be executed, and demeaned as a traitor when apprehended.

On May 5th, 1684, the Council published the fugitive rolls with a proclamation requiring all subjects not only not to comfort or harbour the said persons, but likewise to do their utmost endeavours to apprehend them and to inform against them. There are many mistakes in the rolls, "but they contain a list of very good people persecuted for conscience sake" (Wodrow).

The following is the list applicable to Galloway:—

Wigton.

Thomas Macneilly in Portpatrick parish.
James Semple there.
Andrew Martin of Little Aries, forfeited.
William Kennedy in Barnkirk.
James Stuart, son of Archibald Stuart, in Causey-end.
Patrick Vause in Mochrum parish.
John Hay, brother to Aryalland.
James Macyacky of Kenmuir.
James Macjarrow, servant to Culvennan.
George Stroyan in Kirkowan parish.
Archibald Stuart in Causey-end.
Alexander Clingen in Kilellan.
Alexander Hunter of Culwhassen, forfeited.
James Soffley, merchant, in Wigton.
James Martison in Glenapil, in Peningham parish.
John Hannay at the Mill, Peningham.
John Martison in Glenmougil, in the said parish.
Hugh Macdoual, weaver, in Wigton.
James Cairns in Peningham parish.
John Maclurg, smith, in Monnigaff.
Patrick Murdoch of that ilk.
Patrick Dunbar, younger, of Machrimore.

William Stuart, son to —— Stuart, wadsetter, of
Larg.

Anthony Stuart, his son.

—— Stuart, his son.

Michael Mactaggart, liferenter in Glassock.

Mr. William Hay, brother to the laird of Aryalland.

John Mackilhaffy in Craichley's Land.

James Macyacky there. William Wilson in Stranraer.

William Tarbran, late bailie there.

Joseph Macdoual, servitor to Sir David Dunbar of
Baldoon.

Alexander Hay of Aryalland.

Alexander M'Clellan in Carse of Baltersan.

Stewartry of Kircudbright.

Adam Smart in Kircudbright.

Samuel Gelly, gardener, there.

Samuel Campbell, weaver, there.

John Heuchan.

James Robertson, merchant, there.

Alexander Mackean, tailor, there.

Thomas Paulin there.

Adam Macwhan there.

Gabriel Hamilton there.

John Clark there.

Alexander Morton there.

Robert Grier in Lochinkit.

James Mackartney, flesher, in Kircudbright.

William Kevan in Stockin.

—— Neilson, younger, in Corsack.

Samuel Parker, chapman, in Twinham parish.

Alexander Birnie in Colkegrie.

William Halliday in Glencape.

James Macgowan in Auchingisk.

—— Martin in Kirchrist.

David Braidson in Quarters.

Thomas Sprout in Over-bar-chapel.

—— Halloun in Lairmannoch.

Robert Cadjow in Craig.

Hugh Mitchelson.

Alexander Campbell, weaver, sometime Uroch.

John Charters in Tongland.

—— Welsh in Scar.

Alexander Campbell, miller, sometime in Uroch.

James Durham in Edgarton.

Anthony Macmillan in Stonebrae.

John Rae in Slachgarrie.

Richard Machesny in Moit.

John Carsey in Blackmire.

Archibald Machesny in Balhassie.

James Macdoual, servitor to Henry M'Culloch of Barholm.

John Auchinleck, son to John Auchinleck elder, in Balgraden.

Robert Miller in Laigh Risco.

Alexander Dugalston in Lagan.

David M'Culloch, son to the laird of Ardwel.

Gilbert Gie in Marshalton.

John Campbell in Marbrack.

Alexander Porter in Lag.

John Colton in Nether Third.
George Campbell in Aresalloch.
David Canon in Firmaston.
John Gordon, elder, in Garyhorn.
John M'Call, weaver, in Craigincar.
John Macmillan, sometime servitor to James Ferguson in Trostan.
Fergus Grier in Brigmoor.
James Macmillan in Glenlie.
John Macmillan in Strangassie.
James Gordon in Largmore.
Henry Gordon in Lochsprey.
Andrew Macmillan, servant to New Galloway.
John Crawford, apothecary, there.
William Dempster in Armancandie.
Thomas Murdoch in Barnsalloch.
John Tait, tailor, in Balmaclellan.
Alexander Mein in Armancande.
James Hook in Holm.
James Halliday in Fell.
William Macmillan in Areshalloch.
David Mackile in Dalshangan.
James Clark in Marbrack.
Gilbert Macadam in Craigingilton.
William Grier, servitor to Marion Welsh of Glenhill.
James Anderson in Shalloch.
John Wright there.
James Currie in the Glen.
John Maclachrie in Larg.
John Macjore in Keirland.

Edward Gordon in Blacke.

John Hannay at the Bridge end of Dumfries.

John M'Gee there.

Roger Macnaught in Newton of Galloway.

Mr. William Gilchrist, ⎫
Mr. James Welsh,   ⎪
Mr. John Hepburn,   ⎪
Mr. James Guthrie,   ⎬ Preachers.
Mr. John Forrester,   ⎪
Mr. —— Lennox,   ⎪
Mr. Thomas Wilkie,   ⎪
Mr. Thomas Vernor,   ⎭

Andrew Macmillan who haunts at Monnigaf.

William Sohaw in the parish of Borgue.

—— Mactagart sometime in the said parish.

Robert Gordon in Kilmair.

John Gourley in Mondrogat.

George Short,   ⎫ who haunted in Tongland parish.
Robert Cochran, ⎭

William Macmillan in Bredenoch.

—— Livingstone in Quintinsepy.

Gilbert Caddel in Borgue parish.

John Richardson there.

John Bryce there.

William M'Gavin there.

William Campbell there.

Walter and Gilbert M'Gee there.

James Robertson there.

John Clinton there.

—— Crichton, son to Robert Crichton in Auchin-
shinnoch.

—— Macmillan, son to John Macmillan in Glenlie.
—— Macmillan in Greenan.
—— Gibson, son to Robert Gibson in Overstranga-
shel.
Gilbert M'Ewen, Carsferry.

Fugitives for reset and harbour.

James Macnaught in Newton of Galloway.
—— Gordon of Garrary.
William M'Call in Holm of Daltanachan.
John Hook in Holm.
Robert Hillow in Hillowton.
Andrew Crock in Iron-crogo.
John Macmin in Fuffock.
William Raffie in Iron ambrie.
—— Macjore in Kirkland.
John Herron, sometime in Earlston, now in Hard-
land.
John Barber, elder, in Over-Barley.
John Barber, younger, there.
John Barber in Nether Barley.
James Girran in Clachan.
James Macadam there.
Alexander Gourley in Greenan-Mill.
James Marmichael in Clachan.
George Douglas there.
Edward Ferguson in Auchinshinoch.
John Corsan there.
Robert Grier in Reglen.
William Edgar in Gordonston.

George Macmichael in Carskep.
John Macmillan of Iron-daroch.
Andrew Wilson in Black-craig.
Robert Macmichael in Craiglour.
Alexander Macmillan in Glenrie.
John Brown in Nether Strangassel.
John Macchesny in Hole.
Robert Gordon in Clachan.
Alexander Gordon there.
John Macmillan in Glenlie.
William Houston in Blarney.
John Geddes in Bartagart.
James Mulliken in Knocknoon.
John Mulliken in Barscob.
Samuel Cannon in Barsalloch.
Mr. William M'Millan of Caldow.
Robert Caa in Knocklie.
James Garmorie in Armanady.
Robert Mackartnie in Quintinspy.
James Edgar in Drumakelly.
John Grier of Blackmark.
William Stuart, } both in Crofts.
Patrick Macjore, }
Gilbert Welsh in Bank.
James Turner in Auchingibbet.
John Collin in Auchingibbet.
James Garmarie in the parish of Corsmichael.
John Garmorie in Trouden.
John Graham in Chapelearn.
Thomas and Robert Grahams in Ernefillan.
John Gelly in Iron Grogo.

John Clark in Drum.
John Auchinleck in Dalgredan.
Robert Crichton in Auchinshinoch.
John Hislop in Midardes.
John Macmillan in Dunveoch.

Follow the Women who are fugitives for reset.

Marion Welsh in Glenhill.
Grizel Richardson in Arnworth.
Margaret Gordon in Mayfield.
Elspeth Anderson in Shaw-head.
Rebecca Macmichael at the Black-craig in the Dalry
    parish.
Margaret Tod in Clachan.
Bessie Gordon there.
Jean Thomson at Bridge of Orr.
Grizel Fullarton, good wife of Balmagan.
Grizel Gordon in Over Ardwell in Anworth.
—— Gordon, widow, in Glenlie.
Mary Chalmers, liferentrix, of Clairbrand.

John Welsh in Drumjowan.
Roger Macnaught in Newton of Kells.
Gilbert M'Ewen in Carsfeiry.
William M'Call in Clachan.
James Chapman there.
John Struthers in Monnigaff.
Robert Gaa, smith, in Clachan.
Henry Gordon in Dundeuch.
Alexander Corsan in Newton of Kells.

CHAPTER XXVI.

New Justiciary Courts—Appointments for Wigtownshire, the Stewartry, and Dumfries—Instructions to seize all preachers, to turn out wives and children of forfeited persons, to impose fines and quarter on the stubborn, to suffer no man to travel with arms except gentlemen of known loyalty who have taken the Test; to allow no yeoman to travel three miles from his house without a pass—Hay of Park sent prisoner to Blackness—Liberated a year later on Bond for £1,000—Courts at Dumfries, Kirkcudbright, and Wigtown— A "Cheerful" offer to his Majesty of twenty months' cess— William Martin and James Martin of Dullarg fined at Kirkcudbright—Their sufferings—James Martin dies in prison— The Society's "Apologetical Declaration"—Proclamation against it—Cruel persecutions—James Graham, Crossmichael, executed, and William Auchenleck, Buittle, shot dead without any reason—The Laird of Lagg at Dalry—Courts at Twynholm and Kirkcudbright.

On September 6th, 1684, there was a Commission for new Justiciary Courts, the Treasurer Principal, Lord Drumlanrick, and Colonel Graham of Claverhouse being appointed to Dumfries and Wigtown and the Stewartries of Annandale and Kirkcudbright with detailed instructions. Number 3 of these was as follows:—" You shall seize all preachers, chaplains, or such as exercise as Chaplains, who are not authorised by the Bishops, and send them to our Privy Council to be disposed of as they think fit and see cause." Number 12, " You shall turn out all the wives and children of the forfeited persons and fugitives from their habitations if it shall appear that they have conversed with their parents or husbands, or if they shall refuse to vindicate themselves by their oaths." Number 17, "If you find any part of the country stubborn or contumacious, you shall impose such fines upon them as the law will allow, and in case of non-payment thereof and that you think it fit you are immediately to quarter our Forces on the stubborn and contumacious until the fines imposed shall be exhausted by them." Number 20, "You shall suffer no man to travel with arms excepting gentlemen of known loyalty who have taken the Test and no yeoman to travel three miles from his own house without a pass from his minister or a Commissioner of the Excise."

On September 16th, 1684, the Council ordered Hay of Park and one or two others to be sent to Blackness and kept close prisoners. The reason for this does not appear. In August, 1685, Hay was liberated on Bond for £1,000 sterling to live regularly and orderly. Upon 2nd October, 1684, Queensberry, his son, and Claverhouse held Court at Dumfries, having for their district Dumfries, Galloway, Nithsdale, and Annandale. After some days at Dumfries, they went to Kirkcudbright, and then to Wigtown. Particular gentlemen and officers of the soldiers were sent to parishes at a distance which the judges could not readily reach, and the inhabitants were obliged to swear over again though they had satisfied the judges. The Test was offered to the men and other oaths to the women, and on refusing they were brought to Dumfries Prison to await the judges' return. Fines were also imposed.

On October 13th, the Committee for public affairs transmitted an address from Kirkcudbright to the Secretary with the following letter:—"My Lord, We have this day received an account from my Lord Treasurer of the procedure of the Committee of Council sent to the district of Nithsdale and Galloway here inclosed, whereby you will perceive that by the diligence and influence of the Lord Treasurer that place is brought to make a cheerful offer to His Majesty of twenty months' cess to be paid in four years beginning at Martinmas next, and that by and attour the supply granted by the current Parliament. They have likewise offered themselves to be bound for their tenants and servants that they shall walk regularly in time coming. This is a very good example to the Western and Southern shires, so that if they can be brought up this length there may be a considerable addition to His Majesty's Forces."

When the Lords were at Kirkcudbright, they fined among others William Martin, son of James Martin of Dullarg in the parish of Parton. Besides the severities exercised upon his father, Mr. Martin was put to considerable charges before the Justiciary at Dumfries, 1679, for alleged accession to Bothwell. In 1682, he was charged by a herald to compear at Edinburgh, and there seven times pannelled, and no probation adduced as to his being at Bothwell, yet he was forced judicially to renounce all the lands he was infeft in before the year 1679. Queensberry forced him to dispone lands worth six hundred merks a year for the sum of five thousand merks, which he reckoned a loss to him of £6,333 6s. 8d. In the beginning of 1684, in his absence, his wife was summoned for his alleged baptising a child with a Presbyterian minister, and was forced to give Bond for £100 Scots, which was paid. At different times he had eight dragoons quartered upon him for some days. Colonel Douglas quartered upon him with forty-four horsemen for some time, and being cited to the Circuit at Kirkcudbright, and, knowing the Test was to be offered, he decided to withdraw, and was fined in absence £700 Scots, which he paid. James Martin, his father, was also brought to much trouble at this Court. He had been fined most groundlessly by Middleton's Parliament in five hundred and ten merks. When he refused to pay, almost as much more was taken from him by force, as appears by a discharge under Sir William Bruce's hands. John Maxwell of Milltoun fined him a large sum for his wife's nonconformity, and, upon his refusing to pay, three yoke of oxen and some horses were taken away. At length, he raised an action of reduction against Milltoun, which cost him upwards of £100, and the Council were so sensible of this persecutor's exorbitancy, that for this and other things they for a time took away his commission. Being this year cited before this Court at Kirkcudbright, at the instigation of Mr. Colin Dalgliesh, curate, he was fined £1,000 for his wife's not keeping the Church, and cast into prison till he paid it. He suffered severely, and, receiving no attention in his illness, he died there.

In October, 1684, the Society People, among whom were many Gallovidians, met to draw up their Apologetical Declaration, directed especially against informers. Renwick was employed to draft it, though he argued strongly against emitting such a declaration, but as the others were clamourous and insisted, he yielded for the sake of peace. Its import may be gathered from the following excerpt:—" Call to your remembrance all that is in peril is not lost, and all that is delayed is not forgiven. Therefore, expect to be dealt with as ye deal with us, so far as our power can reach, not because we are acted by a sinful spirit of revenge for private and personal injuries, but mainly because by our fall reformation suffers damage." The Declaration was published on the church doors and market crosses of Nithsdale, Galloway and Ayr. It raised the fury of the Government, but, at the same time, the most venomous malignants were affrighted, informers in the south and west were for some time deterred from their traffic, and the most violent and persecuting of the curates in Nithsdale and Galloway found it convenient to retire for some time to other places. The Privy Council, on 31st December, issued a Proclamation that whoever would own the Society's Declaration, or refuse to disown it, would be tried and executed. Lieutenant General Drummond was instructed to go to the Southern and Western shires with practically full power to quarter the army wherever he thought fit.

A. Commission was granted to John, Viscount of Kenmure, the Laird of Lagg, David Dunbar of Baldoon, Sir Godfrey M'Culloch of Mertoun, and Mr. David Graham, Sheriff Depute of Galloway for the shire of Wigtown and Stewartry of Kirkcudbright, and to the Commanding Officers of the garrisons to proceed against those guilty of being present at conventicles, withdrawing from public ordinances, etc.

Cruel persecution followed.

James Graham, tailor, in the parish of Crossmichael, returning from his work to his mother's house, was overtaken by Claverhouse and a party of soldiers. Searching him, they found a Bible in his pocket, and at once carried him to Kirkcudbright, then to Wigtown, and then to Dumfries. Here he was kept in the irons because he would not answer their interrogatories. He was next taken to Edinburgh and questioned upon the Declaration of the Societies, and, refusing to answer, he was found guilty, condemned, and executed. William Graham, his brother, was cruelly murdered by Claverhouse himself, as we shall afterwards see.

William Auchenleck in Buittle parish had been convoying a friend going to Ireland, and, returning on horseback, met a company of Douglas' foot coming from Kirkcudbright, and they called on him to stand. Auchenleck was a full conformist, but, suspecting the soldiers would seize his horse, he rode off till he came to a public house at Carlingwark, where he called for some ale, and was drinking it on horseback when some of the soldiers, taking a nearer way, came up and shot him dead. A boy happened to be at the house, and was mounting his horse when the shot frightened it and he was thrown off. The soldiers came up, knocked him on the head with their pieces, and seized his horse and what money he had without asking a single question.

The soldiers exacted considerable sums in the parish of Dalry as the rest of the Bonds extorted by Bannatyne and others. The very interest of these notes and Bonds was reckoned up, cattle taken away, and houses rifled, merely upon alleged accession to Pentland. The Laird of Lagg held Courts frequently in Galloway, obliging those who did compear to declare on oath what they knew of those who did not compear, and if they knew where any of the wanderers resorted. At Dalry, he gathered all the men of the parish into the Kirk, and surrounded it with soldiers. Then he forced them to take the Test, and when by fair means or foul he had prevailed with them, he said, " Now you are a fold full of clean beasts. You may go home." Afterwards, getting information from his spies, he harassed several, and fined them though they were legally purged by taking the Test. He exacted upwards of seven hundred merks from three men who had qualified.

David Graham about the same time held Courts at Twynholm. His great interrogatory was, if they kept the Church, and when many could not depone in terms of law, they were fined and the fines exacted with all rigour.

Similar Courts were held at Kirkcudbright, where the curate caused the whole parish to be cited, sat in Court and excused and accused as he thought fit. A private mark was put at the names of those he alleged were backward in keeping the Church. Masters were sworn that if their servants did not keep the Church they should be dismissed, and parents the same way as to their children.

CHAPTER XXVII.

Women as well as men cited and examined on oath—Gavin M'Clymont, Carsphairn, has seven cows taken away—John Corson, Borgue, imprisoned and fined 6,000 merks—Intention to sentence his wife to be drowned at Kirkcudbright—Lagg holds Courts at Carsphairn—Peter Pearson, curate of Carsphairn, sits in Court and informs against the inhabitants —The Glenkens has one visitation after another—Mrs. M'Dowall of Gillespie forced to retire to Ireland—Charles Stewart of Knock apprehended by Claverhouse, and imprisoned in Stranraer—Auchencloy—The troops' oppressions in Galloway—John Hallam executed.

IN other Galloway parishes similar Courts were set up. Women as well as men were cited and examined on oath about themselves and their neighbours, particularly if they knew where any of their goods and gear were or any person who had anything that belonged to them, so that the soldiers could go and seize it.

Seven cows were taken from Gavin M'Clymont in Carsphairn upon his refusal after quartering to pay the cess, amounting to less than £5 Scots.

John Corson of Balmangan, in the parish of Borgue, was imprisoned for nine months for refusing the bond of regularity. He was fined six thousand merks, and paid every farthing as a discharge bears. His lady had been imprisoned by Colonel Douglas, and for refusing the Abjuration received an Indictment, and it was no secret that they intended to sentence her to be drowned within the sea mark at the Ferry at Kirkcudbright, but King Charles' death put a stop to this and some other processes of the same kind.

Claverhouse summoned the whole parish of Borgue to give up all the arms they had, and these were carried to Dumfries and given to the Earl of Nithsdale.

During the harvest of 1684, Lagg held a Court at Carsphairn Church. On his way from Sanquhar, he seized a young man, George Lorrimer, at Holm of Dalwhirran, and would have him drink the King's health. He refused, and was sent to Dumfries prison, but broke out and escaped.

Peter Pearson, curate of Carsphairn, sat in Court with Lagg and informed against those cited, and upon his information parties were sent out throughout the parish to harass them, and seize their goods. The Glenkens district now had one visitation after another. Livingstone came from Nithsdale to Carsphairn with a troop of dragoons. Claverhouse followed with five or six troops, and went through all the hills searching for persons in their hiding. The soldiers often passed the mouths of the caves where those they sought were lurking, and the dogs would smell about the stones under which they were hid, and yet they remained undiscovered. This was the case with Gavin M'Clymont at Cairnsmuir Hill, and others.

The son of an old woman of seventy-three years in Carsphairn had been cited in 1680 for hearing Mr. Cameron, and, not appearing, was intercommuned, and the mother's house spoiled. Later, the soldiers, not finding him, carried his mother to Dumfries. They offered her the Test, and, when likely to comply, they would have her swear further that she would never speak to nor harbour her son. This she refused, and next market day she was scourged through Dum-- fries, and fined 200 merks before being liberated.

M'Dowall of Gillespie was dead sometime before this, and his Lady, Janet Ross, liferentrix, enjoyed the estate. Corporal Murray, with thirteen dragoons and their horses, was sent to quarter upon her at the instigation of the curate, and for mere nonconformity. They stayed several weeks and destroyed almost the whole crop. They shot the sheep in the fields, and at length forced her to retire to Ireland for about twenty months. Her tenants had to appear first at Ayr and then at Edinburgh as witnesses against her for nonconformity.

Charles Stuart, Knock, was apprehended by Claver-house in the harvest, and cast into Stranraer prison, and had to pay three hundred merks for baptising his child with Mr. Samuel Arnot. He was summoned to Edinburgh as a witness against Sir James Dalrymple of Stair, and his lady for her nonconformity, and had to remain there seventy-two days at his own expense.

In December, Claverhouse, when ranging up and down Galloway with a troop, came to the Water of Dee and at Auchencloy captured six men, as afterwards related.

On December 3rd, the Council gave orders to the Lord Advocate to raise a process of forfeiture before. the Parliament by a summons in Latin after the old way under the Quarter Seal upon a charge of sixty days against Thomas Hay of Park, James Dalrymple of Stair and others. In the beginning of 1685, Captain Strachan harassed the parish of Dalry. He had garrison at Earlston, and held Courts in the neighbourhood. At the same time Courts were held by Lagg, and such as he deputed, in other parts, and the Abjuration Oath pressed in several neighbouring parishes.

Captain Douglas and his soldiers oppressed terribly in the parish of Twynholm. A poor tenant there took the oath, so the soldiers left for a little, but after eight or ten days returned and took him to a neighbouring parish to assist them in searching for other wanderers. On the road they met a man who would not answer their questions nor take the oath, and him the Captain ordered to be immediately shot. The other countryman entreated the Captain to examine him further and give him more time before they despatched him. For this they beat him and bruised him to such an extent that in a few weeks he died. The same Captain came through a good part of Galloway with soldiers, and they spoiled all places where they came. They deputed their power to gentlemen in each parish who harassed at their leisure.

In Tongeland, Lieutenant Livingstone and a party of dragoons harassed severely. A youth of eighteen, John Hallam, stepping out of their way, was seized and carried to Kirkcudbright. Refusing the Abjuration there, he was executed.

CHAPTER XXVIII.

Death of Charles—General Election, and members for Galloway
—James grants an Indemnity—Sir James Dalrymple and
others put to the horn—Edward Kyan, from Water of
Minnock, shot dead—Dunbar of Baldoon, M'Culloch of Myreton, and others, to assist Colonel Douglas to put down rebels
—Five men shot at Ingleston cave—M'Kie of Larg with
the rebels—Andrew M'Quhan shot dead—Second Sanquhar
Declaration—David Halliday and George Short shot dead
—Machermore garrison strengthened—Ochiltree, Earlston,
Craighlaw, and other estates annexed to the Crown.

CHARLES died on 6th February, 1685, having received
absolution a few hours before his death, and James
succeeded without taking the Coronation Oath. A
General Election followed his accession. Claverhouse
in Galloway used every exertion to secure the return
of members acceptable to the Government, but, to his
chagrin, Sir Andrew Agnew of Lochnaw and the
Honourable William Stewart of Castle Stewart were
unanimously elected. In the Stewartry, however, the
King's party returned Hugh Wallace of Ingleston,
heritor of the barony of Larg, M'Kie being forfeited
for the time. There was a momentary check to the
horrible persecutions. James signalised his accession
by an Indemnity which, however, was so restricted
as to be hardly worthy of the name. It excepted fines
for which already sentence had been pronounced, and
all those guilty of the assassination of archbishop

Sharp, Pearson of Carsphairn, Thomas Kennedy, and Duncan Stewart.

On 16th February, 1685, George Brown, tailor, John Pollock, and John Wallet in Galloway were before the Council. They refused the abjuration, and their cases were continued. On March 17th, 1685, Sir James Dalrymple of Stair and others, being oft times called, did not compear, though cited according to law, for being accessory "to the late horrid plot against the life of his Majesty, and his late brother Charles II., their Sovereign," being accessory to the Rebellion, 1679, reset and converse with rebels, and doing favour to them, were decerned outlaws and fugitives, and put to the horn, their moveable goods and gear to be escheat and brought in for his Majesty's use. The Advocate declared he was satisfied no Act be extracted against them till May 16th next, when at his instance they were cited to appear before Parliament.

On 28th February, 1685, Lieutenant James Douglas with twenty-four soldiers surrounded the house at Dalwin, in the parish of Barr, having got information that there were fugitives there. Edward Kyan, a youth from Galloway, bargaining to buy corn, fled in betwixt the gable of one house and the side wall of another, but they dragged him out and took him through the yard. He was asked where he lived, and he told them upon the Water of Minnoch. When one of the soldiers had him by the arm dragging him away, Douglas, without any warning, shot him twice through the head. When lying on the ground, struggling with death, one of the soldiers shot him a third time. He was but a youth, and could not have been at Bothwell or any of the Risings, and they had indeed nothing to charge him with but his hiding himself.

On 27th March, 1685, there was a special commission to Colonel Douglas to go with horse south and west, and to be assisted in putting down the rebels by many others throughout the country, including the Viscount of Kenmure, Robert Grierson of Lagg, Sir David Dunbar of Baldoon, Sir Godfrey M'Culloch of Myreton, and Mr. David Graham, Sheriff of Galloway, in the shire of Wigtown and Stewartry of Kirkcudbright.

On 28th April, Colonel James Douglas and Lieutenant Livingstone came suddenly to a cave near Ingliston, in Glencairn, betrayed to them by Andrew Watson, and surprised in it John Gibson, brother to James Gibson of Ingliston, heritor of the ground, James Bennoch in Glencairn parish, Robert Edgar, Robert Mitchell from the parish of Cumnock in Ayrshire, and Robert Grierson, a Galloway man. When the soldiers came up, they shot into the mouth of the cave and wounded one of them, and then rushed in. The rest were immediately taken out and shot dead.*

On 6th May, 1685, John M'Ghie of Larg was found guilty of being in arms in company with the rebels at the Standing Stones of Torhouse, and in the town of Wigtown, when about three score came in there to

* For fuller details see article, " Grierson of Balmaclellan," *infra*.

search for arms in June, 1679. M'Ghie (or M'Kie) was dead long before the trial, but this had no restraining effect on the persecutors.

On 10th May, Lieutenant Colonel Douglas came into a house near Newton of Galloway, and found Adam M'Quhan lying very ill of a fever. Putting questions to him which he was unable or unwilling to answer, the soldiers took him out of bed, carried him to Newton, and next morning shot him without any process or assize. He was buried in Kells Churchyard, where a stone has been erected to his memory.

The Society People published the second Sanquhar Declaration, 25th May, 1685. Renwick, with nearly two hundred supporters, most of them from Galloway, and many of them armed, rode into Sanquhar, read the Declaration, and fixed it to the Market Cross. Its chief interest lay in its protest against the Duke of York as a Roman Catholic succeeding to the Throne. It concluded with a paragraph meant to show that they were not responsible for violence laid to their charge:—

" Finally, we being misrepresented to many, as persons of murdering and assassinating principles, and which principles and practices we do hereby declare before God, angels, and men, that we abhor, renounce, and detest, as also all manner of robbing of any, whether open enemies or others, which we are most falsely aspersed with, either in their gold, their silver, or their gear, or any household stuff. Their money perish with themselves, the Lord knows that our eyes are not after these things.

"And in like manner we do hereby disclaim all unwarrantable practices committed by any few persons reputed to be of us, whereby the Lord hath been offended, his cause wronged, and we all made to endure the scourge of tongues, for which things we have desired to make conscience of mourning before the Lord, both in public and private."

On June 10th, Lord Annandale and Grierson of Lagg, hearing of four wanderers in the parish of Twynholm, went forth with six score of horse in different directions. Lord Annandale and his party fell in with David Halliday in Glengap and George Short. Upon their surrender, he gave them quarter till they should be tried. When Lagg came up, he would have them shot. They begged till to-morrow to be allowed to prepare for eternity. Lord Annandale told Lagg he had promised this. Lagg swore no, and ordered his men to shoot them. For some time they refused, till he swore he would do so himself. They were shot as they lay tied together on the ground, and their bodies allowed to lie till next day.

Argyle's unfortunate attempt on Scotland ended disastrously, and several of the Galloway Presbyterians were implicated. Among the interrogatories put to Argyle at his trial was this:—"If William Clelland was sent by you from any part of Holland, and where he was sent? and if any person be sent to Galloway, with arms, or what officers are sent to Galloway or elsewhere, and what correspondence they have?"

Argyle, as we know, was tried, condemned, and executed June 13th, 1685.

Colonel Richard Rumbold, Maltster at Rye, who had been with Argyle, was taken not long afterwards, tried, condemned, and ordered to be executed, the sentence containing revolting details as to the cruel way in which this was to be carried out. His body was ordered to be quartered, one part to be fixed to the Port or Tolbooth of Glasgow, another at Jedburgh, a third at Dumfries, and a fourth at Newtoun of Galloway.

This year, 1685, the garrisons were strengthened at Earlston, Waterhead, and Machermore.

By Act of Parliament, the lands of Sir John Cochrane of Ochiltree, John Porterfield of Duchal, Mr. William and Alexander Gordon of Earlston, John Gordon, younger, of Craighlaw, were this year annexed to the Crown, not to be dissolved from it, but by Parliament, "and that not upon general narratives, but particular causes and services to be specified that it may appear the same is not granted upon importunity or upon private suggestions, but for true, just, and reasonable causes of public concern." These had justice done to them after the Revolution.

After Argyle's attempt on Scotland, parties of soldiers were continually marching through the west and south. A good number of them traversed the Glenkens district as if it had been an enemy's country. Claverhouse came through Nithsdale into the Stewartry, and forced the people to take what oaths he pleased. Lieutenant Livingstone and a company of soldiers continued a good space at New Galloway, and brought the country under the greatest hardships by searching and seizing whatever they found.

CHAPTER XXIX.

Major Wynram stationed at Wigtown—Barnkirk house stripped
—Tenant's wife imprisoned in Wigtown for eleven weeks
with infant—John Wallace of Knockiebay has his house and
stock despoiled—Remission to Sir James Dalrymple—His son
made King's Advocate—James' Indulgences—The Cameronians hold out—Renwick seized and executed—Invitation to
the Prince of Orange—His Declaration for Scotland—He
lands at Torbay, accompanied by Sir James Dalrymple—
Report of 10,000 Irish Papists burning Kirkcudbright—The
Privy Council's proclamation for the defence of religion—
The Galloway Commanders—The Cameronians in arms—
Grierson of Lagg—William orders a meeting of Scotch
Estates at Edinburgh—The Galloway representatives—The
Convention guarded by the Cameronians—Sir John Dal-
rymple refutes the claim of Divine Right put forward for
James—The Crown settled on William and Mary—Parliament
abolishes Prelacy—Synod of Galloway—General Assembly
meets.

MAJOR WYNRAM was stationed, in the autumn of 1685,
with a company of dragoons at Wigtown, harassing
the neighbourhood, and causing much suffering and
distress. The Burgh Records of Wigtown contain the
following:—

" WIGTOUNE, August
twentie thrie, 1686.

" The qlk day the Magistrates and Councell,
considering that Major Wynram his troop of
Dragounes Did eat up the Wholl meadowes of

the hills and Clay Crops with their horses at Lambas, 1685 yeirs, they therfoir appoynt the sd. Lambas teremes rent of the sd. hills to be allowed to the tenants yrof for the loss of the sds. meadowes and grass, and for their vyr trouble they had yranent."

A party of these soldiers came to Barnkirk, near Newton Stewart, a part of Castle Stewart's lands in Penninghame parish, and apprehended Sarah Stewart, spouse to William Kennedy, who for non-compearance had been denounced. They unroofed the house and seized the plenishing. Then they forced her to go with them on foot to Wigtown, carrying an infant not nine months old, and having to leave her other three children without even a servant to look after them, though the eldest was only eight, the next five, and the other not three years of age. At Wigtown she was with her infant kept in prison eleven weeks, though she was not obnoxious to the then laws, being a conformist. They wanted her to swear she would never converse with her husband, now put to the horn, but would inform against him that he might be apprehended, and this she peremptorily refused.

John Wallace of Knockiebay, in the parish of New Luce, was seized this year for refusing the abjuration. A party of Colonel Buchanan's men spoiled his house and took away everything they wanted, brought in a number of sheep to the church, and kindled a fire with the seats and forms of the church, and roasted them there.

The case of Sir James Dalrymple of Stair was continued from time to time. In February, his son was made King's Advocate. The same day that he was admitted, the father's process was delayed till March 28th, when a remission was granted to free James Dalrymple of Stair for his resetting, harbouring, and receiving maill duty from rebels and traitors upon his ground in the years 1679-80-81-82-83—John Dick in Banban, Quinton Dick in Dalmellington, and many others, and for resetting and harbouring Mr. Alexander Lennox, Mr. Alexander Ross, Mr. Alexander Peden, and Mr. Alexander Hamilton, vagrant preachers, and suffering them to preach and baptise children in his house, and for his drawing a petition for and advising some of the rebels.

In July, 1686, William M'Millan in Barbreck, upon the promise judicially given never to rise in arms against the King on pretext of the Covenant or any other pretext whatever, that he would orderly keep his parish church, and owning Bothwell to be rebellion, was liberated.

James, in order to conceal his real design in favour of the Roman Catholics, granted at his own hand an Indulgence to the moderate Presbyterians, but it was not received with any favour. In 1687, he published his "Declaration for liberty of Conscience," giving further concessions, and in July he issued a Proclamation abolishing all laws imposing penalties for non-conformity, and removing all restrictions except the prohibition of conventicles. Bishop Atken of Galloway, an old man aged seventy-four, made a bold stand against the repealing of the penal laws. He died shortly afterwards—28th October, 1687—otherwise he would probably have been turned out, for Bishop Bruce of Dunkeld was freed from his office on preaching a sermon against the proposals.

Many of the Covenanters accepted the Indulgence, but the Cameronians still held aloof and boldly declared that the King's intention was merely to facilitate the extension of Popery, and they continued to meet for divine worship in conventicles as before.

The leader of the Cameronians was now James Renwick, a gentle youth, but an intrepid preacher, who condemned severely all who accepted the royal Indulgence. Every effort was made to capture him, rewards offered for his seizure, and at last, after many miraculous escapes, he was taken in a house in Edinburgh in the beginning of February, 1688. Before the Privy Council he resolutely disowned the royal authority, and upheld the lawfulness of attending field meetings armed for defence. He was condemned and executed at Edinburgh on the 17th day of February, aged twenty-six years, and was the last of the Scottish martyrs.

Events now shaped rapidly for the downfall of James and his ecclesiastical tyranny. For some time back, certain of the Scottish Presbyterian leaders had been putting their grievances before William, the Prince of Orange, who had married Mary, the eldest daughter of James, and some of the ministers who had fled to the Continent had had an opportunity of meeting him, notably Patrick Warner, one of the

Galloway preachers. As the despotism of the King became more pronounced, pressing invitations were sent to the Prince, desiring his aid in maintaining the civil and religious liberties of the country. On 10th October, 1688, the Prince issued his famous "Declaration for Scotland," in which he narrated the grievances and oppressions of the country, and declared that "the freeing of the kingdom from all hazard of Popery and arbitrary power for the future and the delivering it from what at the present doth expose it to both, the settling of it by Parliament upon such a solid basis as to its religious and civil concerns as may most effectually redress all the above-mentioned grievances, are the true reasons of our present undertakings as to that nation." This was published throughout Scotland in defiance of the Privy Council, and received with the utmost satisfaction. The Prince landed at Torbay on 5th November, 1688, with fourteen thousand men, among his personal attendants being Sir James Dalrymple of Stair, who had refused the Test and gone abroad. For about a week it seemed doubtful whether the country would rise to support him, but when the Rising did start, the tide flowed full in his favour. Every day crowds flocked to his standard, even the King's favourite daughter taking refuge with the insurgents. James soon realised his position, and finally left the kingdom in December, and on 13th February, 1689, William and Mary were proclaimed King and Queen of England.

As soon as it was known that William had landed, the Scotch Council began to change their position, and a Proclamation was issued on 24th December, 1688, requiring all Protestant subjects to put themselves in a state of defence for securing their religious liberties. This was probably occasioned by an unfounded report that ten thousand Irish Papists had landed in Galloway, and burned Kirkcudbright. The following is a copy of a letter written at this time to Crawford of Jordanhill, and addressed, "For the Laird of Jordanhill, in haist, haist."

"PAISLEY, 21st December, 1688.

" SIR,

" This night, yr came to this place ane express, signifying that some Irishes have landed at Kirkcudbright and burnt the toune; and, as is reported, are marching towards Ayre. Wherefore, for the safety of the Shyre, and all concerned yr in, ye are desyred by all in this place, to be here to-morrow to consider what is fitt to be done—where ye shall be attended by

" SIR,

" Your most humble servant, J. IRVING.

" Thir news are just now confirmed, wherefore fail not, for they are burning and destroying as they come along; and, in the mean tyme, acquaint your vassals and tenants to be in readiness, and bring them all along with you."

The heritors of Wigtown were to be commanded by MacDowall of Logan, with the young Laird of

Lochnaw as his Lieutenant, and they were to rendez-
vous instantly at Glenluce. In the Stewartry of
Kirkcudbright the command was given to Viscount
Kenmure.

This Act was the last of the Privy Council of
Scotland. How different from the many Acts they
had previously published.

The alarm, as we have said, was unfounded, but the
Cameronians in Galloway at once took to arms and
were joined by many of the Presbyterians of the West,
and prepared for the defence of the country. Some
of the Papists' houses were rifled, and some burned
to the ground, but there was no bloodshed.

Most of the Scottish nobles at once resorted to
London, doubtless in quest of preferment, and in the
meantime the English curates were ejected from
Galloway, but otherwise the Revolution was very
quietly effected.

Grierson of Lagg was naturally far from favourable
to the new regime, and there is a Bond, dated the fyth
day of May vic four scoor nyne years (5th May, 1689),
by which James Stewart of Castle Stewart, under
penalty of £500 sterling, binds himself that Sir Robert
Grierson of Lagg shall live peaceably with all submission to the present Government under King
William and Queen Mary, and "shall appear and sigt
himself" before the Estates of Parliament when called
upon. Lord Kenmure, on 21st May, 1689, arrested
Lagg in his own house and imprisoned him in Kirkcudbright. He was liberated on finding security in a
large sum to appear when called upon. He was again

arrested in July in Edinburgh, and liberated in the end of August on finding security for £1,500 sterling to live peaceably under King William and Queen Mary. He died on 31st December, 1733, at a very old age. Naturally, his name was detested in Galloway, and the most grotesque traditions have been handed down regarding his death and his funeral. During his latter years he became an object of curiosity to many. Among those eager to obtain a glimpse of the notorious persecutor was the servant of Colonel Vans of Barnbarroch. He made known his request to the Colonel when the latter was on a visit to Lagg, and it was arranged that the servant would carry in an armful of faggots for the fire of the room where Lagg and the Colonel sat. Lagg had been informed of the servant's curiosity, and no sooner did the servant enter the room than Lagg turned round to him and, with a look that he never forgot, demanded in a voice of thunder, " Ony Whigs in Galloway noo, lad?" The terror-stricken youth dropped his bundle of sticks on the floor and bolted from the room.

William called the Scottish nobles together in London early in 1689, and asked their advice, and they presented an address to him that he would take upon himself the civil and military administration and call a meeting of the Estates at Edinburgh for 14th March. He agreed to this. On 5th March, the Prince's letter, dated from St. James, was read at the Market Cross of Wigtown by the Town Clerk, and the barons then proceeded to the Court House, Sir Andrew Agnew being chosen preses. The election of two representatives to the Convention resulted as follows:—Sir Andrew Agnew, 27; Garthland, 21; Sir John Dalrymple, 13; Castle Stewart, 1. The first two were accordingly declared elected. Sir John Dalrymple was elected for Stranraer, being the first instance in Scotland of a baron sitting as a burgess. William Coltraine was elected for the Burgh of Wigtown, and Patrick Murdoch for the Burgh of Whithorn. When Sir John Dalrymple became Lord Advocate on the Government being formed, he had a seat in Parliament *ex officio*, and Sir Patrick Murray was elected in his place for Stranraer. In the Stewartry of Kirkcudbright, M'Guffog of Rusco and Patrick Dunbar of Machermore were elected by the Barons, John Ewart for the Burgh of Kirkcudbright, and Hugh Dalrymple for New Galloway. The Convention met at Edinburgh on 14th March, Lords Cassillis, Galloway, and Kenmure representing the Galloway nobility. The Convention was guarded by the Cameronians, who showed their loyalty by raising in a single day, without tuck of drum, 1,140 men as a regiment for King William's service. Their presence undoubtedly saved the situation, for Edinburgh Castle was still held by the Duke of Gordon, a staunch Papist, who refused to surrender, and Claverhouse was also in the city ready to muster his troopers the moment a favourable opportunity occurred.

The Estates agreed to put the kingdom in a posture of defence, and Sir Andrew Agnew, Sir John Dalrymple, Sir William Maxwell, Sir James Dunbar, Sir Charles Hay, the Lairds of Garthland, Barnbarroch, Castle Stewart, Sheuchan, Dunskey, and Dunragit, were appointed Commissioners for organising and officering the militia in Galloway.

The Convention declared that James had forefaulted the right to the Crown and that the Throne was vacant. A feeble opposition to the vote of forfeiture was made by bishop Paterson of Glasgow and Sir George M'Kenzie who maintained that James was an absolute and irresponsible monarch. All the arguments of these disheartened supporters of the Divine Right claimed by James were ably refuted by Sir John Dalrymple and Sir James Montgomery. The Convention prepared the famous "Claim of Right" and settled the Crown on William and Mary. The Claim of Right narrated the grievances which the country had suffered under James, and declared that he had forfeited the right to the Crown, and that the Throne had become vacant. It further declared that Prelacy and the superiority of any office in the Church above Presbyters is and hath been a great and insupportable grievance and trouble to this nation, and contrary to the inclinations of the generality of the people ever since the Reformation (they having reformed from Popery by Presbyters), and, therefore, ought to be abolished. It concluded by settling the Crown on William and Mary and the heirs of the body of the Queen.

Sir John Dalrymple, Earl of Argyle, and Sir James Montgomery were selected to proceed to London and offer the Crown, and a month later they were received by William and Mary in the Banqueting House,

Whitehall, and the royal pair repeated the Coronation Oath of Scotland clause by clause after Argyle.

Parliament abolished Prelacy, ratified the Confession of Faith, settled the Presbyterian Church Government, and rescinded the fines and forfeitures.

The first meeting of the Presbyterian ministers within the bounds of the Synod of Galloway took place at Minnigaff on 14th May, 1689, and the first General Assembly was held the following year. Civil and religious liberty had again been secured for the Presbyterians, and a brighter day had at last dawned upon Scotland.

CHAPTER XXX.

DALRY—THE PENTLANDS—RULLION GREEN.

Sir James Turner sent into Galloway to collect fines—John M'Clelland of Barscobe, John Maxwell of Monreith, Colonel Wallace, and another rescue Grier from soldiers near Dalry, and induce others to join them—Encounter with soldiers at Balmaclellan—The Covenanters' Rising—March on Dumfries and seize it, Sir James Turner being taken prisoner—They return to Dalry, and proceed north—Welsh, Veitch, and M'Kail join them at Bridge of Doon—Invitation from Clydesdale—March to Muirkirk—Renew the Covenants at Lanark, and issue Declaration—March to Bathgate—Their forlorn appearance—At Rullion Green—The Royal troops come up to them (28th November, 1666) and put them to flight—Proclamation by the Government—John Maxwell's narrow escape—Excerpt from Glasserton Session Records—Document showing William Maxwell had no accession to the Rebellion—Eleven prisoners sentenced to be executed, including M'Culloch of Barholm, Captain Arnot, and the Gordons of Knockbrex--Neilson of Corsock executed, though Turner tries to save him—John Grierson and William Welsh hanged at Dumfries—Memorial stones and inscriptions—The Martyrs' monument and inscription—James Kirk's martyrdom—William Welsh, John M'Call, James Muirhead, and others sent to Ayr to be executed—Rather than carry out the sentence, the hangman flees from the town—Irvine hangman refuses to carry out sentence although threatened to be shot—A condemned man carries out sentence on his own life being spared—Extract from Pennicuik Session Records—The monument near Rullion Green and inscription—Barscobe's violent death.

As we have seen, Presbyterianism was abolished on the restoration of Charles II. in 1660, and Episcopacy put in its place. Patronage was restored, and all ministers ordained since 1649 were required to receive presentation from the bishop or patron. On October 1st, 1662, it was enjoined that all ministers who had not complied were, before 1st November, to remove with their families twenty miles from their respective parishes, six miles from Edinburgh or any cathedral charge, and three miles from any royal burgh, no two of them were to reside in the same parish, and they were to be deprived of their stipend for that year. The ministers of Galloway, almost to a man, refused to submit, and left their all and went forth into the world not knowing where they or their families were to lay their heads. Many of them, indeed, braved the fury of the Government, and continued to preach to the people. The Government issued a series of proclamations against them. The parishioners were to attend their own parish churches and not other religious meetings, under pain of fine and imprisonment. Sir James Turner was sent into Dumfriesshire and Galloway to enforce these orders and to collect the fines. He had once been a Covenanter himself, and had displayed no little zeal in the cause, but at the Restoration he went over and, like most apostates, was more bitter than those he had joined. A sum of £41,282 Scots was levied in Galloway, and this immense sum was the least part of the sufferings endured. The troops acted as in an enemy's country. They lived at free quarters, consumed the produce of the fields and the cattle, and plundered and wasted, with little distinction between what belonged to those who had conformed and those who had not.

On Tuesday, November 13th, 1666, John M'Clelland of Barscobe, whose estates were afterwards forfeited, ventured into Dalry along with young John Maxwell of Monreith, Colonel Wallace, and another, to get refreshments. As they entered the village they met Corporal George Deanes and three soldiers of Sir Alexander Thomson's company of the Guards, then at Dalry, driving a company of people to thresh the corn of an old man named Grier, who had some land near the village, and who fled rather than pay the fines for non-attendance at the parish church. M'Clelland and the others would fain have interfered, but they pressed on to the inn, called Mid-town, in Dalry, and were at breakfast when they were informed that the soldiers had caught Grier, and had brought him to his house and were stripping him, and threatened to set him on a hot girdle to compel him to tell where some of the Covenanters were hidden. This roused their wrath, and they at once set off for the old man's house. They found him lying bound on the floor, and earnestly solicited the soldiers to let him go, and this being refused, they demanded to know why he was being so treated. The soldiers resented this interference, and words soon gave place to blows. The soldiers drew their swords and severely wounded two of M'Clelland's party, and M'Clelland fired his pistol, loaded, it is said, only with part of a tobacco pipe, but one of the soldiers was struck, and fell. The soldiers were secured, and the old man was set free. M'Clelland's party soon recognised that they had taken a step from which there was no turning back. They enlisted the sympathy of a few others, and next day, surprised the soldiers quartered at Balmaclellan, and took about a dozen prisoners, one who resisted being killed in the encounter. Barscobe then persuaded John Neilson of Corsock to join him. Neilson had already been fined for nonconformity; soldiers had been quartered on him; himself and his tenants plundered; and his wife and children turned to the door. Others who had been similarly treated joined M'Clelland, and the company soon numbered about fifty horse and two hundred foot. The command was given to a man named Andrew Gray of Edinburgh, who seems to have had no qualifications for the position. They proceeded rapidly to Irongray— about six miles from Dumfries. Here they held a council of war, and Neilson was given command of the advance party, and, early in the morning, they, marched into Dumfries and captured Sir James Turner almost before he was aware. So little had he dreamed of any attack that he had left all the approaches of the town unguarded. Aroused from sleep by the tramp of armed men, he shouted in terror from his window in Bailie Finnie's house, " Quarter, gentlemen, for God's sake. Quarter, and there will be no resistance." Neilson replied that he would get quarter if no resistance was made, but when Gray came up he declared, with that arrogance so characteristic of the man, that he would get no quarter, and would at once have shot him had not Neilson prevented him, saying, " You shall as soon kill me, for I have given him quarter." Turner was taken prisoner, along with some of his men. The Covenanters also seized some money which had been sent from Edinburgh to pay the troops, as well as some fines recently levied. This money was entrusted to Captain Gray, but he took it with him when he deserted. The Covenanters proceeded to the Cross, where a huge crowd gathered, and the leaders explained to the people that they were only acting in self-defence, and they were not rebels, and as a proof of this they drank the King's health amidst the cheers of the crowd. They swore allegiance to the Covenant, and upbraided the bishops. The town's people were asked to bring their arms, and these were handed to the Covenanters at the Cross.

Increasing numbers joined them, and they retraced their steps by Glencairn to Dalry, taking their prisoners with them. Mr. Henderson, the minister of Dumfries, gave Turner such a good dinner at Dalry that he speaks thus of it in his *Memoirs*:—" Though he and I be of different persuasion, yet I will say he entertained me with real kindness."

Apparently they had not yet decided how to act, and were waiting to see what support they would get. Gray now deserted the company, Colonel James Wallace of Auchans, a soldier of experience, being placed in command. Galloway did not rise as they expected, but the company proceeded north, and on 21st November, at Bridge of Doon, near Ayr, they were joined by three divines, each of whom was yet to suffer in the coming persecution. These were John Welsh, William Veitch, and Hugh M'Kail. Here also they were joined by Major Learmont, Captain Arnot, and the veteran Captain John Paton of Meadowhead. The company were badly armed. "Scythes made straight and put upon long staffs were the most of their arms." They got little assistance in Ayrshire, but there was an earnest invitation from Clydesdale. They marched to Muirkirk, arriving between seven and eight in a November night, drenched with rain. They found no other shelter than the kirk, in which they lay all night without food or fire. On Saturday morning, 24th, it was discussed what was to be done, but word of a reinforcement of three hundred men encouraged them to go on. On Sunday morning, they arrived at Lesmahagow, where the reinforcements reached them, but these were no more than fifty men. Two sons of Gordon of Knoxbrex, Borgue, overtook them with others from Galloway, and intimated that no more assistance need be looked for from there. It was debated whether Sir James Turner should be put to death or kept prisoner, and the latter course was adopted by one vote. On Monday, 26th, they renewed the Covenants at Lanark, and issued a Declaration stating the object of their rising:—

DECLARATION OF THOSE IN ARMS FOR THE COVENANT, 1666.

"THE nature of religion doth sufficiently teach, and all men almost acknowledge the lawfulness of sinless self-defence, yet we thought it our duty at this time to give an account unto the world of the occasion and design of our being in arms, since the rise and scope of actions, if faulty, may render a thing right upon that matter, sinful.

"It is known to all that the King's Majesty at his coronation, did engage to rule the Nation according to the revealed will of God, in scripture; to prosecute the ends of the National and Solemn League and Covenants, and fully to establish Presbyterian Government, with the Directory for Worship; and to approve of all Acts of Parliament establishing the same; and thereupon the nobility and others, his subjects, did swear allegiance; and so religion was committed to him as a matter of trust, secured by most solemn indenture between him and his people.

"Notwithstanding all this, it is soon ordered that the Covenant be burnt, the tie of it declared void and null, and men forced to subscribe a declaration contrary to it; Episcopal government in its height of tyranny is established, and men obliged by law, not to plead, witness, or petition against these things; grievous fines, sudden imprisonments, vast quarterings of soldiers, and a cruel inquisition by the high commission court were the reward of all such as could not comply with the Government by lordly hierarchy, and adjure the Covenants, and prove more monstrous to the wasting their conscience than Nature would have suffered heathens to be. Those things, in part, have been all Scotland over, but chiefly in that poor country of Galloway at this day; and had not God prevented, it should have in the same measure undoubtedly befallen the rest of the Nation ere long.

" The just sense whereof made us choose rather to betake ourselves to the fields for self-defence than to stay at home burdened daily with the calamities of others, and tortured with the fear of our own approaching misery. And considering our engagement to assist and defend all those who entered into this league and covenant with us; and to the end we may be more vigorous in the prosecution of this matter, and all men may know the true state of our cause, we have entered into the Solemn League and Covenant, and though it be hardly thought of, renewed the same, to the end we may be free of the apostacy of our times and saved from the cruel usages these resolved to adhere to this have met with; hoping that this will wipe off the reproach that is upon our Nation, because of the avowed perjury it lies under. And being fully persuaded that this league, however misrepresented, contains nothing in it sinful before God, derogatory to the King's just authority, the privileges of Parliament, or liberty of the people; but on the contrary, is the surest bond whereby all these are secured, since a threefold cord is not easily broken, as we shall make it appear in our next and longer declaration, which shall contain more fully the proofs of the lawfulness of entering into Covenant and the necessity of our taking arms at this time

in defence of it, with a full and true account of
our grief and sorrow for severing from it, and
suffering ourselves to be divided, to the reproach
of our common cause, and saddening the hearts
of the godly, a thing we sorrowfully remember,
and firmly resolve against in all time coming."

They immediately left Lanark, with the Royal troops
under General John Dalziel almost at their heels, and
hoping for assistance from West Lothian and Edinburgh, they marched towards Bathgate. It was night
when they reached it, and rain had fallen in torrents
all the way. No suitable accommodation could be
got, and they were wet and wearied. At eleven
o'clock that night they were alarmed by a report of
the approach of the enemy, and within an hour
they were on the march again. Their numbers were
gradually lessening. Alexander Peden and others had
turned back at Lanark, and every hour saw others
depart. Before they had entered Lanark they numbered nearly two thousand; now at Colinton, only nine
hundred. They got no assistance from Edinburgh,
and hope entirely deserted them.

The following derisive description of their forlorn
appearance is taken from " The Whigs' Supplication,"
a poem by Samuel Colvil (Edinburgh, 1711);—

> " Right well do I the time remember,
> It was in Januar or December,
> When I did see the out-law Whigs,
> Lie scattered up and down the rigs,
> Some had boggars, some straw boots,
> Some legs uncovered, some no coats,

> Some had halberts, some had durks,
> Some had crooked swords, like Turks,
> Some had slings, and some had flails,
> Knit with eel and oxen tails,
> Some had spears, and some had pikes,
> Some had spades which delved dykes,
> Some had fiery peats for matches,
> Some had guns with rusty ratches,
> Some had bows, but wanted arrows,
> Some had pistols without marrows,
> Some had the coulter of a plough,
> Some scythes both men and horse to hough,
> And some with a Lochaber ax,
> Resolved to give Dalzell his paiks,
> Some had cross-bows, some were slingers,
> Some had only knives and whingers,
> But most of all, believe who lists,
> Had naught to fight but with their fists,
> They had no colours to display,
> They wanted order and array,
> Their officers and motion-teachers,
> Were very few, beside their preachers,
> For martial music, every day,
> They used oft to sing and pray,
> Which hearts them more, when danger comes,
> Than others' trumpets and their drums,
> With such provisions as they had,
> They were so stout, or else so mad,
> As to petition once again,
> As if the issue proved in vain,
> They were resolved, with one accord,
> To fight the battles of the Lord."

They sent a letter to Dalziel, but got no reply. They passed the east end of the Pentland Hills and marched to Rullion Green. They had now decided to disband and go home, but the Royal troops came on them (28th November, 1666) and forced an engagement, and though at first the Covenanters held their

own and fought bravely, they were ultimately over-
powered and put to flight. Over fifty were killed and
about a hundred and fifty taken prisoners. Colonel
Wallace escaped to Holland and never returned.
Many of the Covenanters believed that their persecutors were so leagued with Satan as to be invulnerable
to any kind of shot except silver bullets. It was
believed by them that the bullets were seen rebounding
like hailstones off the buff coat and boots of General
Dalziel. The Government issued the following
proclamation on 4th December:—

PROCLAMATION DISCHARGING THE RECEIPT OF THE REBELS, DECEMBER 4TH, 1666.

" CHARLES, by the grace of God, King of Scotland, England, France, and Ireland, defender of
the faith, to all and sundry our lieges and loving
subjects whom these presents do or may concern,
greeting: forasmuch as, upon the first notice given
to our privy council, of the rising and gathering
of these disloyal and seditious persons in the west,
who have of late appeared in arms, in a desperate
and avowed rebellion against us, our government,
and laws, we declared them to be traitors, and
discharged all our subjects to assist, reset, supply,
or correspond with any of them, under the pain
of treason; and the said rebels and traitors being
now, by the blessing of God upon our forces,
subdued, dissipated, and scattered, and such of
them as were not either killed or taken in the

field, being lurking in the country; and we being unwilling that any of our good subjects should be ensnared or brought into trouble by them, have therefore, by the advice of our privy council, thought fit again hereby to discharge and inhibit all our subjects, that none of them offer or presume to harbour, reset, supply, or correspond, hide or conceal, the persons of Colonel James Wallace, Major Learmont, —— Maxwell of Monrief younger, —— Maclellan of Barscobe, —— Gordon of Barbreck, —— Maclellan of Balmageichan, —— Cannon of Barnshalloch younger, —— Cannon of Barley younger, —— Cannon of Mordrochat younger, —— Welsh of Skar, —— Welsh of Cornley, Gordon of Garery in Kells, —— Robert Chalmers brother to Gadgirth, Henry Grier of Balmaclellan, David Scott in Irongray, John Gordon in Midton of Dalry, William Gordon there, John Macnaught there, Robert and Gilbert Cannons there, —— Gordon of Bar, elder in Kirkpatrick-Durham, Patrick Macnaught in Cumnock, John Macnaught his son, —— Gordon of Holm younger, —— Dempster of Carridow, Grier of Dalgoner, —— of Sundywell, Ramsay in the Mains of Arniston, John Hutchison in Newbottle, —— Row, Chaplain to Scotstarbet, Patrick Liston in Calder, William Liston, his son, James Wilkie in the Mains of Cliftonhall, the laird of Caldwell, the goodman of Caldwell, the laird of Kersland, the laird of Bedland-cunningham, —— Porterfield of Quarrelton,

Alexander Porterfield his brother, —— Lockhart
of Wicketshaw, —— Trail, son to Mr. Robert
Trail, David Poe in Pokelly, Mr. Gabriel Semple,
John Semple, Mr. John Guthrie, Mr. John
Welsh, Mr. Samuel Arnot, Mr. James Smith,
Mr. Alexander Peden, Mr. —— Orr, Mr. William Veitch, Mr. —— Patton, Mr. —— Cruikshanks, Mr. Gabriel Maxwell, Mr. John Carstairs, Mr. James Mitchell, Mr. William Forsyth, or any others who concurred or joined in
the late rebellion, or who, upon the account
thereof, have appeared in arms in any part of
that our kingdom; but that they pursue them as
the worst of traitors, and present and deliver such
of them as they shall have within their power,
to the lords of our privy council, the sheriff of
the county, or the magistrates of the next adjacent
burgh royal, to be by them made forthcoming to
law; certifying all such as shall be found to fail
in their duty herein, they shall be esteemed and
punished as favourers of the said rebellion, and
as persons accessory to, and guilty of the same.
And to the end, all our good subjects may have
timeous notice hereof, we do ordain these presents
to be forthwith printed and published at the
market crosses of Edinburgh, Ayr, Lanark,
Glasgow, Irvine, Wigtown, Kirkcudbright, Dumfries, and remnent market crosses of our said
Kingdom: and we do recommend to the right
reverend our archbishops and bishops, to give
orders that this our proclamation be with all

possible diligence read on the Lord's Day, in all the churches within their several dioceses. Given at Edinburgh, the fourth day of December, and of our reign the eighteenth year, one thousand six hundred and sixty six."

John Maxwell of Monreith, when he saw that the day was irretrievably lost, fled from the field on a good grey horse, never halting till he reached his distant home in Galloway. He could not remain here, of course, and, bidding his family a sorrowful good-bye, he went forth a wanderer upon the world. The horse to whose fleetness he owed his life was turned into a field at Monreith still known as "Pentland," and as a reward for having saved its master's life it was never put to work again. The proverb, "As good as Pentland," is current in the district to this day.

The Session Records of Glasserton contain the following entry:—"John Maxwell, brother to Sir William Maxwell of Monreith, was forfeit in his estate for going to Pentland and not joining with Prelacy. He was necessitated to hide himself many a night and day, and to turn his back upon all that he had, and to flee to Ireland for the preservation of his life from bloody persecutors, and died there."

He had many a hairsbreadth escape before he got away. On one occasion he was in Edinburgh when the attempt was made by Mitchell on the life of Archbishop Sharpe, and in consequence of which a search was made for all concerned in the Rising at Dalry. He was closely pursued by some soldiers, so he darted down a close known as the Horse Wynd into a "change-house" kept by his landlord, Nichol Moffat, and the landlady put him in a large meal chest and locked it, keeping the key herself. A moment later the soldiers hurried in, asserting that the fugitive was bound to be in the house. "Seek the hoose as ye will," replied the landlady, "it's no sae muckle as will keep ye lang." This the soldiers did, but could find no trace of Maxwell, and then they called for drink and sat down to it, one of the soldiers actually seating himself on the lid of the meal chest. They began to express their wonder as to where the fugitive could have got to, when the man on the chest' suddenly exclaimed, "I wouldna say but yon d—— Whig is in this vera kist. They hide onygate. Guidwife, gae us the key till we see for oorsels." Maxwell could not help but hear this remark, and it must have caused him the greatest anxiety. However, the landlady was equal to the occasion. Going to the foot of the stairs, she called up, "Jenny lass, rin and ask the guidman for the key o' the girnel till we see if a Whig can lie in meal and no' gi' a hoast." The ruse succeeded. The soldiers laughed, finished their liquor, and then went out, apparently not thinking it worth while to wait for the key. Maxwell eventually escaped to Ireland, where he died in 1668, leaving two children named William and Agnes. The estate went to his younger brother, of whom the present proprietor is the direct descendant. In the Charter Chest at Monreith, the following document is found:—

"Whereas William Maxwell of Mureith, the elder, hath by certificate from the noblemen and clergy in Galloway vindicat himself that he hath had no accessione to the late rebellione, nor no hand in his sones accesione thereunto, and having given sufficient security to me to answer whensoever he shall be called. These are, therefore, discharging all officers and soldiers under my command or any other person or persons whatsomever to trouble or molest the person, goods, or gear of the said William Maxwell, elder of Mureith, as they shall be answerable. Given under my hand at Holyrood House this 14th February, 1667.

" (Sgd.) Rothes."

Orders were given for eleven of the prisoners to be brought immediately to trial, including Major John M'Culloch of Barholm, Captain Andrew Arnot, John Gordon and Robert Gordon of Knockbrex. They were found guilty, and sentenced to be executed on 7th December at Edinburgh. The heads of Major M'Culloch, John Gordon, and Robert Gordon were commanded to be sent to Kirkcudbright for exposure on the principal gate of that burgh, and their bodies to be buried by the Magistrates of Edinburgh in such places as were usually assigned to traitors. The Council ordained that the right arms of Major M'Culloch, John Gordon of Knockbrex, and his brother Robert, and Captain Arnot be cut off by

the Magistrates of Edinburgh to be sent to the
Magistrates of Lanark, and affixed upon the public
ports of that town, being the place where they took
the Covenant. Before proceeding to the scaffold, the
condemned men subscribed a joint testimony which
will be found in Naphtali, 307. John Gordon and
Robert Gordon, when thrown off the executioner's
ladder, clasped their arms round each other, and thus
met death.

When Neilson of Corsock was brought to trial, he
was questioned as to a settled plan of revolution, but
denied all knowledge of the existence of any organised
conspiracy. Not satisfied with this, the instrument
of torture, called the boot, was used on him, and he
suffered terribly. He was sentenced to be hanged at
the Cross of Edinburgh. Sir James Turner endeavoured to save him, moved by the fact no doubt
that on another occasion Neilson had saved him.
Turner's good intentions, however, were frustrated by
Dalgleish, minister of his parish, who represented
Neilson as the very ringleader of the movement, and
urged the necessity of his execution as an example to
others. His son was outlawed, and went into exile,
and Mrs. Neilson was deprived of all her moveables
by way of fine for communicating with him.

Among the other prisoners were John Grier or
Grierson of Four Merkland, and William Welsh,
Carsphairn. The Court at Ayr, on 24th December,
ordered these men to be hanged at Dumfries on 2nd
January, and charged the Magistrates to have their

heads and right arms fixed upon the eminent parts of the burgh. They were accordingly fixed on the bridge-ports, but owing to information of an attempt to take them away by night, they were removed to the top of the Tolbooth. A memorial stone in St. Michael's Churchyard, Dumfries, has the following inscription:—

> " Here lyes William
> Welsh, Pentland
> Martyr, for his
> Adhering to the
> Word of God and
> Appearing for
> Christ's Kingly
> Goverment in His
> House and the Co-
> -venanded Work
> of Reformation
> Against Perjury
> and prelacie. Exe-
> -cuted Janr. 2,
> 1667, Rev. 12, 11.

> Stay, Passenger read
> Here interr'd doth ly
> A witness 'gainst poor
> Scotland's perjury
> Whose head once fix'd up
> On the Bridge Port stood
> Proclaiming vengeance
> For his guiltless blood."

The inscription on Grierson's stone is as follows:—

were re-erected

HERE LYES WILLIAM *
GRIERSON, PENTLAND
MARTYR FOR HIS
ADHERING TO THE
WORD OF GOD AND
APPEARING FOR CHRI
ST'S KINGLIE GOVERME
NT IN HIS HOUSE AND
THE COVENANTED WO
RK OF REFORMATION : A
GAINST PERJURY AND
PRELACY   EXECUTED
JAN. 2-1667.—REV. 12-11.

This and the neighbouring tombstone

and repaired by voluntary subscription

UNDER THIS STONE LO HERE
DOTH LY
DUST SECRIFIC'D TO TYRANY
YET PRECIOUS IN IMMANULE
SIGHT
SINCE MARTYR'D FOR HIS
KINGLIE RIGHT ;
WHEN HE CONDEMNS
THESE HELLISH DRUGES
BY SUFFRAGE SAINTS
SHALL JUDGE THEIR JUDGES.

in March 1873.

* This should be "John."

The Martyrs' Monument, close beside this stone, takes the form of a large granite pyramid. It has the following inscription: —

Near this spot
were deposited the remains
of
WILLIAM GRIERSON *
and
WILLIAM WELSH
who suffered unto death
for their adherence to the
principles of the Reformation
Jany. 2, 1667.

Also of
JAMES KIRK
Shot on the sands of Dumfries,
March, 1685.   Rev. 12. 3.

On the other side is the following:—

The Martyrs'
Monument
erected by the
voluntary contributions
of
persons who revere the memory
and admire the principles
of the sufferers for conscience
sake, during the persecution
in Scotland, aided by a collection made at a
sermon preached on the spot by the Rev.
William Symington of Stranraer.
MDCCCXXXIV.

* The name William has been taken from the tombstone, but "John" seems correct.

The story of Kirk's martyrdom is another example of the treachery of the "killing times." Kirk was a gentleman of considerable means belonging to the parish of Dunscore. After Pentland, he suffered considerable hardships. He was forced to flee the country, and when in Holywell parish, in Dumfries, a person showed him a hiding place and then lodged information with the soldiers at Dumfries. A company of dragoons at once went out and had no difficulty in seizing Kirk. He was offered the Abjuration Oath, but refused. Then he was offered his life if he would reveal the haunts of his fellow wanderers, but he again refused, and he was led to Dumfries sands and instantly shot.

Among the other Pentland prisoners sent to be tried by this Court at Ayr and sentenced to death were the following:—John M'Call, son of John M'Call in Carsphairn; James Muirhead in the parish of Irongray; John Graham in Midtoun of Old Crachan (Dalry); James Smith in Old Crachan; Alexander M'Culloch in Carsphairn; James M'Millan in Marduchat; George M'Cartney in Blairkennie; John Short in Dalry; and Cornelius Anderson, tailor, in Ayr. So unjust was the sentence considered that, before the date of execution, the hangman fled from the town. The authorities had difficulty in finding a substitute. The executioner at Irvine—William Sutherland—was forcibly brought over, but he refused to perform the odious duty, although placed in the stocks and threatened to be shot. At last the authorities prevailed upon Cornelius Anderson, one of the condemned men, to undertake the execution on condition that his own life would be saved. He, too, wished to get out of the job, and had to be kept more or less intoxicated to carry out the execution. Afterwards he went to Ireland, and was burned to death in his house there.

The Covenanters who fled from Rullion Green had little mercy shown them as they passed through the country. Some were said to have been shot, some died from their wounds, and several were buried in nameless graves in Pennicuik and Glencorse churchyards. The Session Minutes of Pennicuik contain the following entry:—" December 9, 1666, Disbursed to John Brown, Bellman, for making Westlandman's graves, 3s. 4d."

A wounded Covenanter sought succour at Blackhill, Lanarkshire, but the inmates were afraid to receive him. He asked to be buried within sight of the Ayrshire hills. Next morning he was found dead, and his request was carried out. Many years after, doubters had the grave opened, and the body was found wrapped in a red cloak, in which were some Dutch silver coins. A stone now marks the grave on the hillside near where the unknown died.

A small monument has been erected to the memory of those Covenanters who fell. It stands on the hillside about seven and a half miles from Edinburgh. It is some three feet high by about two feet broad, and is surrounded by a neat iron railing. The inscriptions are as follows:—

Here
And near to
this place lyes the
Reverend Mr. John Crookshank
and mr Andrew mccormick
ministers of the Gospel and
About fifty other true covenanted Presbyterians who were
killed in this place in their own
innocent self defence and de
fence of the covenanted
work of Reformation By
Thomas Dalzeel of Bins
upon the 28 of november
1666. Rev. 12–11. Erected
Sept. 28, 1738.

Behind—

A Cloud of Witnesses lyes here
Who for Christ's interest did appear,
For to Restore true Liberty
Overturned then by tyranny.
And by proud Prelats who did Rage
Against the Lord's own heritage.
They sacrificed were for the laws
Of Christ their king, his noble cause.
These heroes fought with great renown
And falling got the martyrs crown.

M'Clelland of Barscobe was captured by Claverhouse in one of his night raids. He was imprisoned for a long time, but was released on taking the Oath, which greatly offended some of the more zealous of the Covenanting party. The following notice of his death appears in Law's *Memorials*, November, 1683:—"Some of those men of wild principles go into the house of Barscobe, a gentleman in Galloway, who had been a long time prisoner for joining with the men at Pentland and got free upon his taking of the Bond of Peace (which thing incensed them) and strangles him in his own house." This, however, is erroneous. M'Clelland and William Grierson, Millmark, after attending a funeral, went to a tavern in Dalry, where a woman became very abusive about William Grierson's wife. Grierson, in the heat of the moment, struck her, and M'Clelland interfered to protect the woman, who was in a delicate state of health. Grierson, thoroughly roused, attacked M'Clelland, and in the scuffle the latter fell into the fire and received fatal injuries. A prosecution followed, but the jury found that M'Clelland was subject to epileptic fits, and acquitted the accused.

CHAPTER XXXI.

SAMUEL RUTHERFURD.

A native of Roxburghshire—Professor of Humanity, 1623—
Resigns owing to unfounded rumours—Called to Anwoth,
1627, through influence of Viscount Kenmure--His earnest life
and great enthusiasm—Rutherfurd's witnesses on Mossrobin
farm—Tragic death of dyker—Visit of Archbishop Ussher
and traditions—The eleventh commandment—Rutherfurd
summoned before High Commission Court, 1630—Publishes
his famous work against Jesuits and Arminians, 1636—
Summoned before the High Commission Court at Wigtown—
Lord Lorne, afterwards Marquis of Argyle, befriends him,
but he is deposed and ordered to confine himself in Aberdeen
—Letters to his parishioners—Returns to Anwoth, 1638—
Attends General Assembly of 1638 at Glasgow—Professor of
Divinity at St. Andrews—Letters to people of Anwoth—
Refuses professorship at Utrecht and Harderwick—Appointed
one of the commission to Westminster Assembly—Publishes
Lex Rex—Indicted for high treason—His answer to the
summons—Died 19th March, 1661—Inscription on tombstone
—Monument near Gatehouse and inscription.

No name in the annals of Galloway is held in greater
love and reverence than that of Samuel Rutherfurd,
for though he was not born in our ancient province,
he laboured here so long, so lovingly, and so faithfully
that he may well be claimed as one of Galloway's own.
He was born in 1600, in the parish of Nesbit (now
annexed to Crailing) in Roxburghshire, and after
attending Jedburgh Grammar School, he proceeded
to Edinburgh University in 1617, took his M.A. in

1621, and while yet a young man was elected Professor of Humanity in 1623. Two years afterwards, however, some unfounded reports were made against him, and though these were immediately shown to be the work of evil disposed persons, he determined to resign. He seems to have been licensed to preach while in Edinburgh, and about 1627 he was called to be minister of Anwoth, which was then made a separate parish.

He was entered to this church through the influence of the then Viscount Kenmure and without any engagement to the bishop. He came to the work of the ministry with great enthusiasm. He rose every morning at three o'clock, and spent his whole time reading, praying, writing, catechising, visiting, and in the other duties of his high calling. He found many of the people had little interest in religion, were careless regarding the Sabbath, and preferred playing football to attending the house of God. One Sabbath he proceeded to where they were engaged in their game on a level piece of ground between the church and Skyreburn on Mossrobin farm, and, pointing out the sinfulness of their ways, called on the objects around, especially three large stones, to witness between him and them that he had done his duty, whether they had or not. Mrs. Stewart Monteith tells a weird-like story about these silent witnesses. A new dyke was being built on Mossrobin, and at a certain part stones were wanted. One of the workmen purposed making use of one of Rutherfurd's witnesses which was at hand, but his companions rejected the proposal with horror.

He was not to be deterred, however, and with an oath that the first bite he took might choke him if he did not build the stone into the dyke before breakfast, he broke up the stone and used it in the dyke. Shortly, afterwards, he sat down to his meal, and putting the first morsel into his mouth, he suddenly turned black in the face, fell back, and expired. The other two stones remain untouched to this day.

Rutherfurd's fame as a preacher soon spread, and, coming to the ears of Archbishop Ussher of Armagh, the latter resolved to go and hear for himself what manner of man this Rutherfurd was. There was no place near the church for the bishop to stay in. So he came to the Bush of Beild and asked if Mr. Rutherfurd was at home. Mrs. Rutherfurd said he was. He said he was a stranger, and wished to wait till Monday, but could find no place to stay and asked if he could be put up there. Mrs. Rutherfurd, seeing he was a gentleman, asked him to alight, and in reply to her he said his name was James Ussher. She went and told her husband, but it never occurred to either of them that it was the Archbishop. Rutherfurd welcomed him, and nothing transpired that night to reveal his identity. Early on the Sabbath morning the stranger went out, and, coming to a thicket, retired to pray. It was a spot to which Rutherfurd was in the habit of coming for prayer also, and when Rutherfurd drew near as usual, he was surprised to hear someone there before him. Eagerly listening, he perceived an extraordinary gift of prayer, and waited till the stranger appeared.

Then when he saw him, the recollection of his name flashed across his mind, and he asked: "Are you the great and learned Doctor Ussher?" "I am he whom some are pleased to name so," was the reply. Rutherfurd embraced him most affectionately, and said, "You must preach for me to-day." "Nay," said the other, "I came to hear you preach and to be acquainted with you, and I will hear you." They arranged that Rutherfurd would preach in the forenoon and the Archbishop in the afternoon.

Tradition has preserved another version of the story. It is as follows:—A beggar arrived on a Saturday, at Bush of Beild and craved a night's lodging. He was given a seat at the kitchen fire, and told he could lodge in the barn. Mrs. Rutherfurd soon afterwards came into the kitchen and began to catechise the servants, her husband meantime preparing for the Sabbath services. The beggar was asked how many commandments there were, and on his replying "eleven," Mrs. Rutherfurd lifted up her hands in amazement at the ignorance of the man, and said it was a shame for a man with grey hairs like him and living in a Christian country not to know how many commandments there were. To her surprise, however, he defended his answer by quoting the words of our Saviour, "A new commandment I give unto you, that ye love one another." After he had gone to the barn, he was engaged in prayer when Rutherfurd passed, and heard and listened. The language soon convinced him that it was no beggar, but some good and learned man in disguise. He immediately knocked and entered.

Taking the stranger by the hand, he said, "I am persuaded that you are none other than Archbishop Ussher, and you must certainly preach for me to-day." Ussher explained that, being anxious to see a man of whom he had heard so much, but fearing he might be averse to receiving a visit from an Archbishop, he had been induced to come in disguise. He was cordially welcomed, and was pressed to go and rest at the Manse, but preferred to remain where he was till the afternoon, when he preached to the people, adopting the Presbyterian form of worship, and taking for his text, John xiii., 34—"A new commandment I give unto you, that ye love one another," remarking that this might be called the eleventh commandment.

Rutherfurd was summoned in June, 1630, before the High Commission Court at Edinburgh, but the Archbishop of St. Andrews was unable to attend owing to the inclemency of the weather, and Mr. Colvil, one of the judges, having befriended Rutherfurd, the diet was deserted. About this time, his wife, Euphemia Hamilton, died, and he himself was very ill for over three months.

Sydeserf, the bishop of Galloway, was dissatisfied with his teaching, and more than once threatened a prosecution. In 1636, Rutherfurd published his famous work in Latin against the Jesuits and Arminians, *Exercitationes Apologeticae pro Divina Gratia contra Jesuitas et Arminianos.* In July, 1636, he was summoned to appear before the High Commission Court at Wigtown because of nonconformity, of preaching against the Five Articles of Perth, and of

being the author of *Exercitationes de Gratia,* which,
it was alleged, reflected on the Church of Scotland,
but the truth was that it reflected on the Episcopal
clergy, and so Bishop Sydeserf could not endure it.
He attended the Court, but declined to recognise
it as a lawful judicatory, and refused to give the
Chancellor and the bishops their titles, and denied
their right or competency to sit as judges of his
professional conduct or of his principles. The trial
lasted three days, but the result might have been fore-
seen from the beginning. Lord Lorne, afterwards the
famous Marquis of Argyle, used every exertion on his
behalf, but the bishop of Galloway threatened to write
to the King, so Rutherfurd was deposed and prohibited
under pain of rebellion from exercising any part of his
ministerial functions in Scotland, and ordered to
confine himself within the city of Aberdeen during
the King's pleasure. This sentence he had no alternative but obey. From Aberdeen he wrote many of
his famous letters. The following is an extract from
one written on 7th September, 1637, to his old friend,
Marion M'Knaught, wife of the Provost of Kirkcudbright:—

" I know the Lord will do for your town. I
hear that the bishop (Sydserff) is afraid to come
amongst you, for so it is spoken in this town,
and many here rejoice now to pen a supplication
to the council for bringing me home to my place
(Anwoth). . . . See if you can procure three
or four hundred in the country (Galloway), noble-

men, gentlemen, countrymen, and citizens to
subscribe it; the more the better. It may affright
the Bishop, but by law no advantage can be taken
against you for it; I have not time to write to
Carletoun and Knockbrex, but I would you did
speak to them in it. . . . There are some
blossomings of Christ's Kingdom in this town
(Aberdeen); the smoke is rising and the ministers
are raging, but I like a rumbling and a roaring
devil best. . . . We have been all over-feared,
and that gave the lowns the confidence to shut me
out of Galloway." *

Writing in 1637 to Robert Gordon of Knockbrex,
he says:—

> "I dare not say that I am a dry tree, or that
> I have no room in the vineyard, but yet I often
> think that the sparrows are blest, who may resort
> to the house of God in Anwoth, from which I am
> banished."

The only cause of regret he seems to have had in
Aberdeen arose from his being deprived of his clerical
office. His letters, first published in 1664 under the
title of *Joshua Redivivus,* have passed through many
editions, and translations have been made into Dutch,
German, and French. Dr. Grosart makes the interesting statement that—"Not long since, a travelling
friend met with two editions among the forsaken towns

---

* **Rutherfurd's** *Letters*, part iii., epistle xxxix.

of the Zuider Zee. It went to my heart to meet with
a copy under the shadow of Mount Hermon. In the
back woods of the Far West, the book lies side by side
with the *Pilgrim's Progress.*"

Fortunately, circumstances arose which left the way
open for him to bring his banishment to an end.
Having heard that the Privy Council had accepted
a declinature against the Court of High Commission,
he ventured in 1638 to return to Anwoth, where he was
affectionately welcomed. This step might have been
fraught with great danger but for the decisive and
bold stand taken by the venerable Assembly which
met at Glasgow the same year. The Assembly
abolished Episcopacy and established the Presbyterian
form of worship. Rutherfurd attended the Assembly
as representative of the Presbytery of Kirkcudbright,
and gave an account of his former sufferings, his confinement, and its causes. He was appointed one of
the Committee to take into consideration the grievances
under which they laboured, and was chosen to draw
up objections to the Service Book, the Book of Canons
and Ordination, and the Court of High Commission,
a work which he performed with the greatest ability.
But a still greater honour was conferred on him when
he was appointed Professor of Divinity in the New
College of St. Andrews. He used every endeavour
against the appointment, being reluctant in those days
of trial and difficulty to abandon his flock, many of
whom were endeared to him by personal ties and
associations, but his objections were over-ruled. The
people of Anwoth continued to have a warm place in

his affections, and he kept up correspondence with his many friends in the district with whose names we are familiar, amongst whom are Lady Kenmure, Gordons of Knockbrex, Cardoness and Rusko, M'Culloch of Ardwall, Lennox of Disdow, and Muir of Cassencary. But even at St. Andrews his office was not without its difficulties and responsibilities. It was the seat of the archbishop, the stronghold of Episcopacy, and the University was the most celebrated and most numerously attended in Scotland. Here he fulfilled his duties with that fidelity, enthusiasm, and ability that had become characteristic of the man.

One of his most noteworthy appearances about this time was at the Assembly of 1648, when Henry Guthrie, minister of Stirling, afterwards bishop of Dunkeld, brought forward a motion against private religious meetings. Considerable discussion ensued. Rutherfurd, though not much disposed to speak in these judicatory Assemblies, threw in this solecism, and challenged the whole Assembly to answer it, "What the Scriptures do warrant no Assembly can discharge, but private meetings for religious exercises the Scriptures do warrant."—Malachi, iii. 16. "Then they that feared the Lord spake often one to another, etc."—James v. 16. "Confess your faults one to another, and pray one for another," things which he said could not be done in the Church. Although the Earl of Seaforth and others of Guthrie's party strove hard against it, Rutherfurd's arguments had such an effect on the Assembly that his views prevailed, and all that Guthrie's party could secure was an Act anent the order of family worship. Rutherfurd afterwards wrote a treatise defending the lawfulness and usefulness of private religious meetings.

Rutherfurd's reputation had spread so far that the Magistrates of Utrecht offered him the Divinity Chair in that University when it fell vacant through the death of the learned Dematius. This, however, he declined, as also an invitation to the Chair of Hebrew and Divinity in the University of Harderwick. In 1643, he was appointed one of the Commission from the Church of Scotland to the Assembly of Divines at Westminster, and continued a Commissioner till the principal business of the Assembly was concluded in 1647. Their work was to consider and perfect these four things mentioned in the Solemn League— A Directory for Worship, a uniform Confession of Faith, a Form of Church Government and Discipline, and the public Catechism. While in London, he not only faithfully discharged his duty at Westminster, but he found time to write a number of valuable works, perhaps the most notable of which was *Lex Rex*. It excited deep and universal interest on account of the democratic principles it advanced. The full title of the book is *Lex Rex, the Law and the Prince; a discourse for the just prerogative of King and People, containing the reasons and causes of the most necessary defensive wars of the Kingdom of Scotland, and of their expedition for the ayd and help of their dear brethren of England; in which their innocency is asserted, and a full answer is given to a seditious pamphlet entitled " Sacrasancta Regum Majestas,"* *under the name of J. A. but penned by Jo. Maxwell,** *the excommunicate P. Prelate; with a scriptural con-* *futation of the ruinous grounds of W. Barclay,* *H. Grotius, H. Arnisasus, Ant. De Domi, P. Bishop* *of Spalato, and of other late Anti-magistratical* *Royalists; as the author of Ossorianum, D. Fern,* *E. Symmons, the Doctors of Aberdeen, etc., in XLIV.* *questions.* It struck a deadly blow at the doctrine of absolute monarchy.

It was condemned at the Restoration as treasonable, and whoever should retain a copy of it was to be accounted enemy of the King. King Charles said it would scarcely ever get an answer, and in this he was right. It was ordered to be burned by the hands of the hangman at Edinburgh Cross and at the gates of the New College of St. Andrews, where Rutherfurd was Professor. But, as an old writer remarked, " Books have souls as well as men, which survive their martyrdom, and are not burned but crowned by the

---

* This was John Maxwell, bishop of Ross. He was a son of the Laird of Cavens, in Kirkbean, in the Stewartry. He aimed unsuccessfully at the office of Treasurer, then held by the Earl of Troqueer. He was deposed and excommunicated by the Assembly of 1638 on the ground that he was "a wearer of the cap and rocket, a deposer of godly ministers, an admitter of fornicators to the communion, a companion of Papists, an usual player of cards on Sabbath, and once on communion day, that he had given absolution to persons in distress, consecrated deacons, robbed his vassals of forty thousand merks, kept fasts each Friday, journeyed ordinarily on Sabbath, that he had been a chief decliner of the Assembly, and a prime instrument of all the troubles which befel both Church and State."

flames that encircle them." Probably to please their worthless King, Parliament indicted him for high treason. Most of the members must have known that he was on his deathbed, but notwithstanding this, they cited him to Edinburgh. When the summons arrived, he answered, " Tell them I have got a summons already from a superior Judge, and I behove to answer my first summons, and ere your day come I will be where few Kings and great folk come." His physician and the ministers and magistrates of St. Andrews testified that he could not obey the summons, yet Parliament, not satisfied with this, sentenced him to confinement within his own house till the state of his health might be seen. It was put to the vote whether or not to let him die in the College. It was carried " Put him out," only a few dissenting. Lord Burley said, " Ye have voted that honest man out of his College, but ye cannot vote him out of Heaven." He died on 19th March, 1661, aged 61 years. On the afternoon before his death he used the beautiful expression which has become the subject of one of the finest hymns in the English language, " Glory dwells in Immanuel's Land." The following is the epitaph on his tombstone in St. Andrews:—

> " What tongue, what pen, or skill of men,
> Can famous Rutherfurd commen'?
> His learning justly raised his fame,
> True goodness did adorn his name,
> He did converse with things above,
> Acquainted with Emmanuel's love,
> Most orthodox he was, and sound,
> And many errors did confound,

For Zion's King and Zion's cause,   .
And Scotland's Covenanted laws
Most constantly he did contend,
Until his time was at an end,
At last he won to full fruition
Of that which he had seen in vision."

On a hill on the farm of Boreland of Anwoth, near
Gatehouse, and about half a mile from the church,
a monument has been erected to his memory, and is
a prominent object for many miles around. It is a
grey granite obelisk nearly 60 feet high, and was
erected in 1842, at a cost of £200, raised partly
by public subscription, and partly by a collection taken
at a sermon preached by the side of the monument by
the Rev. Dr. Cook, Belfast, in 1838. On the side of
the monument facing the south is the inscription:—

To the memory of
THE REV. SAMUEL RUTHERFURD,
Minister of the parish of Anwoth,
from 1627 to 1639,
when he was appointed Professor of Divinity
in the University of St. Andrews,
where he died in 1661.

This monument was erected A.D. 1842,
in admiration of his eminent talents,
extensive learning, ardent piety,
ministerial faithfulness,
and distinguished public labours
in the cause of civil and religious liberty.

The righteous shall be in everlasting remembrance.
Psalm cxii. 6.

On the reverse side is an inscription stating that the monument was struck by lightning in 1847 and rebuilt in 1851.

Rutherfurd was small of stature and very fair. He had a shrill voice which became like a "scraich" when preaching, and then his hands were never a moment still. Some of the foregoing incidents show how intense he was. He was usually mild and gentle, but when roused his zeal oft outran discretion, and on some occasions he displayed towards the "Resolutioners" a bitterness which can hardly be justified.

Note.—George Rutherfurd, a brother of above, was appointed schoolmaster and reader of Kirkcudbright in 1629, mainly through the influence of Provost Fullerton. He was summoned before the High Commission Court for nonconformity, and ordered to resign his charge and remove from Kirkcudbright. He retired to Ayrshire, but afterwards had charge of Tongeland parish, where he remained till his death. This fact probably accounts for the tradition mentioned by the Rev. James Reid of Newton Stewart in *Memoirs of the Lives of the Westminster Divines* (Vol. II., 345), that Samuel Rutherfurd was "born of respectable parents in the parish of Tongeland near Kirkcudbright." Other writers have adopted this, but there seems nothing to support it.

CHAPTER XXXII.

ANWOTH CHURCHYARD—THE MARTYRS OF KIRKCONNEL MOOR.

Burial place of Galloway families—Martyr's tombstone and inscription—Bell of Whiteside, his thrilling adventures and hairsbreadth escapes—David Halliday of Mayfield, Robert Lennox of Irelandton, Andrew M'Robert, Beoch, James Clement, and Bell surrender on promise of quarter, but are immediately shot—Viscount Kenmure challenges Lagg for his barbarities—Tombstone in Balmaghie churchyard to Halliday and inscription—Tombstone in Twynholm churchyard to M'Robert and inscription—Tombstone in Girthon churchyard to Lennox and inscription—Tombstone to James Clement and inscription—Monument and inscription—Clement's grave opened and his skull taken away—Poem on the Martyr's grave.

ANWOTH churchyard, near Gatehouse, is the burial-place of some of the great Galloway families, the M'Cullochs, Gordons, Maxwells, and Hannays. Here may still be seen Rutherfurd's little church, now roofless. It was last used for public worship in 1826, just two centuries after Rutherfurd came to Anwoth. His manse, Bush of Beild, was unfortunately razed to the ground, 1826-27, and the stones were built into the present church. In the centre of the churchyard is a martyr's tombstone, with the following inscription:—

OF WHITESYDE WHO WAS BARBAROUSLY SHOT

HERE LYES JOHN BELL

TO DEATH IN THE PAROCH

THIS MONUMENT SHALL TELL POSTERITY
THAT BLESSED BELL OF WHITESYDE HERE DOTH LY
WHO AT COMMAND OF BLOODY LAG WAS SHOT
A MURDER STRANGE WHICH SHOULD NOT BE FORGOT
DOUGLAS OF MORTON DID HIM QUARTERS GIVE
YET CRUEL LAG WOULD NOT LET HIM SURVIVE
THIS MARTYR SOUGHT SOME TIME TO RECOMMEND
HIS SOUL TO GOD BEFORE HIS DAYS DID END
THE TYRANT SAID, WHAT, DEVIL, YE'VE PRAY'D ENOUGH
THIS LONG SEVEN YEARS ON MOUNTAIN AND IN CLUCH
SO INSTANTLY CAUS'D HIM WITH OTHER FOUR
BE SHOT TO DEATH UPON KIRKCONNEL MOOR
SO THUS DID END THE LIVES OF THESE DEAR SAINTS
FOR THEIR ADHERING TO THE COVENANTS.

OF TONGLAND AT THE COMMAND OF LAG 1685.

Bell was proprietor of Whiteside, and after the death of his father, his mother married Viscount Kenmure. Bell was one of the greatest sufferers in the terrible persecution that ensued after Bothwell. In June, 1680, he was charged with many others with murdering Archbishop Sharp, burning the King's laws, and with accession to "the rebellion." He was not present at the trial, but of course he was found guilty. In 1681, Claverhouse quartered his soldiers at Whiteside till they had eaten all the provisions. Then they compelled the people of the district to bring them provisions, and they waited till their horses had consumed all they could get. Everything of value which they could carry they took with them, and drove away the sheep and horses, tore the very timber from the buildings, and destroyed the plantations, and left the place utterly desolate. Bell, of course, had been a fugitive since his trial, and had many miraculous escapes. Simpson narrates a number of these.

One day when Bell was at home, a company of soldiers suddenly appeared near the house. It happened that a female servant was sorting a quantity of crockery, and it occurred to her that he should disguise himself and take in his hand a basket filled with the earthenware and walk slowly away as if he were a dealer. The stratagem succeeded, and he passed the soldiers without discovery, and escaped.

At another time Bell, when surprised by the arrival of dragoons, fled into a retired apartment and hid himself in a large oak chest. To prevent suffocation, one of his attendants in closing the lid inserted a piece of cloth to allow the air to circulate. The soldiers examined every chamber and groped into every corner. They entered the place where Bell was concealed, tossed about the furniture, and pried into every likely retreat but it never occurred to them to lift the lid of the chest.

He formed a cave in a retired spot within his own lands where he secreted himself, but a spy set himself to discover the retreat and betrayed it to the soldiers. Next day a company of troopers was conducted to the place in the expectation that Bell would be seized. At that moment, however, he happened to be in a field and observed the horsemen rapidly approaching. He at once left the spot and fled, but, being seen, he was pursued. He made in the direction of a moss where a number of people were casting peats, and when he approached one of them told him to throw off his coat, take a spade, and dig in the hag with him. Bell at once did this, and when the dragoons approached, all the labourers, though well aware of what was coming, were engaged in their work, apparently unconscious of the presence of the soldiers. The commander of the party asked if they saw a man pass that way. One of the workers answered that a short time ago they saw a man making across the moor in the direction in which they were marching. On hearing this, the soldiers continued their pursuit, and Bell was left undiscovered.

In February, 1685, he and David Halliday of Mayfield, Robert Lennox of Irelandton, Andrew M'Robert, Beoch, and James Clement were being searched for by Lagg and his dragoons. They had taken refuge at Mayfield, but hearing the approach of the pursuers, they fled in the night, and hid in Kirkconnel Moor. Lagg got information of their hiding place and came upon them. Being promised quarter, they surrendered without resistance, but no sooner had Lagg got them into his power, than he gave orders that they were to be shot on the spot. Bell was well known, and Lagg had met him in society on equal terms, and been friendly with him. He besought a short time for prayer, but this was refused, and when Douglas of Morton, one of Lagg's officers, interceded for delay, Lagg exclaimed with an oath, "What the devil! have you not had time enough for preparation since Bothwell?" They were all immediately shot,

and for a time Lagg would not permit their bodies
to be buried. Sometime afterwards, Viscount Kenmure, Claverhouse, and Lagg happened to meet at
Kirkcudbright, when the Viscount challenged Lagg
for his barbarities on one whom he knew to be a
gentleman, and especially for refusing to allow his
body to be buried. Lagg replied with an oath that
he could take him and salt him in his beef-barrel.
The Viscount then drew his sword and would have run
him through had not Claverhouse intervened. Bell,
as we have seen, was buried in Anwoth. Halliday was
buried in Balmaghie. In the same grave was buried
David Halliday in Glengap, who was shot by Lagg
and the Earl of Annandale. The tombstone there has
the following inscrption:—

HERE LYES DAVID HALLIDAY, PORTIONER OF MEIFIELD WHO
WAS SHOT UPON THE 20 OF FEBR 1685, AND
DAVID HALLIDAY ONCE IN GLENGAPE WHO WAS LIKEWISE
SHOT UPON THE 11 OF JULY 1685 FOR THEIR ADHERENCE TO
THE PRINCIPLES OF SCOTLANDS COVENANTED REFORMATIONE.

BENEATH THIS STONE TWO DAVID HALLIDAYS
DOE LY WHOSE SOULS NOU SING THEIR MASTERS PRAISE
TO KNOU IF CURIOUS PASSENGERS DESYRE
FOR WHAT, BY WHOME AND HOU THEY DID EXPYRE
THEY DID OPPOSE THIS NATIONS PERJUREY
NOR COULD THEY JOIN WITH LORDLY PRELACY
INDULGING FAVOURS FROM CHRISTS ENEMIES
QUENCHED NOT THEIR ZEAL, THIS MONUMENT THEN CRYES
THESE WERE THE CAUSES NOT TO BE FORGOT
WHY THEY BY LAG SO WICKEDLY WERE SHOT.
ONE NAME, ONE CAUSE, ONE GRAVE, ONE HEAVEN DO TY
THEIR SOULS TO THAT ONE GOD ETERNALLY.

M'Robert was buried in Twynholm, and his tombstone has the following inscription:—

MEMEN (*Cross-bones*) TO MORI.

HERE
LYES ANDREU
McROBERT WHO WAS
SURPRISED AND
SHOT TO DEATH
IN THE PAROCH.

Other side:—

(*Skull*)

TONGLAND BY
GRIER OF LAGG
FOR HIS ADHERE
ENCE TO SCOT
LANDS REFORMATION
COVENANTS NATION
AL AND SOLEMN
LEAGUE. 1685.

Lennox was buried in Girthon, and his tombstone bears the following inscription:—

WITHIN THIS TOMB
LYES THE CORPS OF
ROBERT LENNOX SOME
TIME IN IRELAND TOUN
WHO WAS SHOT TO
DEATH BY GRIER OF
LAGG IN THE PAROCH
OF TONGLAND FOR
HIS ADHERENCE TO
SCOTLANDS REFORMATION
COVENANTS NATIONAL
AND SOLEMN LEAGUE
1685.

Clement, who is supposed to have been a fugitive from Carrick, was buried where he was shot. On the hillside at Kirkconnel Moor a small tombstone may be seen with the following inscription:—

> HERE LYES
> JAMES CLEMENT
> WHO WAS SURPRIS
> ED AND INSTANTLY SHOT TO
> DEATH ON THIS
> PLACE BY GRIER
> OF LAGG FOR HIS
> ADHERENCE TO

Other side:—

> (*Skull and Cross-bones*)
> SCOTLANDS REFOR
> MATION COVENANTS
> NATIONAL AND SO
> LEMN LEAGUE.   1685.

A monument alongside has the following inscription:—

> SACRED
> TO THE MEMORY OF
> DAVID HALLIDAY OF MAYFIELD
> JOHN BELL OF WHITESIDE
> ROBERT LENNOX
> OF IRLANDTON
> ANDREW McROBERT AND
> JAMES CLEMENT
> WHO SUFFERED MARTYRDOM
> ON THIS SPOT A.D. 1685
> FOR THEIR
> ADHERENCE TO THE COVENANTS
> AND TRUE PRESBYTERIAN
> PRINCIPLES BY THAT WICKED
> PERSECUTOR GRIER OF LAG.

Another inscription tells that on 11th September, 1831, about ten thousand people assembled here, and, after worship, contributed a fund for the erection of the monument.

Clement's remains were not allowed to rest in the grave, though it was not his persecutors who were responsible for this. In 1828, four men went from Kirkcudbright in the dead of night for the purpose of getting his skull, which they believed would prove by its confirmation that Clement was a religious fanatic. Just as they secured the skull, they were startled by a wild screech and fled in terror from the spot, leaving the grave open. On examining the skull, they found a hole in the side, showing where the fatal bullet had entered. Mr. John Morrison, portrait painter, learned from one of the four what had happened, and he went and filled up the grave. He also got possession of the martyr's skull, preserved it carefully to his death, and it was buried with him in his coffin. Morrison wrote a poem on the incident, and it gave offence to those concerned. The poem is not without merit, and, as it has never been printed, we give it here, omitting some of the verses to which objection was taken. It is entitled:—

THE MARTYR'S GRAVE.

KIRKCONNELL MOOR, PARISH OF TONGLAND, GALLOWAY.

"And I saw under the altar the souls of them that were slain for the Word of God, and for the testimony which they held; and they cried with a loud voice, saying, How long, O Lord, holy and true, dost thou not judge and avenge our blood."—Revelation, vi. 9 and 10.

An hundred and fifty years
    Are nearly added to the scroll
Of time, since Scotland was in tears,
    And thou wast numbered on the roll
Of Martyrs, in the cause of God,
That slumbered here beneath this sod.

On this lone spot an altar stood,
    To every passing pilgrim dear ;
This turf was watered by the blood
    Of Martyrs ; those gray rocks that rear
Their peaks, have echoed to the shot
That here consigned their bones to rot,

And their bless'd spirits to the sky.
    Oh ! pause, thou passing pilgrim, pause !
'Twas here five martyrs dared to die,
    Faithful to heaven and freedom's cause.
This lonely grave, this mossy stone,
Is Caledonia's Marathon.

Alone I loved to wander here
    When sank the sun in splendour down,
His parting halo did appear
    To me the blessed Martyr's crown
Of Glory, and a still small sound
Whispered—This grave is holy ground.

And I have lingered later still,
    When rising from the eastern clime
The yellow moon, o'er heath and hill,
    Spread her broad light ; sounds divine
Are sighing, as the night-winds pass
In whispers through the waving grass.

What are the sculptured tombs of kings
   When bats their leathern pinions wave,
The ghastly owl at midnight sings
   Their dirge, while from this lonely grave
The lark soars up to heaven's gate
In emblem of the Martyr's fate.

The purest saint that climbs the sky
   Not higher sits at God's right hand
Than those who for their country die,
   And with their blood reclaim the land.
Revere this patriot's grave, for he
Perish'd that Scotland might be free.

.   .   .

There is also a poem on The Martyr's Grave by James Murray, author of *The Maid of Galloway*. This poem is now to be found only in the hands of collectors, and, as will be seen from the following extracts, it suggests that the martyrs were captured at worship in the early morning.

Hunted from home and hearth, abroad
On this lone moor *above* this sod,
Here met five worshippers of God
   To join in praise and prayer.
As rose to Heaven their song of love,
It woke a voice in glen and grove,
And Angels listened from above,
   Their converse sweet to share.

But scarce the psalm had died away,
Scarce hush'd the lark's responsive lay,
Till other sounds of feud and fray
   Rose in the morning gale.
Fierce, furious men the place surround,—
A flash is seen,—a hurling sound—
Then fell upon the blood-dyed ground,
   These martyrs mute and pale.

.   .   .   .

But scarcely had their heaven-ward song,
The golden portals passed along,
Till seated 'mong the martyred throng,
   Their praise anew they told.

CHAPTER XXXIII.

TWO CURATES: KIRKWOOD OF SANQUHAR AND PIERSON OF CARSPHAIRN.

Kirkwood of Sanquhar helps two Galloway Covenanters to escape —Pierson of Carsphairn a zealous persecutor—Some of the Covenanters go to reason with him—A scuffle—Pierson is shot by M'Michael—M'Michael responsible for a previous tragedy, having inflicted a mortal wound on Roan near Dalry —Engaged in Enterkin Pass rescue—M'Michael killed on Auchencloy Hill—Robert Ferguson, Robert Stuart, and John Grier shot—Martyrs' tombstone in Dalry churchyard and inscription—Tombstone to Ferguson and inscription—Martyrs' monument and inscription—Tombstone in Kirkcudbright churchyard to William Hunter and Robert Smith, who were not allowed to write to their relations, and whose words at the gibbet were drowned by beating of drums so that they could not be heard.

SOME of the Episcopal curates did not make themselves so obnoxious to the Covenanters as others, and Simpson tells the story of James Kirkwood, the curate of Sanquhar, whose shrewdness and sympathy probably saved the lives of two persecuted Covenanters from Galloway. The two were being hotly pursued through Carsphairn, and dashed into the Nith, emerging on the opposite side near the manse, where the curate and some others were playing quoits. "Where shall we hide?" asked the two in desperation. "Doff your coats and join in the game," answered the curate.

This was done, and just then the dragoons dashed up and hurried on in the direction which they supposed the Covenanters had taken.

Of quite another stamp was Peter Pierson, the curate of Carsphairn. He had made himself particularly active in supplying Lagg with all the information he could, even without being asked for it, and he had been very zealous in persecuting the Presbyterians. He lived at the manse alone, without even a servant, and kept a number of firearms loaded in his chambers. He was perhaps more a Roman Catholic than an Episcopalian, and frequently declared that Papists were much better subjects than Presbyterians. Matters at last came to such a head that a resolve was made by some of the Covenanters to reason with Pierson, and get him to promise that he would not instigate their enemies against them again. Accordingly, a party of kindred spirits met one night in the end of 1684 in the house of John Clark of Muirbroke, some three miles from Carsphairn, to arrange their plans. The party comprised James M'Michael, fowler of the Laird of Maxwelton, Roger Padgen of Sanquhar, Robert Mitchell of New Cumnock, William Heron, Glencairn, one Watson, and three or four others. Three of the number, M'Michael, Heron, and Mitchell, were selected to interview Pierson, and proceeded to the manse at night, when they knew he would be in. There are different versions of what happened. One account says that Heron and Mitchell were admitted, and delivered their message, which at once put Pierson

in a rage, and he lifted a gun and threatened to shoot
them, getting between them and the door. They called
out, and M'Michael then pressed into the room and,
seeing Pierson with the gun raised, and fearful for
the safety of his companions, he at once fired a pistol,
and shot him dead. Another account says that, in
the course of a scuffle, M'Michael's pistol accidentally
went off and Pierson was killed. Certain it is in any
case that when the Covenanters went to the manse,
they had no intention of doing the curate any bodily
harm. The Societies held that M'Michael's action was
unjustifiable, and removed his name from the Roll.
This, however, did not interfere with his course of
conduct, but he had now to be more a fugitive than
ever. Unfortunately, he had been responsible for a
previous tragedy. He was a bold fiery man, but a
sincere adherent of the Covenanters. He was asked
with some of the Society People to interview Roan
of Stroanpatrick, near Dalry, whose fidelity as a
Covenanter was suspected. They were not satisfied,
in spite of Roan's assurance, and M'Michael told him
that he was not to attend their meetings till he had
cleared himself of the accusation of being a spy, and
that in the meantime he was to deliver up his arms.
As the interview was proceeding, one of the party
noticed that M'Michael could hardly control himself,
and, fearing some untoward incident, he secretly extracted the shot from M'Michael's musket, which was
lying against the wall. Roan invited them to his
house to receive his arms, and they set out. Suddenly

Roan, watching his opportunity, darted aside, crossed a stream, and made off. M'Michael with drawn sword pursued, but finding he was not gaining ground, he threw his sword after Roan with all his might, and it struck him and inflicted a mortal wound.

M'Michael is said to have been engaged in the daring Enterkin Pass rescue, when a number of countrymen took up a position commanding the Enterkin Pass in Dumfriesshire, and rescued eight Covenanters from an escort of twenty-eight soldiers, killing the commander. The soldiers in the confusion managed to carry off one of their prisoners, named John M'Kechnie, belonging to Galloway, "a singularly pious man." They got orders to shoot him soon after, but the bullet only passed through his arm, and he was carried to Edinburgh and thrown into prison. He was refused surgical aid, and the wound gangrened, and he died three months afterwards.

Some of those who had met at Muirbroke the night of the Carsphairn tragedy were afterwards discovered to have been playing the part of spies. Watson was treacherous enough to go over to the persecuting party, and Padgen became one of Strachan's dragoons. He had apparently been in the pay of the Government while associating with the Covenanters. M'Michael, Heron, and Mitchell, were all slain within the year. Claverhouse got information that M'Michael and a few others were hiding somewhere about Auchencloy Hill, on the northern shore of Loch Skerrow, and his search there soon proved successful. M'Michael and his associates—eight in all—were taken by surprise on 18th December, 1684. Two managed to get away in the confusion, but the others had to defend themselves. Claverhouse had a hand to hand contest with M'Michael, and was only saved from M'Michael's sword by his steel bonnet. As it was, he was getting the worst of it when he called for assistance. M'Michael taunted him with these words, "You dare not bide the issue of single combat. Had your helmet been like mine—a soft bonnet—your carcase had now found a bed upon the heath." Meantime a dragoon had stolen up behind him and cleft his skull with his sword. Robert Ferguson, Robert Stewart, and John Grier were shot. The soldiers then pursued the other two, and learned that they had been seen to enter a certain house. Rushing into it, they searched it thoroughly, but the fugitives had never rested in it, yet the soldiers took all in it prisoners, and burned it to the ground. A little before this, some prisoners had been rescued at Kirkcudbright, and this was the pretext for so great cruelty. Stewart's excellent character must have been known to Claverhouse, for he is said to have exclaimed in derision after he shot him, "Stewart's soul in Heaven doth sing!" Ferguson was buried in the moor where he fell. The other three were buried in the churchyard of Dalry, where there is a martyrs' tombstone to their memory. It is about six feet in length by three in breadth, lying upon supports that raise it about a foot from the ground, and has the following inscription:—

Memento Mori.

Here lieth Robert Stewart
(Son to Major Robert Stewart of Ardoch)
And John Grierson, who were murthered by
Graham of Claverhouse,
Anno 1684, for their adherence to Scotland's
Reformation and Covenants,
National and Solemn League.

This narrative runs round the outer edge of the stone, forming a framework for the following lines:—

Behold ! Behold ! a stone's here forced to cry,
Come, see two martyrs under me that ly.
At Water of Dee they ta'en were by the hands
Of cruel Claverhouse and's bloody bands.
No sooner had he done this horrid thing
But's forced to cry, " Stewart's soul in Heaven doth sing ";
Yet, strange, his rage pursued even such when dead,
And in the tombs of their ancestors laid ;
Causing their corpse be raised out of the same,
Discharging in churchyard to bury them,—
All this they did, 'cause they would not perjure
Our Covenants and Reformation pure ;
Because like faithful Martyrs for to die
They rather chose than treacherously comply
With cursed prelacy, this nation's bane
And with indulgence, our Churches stain
Perjured intelligencers were so rife
Shew'd their cursed loyalty—to take their life.

Robert Stewart was the son of Major Stewart of Ardoch, about two miles north of Dalry. The inscription plainly implies that the bodies of Robert Stewart and John Grierson had been buried in the graves of their ancestors, but that Claverhouse had ordered them to be disinterred as traitors. They were re-interred in the most northern part of the church-yard, the part assigned to criminals.

A small moss grown stone marks the spot where the dust of Ferguson lies in the loneliest of graves. It has the following inscription:—

Memento Mori.

Here lyes Robert Ferguson
who was surprised and instantly shot
to death on this place by Graham
of Claverhouse for his adherence
to Scotland's Reformation Covenants,
National and Solemn League,
1684.

A handsome monument has been erected near by, bearing the following inscription:—

Erected
in memory of the martyrs
R. Ferguson, J. McMichan,
R. Stewart & J. Grierson,
who fell on this spot 18 Dec. 1684,
from a collection made here
on the 18th August, 1835,
and the profits of a sermon, afterwards
published, preached on that day
by the Rev. R. Jeffrey of Girthon,
Daniel 3, 17-18.

Two other prisoners were taken to Kirkcudbright, and there hanged and beheaded. They were buried in Kirkcudbright churchyard, and a stone was afterwards erected to their memory. It is a flat stone about six feet long by two feet six inches. The inscription on it shows that they were not allowed to speak when brought to the gibbet, and they were not allowed to write to their relations. The following is the inscription:—

WILLIAM HOUNTURE
ROBERT SMITH. 1684.

This monument shall shew posterity
Two beadles martyres under it doth lie
By bloody Grahame were taken and surprised
Brought to this toun and afterwards were saiz'd
By unjust law were sentenced to die.
Them first they hanged then headed cruely
Captans Douglas Bruce Grahame of Claverhouse
Were these that caused them to be handled thus
And when they were unto the Gibbet come
To stope there speech they did beat up the drum
And all becaus that they would not comply
With indulgence and bloody prelacie
In face of cruel Bruce Douglas and Grahame
They did maintaine that Christ was Lord supream
And boldly ouned both the covenants
At Kirkcudbright thus ended these two saints.

CHAPTER XXXIV.

PEDEN, THE PROPHET.

Born in Ayrshire about 1626—Minister of New Luce, 1659—
Ejected by the Drunken Act, 1662—Farewell services—A
wanderer among the wilds of the South-west of Scotland—
Charged with conventicle keeping—Joined Dalry rising but
left them at Lanark—Forfeited by Act, 1669—Miraculous
escapes—Arrested by Major Cowburn and sent to Bass
Rock—Transferred to Edinburgh Tolbooth—Sentenced to be
transported to Virginia—Sails from Leith with sixty others
banished—Foretells their delivery—Liberated—Returns to
Scotland—Foretells the Covenanters' defeat at Bothwell—
Preaching in Galloway—Predicts his own death, and that his
body will be raised from the grave—His prophecy of the
death of John Brown fulfilled—His last illness, death, and
burial—His body raised from the grave, and re-interred
by the soldiers at Cumnock—Tombstone and inscription—
Monument and inscription.

ONE of the most inspiring patriots of the Covenanting
times was Peden the Prophet. He was born at the
farmhouse of Auchenloich in Sorn, Ayrshire, about
1626. Where he received his earlier education is not
known, but he studied at Glasgow University, and was
afterwards School-master and Precentor and Session
Clerk to the Rev. Mr. Guthrie at Tarbolton.

Having been licensed to preach, he was, in 1659,
appointed minister of New Luce which, twelve years
before, had been separated from Glen Luce.

Here he continued for three years until ejected by, the Drunken Act of Glasgow in 1662. He was greatly beloved by his people, and when he preached his farewell sermon, they were much affected and could scarcely drag themselves away, continuing with him at the church till darkness fell. His farewell sermon was from Acts xx. 31:—"Therefore, watch and remember that by the space of three years I ceased not to warn every one night and day with tears," asserting that he had declared unto them the whole counsel of God, and professing that he was free from the blood of all men. In the afternoon, he preached from the 32nd verse:—"And now, brethren, I commend you to God and to the word of his grace."

When he left, he closed the door behind him, raised the Bible and knocked with it three times on the door, saying in the hearing of them all, "I arrest thee in my Master's name that none enter thee but such as come in by the door as I have done." It is remarkable that no curate or minister who had accepted the hated Indulgence ever entered the pulpit.

Peden took to wandering among the people of the South-west of Scotland, preaching, baptising, and generally carrying out the office of the ministry. He was cited in 1665 to appear before the Council in Edinburgh, but paid no attention, and was declared a rebel. In the preamble of a letter issued against him by the Council, conventicles are declared to be seminaries of rebellion, and the not joining with the public ordinary meetings for divine worship to be seditious, and after reciting the names of Welsh, Blackader,

Peden, and others, their seditious practice and example is specified. Of Peden it is affirmed—" The said Mr. Alexander Peden did keep a conventicle at Ralston in the parish of Kilmarnock, about the 10th of October last, where he baptised the children of Adam Dickie, Robert Lymburner, and many others; as also kept a conventicle in Cragie parish, at the Castle-hill, where he baptised the children of William Gilmor in Kilmarnock, and Gabriel Simpson, both in the said parish, and that besides twenty-three children more; both which conventicles were kept under cloud of night, with a great deal of confusion: as also the said Mr. Alexander rides up and down the country with sword and pistols, in grey cloths."

Peden joined the rising at Dalry, but left them at Lanark. Afterwards, when one of his friends said to him, " Sir, you did well that left them, seeing you were persuaded that they would fall and flee before the evening," he was offended, and replied, " Glory, glory to God that he sent me not to hell immediately, for I should have stayed with them though I had been cut to pieces."

Though not at Rullion Green, his name was included amongst those against whom the doom of forfeiture was pronounced by the Act of Parliament in 1669, as participators in the outbreak.

About this time he had a wonderful deliverance. He was riding with Welsh, the Laird of Glenover, when they met a party of horsemen whom there was no avoiding. The Laird was terrified, but Peden said, " Keep up your courage, for God hath laid an arrest on these men that they shall do us no harm." When they met, they were courteous, and asked the way. Peden went off his road to show them the ford on the water of Titt. When he returned, the Laird said, " Why did you go? You might have let the lad go." " They might have asked the lad questions and might have discovered us," replied Peden. " As for me I knew they would be like Egyptian dogs. They could not move a tongue against me, my time not being yet come."

Tradition records many of Peden's weary wanderings and marvellous and miraculous escapes during the next seven years. In 1673, however, he was arrested in the house of Hugh Ferguson of Knockdoon, Colmonell, Ayrshire. Ferguson was fined a thousand merks for sheltering him, and Peden was sent to the Bass Rock, then the State prison, where he remained till October, 1677, when he was transferred to Edinburgh Tolbooth. Major Cowburn got £50 for arresting him. In a petition to the Council on November 14th, 1678, Peden tells that he had lain in Edinburgh Tolbooth for a long time, and asks permission to go to Ireland, where he had formerly lived for some years.

He was sentenced to be transported to Virginia.

Along with sixty others, he was sent from Leith in the *St. Michael* of Scarborough on the voyage to London. It was a sad party that set sail from the Scotch port. Peden, however, assured his fellow passengers that they would be set at liberty, and, owing to some mismanagement in the arrangements, or, as others state, through the good offices of Lord Shaftsbury, they were all set free when they got to London. Returning to Scotland in June, 1679, Peden at once set himself to the work so dear to his heart. On the way to Scotland, he waited a Sabbath at a Border village, and kept himself retired till about the middle of the day, when some of his friends told him they were waiting expecting him to preach. He said, "Let the people go to their prayers. As for me I neither can nor will preach this day, for our friends are fallen and fled before the enemy at Hamilton, and they are hashing and hagging them down, and their blood is running like water." This was the 22nd of June, the day of the Covenanters' defeat at Bothwell.

When he arrived in Galloway, much of his time was taken up praying earnestly for those taken prisoners at Bothwell, for with prophetic vision he declared that "the wild sea billows would be the winding sheet of many of them." The vessel on which they were sent to America was wrecked among the Orkney Islands, and nearly two hundred and fifty souls found a watery grave.

He also predicted his own death, and that his body would be taken out of the grave again. "I shall die in a few days," he said, "but having foretold many things which will require some time before they are verified, I will give you a sign which will confirm your expectation that they shall as truly come to pass as those you have already seen accomplished before your eyes. I shall be decently buried by you, but if my body is suffered to rest in the grave where you will lay it, then I shall have been a deceiver, and the Lord hath not spoken by me, whereas if the enemy come a little time afterwards to take it up and carry it away to bury it in an ignominious place, then I hope you will believe that the God Almighty hath spoken by me, and consequently shall not one word fall to the ground."

Nothing is better authenticated than that when John Brown of Priesthill and Marion Weir were married by Peden, he turned to the latter and said, " You have got a good man to be your husband, but you will not enjoy him long. Prize his company and keep linen by you to be his winding sheet, for you will need it when you are not looking for it, and it will be a bloody one."

This was in June, 1682. In the end of April, 1685, he came to the house of this worthy couple and remained for the night. In the morning, when taking farewell, he muttered as if speaking to himself, " Poor woman, a fearful morning, a dark misty morning, poor woman!" Next morning, between six and seven o'clock, Brown was shot by Claverhouse at his door in presence of his young wife and children. Peden, who had been out in the fields all that night, was then eleven or twelve miles distant. Coming to a house in the morning, he called the family together that he might pray with them, and in the course of his prayer he used these words, " Lord, when wilt thou avenge

Brown's blood, and let Brown's blood be precious in Thy sight." When he had finished, he was asked what he meant. "What do I mean?" he replied. "Claverhouse has been at Priesthill this morning, and has cruelly murdered John Brown. His corpse is lying at the end of the house, and his poor wife is weeping by it, and not a soul to speak comfort to her."

Many and varied were the prophecies of Peden that literally came to pass; many the judgments he pronounced that were fulfilled, and many the prayers he breathed that seemed to be instantly answered. It has been said by M'Gavin in connection with his prophecies that "sagacious foresight was made to have the appearance of the prophetic spirit," and Dr. John Ker speaks of "the keen insight of his sayings, which amounted to foresight," but it requires something far above and beyond all this to explain many of his prophecies which undoubtedly happened as he foretold. There was the prophecy of the martyrdom of John Brown, the prophecy of his own burial, of his body being raised again and re-buried, and the sign he spoke of in connection with it. No sagacious foresight can possibly account for these, and "although these things are now made to yield to the force of ridicule, the sarcasm of the profane, and the fashions of an atheistical generation, yet one must conclude with the spirit of God that the secrets of the Lord both have been, are, and will be with them who fear His name." *

* *Scots Worthies*, article Peden, p. 517 of fourth edition.

After wandering about through Galloway and Ayr-shire, he arrived back at his native parish, and near the Lugar he had a cave dug with a willow bush covering the mouth of it. This was not far from his brother's house at Ten Shillingside, and for a while it proved a safe retreat. At length, however, feeling his end drawing near, he left the cave and went to his brother's house, which was only a little distance from Auchenleck House, the seat of the Boswells. His brother and family, knowing that he was being searched for, implored him to return to the cave. "That," he said, "is discovered, but no matter, for within forty-eight hours I shall be beyond the reach of them all." A few hours after this, his pursuers came, found the cave, but no one in it, and then advanced to the house, expecting to find him there. The family, however, had hid him, and the soldiers did not discover him.

Peden died as he foretold on 26th January, 1686, and was buried in the churchyard of Auchenleck, but the soldiers came soon afterwards to the grave, broke open the coffin, drew off his shirt, and threw it on a neighbouring bush. They carried his body to Cum-nock with the intention of hanging it on the gallows tree, but the Earl of Dumfries told the officers in command that the gallows had been erected for thieves, robbers, murderers, and not for men like Peden. His remains were accordingly buried beside it. This ground afterwards became the burial-place for the parish, and a tombstone was erected over his remains, with the following inscription:—

Here Lies

Mr. ALEXANDER PEDEN,
A Faithful Minister of the
Gospel sometime
of Glenluce
who departed this life
26th. of January 1686,
And was raised after six weeks
out of the grauf,
and buried here,
out of
Contempt.

MEMENTO MORI.

In 1891, a handsome monument of Aberdeen granite was erected beside the grave, mainly through the exertions of Mr. A. B. Todd, that Grand Old Man of Covenanting lore. At the inauguration ceremony, Mr. Todd said that the corroding tooth of time might cause that granite pile to crumble into dust, " but even though such should be the case, or though the thunder-bolts of the sky should shiver it to pieces, still the memory of Peden and of the martyrs of the Covenant can never perish, for they are star-traced in the heavens." The late Professor Blackie took a prominent part in the proceedings.

The monument has the following inscription :—

In Memory

of

ALEXANDER PEDEN

(A Native of Sorn)

THAT FAITHFUL MINISTER OF CHRIST, WHO,
FOR HIS UNFLINCHING ADHERENCE TO THE
COVENANTED REFORMATION IN SCOTLAND, WAS
EXPELLED BY TYRANT RULERS FROM HIS PARISH
OF NEW LUCE, IMPRISONED FOR YEARS ON THE
BASS ROCK BY HIS PERSECUTORS, AND HUNTED
FOR HIS LIFE ON THE SURROUNDING MOUNTAINS
AND MOORS, TILL HIS DEATH ON 26th. JANUARY 1686
IN THE 60th. YEAR OF HIS AGE, AND HERE
AT LAST, HIS DUST REPOSES IN PEACE, AWAITING
THE RESURRECTION OF THE JUST.

"SUCH WERE THE MEN THESE HILLS WHO TRODE
STRONG IN THE LOVE AND FEAR OF GOD,
DEFYING THROUGH THE LONG DARK HOUR,
ALIKE THE CRAFT AND RAGE OF POWER."

ERECTED

IN

1891.

Peden was never married. His brother's descendants
however are very numerous, and naturally take a great
interest in all that pertains to the history of Peden the
Prophet.

CHAPTER XXXV.

LOCHENKIT — IRONGRAY.

Martyrs' tombstone to John Wallace, William Heron, John Gordon, and William Stuart—Monument and inscription—Story of their martyrdom—Edward Gordon and Alexander M'Cubbin hanged at Irongray—Tombstone and inscription—Robert Grierson banished to West Indies, and returns after the Revolution.

LOCHENKIT is a small sheet of water in the parish of Kirkpatrick-durham, in the Stewartry. About half a mile to the west is a martyrs' tombstone, with the following inscription:—

HERE LYES

Four martyrs, John Wallace, William
Heron, John Gordon, and William
Stewart, found out and shot dead
upon this place by Captain Bruce
and Captain Lag for their adhearing
to the Word of God, Christ's Kingly
Government in his house and the
Covenanted work of reformation
against Tyranny, Perjury, Prelacy,
2 March MDCLXXXV.
Rev. Chap. xii. ver. 11.

22

> Behold
> Here in this wilderness we lie
> Four witnesses of hellish cruelty
> Our lives and blood could not their ire assuage
> But when we're dead they did against us rage
> That match the like we think ye scarcely can
> Except the Turk or Duke de Alva's men.

> Repaired by the friends of civil and
> religious Liberty.

Close by, a handsome monument has been erected on an eminence that enables it to be seen from a great distance. It is a square obelisk of gray granite, surmounted by a hand pointing to Heaven. On the side facing the martyrs' tombstone is the following inscription:—

YONDER LIE

WILLIAM HERON FROM GLENCAIRN
JOHN GORDON   ⎫
WILLIAM STEWART ⎬ GALLOWAY
JOHN WALLACE   ⎭
MEN WHO WERE FOUND OUT AND SHOT
DEAD HERE 2ND MARCH 1685
BY CAPTAIN BRUCE FOR THEIR
ADHERENCE TO SCOTLANDS
COVENANTED REFORMATION.
TO COMMEMORATE THE
PRINCIPLES FOR WHICH THESE
MARTYRS SUFFERED THIS
MONUMENT IS ERECTED BY
SUBSCRIPTION AFTER SERMONS
1843.

In February, 1685, Captain Bruce and a party of dragoons, who had been hunting the hills and moors of Galloway for Covenanters, came upon some at Lochenkit. Four of them, John Gordon, William Stewart, William Heron, and John Wallace, were shot on the spot. Two others, Edward Gordon and Alexander M'Cubbin of Glencairn, were taken prisoners, and carried to the Bridge of Urr, where Lagg was pressing the abjuration oath upon the country people. These two refused to take the oath, and Captain Bruce interceded for them and desired that an Assize should be called at once to try them. Lagg swore he would seek no Assize, and in a bravado said that all who had taken the oath had sworn these men's doom. The Captain, however, got the matter put off till the morning, and then they marched to Irongray, where the two were hanged upon a growing tree near Irongray Church, and left hanging for some time. They were afterwards buried at the foot of the tree. Just before his execution, M'Cubbin was asked by a friend if he had any word to send to his wife. " I will leave her and the two babes upon the Lord and to His promise. A father to the fatherless and a judge of the widows is God in His holy habitation." When the person employed to carry out the sentence asked his forgiveness, he replied, " Poor man, I forgive thee and all men. Thou hast a miserable calling upon earth."

A stone was afterwards erected to their memory, with the following inscription:—

Here lyes Edward Go
rdon and Alexander
M'Cubine, Martyres
hanged without
Law by Lag and Cap.
Bruce for adhereing
To the word of God
Christ's Kingly Gover
ment in His House
And the covenanted
Work of Reformation
Against tyranny
Perjury and Prelacy
Rev. xii. 12.   March 3. 1685.

As Lagg and bloodie
Bruce command
We were hung up by
Hellish hand
And thus the furio
Us rage to stay
We dyed near Kirk
Of Irongray.
Here now in peace
Sweet rest we take
Once murder'd for
Religion's sake.

Tradition tells us that the reason these men were
executed near Irongray Church was that it might be
within sight of Hallhill, then occupied by a family
named Ferguson, well known for their attachment to
the principles of the Covenanted Reformation.   It was

thought that the sight of the execution would over-awe the Fergusons. It had quite the opposite effect. A young daughter of the family came to the martyrs when they were brought to the place of execution, and tied a handkerchief over their eyes. For this she was banished, and went to Lisbon, where she married a carpenter, and lived to a ripe old age. It is said that seventy years after the execution, on 1st November, 1755, the day of the great earthquake, when the city was all but entirely destroyed, and when from thirty to sixty thousand people lost their lives, she was sitting on a plank by the riverside when the sea came up, rising like a mountain. Multitudes of people were swept back to a watery grave when it retired, but it carried her on before it, and left her high and dry, on the land.

The two others who were taken prisoners were banished to the West Indies. One of the two was Robert Grierson, farmer, in Lochenkit. He had for long been mourned as dead, but one night after the Revolution, his wife thought she heard a footstep outside the house, and going to the door, the dog left her and bounded forward. She heard a voice addressing it, and said to herself, " If my husband had been alive, I would have said that is he with the dog." In a few minutes she was in his arms. He lived and died at Lochenkit, and the late Rev. Alexander Grierson, M.A., minister of the Free Church, Irongray, was one of his descendants.

Mr. James M'Cubbin, Ivy Lodge, Crawford, is a descendant of Alexander M'Cubbin, and possesses his

Bible. Needless to say, it is carefully preserved. **It** is a small folio, dated " Edinburgh. Printed· by Andro Hart, and are to be solde at his Buith, on the North Side of the Gates, a little beneath the Crosse. Anno Dom., 1610."

CHAPTER XXXVI.

THE GORDONS OF AIRDS AND EARLSTON.

Earlston Castle—Disciples of Wickliffe welcomed to Earlston—
Religious meetings in Wood of Airds—Alexander Gordon,
refusing to receive curate at Dalry, is fined and banished to
Montrose—Member of General Assembly of 1638—The Bishop
unsuccessfully objects to him—Some of Rutherfurd's letters
addressed to his son William—William refuses to assist
Commission to settle curate at Irongray, and himself claims
the right of patronage—Indicted for conventicle keeping
and banished—Returns to Scotland—Prepares to join
the Covenanters at Bothwell, but, being delayed, sends his
son and follows later—Not knowing of the Covenanters'
defeat, he encounters a body of English dragoons at Crookitstone, and refusing to submit is killed—Buried in Glassford
churchyard—Monument to his memory and inscription—His
son's narrow escapes—Alexander Gordon elected by the
Societies to advocate their cause abroad—He is apprehended
while setting sail at Newcastle, and casts his papers overboard—He is taken to London, sent to Scotland, and condemned to be beheaded—Intention to torture him to get
confessions and implicate others—Thrice reprieved, and then
sent to Bass Rock—The Revolution sets him free—*Lady
Earlston's Soliloquies*—Earlston a member of the Convention
which settled the Crown on William and Mary.

EARLSTON Castle occupies an attractive position in the
Glenkens of Galloway, and is the ancient home of
the Gordons of Earlston, who played a prominent part
in the troublous times in Galloway. They were indeed
among the first in Scotland to imbibe the tenets of the

Reformation. Some of the disciples of Wickliffe were welcomed to Galloway by Alexander Gordon of Airds about the beginning of the sixteenth century, and the Gordons had a copy of the New Testament, which was read at some of their meetings in the Wood of Airds. At that time to have a copy of the sacred law was illegal, and entailed severe punishment. Alexander Gordon was a man of great size and strength. Living in the same house with his son, grandchildren, and great-grandchildren till he was over a hundred years old, he became known as "The Patriarch." When the Roman Catholics got an Act passed for the better observance of Saint and other days, prohibiting all labour, and enacting that beasts of burden, if employed, would be forfeited, he very shrewdly outwitted the legislators by yoking one Christmas day ten of his sons to the plough with the youngest as driver, he himself holding the stilts, and thus turned over the soil, breaking the law without forfeiting his team. He had a family of eleven sons and nine daughters. He died in 1580, and was succeeded by his son John.

In 1635, Sydeserf, the bishop of Galloway, appointed a curate to Dalry without consulting the people. Alexander Gordon of Earlston, great-grandson of the Patriarch, refused to receive him, and was summoned before the Diocesan Commission Court. He failed to appear, was fined, and banished to Montrose. Although he had the superintendence of Lord Kenmure's Estate, and Lord Lorne, one of Kenmure's tutors, requested the remission of the sentence, the

Bishop remained inexorable, and insisted on it being
carried out. Ever afterwards, Gordon took an active
part with the Covenanters. He was appointed one of
the elders sent by the Presbytery of Kirkcudbright to
the Assembly of 1638. Along with Dickson of Irvine,
and Samuel Rutherfurd of Anwoth, he was objected
to by the bishops as incompetent because lying under
the censure of the Church. These three were heard in
their defence, and Argyle supported Earlston's statement. The result was that the Assembly accepted the
defence, and the three took a prominent part in the
Assembly proceedings. Gordon was one of the Commissioners for the Stewartry in the Parliament of
1641. He and his son John were members of the
Covenanters' War Committee for the Stewartry. He
died in 1654, and John having predeceased him, he
was succeeded by his second son William.

It may be noted in passing that five of Rutherfurd's
letters are addressed to William. Indeed, as early as
1637, Rutherfurd thus admonished him:—" Sir, lay
the foundation thus, and ye shall not shrink nor be
shaken; make tight work at the bottom, and your ship
shall ride against all storms; if withal your anchor be
fastened on good ground, I mean within the vail."

William was educated for the Church of Scotland.
When the Civil War broke out, he had command of
a company under Leslie. He was fined £3,500 for
his adherence to the Covenanters.

In 1663, when a commission was appointed to
enquire into the question of the settlement of curates

at Irongray and Kirkcudbright, on account of the
opposition offered by the women of these places,
William Gordon was ordered by the commission to
assist the bishop in settling a curate at Dalry in room
of John M'Michan who was evicted. The letter is in
the following terms:—

" KIRKCUDBRIGHT, 21st May, 1663.

" SIR,

" We doubt not but you heard, that the lords
of his Majesty's privy council have commissioned
us to come to this country, as to take course with
the seditious tumult raised in this place so as to
do everything that may contribute to the settling
of the peace here, and to be assisting to the Bishop
for the planting of other vacant churches, by the
withdrawing of the respective ministers: and
finding the church of Dalry to be one of those,
and that the bishop hath presented an actual
minister, Mr. George Henry, fit and qualified for
the charge, now being, according to the Act of
parliament, fallen into his hand, jure devoluto,
and that the gentleman is to come to your parish
this Sabbath next to preach to that people, and
that you are a person of special interest there;
according to the power and trust committed to us,
we do require you to cause his edict to be served,
and the congregation convene, and to countenance
him so as he be encouraged to prosecute his

ministry in that Place. In doing whereof, as you will witness your respect to authority so oblige us to remain,

" Sir,

Your loving friends and servants,

" LINLITHGOW,   ANNANDALE,
" GALLOWAY,   DRUMLANERK."

He replied that, as patron, he had with the approval of the people already taken steps to secure " a truly worthy and qualified person. I have ever judged it safest to obey God, and stand at a distance from whatsomever doth not tend to God's glory and the edification of the souls of his scattered people, of which this congregation is a part. And besides, My Lords, it is known to many that I pretend to lay claim to the right of patronage of this parish and have already determined therein, with the consent of the people, upon a truly worthy and qualified person and an actual minister that he may be admitted to exercise his gifts amongst that people; and for me to condescend to countenance the bearer of your Lordship's letter were to procure me most impiously and dishonourably to wrong the majesty of God, and violently to take away the Christian liberty of his afflicted people, and enervate my own right." He was cited to appear before the Council in July to answer for his seditious and factious carriage, but nothing seems to have followed, and in

November following he was cited on a charge of keeping conventicles and private meetings in his house, " to answer for his contempt under pain of rebellion," and the following March an indictment was drawn up against him, as follows:—

" That he had been at three several conventicles, where Mr. Gabriel Semple, a deposed minister, did preach, viz., one in Corsock Wood, and the other two in the Wood of Airds, at all which there were great numbers of people; that he did hear Mr. Robert Paton, a deposed minister, expound a text of Scripture, and perform other acts of Worship in his mother's house; and that Mr. Thomas Thomson, another deposed minister, did lecture in his own house to the family on a Sabbath day; and that being required to enact himself to abstain from all such meetings in time coming, and to live peaceably and orderly conform to law, he refused to do the same."

The punishment was:—

" To be banished, and to depart forth of the kingdom within a month after date hereof, and not to return under pain of death; and that he enact himself to live peaceably and orderly during the said month under the pain of ten thousand pounds, or otherwise to enter his person in prison."

He seems to have gone into banishment for some time, but after Pentland he was allowed to return to Scotland.

Hearing of the rising after Drumclog, he prepared to join the Covenanters, but was delayed by circumstances at home, and sent his son Alexander. He collected some friends to go with him to join the Covenanters, and as he was passing the Castle of Threave with some of them, he said, "Gentlemen, I was the man that commanded the party which took this Castle from the late King, who had in it two hundred of the name Maxwell, of whom the greatest part being Papists, we put them all to the sword, and demolished the Castle as you see it, and now (though an old man) I take up arms against the son, whom I hope to see go the same way that his father went, for we can never put trust in a Covenant-breaker; so, gentlemen, your cause is good—you need not fear to fight against a foresworn king."

He was met at Crookitstone by a party of English dragoons, and, unaware of the Covenanters' defeat at Bothwell, he refused to be sworn, and was shot down. Permission was denied to have him buried at Earlston, and he was buried in the churchyard of Glassford, the parish where he fell. A monument was erected shortly afterwards, but the times were too troublesome for an inscription to be put on it, and it remained without one till 1772, as the inscription shows:—

To the memory of the very Worthy Pillar of the
church, Mr. William Gordon of Earliston in Gallo-
-way, shot by a partie of dragoons on his
way to Bothwellbridge, 22nd June 1679,
aged 65, inscribed by his great grand-
son, Sir John Gordon, Bart, 11 June, 1772.

Silent till now full ninety years hath stood,
This humble Monument of Guiltless Blood,
Tyranick Sway, forbad his fate to name
Least his known worth should prove the Tyrant's shame
On Bothwell road with love of Freedom fir'd
The tyrant's minions boldly him requir'd
To stop and yield, or it his life would cost,
This he disdained not knowing all was lost,
On which they fir'd. Heaven so decreed his doom,
Far from his own laid in this silent Tomb.
How leagu'd with Patriots to maintain the Cause
Of true RELIGIOUS LIBERTY and LAWS,
How learn'd, how soft his manner, free from Pride,
How clear his Judgment, and how he liv'd and dy'd,
They well could tell who weeping round him stood,
On Strevan plains that drank his Patriot Blood.

REPAIRED
By Sir John Gordon, Bart.,
of Earlston.
His Representative.
1842.

On the other side of the monument, facing the road
that runs past the manse, are the lines—

IF A HARD FATE DEMANDS,
OR CLAIMS A TEAR,
STAY, GENTLE PASSENGER,
AND SHED IT HERE.

His son, Alexander Gordon, had a narrow escape after the battle. Riding through Hamilton, he was recognised by one of his tenants and was persuaded to dismount and disguise himself in female attire, while the horse's harness was concealed in a dunghill. In this disguise he betook himself to the rocking of a cradle in which a child lay asleep, and so escaped detection; but for several years afterwards he had to remain in concealment. His house at Earlston was made a garrison for the soldiers so that he durst not enter it, but he found a refuge in a small building in the thickest part of the woods, not far from his home.

After Bothwell, he had many narrow escapes from capture. On one occasion when troopers came to the house, he hastily arrayed himself in the clothes of a workman, and was busily employed cleaving wood with the assistance of a female servant. The commander asked the wood cleavers if Earlston was within, and receiving an answer in the negative, ordered Gordon to throw down his axe and assist in the search. He complied with an air of indifference as if it were all the same to him whether he was splitting firewood or searching for fugitives. He conducted them through the house, but their search was in vain.

On another occasion he escaped detection by climbing an enormous oak tree, to which he had a rope attached for the purpose, and hiding among its leafy branches.

In 1680, the Government made the rising at Bothwell a pretext for persecuting all who refused to conform to Episcopacy. Galloway was the first to suffer. On 18th February, Patrick M'Douall of Freugh, William Ferguson of Kaitlock, William Gordon, elder, and Alexander Gordon, younger, of Earlston, James Gordon, younger, of Craichlaw, William Gordon of Culvennan, Patrick Dunbar of Machermore, and —— M'Ghie of Larg were called before the Justiciary Court, and hired witnesses having deponed to their accession to the rebellion, they were found guilty, and ordered to be executed when taken, and their property confiscated to his Majesty's use. William Gordon of Earlston had been killed after the action, but the prosecution was conducted against him, that his estates might be forfeited. Alexander Gordon and his wife retired to Holland for some time, returning in 1681.

At a general meeting of the Societies, originally, formed to oppose the Test Act, on March 15th, 1682, Alexander Gordon was elected to go to foreign nations to represent their case to the Reformed Churches there. Supplied with money collected by the Societies to defray the expenses, he went by London to the Netherlands.

Earlston was soon associated with Sir Robert Hamilton, who was brother to the Laird of Preston, to whose sister Earlston was married, and they seem to have been stationed at Leewarden in Fries-land. One result of their labours was that James Renwick went over to Holland, finished his studies for the ministry, and received ordination.

In 1683, Earlston returned home, and at the eighth general meeting of the Societies, held in Edinburgh on

May 8th, he gave an account of his labours, greatly to the satisfaction of those present.

He was again elected to be sent abroad, and set sail from Newcastle for Holland, but just as the ship was leaving, it went aground and some officers came on board, and challenged Earlston and his servant,* travelling under the names of Alexander Pringle and Edward Livingstone. For some reason, they threw their papers overboard, and the officers, expecting great discoveries from these, recovered them at great trouble and danger. Earlston and his servant were sent to London, but nothing of any importance was found in their papers.

Soon afterwards, Earlston was sent back to Scotland, and was examined by the Council again and again to see if he had any connection with the Ryehouse Plot, but nothing was found against him. At last, on 21st August, they condemned him to be beheaded at the Cross on the 28th. After sentence, the idea of torture suggested itself to the Council, but they were in a difficulty as to whether there was law for torturing a criminal under sentence of death. As there were only three members in Edinburgh, they wrote to London for guidance. A month passed before the answer came that, although he could not be put to torture for matters relating to the cause for which he was condemned, yet he might be tortured with respect to conspiracies and crimes that had happened since. Accordingly, the Council met to examine him, with

* Edward Aitken. See page 209.

the instrument of torture standing by, but it was not applied, as he satisfied them he would be more full in his answers without the torture than with it. The answers contained nothing that implicated either Earlston or the Society People in any attempt against the King.

On November 23rd, another letter came from the King, ordering the Council to put him to the torture, but when he was brought in and ordered to the boots, he became furious and tossed the soldiers about the room, to the terror of the Council, who bolted till he was secured. Physicians declared that he was too ill to undergo torture, and he was afterwards reprieved three times, and in May was sent to the Bass where he was kept till the Revolution set him free.

His wife, Janet Hamilton, daughter of Sir Thomas Hamilton of Preston, was no ordinary woman. She was a correspondent of James Renwick, and many of his letters were addressed to her. Her religious meditations have been frequently published under the title of *Lady Earlston's Soliloquies*.

Earlston was a member of the Scottish Convention which declared the Throne vacant, and settled the Crown on William and Mary. He became the commander of the Stewartry Militia, commissioner of supply, and lived till after 1726.

CHAPTER XXXVII.

THE M'MILLANS.

·William M'Millan of Caldow persecuted and becomes fugitive—
Goes to Ireland—Licensed to preach—Arrested in Galloway—
Extract from Kirkcudbright Burgh Records, showing an
order for his removal to Edinburgh Tolbooth—Imprisoned
at Dumfries for thirty-five months without any charge—
Liberated—Failing to appear is denounced rebel—Arrested
and taken to Wigtown—Sent to Kirkcudbright and then to
Dumfries Castle—Imprisoned in Edinburgh and afterwards
at Dunottar.

WILLIAM M'MILLAN of Caldow, in the parish of
Balmaclellan, after the re-introduction of Prelacy, was
persecuted by Mr. Robert Moir, curate of Balmaclellan, assisted by Sir James Turner. He was
obliged to leave his mother's house for mere nonconformity, and to live as a fugitive. He took no part
in the Dalry rising, yet Sir William Bannantyne
quartered his men upon his family, apprehended himself, and kept him prisoner for some time in the house
of Earlston then held as a garrison. His goods and
furniture were seized, notwithstanding he had given
bond for £1,000 to answer for anything that could be
laid to his charge. He went frequently to Ireland to
escape persecution, and was prevailed upon by the
Presbyterian ministers of the County of Down to
qualify as a minister, and was licensed to preach about

the year 1673. When in the most peaceable manner he
was preaching in Galloway, he was informed against
by the prelates, and the Earl of Nithsdale sent two
of his militia troop—Alexander Maxwell, afterwards
of Cowheath, and William Glendoning of Parton—
with some other violent Papists, who seized him and
carried him to Kirkcudbright. The following extract
regarding him is taken from the Burgh Records of
Kirkcudbright:—

"At Kirkcudbright, the 13th day of November,
1676. The quhilk day, Thomas Lidderdaill of
St. Marie's Isle, Stewart deput of the Stewartrie
of Kirkcudbright, presented to Samuel Carmont,
ane of the bailzies of the said Burgh ane order
direct from the Lords of his Majestie's Privie
Counsell, Quhairby the said Lords doe ordaine
Maister William M'Millan, ane noted keiper of
field conventicles, now prisoner in the tolbooth
of the said Burgh of Kirkcudbright, to be transported to the tolbooth of Edinburgh. And for
that effect, grants order and warrand to the
Stewart of the Stewartrie of Kirkcudbright and
his deputes, within the boundes of whose jurisdictione he is incarcerat, to tak the said Mr.
William M'Millan into his custodie, and to carrie
him prisoner to the Sheriff of the next adjacent
shyer, and so furth from shyer to shyer till he
be brought prisoner to the said tolbooth of Edinburgh. And ordaines the Magistrates of Edinburgh to receive and detain him prisoner therein

until further order: as the said order subscribed by Mr. Alexander Gibson, and datit at Edinburgh the elevint day of October, now last bypast. Conforme and in obedience quhairunto the said Thomas Lidderdaill, Stewart-deput, hes received from the said Samuel Carmont, Bailzie, the said Master William M'Millan furth of the said tolbooth of Kirkcudbright, and the said Stewart deput hath delyvered him to William Herries of Cloik, conform to ane order direct from Robert, Lord Maxwell, principal Stewart. And the said William Herries with his partie, is to convey the said Mr. William M'Millan to the Sherff of Nithisdaill or his deput, who is the next adjacent Sherff; and to get ane ressait of him from them, for the said principal Stewart and his deput, their exoneratione. As witness their following subscriptions.

"Tho. Lidderdaill,
William Herries."

He was taken to Dumfries, where he was kept prisoner without a charge for nearly three years. After many applications to the Council, he was liberated. He was cited to the first Circuit at Dumfries after Bothwell for reset and converse. He failed to appear, and at the Cross of Dumfries was denounced rebel and fugitive, and his goods confiscated to the King's use. He was obliged to lurk many months in the open fields, to the injury of his health, which at best was infirm. Those hardships brought on fever, and when still suffering from it, he was, with his infirm wife, dragged by the soldiers to the Court at Dumfries. Refusing the Test, he was ordered to be carried to Wigtown to abide trial there. The soldiers forced him to walk till he fainted, and when he fell down they seized a young wild colt and set him upon it, without saddle or anything under him, to the great danger of his life. At Wigtown he had no lodging but the open guard house, without any bed for eight days, and no place to retire to. When the Lords came to Wigtown, he petitioned that he might not have the guards continually about him, or that he might be allowed to give bond to appear at Edinburgh, but both were refused. From Wigtown he was sent to Kirkcudbright, where Lagg, by orders, as he said, from Queensberry, threatened him most severely if he would not take the Test. He refused, and was sent to Dumfries Castle, where he was detained with others from 22nd October till 22nd November. On 22nd November they were carried to Moffat Kirk, where they lay all night cold and wet, and then they were taken to Leith. By order of the Council, M'Millan and thirty-four more were distributed to several prisons in Edinburgh. About 18th May the following year, they were sent to Dunottar.

A petition was presented to the Privy Council by "Grizel Cairns and Alison Johnstone in behalf of Mr. William M'Millan and Robert Young, wright in Edinburgh, their husbands, and the rest of the prisoners," setting forth the lamentable condition in which the prisoners were kept. The Privy Council gave orders to the Deputy Governor "to permit meat and drink and other necessaries to be brought in to the petitioners at the ordinary easy rates, and to allow the said Mr. William M'Millan and Robert Young a distinct room from the rest."

It would seem that M'Millan took the Oath of Allegiance, and was liberated on an undertaking to appear when called on, under penalty of five thousand merks.

Professor Reid asks the question, "Is Caldow an error for Caldons?" There is a stone in Minnigaff churchyard which refers to "James M'Millan and Anthony, his son, in Caldons," Caldons, of course, being in Minnigaff parish. It would appear that the M'Millans were connected with both places, for we find that, on 10th June, 1674, William M'Millan of Caldonis had principal sasine of the land of Caldow in Balmaclellan, and in 1682, Thomas, probably the son of William, was owner.

The famous John M'Millan was connected with the same family. On the fly-leaf of an old copy of the Confession of Faith, in the possession of Mr. John M'Millan, Glenhead, the following names have been written, evidently as a family register:—

(1) (part destroyed), born 1664.
(2) John M'Millan, do., 1682.
(3) James M'Millan, do., 1692.
(4) Mary M'Millan, do., 1715.

It has been suggested that this John may have been the future minister, but this is extremely doubtful.

He is believed to have been born at Barncaughla in Minnigaff parish in 1669, and he became minister of Balmaghie in 1701. He had, while a student, joined "the Societies," and he presented a Statement of Grievances to the Presbytery in 1703, complaining that The Solemn League and Covenant was ignored, and that the Church's freedom was invaded by the State. He was deposed, but continued to occupy the church. He became the pastor of "The Societies," and for nearly half a century discharged the onerous duties with matchless zeal and unsurpassed fidelity. Some of the chief incidents of his life may be gleaned from the following inscription on his monument at Dalserf churchyard:—

East side —:

A public tribute to the memory of the Rev. John Macmillan, minister of Balmaghie in Galloway, and afterwards first minister to the United Societies in Scotland, adhering at the Revolution to the whole Covenanted Reformation in Britain and Ireland, attained between 1638 and 1649. An exemplary Christian; a devoted minister; and a faithful witness to the Cause of Christ: died December First, 1753, aged eighty-four.

"Look unto Abraham your father; for I called him alone, and blessed him and increased him."—Isa. li. 2.

North side:—

Mr. Macmillan acceded to the Societies in 1707. The Reformed Presbytery was constituted in 1743; and the Synod of the Reformed Presbyterian Church in Scotland in 1811.

"Hitherto hath the Lord helped us."—I. Sam. vii. 12.

South side:—

Erected at the grave of Mr. Macmillan by the inhabitants of the surrounding Country of all denominations, who testified their respect to his much venerated memory, by attending and liberally contributing at a Sermon Preached on the spot, September eighth, 1839, by the Rev. A. Symington, D.D., Paisley.

> "Why should not my countenance be sad, when the city, the place of my fathers' sepulchres, lieth waste."— Nehemiah ii. 3.

West side:—

Mr. Macmillan was succeeded in the ministry by his son, the Rev. John Macmillan of Sandhills, near Glasgow, who died February Sixth, 1808, aged seventy-nine; and by his grand-son, the Rev. John Macmillan, of Stirling, who died October Twentieth, 1818, aged sixty-eight. These preached the same Gospel, and ably advocated the same public cause, adorning it with their lives, and bequeathing to it their Testimony and the Memory of the Just.

> "Instead of thy fathers should be thy children."— Psalm xli. 16.

In Balmaghie church a memorial brass has been erected, bearing the following inscription:—

To the Glory of God
and in memory of
JOHN MACMILLAN, A.M.,

Born at Barncauchlaw, Minnigaff, 1669:
Ordained minister of the Parish of Balmaghie 1701:
Accepted the Pastorate of the United Societies 1706:
Which office he laboriously discharged for 47 years:
Died at Broomhill, Bothwell, 1753. Buried in
Dalserf Churchyard.

"A Covenanter of the Covenanters:
A Father of the Reformed Presbyterian Church:
A Faithful Minister of Jesus Christ."

This Tablet is placed here by his Great-great-grandson,
John Grieve, M.D., Glasgow, 1895.

CHAPTER XXXVIII.

THE STEWARTRY WAR COMMITTEE.

Names of Committee and of those who received their instructions
—Commissioners—Gold and silver plate surrendered for the
cause—List of those delivering up silver work with details—
Assessment ·imposed,· and crops valued—Valuers—Definition
of "cold covenanter"—Reports by members of Committee
of cold covenanters in their respective parishes.

WHEN the Covenanters found it necessary to resort to
arms, a War Committee was formed, and the chief
covenanting nobleman in each county was placed at
the head of his regiment with the title of "Crowner,"
and the principal gentry were appointed to act under
him. The Minute Book of the War Committee of the
Covenanters in the Stewartry in the year 1640-41 has
been published, and affords much interesting information. The records show that the following
gentlemen acted on the Committee or received their
instructions:—Sir Patrick M'Kie of Larg; John,
third Viscount Kenmure; Alexander Gordon of Earlston; John Macghie of Balmaghie; William Grierson
of Bargalton; Robert M'Clelland, first Lord Kirkcudbright; John Lennox elder of Cally, and Alexander
Lennox, his son; John Fullerton of Carelton; John
Gordon of Cardoness; Lord Galloway; John Mac-
knacht of Kilquhennatie; Robert Maxwell of Cavence;

Richard Muir of Cassincarrie (some of these received instructions to arrange about providing horses for the troops, with arms, etc.); John Cutlar of Orroland, John Reddick of Dalbeattie; William Gordon of Sherness; William Gordon of Kirkconnel; Thomas M'Clellane of Collyn; Lancelot Grier of Dalskearthe; George Glendonyng in Mochrum; David Arnot of Barcaple; William Glendonyng, late Provost of Kirkcudbright; Alexander Gordon of Knockgray; Alexander Gordon of Garlarge; Robert Gordon of Knockbrex; John Ewart, bailie of Kirkcudbright; William Lyndsay in Fairgirthe; Hew Maxwell in Mersheid; and Robert Gordon, brother germane to John Gordon of Caronnell. Commissioners were appointed to the different parishes on behalf of the Committee to recover payment for the soldiers and otherwise to carry out the Committee's instructions, and the following are the names of some of the commissioners:—Thomas Roney of Irongray, Commissioner for that parish; William Lindsay for Colvend and the Suddick; Robert Maxwell of Cavence for Lochrutton; John Stewart of Shambellie for New Abbey; John Charters of Barnecleuche for Terregles; John Brown for Troqueer; Hugh Maxwell in Torrorie for Kirkbean; David Cannon of Knocks for Buittle.

The Committee were charged with the raising of funds, and those who supported them had to lend what money they had, and when this was not sufficient they had to hand in whatever gold and silver plate and silver work they possessed, and among those who are entered as delivering up silver work, the weight and

details of which are given, are the following:—John
Lennox of Kellie; Robert Gordon of Knockbrex;
George Glendonyng, Mochrum ; Grissell Gordon, spouse
of Umqle, minister of Urr; Marione M'Clellane, wyff
of late James Ramsay (ordained to present her Bairnes
silver work, and that notwithstanding of any reasones
proponit in the contrair); Erlistoun; Alex. Gordon,
Carstraman; Kirkconnell; Dabtoun—Andro Chalmers
of Watersyde—John Charters of Barnacleuche; Robert
Gordon of Knockbrex, in name of Mrs. Gordon of
Robertoun; George Livingston of Quintenespie; John
Fullarton of Carletoun; William Grierson of Bargal-
toun; Lady Cardyness for her husband.

As a local writer remarks, great indeed must have
been the enthusiasm, and equally great the necessity,
that called for such sacrifice.

A regular assessment was also imposed, and crops
were formally valued to ascertain the proportion pay-
able by the owner to the War Fund.

Among those appointed as valuers of crops we find
the following:—John Martin in Newtoun; Gilbert
Rain in Bishopton; William Rain there; John Robeson; Robert Conquhar in Balgreddan; Donald Wilson
in Halkit, Leaths; John Maxwell in Guffogland;
Roger Morrisone in Cassillgour; Adam Wright in
Dundrennan; John Cultrain and James Malcolm
there; William Martin of Dullarg; William Gordon
in Crachie; Alexander M'Kill in Arnemabbock; and
Fergus Neilson in Glenlair; William Clinton in Carleton; John Shaw; John M'Dowall in Barholm; and
Thomas Robeson, Maltman, in Kirkcudbright.

This Committee carried out its operations in a thorough, business-like manner, and was undoubtedly the best organised in Scotland.

The following excerpt from one of the Minutes shows that they kept an eye on every person in the Stewartry:—

" The quhilk day, the Committee foirsaid finds and declares ane cold covenanter to be suche ane persone quha does not his dewtie in everie thing committed to his charge, thankfullie and willinglie, without compulsion for the furtherance of the publict.

" The quhilk day, Alexander Gordon of Knockgrey, Captain of the parochen of Carsfarne, declares ˉno cold or uncovenanters within that parochen.

" Alexander Gordon of Erlistone declares no cold or uncovenanters to be within the parochen of Dalry, whereof he is Captain, except Johne Newall.

" Alexander Gordon of Gairlarg, Captain of the parochen of Kelles, declares no cold or uncovenanters to be within the said parochen of Kelles.

" William Gordon of Shirmers, Captain of the parochen of Balmaclellan, declares no cold or uncovenanters within his parochen.

" George Glendonyng of Mochrum, Captain of the parochen of Partone, declares the lyke.

" George Livingstone, Captain of the parochen of Balmaghie, declares the lyke.

" William Gordon of Kirkconnell, Captain of
the parochess of Buittle, Corcemichael, and others,
declares no cold or uncovenanters within his
bounds except John Maxwell of Mylnetone,
William Maxwell of Midkeltone, Gilbert Maxwell of Slognaw, Mr. Patrik Adamsone, sum-
tyme Minister at Buittle, Mr. James Scott,
symtyme Minister at Tungland, George Tait,
Paul Reddik, Johne Browne of Mollance, Robert
Browne, his brother, Johne Maxwell of Colignaw,
James Maxwell of Brekansyde, Thomas M'Gill
of Keltone.

" William Lindsay, Captain of the paroches of
Colvend and Suthik, declares that no cold or non-
covenanters within these parochess, except James
Lindsay of Auchenskeoch; Andro Lindsay, his
sone, Robert Lindsay, his sone, Charles Lindsay,
his oy *; Johne Lindsay of Wachope; Charles
Lindsay, his uncle; Lancelot Lindsay, brother
naturall to Wachope; Johne Lindsay, his brother
naturall; Roger Lindsay of Maynes; Johne and
James Lindsayes, his sones; Charles Murray of
Barnhurrie; David Lindsay, sone to James Lindsay of Fairgirthe; Richard and William Herreiss,
brethren to Robert Herreis of Barnebaroche; and
the said Robert, late covenanter.

" Robert Maxwell of Cavens, Captain of the
parochen of Lochruttone, declares no cold or uncovenanters within his bounds except Edward

* Grandson.

Maxwell of Hills; William Maxwell, his sone;
Alexander Maxwell, his naturall sone; Lady
Auchenfranko; Richard Herreis, hir sone;
Edward Maxwell, callit of Carswada; Gudewyfe
of Hills; and John Welshe in Langwodheid.

"Johne Cutlar of Orroland, Captain of the
Parochen of Rerrik, declares no cold or un-
covenanters within his bounds except Robert Max-
well of Orchardtone; William Makclellane of
Airds; William Makclellane of Overlaw; Robert
Maxwell of Culnachtrie; Harie Lindsay of Ros-
carrell; John Makclellane of Gregorie; William
Makclellane of Meirfield.

"Lancelot Grier, Captain of the Parochen of
Troqueer, declares no cold or uncovenanters within
his bounds, except Johne Maxwell of Kirkconnell; Elizabeth Maxwell, his mother; Helene
Maxwell, Lady Mabie; John Herreis of Mabie,
hir sone.

"Captain of the Parochen of Newabbay declares no cold or uncovenanted within his bounds,
except James Maxwell of Littlebar.

"Captain of the Parochen of Kirkbeane declares the lyke, except Johne Sturgeon of
Torrerrie; Johne Sturgeon in Cowcorse.

"James Smithe, Captain of the Parochen of
Irongrey, declares no non-covenanters within his
bounds.

"Johne Reddik of Dalbeattie, Captain of the
Parochen of Urr, declares the lyke.

"Roger Maknacht of Killquhenatie, Captain of the Parochen of Kirkpatrick, declares the lyke.

"Johne Fullartone of Carletone declares the lyke.

"David Arnot of Barcaple declares the lyke.

"Richard Muir of Cassincarrie declares the lyke."

CHAPTER XXXIX.

ANDREW FORSYTH.

Blames his father for harbouring Covenanters—Meets Renwick—
Throws in his lot with the Covenanters—Father's opposition
—Leaves home—Adventures and escapes—Returns to Kirk-
cowan after the Revolution.

ANDREW FORSYTH, the Galloway drover, belonged to
the parish of Kirkcowan, where his father was a
farmer. Andrew had once regarded the non-conformists as fanatics and rebels, but he did not take
any part in persecuting or informing against them,
particularly as his father sympathised with the
Covenanters, and frequently afforded them shelter.
One day a conventicle had been dispersed in the neighbourhood of Newton Stewart, and the preacher and two
others sought safety in Andrew's father's house.
Andrew was out at the time, but when he returned he
was much displeased to find the fugitives there, and
blamed his father for receiving them and exposing
himself to persecution. His father replied that he
could not find it in his heart to put them away, adding
that he was sure they would make a favourable impression on him. Andrew scouted the idea of such a
thing, but agreed to meet them, and the demeanour of
the youngest arrested his attention. " His countenance
was fair, and suffused with a sweet placidity. His

24

voice was soft and plaintive. His conversation cheerful and full of heavenliness. No man could look on him without loving him." This was James Renwick, and after hearing him, Andrew became another man, and soon afterwards resolved to join the Covenanters.

On returning home from a conventicle, he informed his father of his resolution but, to his surprise, he met with the strongest opposition. His father by this time had become a suspected person through harbouring the intercommuned, and his laird had let him know that, unless he desisted, he would have to go. He, therefore, raised every objection to his son's proposal, but in vain. The laird had threatened to eject the father, and now the father threatened to eject the son. Andrew resolved to move to a distance, so that no injury might come to his father through him, and he got employment as a shepherd at Glenlee. He soon became prominent on the side of the Covenanters, and was in consequence sought after by the persecutors. On one occasion he was at Fingland when a party of dragoons came to his house in search of him, and as he was returning, he met them in the moor. Escape was impossible, so he assumed an air of indifference, and asked if they were in search of the drover. They replied that they were, and he then informed them that he had seen him a short time before at Fingland. They galloped off without further enquiry, and he at once sought a place of safety till they had left the neighbourhood. After this he formed a retreat in the heart of a great moss, to which he retired in time of danger.

He was ultimately taken by surprise in the farm house one night, and placed on horseback behind one of the troopers, his feet tied together below the horse's belly with a straw rope. The night was dark and the track extremely rough. With the violent motions of the horse in leaping the ditches, the rope broke and Andrew's feet were free. Immediately afterwards, the horse fell, and the two riders were thrown to the ground, but the darkness prevented the others, who were in advance, from seeing what had happened, and Andrew made good his escape. He then found a retreat near Fingland.

He attended a conventicle held by Mr. Renwick, and as it was dispersing, the troopers arrived on the scene. Andrew fled, but was fired at and wounded in the arm. He managed to escape, and found a hiding place in the moss. Shortly afterwards, a flock of sheep losing their way in the mist came near him, followed by two shepherds, to whom he made known his situation, and they gave him every assistance. He had several narrow escapes after this, and at the time of the Revolution he was hiding in the house of a shepherd named Ker, who was himself a Covenanter. When peace was restored, he returned to Kirkcowan, and lived there to an advanced age.

CHAPTER XL.

PATRICK LAING.

Patrick Laing—John Ferguson of Weewoodhead—John Clark—
Escape from Edinburgh prison—Samuel Clark—John Fraser
—John Clement — John Dempster — Retribution — David
M'Briar—Bailie Muirhead of Dumfries—M'Roy of Half Mark
—The Gordons of Largmore—Renwick in Galloway—His
adventures and escapes—M'Lurg shoots a spy and wields
the Galloway Flail—Kirkcudbright Burgh Records—Robert
M'Whae—The Kirkandrew Martyr—Alexander Linn—Craig-
moddie, Kirkcowan.

PATRICK LAING of Blagannoch, born 1641, enlisted in
the Scots Grey, but, although serving the King, his
sympathies were with the Covenanters. He was sent
with his company to arrest certain Covenanters who
had fled to the north of England. He was not successful, and it was whispered that the affair had been
mismanaged, and that he was to blame. He was
arrested, tried, and sentenced to banishment. Repre-
sentations were made on his behalf, and ultimately he
was liberated after much suffering. He retired to the
Glenkens, where he soon came under the notice of Lagg
through professing covenanting principles and not
attending the services of the curates. Many efforts
were made to apprehend him. Simpson narrates that
on one occasion he was returning home leading his
pony, with a load of meal across its back, when he

noticed a party of dragoons approaching. He at once dropped the meal, mounted the pony, and fled along the moor. The dragoons followed. Laing made for the foot of a precipice called Lorg Craig. It seemed impossible that any man could climb it, but he made the attempt and succeeded. When he reached the top he gave three loud cheers in mockery of his pursuers, for he knew that they durst not attempt to scale the dangerous height. He was declared an outlaw, and retired to the north of Scotland. He returned to the Glenkens, and died at Cleuchfoot at the age of eighty-five, and was buried in the old churchyard of Kirkconnell.

JOHN FERGUSON OF WEEWOODHEAD.

John Ferguson of Weewoodhead, in Carsphairn parish, was at Pentland, mounted on a Galloway pony. He fled, but the pony, wearied with the fatigue of the previous days, was not making such speed as a man fleeing for life would desire. A riderless horse belonging to the pursuers galloped up, and Ferguson at once mounted it, and made rapid progress, avoiding the direct road home. While his horse was drinking in the water of Clyde, he was surprised to find that his own pony, now able to go quicker from being free of a rider, galloped up to him, and thence followed him home.

On one occasion he was working at the hay in a meadow alongside the Lane of Carsphairn, when he noticed at some distance a company of troopers approaching. He at once plunged into a deep pool, and kept his head above the water among some bushes. The troopers searched, but were not successful in finding him.

JOHN CLARK—ESCAPE FROM EDINBURGH PRISON.

John Clark of Carsphairn is supposed to be the John Clark mentioned as a frequent companion of Peden. Once when the two were hiding in a cave in Galloway, and had had no food for some time, Peden said, " John, better be thrust through with.a sword than pine away with hunger. The earth and the fulness thereof belongs to my Master, and I have a right to as much of it as will keep me from fainting in His service. Go to such a house and tell them plainly that I have wanted food so long, and they will give it willingly." John did as requested, and the food was readily supplied.

Cannon of Mardrochat frequently lodged information against Clark. On one occasion, Clark and John Fraser of Upper Holm of Dalquhirn, were concealed in Straquhanah Cave, in the upper valley of the Ken, when word was taken to Lagg at Carsphairn, and he at once sent troopers to apprehend them. The approach of the dragoons was observed, and the two fled. They noticed a man mowing, and as the pursuers were at that moment out of sight, they hid themselves beneath the long rows of the new cut grass. The soldiers hurried through the fields, and pressed on in pursuit.

Clark, Fraser, and others were subsequently captured and sent to Edinburgh. There the jails were full, and Clark and others were accordingly imprisoned in the upper storey of a neighbouring house. The wife of one of them contrived to effect their escape. Having seen the place where they were kept, she bought a rope strong enough to sustain the weight of one man, and this she coiled as closely together as possible and placed it in the heart of a quantity of curds which she formed into an ordinary sized cheese. This she carried to Edinburgh, and had it conveyed to her husband. It was received with much thankfulness, and of course the rope was found and its purpose instantly understood. The prisoners watched their opportunity, and, fixing the rope, speedily descended to the street. The heaviest of the party came last, as it was feared the rope might break under his weight. This indeed happened, but those beneath broke his fall as well as they could by stretching out their arms to catch him, but he was so seriously injured that he was unable to walk. They carried him to a cottage and left him there, while they themselves fled to the south. He was unfortunately discovered, and it is said was executed the same day.

SAMUEL CLARK.

Samuel Clark of New Luce was one of Peden's flock, and often accompanied him in his wanderings among the wilds of Galloway. On one occasion, on the dispersion of a conventicle, when numbers of the worshippers were seized, Clark escaped and fled to a friend's house, where he resided for some time, but the soldiers found this out, and he was obliged to flee again. He ran in the direction of Cairnsmore, from the summit of which the greater part of Galloway can be seen. He was pursued by the troopers, and being out of their sight for a moment, he crept in among the heather to hide himself. The horsemen advanced, spreading themselves out that they might not miss him. The main body passed the spot without noticing him, but a single man, slower in his movements than the rest, happened to ride up to the spot where Clark lay. His eyes caught sight of his legs, but he merely touched him gently on the feet, saying, "Creep further in for your limbs are seen."

On another occasion, Clark had been at a meeting at Irlington when the troopers appeared and he was pursued. At length, wearied out with fatigue and want of food, he sat down beside a bush, and, taking off his bonnet, addressed the great Preserver of life in the following strain, "Oh Thou, who didst shield Thy servant Peden in the day of his distress when he called upon Thee, and didst throw over him and me, Thy unworthy follower, the misty covering which hid us from the face of our pursuers, hide me now in the hollow of Thine hand from my enemies who are hunting for my life." The soldiers came up, but they passed by the other side of the bush, and thus his prayer was answered.

Hearing that Mr. Peden was at Sorn, he longed to see him, and set out from his residence in the wilds of Galloway. As he approached his destination, he encountered a company of Claverhouse's troopers who seized him on suspicion as a rebel. They lodged during the night in the Kirk of Sorn, indicating that he would be executed next day. In the early hours of the morning he heard a great tumult outside the church, and the soldiers made off. He began to look round him, and, seeing no soldiers guarding the church, he stole out and fled with all speed. It appears that the soldiers had heard of a conventicle being held in the neighbourhood, and in their eagerness to get to it they had either forgotten their prisoner or thought he would be safe till they returned. Clark was often pursued among the hills, but he evaded his foes, hiding in the glens and caves of Upper Galloway. He survived the persecution. and died in peace in 1730.

JOHN FRASER.

John Fraser of Upper Holm of Dalquhirn in Carsphairn, and Cannon of Mardrochat, were in their early life friends and companions, and both were present at Pentland. Cannon, however, was bought over by the enemy, and embraced every opportunity to betray the hiding places of the Covenanters and to give information when any of them were at home. He was particularly zealous in seeking the ruin of his former friends, especially John Fraser and John Clark, because of their harbouring Richard Cameron. On one occasion when Fraser was surprised in his house by a company of dragoons, escape seemed impossible, but he ran into a small closet and got into bed. One of the inmates quickly heaped a quantity of wet peats on the fire, which in those days was in the middle of the kitchen, and immediately the place was filled with a dense blue smoke, so that it was impossible to see clearly anything in the apartment. The smoke penetrated to the closet and filled it. The dragoons searched as well as they could, and one of them found Fraser in the bed, but was not able to see him distinctly, and did not disclose his presence to the others.

Fraser experienced several other narrow escapes. On one occasion, when surprised in his own house, he took refuge in "the poor man's bed," reserved in those days in almost every house for the wandering poor. His wife covered him with tattered clothing and an old rug, and here he lay while the dragoons searched the house. Once he was seized at dinner and was bound firmly with ropes and cast into one of the stalls of the stable, while the dragoons returned to the house and helped themselves to whatever they could get, having locked the stable door and taken the key with them. They came upon a quantity of brown ale, which the houses of the farmers were plentifully supplied with from their own malt in those days. This the soldiers drank with right good will, and remained in the house eating and drinking and enjoying themselves all the afternoon. Fraser in the meantime had managed to creep into a dark corner of the stable.

At length the soldiers prepared to take their departure, and, staggering and reeling under the influence of the great quantity of drink they had consumed, they came into the stable for their horses. They led them outside, mounted, and rode off in a noisy and disorderly manner, quite oblivious to the fact that their prisoner was left behind. When they had gone some distance, Fraser's wife came and cut the cords that bound his hands, and he at once made off. The soldiers had not gone far on their way when they discovered their mistake, and returned with all speed, but by this time Fraser was nowhere to be seen, and after searching the house and stable, they had to leave without him.

JOHN CLEMENT.

John Clement, although a native of Barr, lived most of his years in the neighbourhood of New Galloway. A conventicle at Fingland, Carsphairn, which he was attending was dispersed by the troopers who pursued him. He fled along the Water of Ken till he came to a small sheep fold with a plaid across it to keep in a lamb, and being for the moment out of sight of his pursuers, he threw the plaid across his shoulders, and, catching a ewe by the horns, was in the act of putting the lamb to suck as the horsemen galloped up. They asked him if he had seen a man fleeing past. He answered that he had not, but advised them to ride to Holm Glen as a likely place for a fugitive, and they at once made off in that direction.

On another occasion, when returning from a conventicle in Carsphairn, he was hotly pursued. When out of sight of the pursuers for a moment, he saw a dead sheep, and instantly doffing his coat, he seized it by the legs, threw it across his shoulders, and then leisurely advanced towards the dragoons as if unaware of their presence. They had not the slightest suspicion that he was the person they were seeking, and asked him if he had seen a man crossing the moor. "I did," he replied, "but he made a short turn in the hollow there, and has taken a different road." He advised them to ride in the direction of Minnigaff, and this they at once did. He survived the persecution, and lived to an old and honoured age in the neighbourhood of New Galloway.

JOHN DEMPSTER.

John Dempster, the tailor of Garrieyard, in Dalry, fought at Bothwell Bridge, and was ever afterwards a marked man. Early one morning, he saw a band of dragoons approach his house, and he at once made off, the dragoons firing at him and then following as fast as they could. He fled in the direction of Earndarroch Wood, about half a mile from his house. A moss lay between his house and it, and while Dempster was able to make his way across, the dragoons soon found their horses sinking into the soft ground, and unable to proceed. One horseman, however, rode round, and reached Dempster as he was scrambling over a dyke into a wood. Dempster was without any weapon, but he had his scissors in his pocket, and quickly drawing these out, he drove the sharp points into the horse's forehead, and it suddenly reared back, throwing its rider, and thus Dempster was able to escape into the wood, and he speedily crossed a ravine and found a hiding place on the other side before his pursuers were in sight. Some time after this, Dempster learned that his place of retreat had been revealed to the enemy, and he accordingly found refuge in a cave above New Galloway. While there, he learned that the dragoons had been informed that he was somewhere in the neighbourhood, and that an organised search was to be made. He at once left the cave along with a friend who was in hiding with him, and just as they did so they observed the dragoons approaching, guided by the informer. The two at once made off in the direction of Loch Ken, and after running for some distance, they wheeled towards Balmaclellan. As they were about to ascend an eminence that leads to the village, they noticed that they were out of the enemies' view, and seizing the opportunity, they turned to a linn in Garpel Glen, and found safety in a cave there. The troopers, on reaching Balmaclellan, searched every house, but, of course, in vain. On another occasion Dempster was met in the evening by Lagg's men on Knockgray Hill, and at once took to flight followed by the dragoons. The falling darkness, however, was much to his advantage, and he had no difficulty in making good his escape for the time. Unfortunately, he remained all night on Craighit, which was in full view of Garriehorn, where Lagg lay with his troopers. In the morning Lagg was searching the hill with his telescope, and saw Dempster hiding behind a rock. He at once divided his men so as to surround the hill, and Dempster, noticing his intention, instantly set off. He crossed the Garrie burn, hurried on towards Bowhill, with the intention of getting to Loch Doon, but when he reached Bowhill, he realised that escape seemed impossible. He reached Muill Hill, but here the dragoons closed in on him, and shot him on the spot.

RETRIBUTION.

About the year 1668, David M'Briar, heritor in Irongrey, who had accused his minister, John Welsh, of preaching treason, became a violent persecutor. Soon afterwards, he found himself in financial difficulties, so he lived in concealment amongst his tenants lest he should be imprisoned for debt. He was met by John Gordon, a north country merchant, agent of a curate who had come from the north to Galloway. Gordon, observing M'Briar's suspicious movements, concluded that he was one of the outlawed Covenanters, and requested him to go as a suspected person with him to Dumfries. This the other, dreading imprisonment for his debts, refused to do, and Gordon drew his sword to compel him. In the struggle M'Briar was killed. Gordon boasted that he had killed a whig, but, when the people saw the body, they told him he had killed a man as loyal as himself. He was seized, carried to Dumfries, and immediately executed.

BAILIE MUIRHEAD OF DUMFRIES.

Some of the Covenanters found a retreat in the neighbourhood of Carbelly Hill, on the west side of the Nith opposite Dumfries. James Muirhead, bailie of Dumfries, after many narrow escapes in other places, sought shelter here in 1684, but was discovered and was taken with about eighy others * to Moffat

---

* William M'Millan of Caldow was one of this company.

Kirk, where they lay all night wet and cold.. The next day—Sunday—they were removed to Peebles, and had to wade the water in spate. The following day, they were carried to Leith Tolbooth, where they were thronged so closely that they could scarcely stand. Here Muirhead took ill, no doctor was allowed to see him, and he died, as much a martyr as those who received their death violently by the hands of the persecutors.

M'ROY OF HALF MARK.

M'Roy of Half Mark, in the parish of Carsphairn, was one Sabbath morning sitting in one of his fields studying the Word of God when Lagg and his troopers came upon him before he was aware. Lagg demanded what he was reading. M'Roy replied, "The Bible." Lagg exclaimed that his cattle must find another herd, and immediately shot him dead.

THE GORDONS OF LARGMORE.

John Gordon of Largmore, in the parish of Kells, received several wounds at Pentland. He managed to reach home, but so exhausted that his life was despaired of. Sir William Bannatyne received information that he was at home, and at once ordered him to be brought to him dead or alive. The soldiers took a cart with them, knowing he would not be able to ride or walk. He was told he must go with them. Raising himself a little in his bed, he answered that he now defied Sir William and all his persecutors, but he forgave them, and then he added that he would soon be in better company. He lay down again, and in a few minutes died. His son, Roger Gordon, and some friends were at Bothwell, and fled south, travelling by night and hiding by day. Suddenly they met a company of troopers sent out to disperse a conventicle at Craggy Mains. Taking to flight, a heavy mist hampered the troopers following them, and they reached Knockalloch on Craigdarroch Water, where they were heartily welcomed. As they were about to retire for the night, the sound of horsemen was heard, and the house was immediately surrounded. The dairy at Knockalloch was a small apartment toward the back of the house, and beneath this was a cellar, the entrance to which was through a small trap door in the floor. When the dragoons rode up, the mistress of the house hastened to show the fugitives this place of concealment, while her husband met the soldiers at the door. The latter made a thorough search, entering even the dairy, but never thought that there was another apartment under their feet.

On another occasion, when Roger Gordon with his wife and some others were proceeding to a conventicle in the wilds of Minnigaff, they met a company of soldiers on foot, and a struggle at once began. The Covenanters had neither swords nor fire-arms, but they made good use of the sticks and clubs they had. Roger Gordon, who was a big strong man, assailed the leader, and a fierce fight ensued, so that the others on both sides stood to watch it. At length Gordon, having broken the sword of his opponent with his club, struck him a severe blow on the arm, which fell powerless by his side. Gordon then seized him and flung him with such force to the ground that he was quite stunned. The troopers went to render what assistance they could to their chief, and allowed the Covenanters to go. After this, Gordon was more severely persecuted. On one occasion, a party of dragoons drove up to the door. He speedily doffed part of his apparel and arrayed himself in the coarser and more tattered clothes of a servant, and went to meet the soldiers. He held their horses while they dismounted, and then led them to the stable, the soldiers in the dark supposing that he was a servant. He took the first opportunity to slip away to a solitary retreat in the Galloway mountains.

On another occasion, Gordon when pursued sought refuge in a cave in a deep ravine. The edges of the ravine seemed even at a short distance to come together and make a uniform surface, and it was not till the traveller was almost on the very brink of the descent that he would suspect that there was any opening. One of the dragoons, more eager than the others, came spurring on in his headlong career, eager to catch sight of Gordon, and not till it was too late did he notice the yawning gully in front. In vain he tried to pull up his charger. Horse and rider went crashing over, right past where Gordon was concealed, and were dashed to pieces in the rocky stream below.

Gordon survived the persecution, and enjoyed many happy days of peace and prosperity. He presented Kells Church with a bell in 1714, and also a pair of communion cups.

In Kells churchyard may be seen a stone with the following inscription:—

> Here lyes the corps of Ro
> ger Gordon of Largmore
> who dyed March 2nd 1662
> aged 72 years and of John
> Gordon of Largmore his
> grandchild who dyed Jan
> uary 6, 1667 of his wounds
> got at Pentland in Defence
> of the covenanted Refor
> mation.

The rest of the inscription refers to other members of the family. The stone also shows the Gordon motto, "Dread God," and three boars' heads.

William Gordon of Roberton, in Borgue, who was connected with the above by marriage, was also a zealous Covenanter, and in 1640 presented the War Committee of the Stewartry with "sex silver spoones and uther work, weght, IX unce, ane drope." He was killed at Pentland, and his family suffered severely.

RENWICK IN GALLOWAY—ADVENTURES AND ESCAPES.

Renwick held many conventicles in Galloway. Simpson tells the following story regarding him. He was at a conventicle in the mountainous district, some distance from Newton Stewart. Information was sent to the nearest party of dragoons, and they at once set off in the hope of surprising the meeting and seizing

Renwick. The latter, however, was warned and fled. Arriving in the evening at Newton Stewart, he found lodging in the Inn. The leader of the dragoons, after a tedious and fruitless search, also reached Newton Stewart, and went to the Inn for the night. It was winter, and the commander, feeling lonely, asked the landlord if he could introduce him to anyone with whom he could spend the evening. The landlord told Mr.. Renwick, and he agreed to spend a few hours in the company of the trooper. The evening passed agreeably, and they parted with many expressions of goodwill on the part of the officer, who retired to rest with the intention of resuming his search in the morning. Some hours later, when all was quiet in the Inn, Renwick took leave of the landlord and went off to seek some secluded retreat. When morning came, the commander asked for the intelligent stranger who had afforded him so much gratification. The landlord informed him that he had left hours before to seek a hiding place among the hills. " A hiding place!" exclaimed the soldier. " Yes, a hiding place," replied the Innkeeper. " This gentle and inoffensive youth is no other than the James Renwick you have been pursuing." " James Renwick! impossible! If he is James Renwick, I for one will pursue him no longer."

On another occasion, Renwick agreed to hold a conventicle among the hills near Balmaclellan. Information was given with all possible secrecy, and on the day appointed a huge assembly gathered from all parts. The morning was lowering, and heavy showers were falling on the distant heights. Notwithstanding the care with which information had been communicated, the enemy learned of the meeting and came upon the conventicle just as worship was beginning. The people at once fled in all directions. Renwick, accompanied by John M'Millan and David Ferguson, fled towards the Ken, hoping to escape to the house of a friend in the parish of Penninghame. They intended to ford the stream above Dalry village, but before doing so engaged in prayer among the thick bushes that grew on its margin. When they rose from their knees they observed, to their amazement, a party of dragoons landing on the opposite bank. They had reached the place in pursuit while the three were engaged in prayer, and, without noticing them or hearing their voices, they had rushed into the water, which was fast rising, and crossed to the other side. John M'Millan, who used to tell the story, said that he was never so much impressed as by the remarks made by Renwick on that occasion. His two friends resolved to see him safely to the other side. The current was becoming more powerful every moment. They provided themselves with long branches of the mountain ash, which were grasped by the three at equal distances, so that if one should be carried off his feet by the water, the others standing firm might accomplish his rescue. In this way Renwick reached the other side in safety, but no sooner had he crossed than the flood descended with great violence, covering the banks on both sides and sweeping every obstacle before it. Renwick afterwards got shelter in the cottage of James M'Culloch, whose wife was a firm supporter of the Covenanters. While he slept, she took his clothes away to dry them, but in the morning they were not sufficiently dried, and she brought some of her husband's, which Renwick put on. In the morning he threw a shepherd's plaid over his shoulders and ascended a gentle eminence near the house. From this he noticed a company of dragoons approaching. He expected to be instantly seized. The troopers rode up to him, and, not recognising him in the strange clothes, asked if he was the master of the cottage. He replied that he was not, but informed them where he was to be found. After some further conversation about rebels and fugitives, they concluded there would be none on their side of the river as the stream had been so greatly swollen since the dispersion of the conventicle, and accordingly they departed without further enquiry. John M'Millan and David Ferguson, after they parted from Renwick, were met by a company of horsemen. David Ferguson concealed himself near the water's edge, and John M'Millan retreated to a thicket. The soldiers, observing the latter, pursued him, but he escaped. Ferguson, however, was never heard of again, but it was supposed that he must have been drowned by the rising stream.

When Renwick was addressing a conventicle at Irlington during the night, a dog bounded several times round the assembly, and then darted in among the crowd. The preacher expressed his fear of approaching danger, as the dog seemed to have come from a distance, and not to be known to anyone there. Suddenly the watchman gave warning of the approaching enemy. In an instant the company dispersed. John Paterson of Penyvenie, David Halliday, John Bell, Robert Lennox, Andrew M'Roberts, and James M'Clymont took refuge in the barn of Irlington, and hid themselves in a quantity of wool piled up in a corner of the building, and thus escaped detection.

M'LURG SHOOTS A SPY, AND WIELDS THE GALLOWAY FLAIL.

The Sanquhar Declaration of 1685 was supported by the Covenanters of Galloway. As a company of the Galloway men proceeded along the Ken to meet Mr. Renwick at Sanquhar, they were informed that a spy named Grier was dogging their footsteps. This man had formerly been one of the Covenanters, and was therefore well acquainted with them and their hiding places. One of the Covenanters, named M'Lurg, was going along the west side of the Ken, not having yet joined the others, and observing a spy lurking about and following, he hid himself behind a rock. As the spy passed the hiding place full in view, M'Lurg discovered that he was an old acquaintance who had deserted and turned their greatest enemy. He had been the cause of much anxiety and distress to the non-conformists, and was at that very moment tracing their steps to do them mischief. M'Lurg thought this a fitting opportunity to avenge the wrongs this man had done, and he immediately lifted his gun and fired, and Grier fell dead. M'Lurg then stripped him of his armour, which was of great account in those days. He had a Galloway flail, which was a formidable weapon when wielded by a strong arm. The handle was of tough ash, about five feet in length, the soople or part which strikes the barn floor was of iron, about three feet long, and had three joints. Thus, when it was vigorously applied, it doubled over the body of a man like a thong, and crushed the ribs after the manner of a boa-constrictor. M'Lurg crossed the stream and joined the others, and shortly afterwards a company of Lagg's men emerged suddenly from a glen, and a struggle between the two parties at once began. M'Lurg with the flail fiercely attacked the leader of the dragoons, who received a fracture of the skull and a broken arm. Then M'Lurg turned on the rest of the soldiers in the same furious manner, and they soon took to flight, leaving the Covenanters to pursue their way to Sanquhar.

Similar traditions are related of James M'Michael of Carsephairn fame, and J. S. M'Culloch, in his poem on "The Galloway Flail," has the following verse:—

" Our Covenant Fathers got haud o' the Flail,
    At the ire o' M'Michael his enemies quail,
    When through turncoats an' troopers, heid, helmet an' mail,
    Crashed the terrible Galloway Flail."

KIRKCUDBRIGHT BURGH RECORDS.

The Burgh Records of Kirkcudbright bear frequent reference to the troublous times then prevailing. Under date 7th September, 1643, the Bailies and Council elected William Glendonyng their Provost to be Captain; John Carson, Bailie, to be Lieutenant; Patrick Carson, ensign; George Callander, Robert

Hughan, John Clark, and George Meik to be sergeants. Then under date 4th April, 1644, we have this entry, " The quhilk day, John Ewart and John Carson, Bailies, and George Meik, merchant, has undertaken to furnish the town sufficiently in arms, to wit:—in musket, pike, sword, match, powder, and ball, and shall bring the same to the said town betwixt and the —— day of May next to come." Under date 26th September, 1644, it is statuted and ordained that John Clark, merchant, "shall go to Edinburgh and buy for the town's use the ammunition following, namely:—3 cwt. of powder, 300 lbs of ball, and 6 cwt. of match, and that he goes away upon Monday next." Under date 29th May, 1645, we have the following:—" The quhilk day, the Provost, Bailies, and Council, taking to their consideration the great danger may befall the town in their dangerous and troublous times through not keeping of a strict watch, have for preventing thereof statuted and ordained it that there be ten persons upon the watch ilk four and twenty hours," and details are then given as to how the watch is to be kept. On 9th October, 1650, the Provost, Bailies, and Council " took a list of arms and nominated the haill fencible persons to be in readiness on advertisement," and this was done in respect of the approaching of the Englishmen to this kingdom.

THE KIRKANDREWS MARTYR.

The martyrdom of Robert M'Whae of Kirkandrews is one of the few to which no reference whatever will be found in Wodrow. In the old parish churchyard a stone has been erected to his memory, bearing the following inscription:—

> HERE LYES
> ROBERT M'WHAE
> WHO WAS BARBAROUSLY
> SHOT TO DEATH BY
> CAPTANE DOUGLAS IN
> THIS PAROCH FOR HIS
> ADHERENCE TO SCOTLANDS
> REFORMATION COVENANTS
> NATIONAL AND SOLEMN
> LEAGUE 1685.

On other side:—

> ERECTED BY THE INHABITANTS
> OF THIS PARISH 1855

This stone is a facsimile of an older one which had fallen down and been broken. It is about three feet high by two feet six inches in breadth. The inscription is given in the appendix of the first edition of *The Cloud of Witnesses*. Tradition tells that M'Whae failed to attend to take the abjuration oath, and had to flee to the hills and moors for safety. He managed to escape detection for some months, but, venturing home, he was surprised in his own house at Kirkandrews by Colonel James Douglas and a troop of dragoons. He fled through a window into the garden, but was seen by the dragoons, and shot dead. He was buried in the Kirkandrews churchyard. A window is pointed out in one of the old cottages from which, it is said, M'Whae was trying to escape when shot.

In *The Laird of Lagg* there is a story of a martyrdom which probably refers to Mowat, a tailor, of whom little is known, except that he was shot by Captain Douglas between Fleet and Dee.

It is narrated that "a party o' Grier o' Lag's dragoons" met a tailor in the parish of Borgue, which now includes the old parish of Kirkandrews. He had no weapon but his needles and ellwand; but he was closely searched. In those days the tailor made the clothes of both male and female, and acted as mantua-maker to the ladies, whose dresses, to be in the fashion, had pieces of lead at certain parts to make them hang right. The tailor was found to have his pockets stored with such pieces of lead, and was instantly charged with the intention of casting bullets. It was in vain that he tried to explain the demands of fashion. They would not hear him, and the proceedings were very short.

CRAIGMODDIE, KIRKCOWAN.

Craigmoddie is in the upland district of Kirkcowan, in Wigtownshire, some ten miles from Kirkcowan village, and is about as lonely and secluded a spot as could well be imagined. Here may be seen a stone erected to the memory of a Covenanter who was discovered hiding in the moor and shot down on the spot. Tradition tells that Alexander Linn was a shepherd and belonged to Lairis, New Luce. Doubtless he was one of Peden's parishioners. General Drummond's soldiers were crossing from Colmonell to Glenluce, and had reached Craigmoddie when some of the soldiers noticed the peesweeps gyrating and always sweeping down at one particular spot. This let the soldiers know that there was something there. Hurrying forward, they found Linn trying to conceal himself, and without ceremony shot him down. In 1827, a stone was erected over the lonely grave, to take the place of an older one which had become damaged and broken. It is a small erect stone, about three feet high and about two feet across. The original inscription has been preserved. It is:—

HERE LYES
THE BODY OF ALEX-
-ANDER LIN, WHO WAS
SURPRISED AND INSTAN-
-TLY SHOT TO DEATH
ON THIS PLACE BY
LIEUTENANT GENERAL
DRUMMOND FOR HIS
ADHERENCE TO SCOT-
LAND'S REFORMATION
COVENANTS NATION-
-AL AND SOLEMN LEAGUE
1685.

A curious tradition has been handed down in connection with the tombstone. A man engaged by the farmer to mow was passing the grave, and it occurred to him that as he had no stone with which to sharpen his scythe, a part of the gravestone was just the thing he wanted. He accordingly broke off a piece, but the farmer asked where he got it. He replied, "Oh, I just took it off Sandy Linn's headstone." "If that is the way," replied the farmer, "you have got your scythe stone, you will mow no hay for me. You can go home as you came." The man saw that the farmer meant what he said, and that he was greatly displeased at what he had done. He had, therefore, no alternative but to tramp away home. On the way, he was climbing a dyke and fell, and seriously injured one of his legs, so that he mowed no hay that year.

CHAPTER XLI.

IRONGRAY COMMUNION.

Awe inspiring circumstances—Difficulties—John Welsh asked to carry it through—John Blackadder to take part—Preliminary services at Micklewood—Congregation of 3,000 to 6,000—Natural surroundings—Sentinels posted—The memorials of the communion—Samuel Arnot preached in the morning—Welsh preached "the action sermon," and Blackadder and John Dickson of Rutherglen took part—Blackadder's simple and impressive eloquence—"The enemy are coming, make ready for the attack"—The Clydesdale men form in battle array—The men of Galloway and Nithsdale follow their example—Rumours that the enemy are about, but no trace of them can be got—The assembly disperses, guarded to different points by horse and foot—Torrential rainfall—Huge conventicle next day with horse and foot on guard—Monument and inscription—Communion cups amissing—The Old Jail at Scaur and its tradition—Escape of Welsh of Scaur—Similar story about John Clark of Drumcloyer—The Rev. John Blackadder, minister of Troqueer, 1652—Expelled by Drunken Act, 1662—Preaches in the fields—Goes to Holland, 1680—Returns 1681—Arrested and sent to Bass Rock—Dies there, 1685—Buried in North Berwick churchyard—Tombstone and inscription—Tablet in Troqueer Church with inscription.

SURELY never was Communion observed under more awe inspiring circumstances than that at Irongray in 1678. It was the outcome of an intense desire on the part of the Covenanters to meet once more with their outed ministers to celebrate the Lord's Supper. There were difficulties in the way, almost insuperable, for the troops of the enemy were scouring the district, eager for blood, and any gathering on a large scale was sure to attract attention, yet it was resolved to proceed with the arrangements, and John Welsh, the outed minister of Irongray, was asked to carry it through. John Blackadder, the outed minister of Troqueer, was invited to take part, and he rode all the way from Culross in Fifeshire where he was when he received the invitation. The preliminary services were held on a Saturday at Meiklewood, about seven miles from Dumfries. Blackadder preached from First Corinthians, xi., 24:—" This do in remembrance of me," showing that the ceremony was not left arbitrarily to the Church, but was a divine command still in force, notwithstanding the laws of man against it. Welsh preached in the afternoon, and intimated the Communion to take place next day.

Early on Sabbath morning, the people gathered at Bishop's Forest of Irongray, their numbers estimated at from 3,000 to 6,000 people. The difference in the estimates may arise from some taking the number who actually took part in the Communion, and others the number who were present, whether taking part or not. The place was peculiarly adapted by nature for such a gathering, for, except to the south, it was surrounded by high hills, from the summits of which the surrounding country could be seen for a good distance. Sentinels, indeed, were posted on Cornlea, on Forest, and other points to give warning should the enemy be seen.

The memorials of the Communion, in the sacramental tables, remain to this day, and are the only specimens of the kind to be found in Scotland. It is said that long ago some of the stones were removed, but for very many years they have not been interfered with, and are regarded with the greatest reverence all through the district. They consist of four parallel rows of large, flat, oblong whinstones, each row some twenty yards in length, and containing some thirty seats. Between each two rows there is a large stone here and there, believed to have been a support for a plank on which the emblematic bread and wine may have been passed along, and at the south end there is a circular heap of stones a few feet high where the bread and wine were laid, and beside which the officiating ministers stood.

Samuel Arnot, the persecuted minister of Tongland, preached in the morning, and John Welsh then preached "the action sermon," dwelling on the sufferings of Christ and the glory that should follow. Blackadder took part in the services, and also the Rev. John Dickson of Rutherglen.

The day had been dull and overcast, threatening rain from morning, but not a drop fell during the protracted services. They were near a close, and Blackadder, in a last earnest appeal, was holding his audience spellbound by his simple but impressive eloquence. The thoughts of his hearers were lifted from this world to the glories of the life everlasting. All was hushed but the voice of the preacher. He had paused after a powerful exhortation, and ere he could resume, there burst across the gathering, like a clarion call, the warning from the sentinels, "The enemy are coming, make ready for the attack." There was no panic, no confusion, no fear even, except for the women and children. These men were made of sterner stuff, and were prepared for victory or death. The Clydesdale men at once took to horse and formed in battle array. The men of Galloway and Nithsdale did not at first take up any position, intending to wait till they saw imminent danger, and believing that the enemy were some distance away, but they followed the example of the Clydesdale men. Alexander Gordon of Earlston, who had served as a captain in the Civil War, drew up a large body of Galloway horse, and Nithsdale's leader also drew up his men. There they waited, expectant, grim, and determined, ready for any emergency. Had an attack been made that day, a greater Drumclog would have been added to the history of Scotland. The cause of the alarm proved to be that the Earl of Nithsdale—a keen Roman Catholic—and Sir Robert Dalziel of Glenae, a great enemy of these gatherings, had sent some servants to see what was being done, and these from their numbers had been taken for the advance of the enemy. Blackadder resumed and finished his discourse, while careful guard was kept against surprise. The soldiers sent out on horseback to enquire returned with the information that there was a rumour that the enemy were about, but they could not discover where. The assembly remained in defensive posture for some time, and then dispersed, guarded to different points by horse and foot. As they parted, the rain began to fall in torrents and continued for hours, to the great discomfort of the people, for soon the streams were overflowing their banks, making travelling difficult and dangerous, for there were no bridges in the neighbourhood.

Nothwithstanding this, the next day there was another conventicle at the head of the parish, some four miles from the Sabbath meeting, and the numbers attending were little less than those of the previous day. The horse and foot as usual drew round about the congregation, the horse being on the outside. Blackadder closed the day by a discourse from Hebrews xiii. 1 :—" Let brotherly love continue."

Near the Communion stones a beautiful granite monument has been erected, surmounted by a Communion Cup. The inscription on the monument is as follows:—

ERECTED

By Voluntary Subscription in 1870,

To Mark the Spot

Where a large number of Covenanters met in the summer of 1678 to Worship God, and where about 3000 Communicants on that occasion celebrated the Sacrament of THE LORD'S SUPPER. The following ejected Ministers officiated :—John Welsh of Irongray, John Blackadder of Troqueer, John Dickson of Rutherglen, and Samuel Arnot of Tongland—the adjacent Stones being used as the Communion Table. These Stones are significant memorials of those troublous times, in which our Fathers, at the peril of their lives, contended for the great principles of civil and religious freedom.

The last sentence of the inscription greatly dissatisfied many of the subscribers, who complained that it did not set forth explicitly the principles for which the Covenanters contended even to death.

There is a tradition that the Communion Cups which originally belonged to the Church were used at this Communion, and that in the dispersion they were hid somewhere in the neighbourhood and were lost. In the Kirk Session Record, dated July 4th, 1697, there is this reference to them:—" The cups, table cloths, and other utensils belonging to the Church, being amissing, and there being need of them because of the sacrament of the Lord's Supper which shortly is to be administered, it is laid upon every Elder to lay out themselves as much as they can in making inquiry after them to see if they can be found." The Elders gave in their report at the next meeting, July 11th, 1697, when it is recorded, "Several members of this judicatory having made search after the utensils of the Church, can hear nothing anent them, only that they were carried away with Mr. John Welsh his plenishing."

At the farmhouse of Scaur near by may be seen a small building called the Old Jail. Its walls are at least three feet thick, the roof is of stone and arched, and there is but one window, very small and high up from the floor. Tradition relates that here a pious Covenanter was imprisoned and starved to death. Another tradition tells that the farmer—Mr. Welsh—who was greatly persecuted for non-conformity, had a wonderful escape from capture. He was in the field with one of his servants named M'Lauchrie, who was ploughing, when soldiers were seen rapidly advancing. There was little doubt they were searching for Welsh. What was to be done? Escape indeed seemed impossible, but M'Lauchrie unyoked his horses, bade his master ride fearlessly home with them, as if he were the servant, while M'Lauchrie took to the hills in full view of the soldiers. The latter at once gave chase, but M'Lauchrie knew the country too well to be captured even by horsemen. A mist enveloped him and he not only saved his master's life but escaped himself. Mr. Welsh repaid him with a favourable lease of the farm of Glenkill, which belonged to him.

A somewhat similar anecdote is related by Simpson regarding John Clark of Drumcloyer, in Irongray parish. He was frequently sought for by the soldiers. One day, when at home, he saw dragoons approaching, and at once fled, but was noticed and pursued. He entered a field where a servant was ploughing and, being for the moment out of sight of the dragoons, he was induced to hold the plough while the ploughman continued the flight. When the dragoons came in sight, they never thought but the man they saw fleeing was Clark, and followed as fast as they could. There was a cave in the rocks underneath the bridge that crosses the Scaur. When the stream was in flood, there was no access to the cave except by seizing the branch of a tree and swinging oneself down into it. Even then the effort was full of danger. The ploughman, however, knew the cave, and was soon safely within it. The troopers speedily approached, and he could hear the feet of the horses as they passed along the bridge in the belief that he was in front. After going a short distance, the dragoons were satisfied that he could not be in front, and returned to the thicket about the bridge and began to search it, now and again firing a shot at random into the trees. He, however, felt quite safe. They could not discover the cave unless they knew it before, and even if they did only one could attempt to enter it at a time, and he could push them one by one into the roaring flood beneath, for in his position one man could master any number. The soldiers wearied themselves out with their fruitless efforts, and the man left the cave at his own convenience.

The Rev. John Blackadder belonged to the more moderate section of the Covenanters, yet he was one of the most zealous preachers of these trying times. It is said that he belonged to the family of Blackader of Tullialan, and that he was entitled to the rank of Baronet. He received his education in Glasgow University, of which the Principal, the Rev. Dr. Strang, was his uncle. He was ordained minister of Troqueer in the Stewartry in 1652, and continued there till expelled by the Drunken Act of 1662. Thereafter for nearly twenty years he preached in houses and fields, as opportunity offered, and took a chief part in many of the great Communions of these times. He was not present at any of the encounters with the Royal forces, and did not accept the position taken up by Cameron in the Sanquhar Declaration. He went to Holland in 1680, but returned in 1681, and was arrested in his house in Edinburgh. He was sentenced to imprisonment on the Bass Rock, but, his health failing, efforts were made for his release, and authority had actually been granted for his return, but before it could be given effect to, he died on the Bass in 1685. He was buried in North Berwick churchyard, where a large flat stone resting on short pillars has been placed over his grave. It bears the following inscription:—

Here lies the body of Mr. John Blackader, minister of the Gospel at Troqueer, in Galloway, who died on the Bass, after five years' imprisonment, anno Dom., 1685, and of his age sixty-three years.

" Blest John, for Jesus' sake, in Patmos bound,
His prison Bethel, Patmos Pisgah found ;
So the blest John on yonder rock confin'd,
His body suffered, but no chain could bind
His heav'n-aspiring soul : while day by day,
As from mount Pisgah top he did survey
The promised Land, and view'd the crown by faith
Laid up for those who faithful are till death :
Grace form'd him in the Christian hero's mould,
Meek in his own concerns, in's Master's bold,
Passions to reason chain'd, prudence did lead,
Zeal warm'd his breast, and reason cool'd his head.
Five years on the bare rock, yet sweet abode,
He Enoch like enjoy'd, and walk'd with God,
Till, by long living on this heavenly food,
His soul by love grew up, too great, too good,
To be confin'd in jail, or flesh, and blood ;
Death broke his fetters, off then swift he fled
From sin and sorrow, and by angels led,
Entered the mansions of eternal joy.
Blest soul ! thy warfare's o'er ; praise, love, enjoy.
His dust here rests till Jesus come again,
Ev'n so, bless'd Jesus ! come, come, Lord ! Amen."

Some years ago a mural brass tablet was placed in Troqueer Church, bearing the following inscription:—

To the Glory of God and in memory of
THE REV. JOHN BLACKADER
Born 1615.
Ordained minister of the Parish of Troqueer 1653.
Extruded 1662. Outlawed for preaching in the fields 1674.
Imprisoned on the Bass Rock 1681.
Died after cruel confinement 1685.
" Faithful unto Death."
Erected A.D. 1902.

CHAPTER XLII.

GLENTROOL MARTYRS.

Tombstone at Caldons Wood and inscription—The first erected by Old Mortality—James and Robert Dun, Thomas and John Stevenson, James M'Clive, and Andrew M'Call—Tradition of their martyrdom—Captain Urquhart's dream and death—Letter from privy council—A romantic story—Narrow escape —The Duns of Benwhat.

GLENTROOL is in the heart of Raiderland, and within recent years has from the beauty of its surroundings become well known to all visitors to Galloway. One of the weekly excursion drives from Newton Stewart has Glentrool as its destination, and apart from that it is a place of frequent pilgrimage. At the Caldons Wood a monument has been erected to the memory of six Covenanters slain here in 1685.

As Sir Walter Scott tells us in the introduction to *Old Mortality*, there is a small monumental stone on the farm of Caldons, near the House of the Hill in Wigtownshire,* which is highly venerated as the first erected by Old Mortality, to the memory of several persons who fell at that place in defence of their religious tenets in the Civil War in the reign of Charles II. The stone stands in a walled enclosure,

* It is, however, on the Stewartry side of the Cree.

and is about two and a half feet high by two feet in breadth. The inscription is as follows:—

                HERE LYES
            JAMES AND ROBERT
            DUNS, THOMAS AND
            JOHN STEVENSONS,
            JAMES McCLIVE
            ANDREU McCALL WHO
            WERE SURPRISED
            AT PRAYER IN THIS
            HOUSE BY COLONELL
            DOUGLAS LIEVTENANT
            LIVINGSTON AND

Other side:—

                CORNET
            JAMES DOUGLAS, AND
            BY THEM MOST IMPIOVS
            LY AND CRUELLY
            MURTHER'D FOR THEIR
            ADHERENCE TO SCOT-
            -LAND'S REFORMATION
            COVENANTS NATIONAL
            AND SOLEMN LEAGUE.
                1685.

There are also two oblong stones on the wall with the following inscriptions:—

IN MEMORY
OF
SIX MARTYRS
WHO
SUFFERED AT THIS SPOT
FOR THEIR
ATTACHMENT TO THE COVENANTED CAUSE
OF CHRIST
IN SCOTLAND
JAN-23. 1685.

ERECTED
BY THE VOLUNTARY CONTRIBUTIONS
OF A CONGREGATION
WHO WAITED ON THE MINISTRATIONS
OF THE REV. GAVIN ROWATT OF WHITHORN.
LORD'S DAY AUG. XIX.
MDCCCXXVII.

Little is known about the martyrs. Tradition tells that a number of Covenanters had gathered one Sabbath morning in the Caldons Wood, and were engaged at worship, when they were suddenly surprised by a company of dragoons under Colonel James Douglas. A few of the Covenanters had arms and defended themselves, but were speedily overcome. Most of them escaped, but the six already mentioned could not get away, and sought refuge in the Caldons farmhouse. They were shot dead, and buried where they fell. One dragoon was killed in the encounter,

besides Captain Urquhart, of whom we read:—
" Tradition asserts that he had dreamed he would be
killed at a place called the Caldons, and while
approaching the cottage of a shepherd in search of
the fugitives, he enquired the name of the place. On
being informed, he gave utterance to a fearful oath,
and with the superstitious feeling of the age, drew up
his horse, but ere he could determine whether to
advance or retire, a shot fired from a window brought
him to the ground." At the same time one of the
Covenanters levelled his musket at Colonel Douglas,
but it would not go off, and so that officer had a
providential escape. There were some women among
the Covenanters, and it was probably on their account
that such fierce resistance was offered. From Kirkinner Session Records we learn that May Dunbar,
second daughter of Sir David Dunbar of Baldoon, of
known piety all her life, " very providentially and
narrowly escaped the enemy's fury at the Caldons."

In *The Cloud of Witnesses* and in Wodrow, two of
the names are given as Andrew M'Aulay and John
M'Clude. On the stone they are Andrew M'Call and
James M'Clive. But for the difference of John and
James it might have been said that these were only
different forms of the same name, but probably, as
another writer suggests, there may be an error in the
first transcription, and the likelihood is that the names
on the tombstone are correct.

On January 28th, 1685, the Council sent the
following letter to those they had commissioned for
Wigtown and Kirkcudbright:—

"Right Honourable,—His Majesty's Privy Council, being certainly informed that Captain Urquhart hath been killed, and some others of His Majesty's Forces killed and wounded by some desperate rebels in your bounds, who had the boldness to attack them, whereof three were taken alive and made prisoners. The Council thinking it fit that justice may be done upon these notorious, desperate rebels, upon the place, for greater terror and example to others, do therefore require you immediately upon receipt of this to proceed and do justice upon them according to your commission, you being first convened to this purpose by Colonel James Douglas, Colonel of the Footguards, whom we have added to your commission, and punish them according to law and your instructions. And where they shall be found guilty, you shall forthwith cause burn their houses and the materials thereof, and secure their goods for His Majesty's use. And particularly if you find any of those rebels have been maliciously and wilfully reset at the Houses of Star or Lochhead lying towards Kilrine and Craigmalloch, inquire into it. Your punctual and exact obedience is required.

"(Signed)   Perth."

A romantic story has been handed down regarding Roger Dun, a brother of the two Duns killed. In fleeing from the soldiers he made for Loch Trool. For a few moments the formation of the ground hid him from view, and he took advantage of this to jump into the loch and get in among some reeds and bushes, where he stood with only his head out of the water.

His pursuers could not see him, and after an unsuccessful search, they fired some shots at random and went away. Dun had to remain in the water for a considerable time. When he ventured out, he sought refuge in a house close to the loch, where the inmates put him to bed while his clothes were being dried at the fire. Soon, however, he was in a raging fever, owing to the long wait in the cold water, for it was the month of January, and for a time his life seemed to be hanging in the balance. He was carefully nursed by a young woman in the house, and ultimately recovered, and the story ends with the marriage of Dun to his faithful attendant. The spot where he was concealed is still pointed out, and retains the name of " Roger's Bush." M'Kerlie and other writers give a somewhat different version of the story, and say that Roger was shot the following day. This, however, is erroneous, as we shall see.

The three Duns, there is every reason to believe, were the sons of James Dun, the farmer of Benwhat, in Dalmellington parish. Roger was born in 1659, and early identified himself with the cause of the Covenanters. He was frequently pursued, and had many narrow escapes. On one occasion, when returning home with his brothers Andrew and Allan from a conventicle at Craigview, in Carsephairn, a company of troopers suddenly pounced on them. Andrew and Allan were captured, but Roger, by a sudden and unexpected spring, eluded the grasp of the soldier who attempted to take him, and got away. He lived till after the Revolution, but was killed at Brockloch, a short distance from Carsephairn, having been mistaken for another man. It appears that the farmers of Camlar, Carse, and Borland were at enmity with the Laird of Lochhead, and on the night of Carsephairn fair, having imbibed too freely, they formed the design of murdering Lochhead on his way home. In the failing light, and mad with drink, they came upon Roger Dun, and, believing him to be Lochhead, they stabbed him to death before they realised their mistake. "Roger Dun's Cairn" still marks the scene of the tragedy. In Carsephairn churchyard a stone has the following inscription:—

ERECTED

In Memory of Roger Dun, who was born at Benwhat, parish of Dalmellington 1659. He suffered much persecution for the cause of Christ, and was Killed on the night of Carsephairn Fair, June 1689, on the Farm of Brockloch.

"Pluck'd from Minerva's breast here am I laid,
Which debt to cruel Atropos I've paid;
Resting my clayey fabric in the dust,
Among the holy ashes of the Just,
My Soul set sail for the celestial shore,
Till the last trump the same with joy restore."

CHAPTER XLIII.

THE WIGTOWN MARTYRS.

Wodrow's narrative—The Wilsons of Glenvernock—Their children would not conform and fled—Margaret and Agnes Wilson, venturing to Wigtown, are betrayed and arrested—Margaret M'Lauchlan seized at worship and imprisoned—Tried before the Laird of Lagg and others for rebellion—Found guilty and sentenced to be drowned—Agnes Wilson liberated on a Bond for £100—The execution on 11th May, 1685—Scenes at the Bladnoch—Buried in Wigtown churchyard—Tombstones and inscriptions—Napier's *Case for the Crown in re. the Wigtown Martyrs proved to be Myths*—Petition by Margaret M'Lauchlan for recall of sentence of death—A reprieve granted, but not given effect to—Procedure in another case showing pardon granted—Wigtown case had no such ending —Proof of martyrdom shown by (1) Tradition, (2) Early pamphlets, (3) Earlier Histories, (4) Minutes of local Church Courts, Kirkinner, Penninghame, and Wigtown, (5) Monumental evidence—Miscellaneous—Singular dream of Margaret M'Lauchlan's daughter re. Provost Coltrain of Drummorral —The Stirling monument—The Wigtown monument.

No fact connected with "the killing times" in Scotland is better known than the story of the Wigtown martyrs. Various circumstances have contributed to this result, not the least important of which has been the fierce but futile attack made on the truthfulness of the story by Mark Napier, Sheriff of Dumfries, in *The Case for the Crown in re. the Wigtown Martyrs*

proved to be Myths." This bitter and bombastic
pamphlet was answered by the Rev. Dr. Stewart of
Glasserton, Mr. David Guthrie, Stranraer, the Rev.
Dr. Thomas Gordon, Newbattle, and Sir Andrew
Agnew, Bart., of Lochnaw, and many others, with
such an accumulation of proofs, hitherto known only
to the few, that the reality of the martyrdom was for
ever placed beyond the region of doubt. We shall
return to *The Case for the Crown* later. Meantime
we give the story of the Wigtown martyrs as narrated
by Wodrow:—" Upon the 11th of May, we meet with
the barbarous and wicked execution of two excellent
women near Wigtown, Margaret M'Lauchlan and
Margaret Wilson. History scarce affords a parallel
to this in all its circumstances; and therefore I shall
give it at the greater length, and the rather, because
the advocates for the cruelty of this period, and our
jacobites, have the impudence, some of them to deny,
and others to extenuate this matter of fact, which can
be fully evinced by many living witnesses. And I
shall mostly give my narrative of it, from an account
I have from the forementioned Mr. Rowan, now with
the Lord, late minister of Penningham, where
Margaret Wilson lived, who was at pains to have its
circumstances fully vouched by witnesses, whose
attestations are in my hand; and I shall add, to make
the account more full, the sufferings of the said
Margaret's relations, though not unto death, as coming
in natively enough here, and what will hand me in
to what I have most in view.

THE WILSONS OF GLENVERNOCK.

"Gilbert Wilson, father to the said Margaret, lived in Glenvernock, belonging to the laird of Castlestewart, in the parish of Penningham, and shire of Wigtown, and was every way conform to episcopacy; and his wife, without anything to be objected against her as to her regularity. They were in good circumstances as to the world, and had a great stock upon a good ground, and therefore were the fitter prey for the persecutors, if they could reach them. Their children to be sure, not from their education but a better principle, would by no means conform or hear the episcopal incumbent. This was a good handle to the persecutors; so they were searched for, but fled to the hills, bogs, and caves, though they were yet scarce of the age that made them obnoxious to the law. Meanwhile their parents are charged at the highest peril not to harbour them, supply them, or speak to them, or see them without informing against them, that they might be taken; and their father was fined for his children's alleged irregularities and opinions, which he had no share in, and harassed by frequent quarterings of the soldiers, sometimes an hundred of them upon him at once, who lived at discretion, upon anything in the house or field belonging to him. Those troubles continuing upon him for some years together, with his attendance upon courts at Wigton almost once a week, thirteen miles distant from his house, his going to Edinburgh, and other harassings, brought him under exceeding great losses. At a modest calculation, they were about five thousand merks, and all for no action or principle of his own, for he was entirely conformist. He died some six or eight years ago in great poverty, though one of the most substantial countrymen in that country. And his wife (1711) lives a very aged widow, upon the charity of friends. His son Thomas Wilson, a youth of sixteen years of age, this February 1685, was forced to the mountains and continued wandering till the revolution, at which time he went to the army, and bore arms under King William in Flanders, and after that in the castle of Edinburgh. He never had a farthing from his parents to enter that ground which they possessed, but having got together somewhat by his own industry, lives now in his father's room, and is ready to attest all I am writing.

MARGARET AND AGNES WILSON.

"It is Gilbert's two daughters, who fell into the hands of the persecutors, Margaret Wilson of eighteen years of age, and Agnes Wilson a child not thirteen years, that have led me to this account. Agnes, the youngest, was condemned with her sister by those merciless judges, but her father obtained a liberation from prison, under a bond of 100 pounds sterling to present her when called. However Gilbert had to go to Edinburgh before she was let out; but to all on-lookers and posterity, it will remain an unaccountable thing to sentence a child of thirteen years to death, for not hearing and not swearing. In the beginning of this year, those two sisters for some time were obliged to abscond and wander through Carrick, Galloway, and Nithsdale, with their brothers, and some others. After the universal severities slackened a little at King Charles' death, the two sisters ventured to go to Wigton, to see some of their suffering acquaintances there, particularly

MARGARET M'LAUCHLAN,

of whom just now. When they came to Wigton, there was an acquaintance of theirs, Patrick Stuart, whom they took to be a friend and well-wisher, but he was really not so, and betrayed them; being in their company, and seeking an occasion against them, he proposed drinking the king's health; this they modestly declined; upon which he went out, informed against them, and brought in a party of soldiers, and seized them. As if they had been great malefactors, they were put in the thieves' hole, and after they had been there some time, they were removed to the prison where Margaret M'Lauchlan was, whom I come next to give some account of.

" This woman was about sixty-three years of age, relict of John Mulligen, carpenter, a tenant in the parish of Kirkinner, in the shire of Galloway, in the farm of Drumjargan, belonging to Colonel Vans of Barnbarroch; she was a countrywoman of more than ordinary knowledge, discretion, and prudence, and for many years of singular piety and devotion; she would take none of the oaths now pressed upon women as well as men; neither would she desist from the duties she took to be incumbent upon her, hearing presbyterian ministers when providence gave opportunity, and joining with her Christian friends and acquaintances in prayer, and supplying her relations and acquaintances when in straits, though persecuted. It is a jest to suppose her guilty of rising in arms and rebellion, though indeed it was a part of her indictment, which she got in common form now used. For those great crimes and no other, she was seized some while ago upon the Lord's day, when at family worship in her own house; which was now an ordinary season for apprehending honest people. She was imprisoned, after she had suffered much in her goods and crop before she was apprehended. In prison she was very roughly dealt with, and had neither fire, nor bed to lie upon, and had very little allowed her to live on.

THE TRIAL.

" Jointly with Margaret M'Lauchlan, or M'Lauchlison, these two young sisters, after many methods were taken to corrupt them, and make them swear the oath now imposed, which they steadily refused, were brought to their trial before the laird of Lagg, colonel David Graham, sheriff, major Windram, captain Strachan, and provost Cultrain, who gave all the three an indictment for rebellion, Bothwell-bridge, Ayr's Moss, and being present at twenty field conventicles. No matter now how false and calumnious poor people's indictments were. None of the pannels had ever been

within many miles of Bothwell or Ayr's Moss: Agnes
Wilson could be but eight years of age at Ayr's Moss,
and her sister but about twelve or thirteen; and it was
impossible they could have any access to those risings:
Margaret M'Lauchlan was as free as they were. All
the three refused the abjuration oath, and it was unaccountable it should be put to one of them. The
assize bring them in guilty, and the judges pronounce
their sentence; that upon the 11th instant, all the
three should be tied to stakes fixed within the flood-
mark, in the water of Blednoch near Wigton, where the
sea flows at high water, there to be drowned. We
have seen, that Agnes Wilson was got out by her
father upon a bond of an hundred pounds sterling,
which, I hear, upon her non-production, was likewise
exacted. Margaret Wilson's friends used all means
to prevail with her to take the abjuration oath, and
to engage to hear the curate, but she stood fast in her
integrity, and would not be shaken. They received
their sentence with a great deal of composure, and
cheerful countenances, reckoning it their honour to
suffer for Christ and His truth. During her imprisonment Margaret Wilson wrote a large letter to her
relations full of deep and affecting sense of God's love
to her soul, and an entire resignation to the Lord's
disposal. She likewise added a vindication of her
refusing to save her life by taking the abjuration,
and engaging to conformity; against both she gives
arguments with a solidity and judgment far above
one of her years and education.

THE EXECUTION.

" This barbarous sentence was executed the foresaid day, May 11th, and the two women were brought from Wigtown, with a numerous crowd of spectators to so extraordinary an execution. Major Windram with some soldiers guarded them to the place of execution. The old woman's stake was a good way in beyond the other, and she was first despatched, in order to terrify the other to a compliance with such oaths and conditions, as they required. But in vain; for she adhered to her principles with an unshaken steadfastness. When the water was overflowing her fellow-martyr, some about Margaret Wilson asked her, what she thought of the other now struggling with the pangs of death. She answered, ' What do I see but Christ (in one of his members) wrestling there. Think you that we are the sufferers? No, it is Christ in us, for he sends none a warfare upon their own charges.' When Margaret Wilson was at the stake, she sang the 25th Psalm from verse 7th, downward a good way, and read the 8th Chapter to the Romans with a great deal of cheerfulness, and then prayed. While at prayer, the water covered her: but before she was quite dead they pulled her up, and held her out of the water till she was recovered, and able to speak; and then by major Windram's orders, she was asked, if she would pray for the King. She answered, ' She wished the salvation of all men, and the damnation of none.' One deeply affected with the death of the other and her case, said, ' Dear Margaret, say God save the King,

Say God save the King.' She answered in the greatest steadiness and composure, "God save him, if he will, for it is his salvation I desire.' Whereupon some of her relations near by, desirous to have her life spared if possible, called out to major Windram, ' Sir, she hath said it, she hath said it.' Whereupon the major came near, and offered her the abjuration, charging her instantly to swear it, otherwise return to the water. Most deliberately she refused, and said, ' I will not, I am one of Christ's children, let me go.' Upon which she was thrust down again into the water, where she, finished her course with joy. She died a virgin-martyr about eighteen years of age, and both of them suffered precisely upon refusing conformity, and the abjuration oath, and were evidently innocent of anything worthy of death."

The martyrs were buried in Wigtown old church-yard at the foot of Bank Street. The ruins of the old church are to the north-west of the present building which was erected in 1853, and the martyrs' grave-stones are to the north of the old church—the place assigned to criminals. They are enclosed by a neat iron railing, and are carefully looked after, in agree-able contrast to some of the martyrs' tombstones we have seen elsewhere in Galloway. The largest of the stones is to the memory of Margaret Wilson. It is a thin flat stone resting upon four pillars about a foot high, and has the following inscription:—

HERE LYES MARGARET
WILLSON DOUGHTER
TO GILBERT WILLSON
IN GLENVERNOCH
WHO WAS DROUND
ANNO 1685 AGED 18.

LET EARTH AND STONE STILL WITNESS BEARE
THEIR LYES A VIRGINE MARTYRE HERE
MURTHER'D FOR OUNING CHRIST SUPREAME
HEAD OF HIS CHURCH AND NO MORE CRIME
BUT NOT ABJURING PRESBYTRY
AND HER NOT OUNING PRELACY
THEY HER CONDEM'D BY UNJUST LAW
OF HEAVEN NOR HELL THEY STOOD NO AW.
WITHIN THE SEA TYD TO A STAKE
SHE SUFFERED FOR CHRIST JESUS SAKE
THE ACTORS OF THIS CRUEL CRIME
WAS LAGG, STRACHAN, WINRAM, AND GRHAME
NEITHER YOUNG YEARES NOR YET OLD AGE
COULD STOP THE FURY OF THERE RAGE.

Near to Margaret Wilson's stone is that erected to
the memory of her aged fellow-sufferer—Margaret
Lauchlane. It is of small size, upright, and rests
upon a socket of stone. The top edge is waved, and
at one corner is a terminating scroll, the scroll at the
other corner having apparently been broken off. On

this waved top the words ME MENTO MORI are engraved. On the other side of the stone we read:—

> HERE LYSE
> MARGARET LACHLANE
> WHO WAS BY UNJUST
> LAW SENTENCED TO
> DIE BY LAGG STRACHANE
> WIN RAME AND GRHAME
> AND TYED TO A
> STAKE WITHIN THE
> FLOOD FOR HER

On the other side, below a sketch of two bones and a skull, the inscription is continued thus:—

> ADHERENCE
> TO SCOTLAND'S RE
> FORMATION COVE
> NANTS NATIONAL
> AND SOLEMN LEAGUE
> AGED 63, 1685.

The lettering on the stones is in the antiquated style of the period of the Revolution, all the letters being capitals, and many of them being joined together.

NAPIER'S CASE FOR THE CROWN.

The arguments advanced by Sheriff Napier may be briefly noticed. His whole case is built up on the fact that a reprieve was granted. While Margaret M'Lauchlan was in prison, a petition was presented to the privy council on her behalf, for recall of the sentence of death passed upon her. A copy is given below, and it will be noticed from the Notary's docquet that the petition does not bear to have been read to her or subscribed in her presence. Neither in form nor in substance can it be said to be the petition of Margaret Lauchlan. She may have consented to a petition being made on her behalf, but never to the views set forth in this one:—

"Unto his Grace my Lord High Commissioner, and remanent Lords of his Majesties Most Honourable Privie Counsell;

"The humble supplication of Margaret Lachlisone, and now prisoner in the Tolbuith of Wigton—

"Sheweth;

"That whereas I being justly condemned to die, by the Lords Commissioners of his Majesties Most Honourable Privie Counsell and Justiciore, in ane Court holden at Wigtoune, the threttein day of Apryle instant, for my not disowning that traiterous apollogetical declaration laitlie affixed at several paroch churches within this kingdom, and my refusing the oath of abjuration of the saymein, which was occasioned by my not perusing the saymein: And now, I having considered the said declaratione, doe acknowledge the saymein to be traiterous, and tends to nothing but rebellione and seditione, and to be quyt contrair unto the wrytin word of God; and am content to abjure the same with my whole heart and soull:

"May it therefoir please your Grace, and remanent Lords as said is, to take my cais to your serious consideratione, being about the age of thre scor ten years, and to take pitie and compassione on me, and recall the foresaid sentence so justlie pronouncet against me; and to grant warrant to any your Grace thinks fit to administrat the oath of abjuration to me, and upon my taking of it to order my liberatione; and your supplicant shall leive, heirafter ane good and faithful subject in tyme cuming; and shall frequent the ordinances and live regularly, and give what other obedience your Grace and remanent Lords sall prescryve thereanent; and your petitioner shall ever pray.

"De mandato dictae Margaretae Lauchlisone scribere necien, ut asseruit, ego Gulielmus Moir, notarius-publicus, subscribo testante hoc meo chyrographo.

"WILLIAM MOIR."

"J. Dunboir, witness.
"Will. Gordoun, witness."

Doubtless Margaret Wilson's father, Gilbert Wilson of Glenvernoch, exerted himself on behalf of his daughter. Certain it is that a reprieve was granted in the following terms:—

"Edinburgh, April 30th, 1685. The Lords of his Majesty's Privy Council do hereby reprieve the execution of the sentence of death, pronounced by the Justices against Margaret Wilson and

Margaret Lauchlison, until the   day of
and discharge the magistrates of Edinburgh from
putting of the said sentence to execution against
them until the foresaid day, and recommend the
said Margaret Wilson and Margaret Lauchlison
to the Lords Secretaries of State, to interpose
with his most sacred Majesty for the royal
remission to them."

It will be noticed that the above reprieve leaves the
date blank—significant enough when it is contended
that nothing was done to give effect to it. From the
fact that the magistrates of Edinburgh were discharged
from executing the sentence Sheriff Napier concludes
that the two women must have been removed to Edinburgh, and that the drowning at Wigtown in May
could not have occurred. Dr. Stewart points out the
procedure in the case of three men sentenced to be
hanged on 20th April at Cumnock. Their case was
brought before the Council on 9th April, when this
deliverance was granted:—" The Lord Commissioner
his Grace hath reprieved and hereby reprieveth the
execution of the foresaid sentence of death until the
20th day of May next at which time the same to be
put in execution in case there be no further order to
the contrary." Following on this the men took the
abjuration oath, and on 8th May the Council ordained
a letter to be written in their favour to the Lord
Secretaries of State, recommending them to apply to
the King for their pardon. No such letter was written,
and the men again presented an address, and on 15th

June the Council "ordains a letter to be written to the Secretaries of State recommending them to mercy." This time the letter is written, and accordingly the minute contains a copy of it. Following on this, the Council Minute of 30th June shows that his Majesty's pardon was produced by the Lord Chancellor. As Dr. Stewart says:—"Here, then, is a case in which a petition for mercy, and an offer to take the Government oaths, ended in a pardon; and the minutes of the Privy Council show the steps by which it went on to this termination. But these minutes show that the Wigtown case, though it had a beginning, had no continuation, and had no such ending. It stopped short, from some cause, at the very first stage—at the mere permission to administer the oath, and forward the prisoners. No proof do these minutes furnish that the oath was administered, as in the case of the Cumnock men; no proof, deserving the name, that the women were actually sent to Edinburgh; no proof that a recommendation to mercy was actually forwarded to London; and, above all, *no proof that a pardon came.*" In the London State papers there is no record of the Wigtown case, but there we find the Cumnock case undergoing its usual course and ending in a formal pardon. Further, when the Edinburgh rulers got into a state of panic at Argyle's invasion and cleared the Edinburgh and Leith jails of "all the prisoners for religion, especially those from the South and West," and sent them to Dunottar, we find the names of the three Cumnock men among the prisoners, but the names of the Wigtown martyrs do not appear. There is not a scrap of evidence to show that the two women were ever in Edinburgh, and there is no record to show that the reprieve ever went beyond the first step.

On the affirmative side of the question the proof has been arranged by Dr. Stewart, under the following headings:—(1) Tradition; (2) Early Pamphlets; (3) Earlier Histories; (4) Minutes of Local Church Courts; (5) Monumental Evidence.

Tradition has been handed down from sire to son of the drowning of these two women, pointing to the very spot where the tragedy took place. The course of the Bladnoch was different then from what it is to-day. Then the mouth of the river was near the Church, and it was in this part that the women were drowned. In the family of the Wilsons, the fact of Margaret Wilson's martyrdom has been preserved as part of the family history. The descendants of Gilbert Wilson were farmers in Penninghame parish till within quite recent times.

The Informatory Vindication, published by the Societies in 1687 undoubtedly refers to the Wigtown martyrs in these words:—" Drowning women, some of them very young, and some of exceeding old age." *The Hind Let Loose*, first published in 1687, also refers to the Wigtown martyrs:—" Neither were women spared, but some were hanged, some drowned, tied to stakes within the sea-mark, to be devoured gradually with the growing waves, and some of them of a very young, some of an old, age."

The following passage from the Prince of Orange's

Declaration for Scotland, dated at The Hague, 10th
October, 1688, shows that he believed that drowning
was one of the barbarities. of the Government:—
" Empowering officers and soldiers to act upon the
subject living in quiet and full peace, the greatest
barbarities in destroying them by hanging, shooting,
and drowning them without any form of law or respect
to age or sex." In *A Short Memorial of the Sufferings
and Grievances* (1690), there is this passage:—" Item,
The said Colonel or Lieutenant-General James
Douglas, together with the Laird of Lagg and Captain
Winram, most illegally condemned and most uncere-
moniously drowned at stakes within the sea-mark, two
women of Wigtown, viz.:—Margaret Lauchlan, upwards of sixty years, and Margaret Wilson, about
twenty years of age, the foresaid fatal year 1685."
In *A Second Vindication of the Church of Scotland*
(1691), by Dr. Gilbert Rule, Principal of the University of Edinburgh, and minister of Old Greyfriars,
there is this passage:—" Some gentlemen, whose
names, out of respect for them, I forbear to mention,
took two women—Margaret Lauchland and Margaret
Wilson—the one sixty, the other twenty years, and
caused them to be tied to a stake within the sea-mark
at Wigtown and left there till the tide overflowed
them and drowned them, and this was done without
any legal trial, 1685."
A Short Character of the Presbyterian Spirit,
published in 1703, in reply to a pamphlet entitled
Toleration's Fence Removed, by the Rev. James
Ramsay of Eyemouth, afterwards Moderator of the

General Assembly, has this reference to the Wigtown case. "He (the author of *Toleration's Fence Removed*) says:—'Others were tyed to stakes within the flood-mark till the sea came up and drowned them, and this without any form or process of law.' He durst not instance any so treated. I know they generally talk of two women in Galloway—drowned they were indeed, but not tyed to stakes within the flood-mark till the sea came up, as this Malacious Vindicator misrepresents." Mr. Ramsay replied, "He takes upon him to deny that the poor women spoken of, *T. F. R.* p. 8, were tyed to stakes within the flood-mark till the sea came up and drowned them; and yet I have a paper from eye and ear witnesses of that abominable fact." The value of the extract from *A Short Character of the Presbyterian Spirit* lies in the fact that it was written by Mr. Matthias Symson, a son of the Rev. Andrew Symson, author of *A Large Description of Galloway*, etc., and afterwards printer in Edinburgh. Andrew Symson was the Episcopal minister of Kirkinner when the martyrdom took place, and in October, 1684, he had marked the name of Margaret Lauchlison as disorderly in regard to Church laws in the list of parishioners over twelve years of age which he had to send to the authorities. Then this pamphlet written by Symson, junior, was issued from the press of his father, who at the time of the execution was living within three miles of Wigtown. What further proof than this admission of the martyrdom would any reasonable man require?—"Drowned they were indeed!"

In regard to " Earlier Histories," it need only be mentioned that the case of the Wigtown martyrs is fully given in *A Cloud of Witnesses*, 1714, and in Defoe's *History of the Church of Scotland*, 1717.

The Minutes of the Local Church Courts prove the martyrdom conclusively. In the Minutes of the Kirk Session of Kirkinner, of 15th April, 1711, there is this reference to it:—The minister gave in the account of the " sufferings of honest godly people in the late times which was read, and is as follows:—Margaret Laughlison, of known integrity and piety from her youth, aged about 80, widow of John Milliken, wright in Drumjargan, was, in or about the year of God, 1685, in her own house, taken off her knees in prayer, and carried immediately to prison, and from one prison to another without the benefit of light to read the Scriptures; was barbarously treated by dragoons, who were sent to carry her from Mahirmore to Wigtown; and being sentenced by Sir Robert Grier, of Lagg, to be drowned at a stake within the flood-mark just below the town of Wigtown, for conventicle keeping and alleged rebellion was, according to the said sentence, fixed to the stake till the tide made, and held down within the water by one of the town-officers by his halbert at her throat till she died."

The following were the members of the Session present:—the Rev. William Campbell, minister of Kirkinner, a Wigtownshire man, and son of the minister of Stoneykirk; William M'Haffie, in Kildarroch, who was an elder in Kirkinner when the Rev. Mr. Campbell came to the parish. From Mr.

Andrew Symson's list above referred to we learn that he was living at Kildarroch in 1684, the year before the martyrdom. Gilbert Milroy, who was a member of Session before 1702; George Dunn, who was an elder before 1698; John Martin of Little Aires, who was ordained in 1703. The Kirkinner Minute of sufferings states that Andrew Martin of Little Aires— probably John's father—was declared rebel for going to Bothwell. Alexander Martin, younger of Cutloy. He was probably tenant of Meikle Aires, as he represents the proprietor—Henry Hawthorn—at parish meetings. He was twelve years of age at the time of the martyrdom. John Martin elder in Airles. There is the name of John Martin in Symson's list, but the residence is different, and he may not be the same. John M'Dowall in Ballaird. There are two John M'Dowall's in Symson's list, but neither of them resides at Ballaird. John Kirkpatrick, chamberlain to Hamilton of Baldoon. He was ordained in 1707, and though he may have had no personal knowledge of the martyrdom, he was doubtless satisfied of its truth on the testimony of others; Robert Heron, Barglass, was previously an elder in Mochrum, and it is probably his name which appears on the roll of the synod, 20th April, 1697; Andrew Gray, ordained Deacon in 1705.

The following is the reference to the case in the Penninghame records of 19th February, 1711:—

"Gilbert Wilson of Glenvernock, in Castle-stewart's land, being a man to ane excesse conform to the guise of the tymes, and his wife

without challenge for her religion, in a good
condition as to worldly things, with a great stock
on a large ground (fitt to be a prey), was harassed
for his childrene who would not conform. They
being required to take the test, and hear the
curats, refused both; were searched for, fled, and
lived in the wild mountains, bogs, and caves.
Their parents were charged, on their highest peril,
that they should neither harbour them, speak to
them, supplie them, nor see them, and the country
people were obliged by the terror of the law, to
pursue them, as well as the soldiers, with hue and
cry.

" In February, 1685, Thomas Wilson of sixteen
years of age, Margaret Wilson, of eighteen years,
Agnes Wilson of thirteen years, children of the
said Gilbert—the said Thomas keeping the mountains, his two sisters Margaret and Agnes went
secretly to Wigtown to see some friends, were
there discovered, taken prisoners, and instantly
thrust into the thieves hole as the greatest malefactors; whence they were some tymes brought
up to the tolbooth, after a considerable tyme's
imprisonment, where several others were prisoners
for the like cause, particularly ane Margaret
M'Lauchland of Kirkinner paroch, a woman of
sixty-three years of age.

" After their imprisonment for some considerable tyme, Mr. David Graham, sheriff, the laird
of Lagg, Major Winram, Captain Strachan, called
ane assize, indicted these three women, viz.:—

Margaret M'Lauchlan, Margaret Wilson, Agnes Wilson, to be guilty of the rebellion at Bothwell-bridge, Airds Moss, twenty field conventicles, and twenty house conventicles. Yet it was weel known that none of these women ever were within twenty miles of Bothwell or Airds Mosse; and Agnes Wilson being eight years of age at the time of Airds Mosse, could not be deep in the rebellion then, nor her sister of thirteen years of age, and twelve years at Bothwell-bridge its tyme. The assize did sitt, and brought them in guilty, and these judges sentenced them to be tied to palissados fixed in the sand, within the flood-mark of the sea, and there to stand till the flood over-flowed them, and drowned them.

" They received their sentence without the least discouragement, with a composed smiling countenance, judging it their honour to suffer for Christ's truth, that He is alone King and Head of his Church. Gilbert Wilson, forsaid, got his youngest daughter, Agnes Wilson, out of prison, upon his bond of ane hundreth pounds sterling, to produce her when called for, after the sentence of death past against her, but was obliged to go to Edinburgh for this be-fore it could be obtained. The tyme they were in prison no means was unessayed with Margaret Wilson to persuade her to take the oath of abjuration, and hear the curats, with threatenings and flattery, but without any success.

"Upon the eleventh day of May 1685, these two women, Margaret M'Lauchland and Margaret Wilson, were brought forth to execution. They did put the old woman first in to the water, and when the water was over-flowing her, they asked Margaret Wilson what she thought of her in that case? She answered, What do I see but Christ wrestling there? Think ye that we are the sufferers? No, it is Christ in us, for He sends none a warfare on their own charges. Margaret Wilson sang Psalm xxv., from the 7th verse, read the eighth chapter of the Epistle to the Romans, and did pray, and then the water covered her. But before her breath was quite gone, they pulled her up, and held her till she could speak, and then asked her if she would pray for the King. She answered that she wished the salvation of all men, but the damnation of none. Some of her relations being on the place, cried out, She is willing to conform, being desirous to save her life at any. rate. Upon which Major Winram offered the oath of abjuration to her, either to swear it, or return to the waters. She refused it, saying, ' I will not. I am one of Christ's children, let me go.' And then they returned her into the water, where she finished her warfare, being a virgin martyr of eighteen years of age. suffering death for her refusing to swear the oath of abjuration and hear the curats."

The members of the Session present were:—

1. Robert Rowan, Minister.
2. John M'Caul, Corsbie. He was at Bothwell, and was taken and imprisoned. His landlord—Castle Stewart—gave Claverhouse a Bond for 1,000 merks for his compearance, and he was liberated. The list by Mr. Colquhoun, Episcopal minister of Penninghame, shows that he was residing at Corsbie at that time (1684).
3. John Martin, Glenvogie. His wife and son are in the list, but he had sought safety in flight.
4. John Heron, Grange of Cree. His name appears in Mr. Colquhoun's list.
5. Alexr. M'Gill, Barvennan. He also is in the list.
6. Thomas M'Caw, Challoch.
7. John M'Keand, Balsalloch. In Mr. Colquhoun's list there are two of this name resident at Balsalloch.
8. William Douglas, Balsalloch. He was 17 years of age at the date of the martyrdom.
9. James M'Geoch, Barwhirran. His name appears in Mr. Colquhoun's list. He was 18 in 1685.
10. John M'Clelland, bailie in Newton Stewart. He was previously an elder in Monigaff.
11. Alexander M'Clinger, Barachan. His wife was at Wigtown sentenced to banishment in 1684 for " converse " with him. In 1684 his residence was Thrive.
12. Patrick Milroy, Glenhapple.
13. James M'Millan, Fintilloch.

In the Wigtown Session Records, under date 8th
July, 1704, it is minuted:—

"Post preses sederunt, the minister and all the
elders and deacons." *Inter alia.* "This day
Bailie M'Keand, elder, in Wigtown, addressed
the session for the privilege of the sacrament,
declaring the grief of his heart that he should
have sitten on the seize of these women who were
sentenced to die in this place in the year 1685,
and that it had been frequently his petition to
God for true repentance and forgiveness for that
sin. He being removed, and the session enquiring
into this affair and the carriage of the said bailie
since that time, and being satisfied with his
conversation since, and the present evidence of
repentance now, they granted him the privilege.
He was called in, admonished, and exhorted to
deliberation, and due tenderness in such a solemn
address unto God."

It may be imagined that Bailie M'Keand's "grief
of heart" would not have been so great as it appears
to have been, and that he would not have been denied
the "privilege of the sacrament" for nineteen years,
had the women, at whose condemnation to death he
assisted, not been actually executed.

The inscriptions on the tombstones must have
appeared at the very latest before 1730, as they are
given in the third edition of the *Cloud of Witnesses,*
published that year, and there is every reason to believe

that the tombstones with the inscriptions were put up much earlier. As Dr. Stewart pertinently asks, " Is it possible to believe anyone capable of ' committing such an outrage on truth and propriety as to inscribe on a tombstone in a churchyard visited every Sunday by the whole population of the County town, what they all would have known to be a mere fable?' "

There are many other circumstances and incidents that go to support the truth of the martyrdom. Some of these we give, not that we think them at all necessary, but that everything connected with the story is of interest.

The following declaration was published in 1861:—

" I, Margaret Wilson, residing in Wigtown, do hereby solemnly and sincerely declare, that the late Mr. William M'Adam, of Woodside, called upon me soon after I came to Wigtown, and read over the annexed paper, and said that his grandfather gave it to him, saying it was a copy of the petition written by himself, signed by him and others, and forwarded to Parliament, against Sir Robert Grierson of Lagg, as stated therein, and that his grandfather was married to one of the Wilsons of Glenvernock.

" (Signed)　　Margaret Wilson."

" Declared before me at Wigtown this 14th day of March, 1861.

" (Signed)　　Thomas Murray,
Sheriff-Substitute of Wigtownshire."

The following is the paper referred to in the above declaration:—

"Memorandum anent ane Petition to be presented to the Parliament against Sir Robert Grierson of Lagge.

"Sir Robert having in the late evill times the command of several troops of dragoons, and being Steuart of the Steuartry of Kirkcudbright does, without any process or sentance of law, cause comite severall barbrous and inhuman murders, and that upon no other account but upon Church irregularities, and does execute his fury against this poor people in such a manner as cannot well be expressed. A particular account of all his barbarities is not designed in this place, but only such of them as are most notour and deserve best the consideration of the honourable states of Parliament, which are as follows:—

"1st. Sir Robert, after he had apprehended two women to wit, Margaret Lauchlison and Margaret Wilson—upon no other account but for alleged nonconformity, did, without any conviction or sentence, cause bind them to a stake within the sea-mark at Wigtoune till the flood returning drowned them both, and that without any consideration of the age of the one or the youth of the other, and the said Margaret Lauchlison being above 63 years of age, and the other 18 years old. This was done in the month of May, 1685."

Sir Andrew Agnew in *The Hereditary Sheriffs of Galloway* says:—" Local traditions traceable to almost contemporaneous times, even if they seem childish, stand in corroboration of the deed, in so far as they show that the reality of the tragedy was never for a moment doubted in the district." He gives the following incidents:—

The man by whose information the women were arrested was well known, and his memory is execrated still. One of his descendants, getting into an altercation with a person in the town, was thus taunted, " I wadna like to have had a forbear who betrayed the martyrs; I wadna be com'd o' sic folk."

The late Miss Susan Heron, Wigtown, often told how her grandfather, who had seen the execution, spoke of it in these words:—" The sands were covered wi' cluds o' folk, a' gathered into clusters, many offering up prayers for the women while they were being put down." Miss Heron died 19th February, 1834, aged eighty-seven, and her grandfather, James Heron, died 31st October, 1758, aged ninety-four, so that he was twenty years of age when the women were drowned. The Herons were buried at the old churchyard of Penninghame, and these dates are taken from their tombstones.

A town sergeant, who had been officiously active— when the women finally refused Lagg to take the test —pressed down their heads with his halbert, and cried with savage glee, " Tak' another drink o't, my hearties." Hardly had he returned home when he was troubled by an extraordinary thirst. No amount of drink could satisfy it. His unnatural craving forced him, when obliged to go about, to carry a pitcher on his back. If crossing a stream, he was irresistibly impelled to kneel down and lap water like a dog. Medical skill was of no avail: as the wretch wandered about the country, now turning to curse a group of urchins who followed to mock his sufferings, now sprawling to moisten his tongue in the gutter, even his ribald companions shrank from him with horror, and the people, whose sympathies were with his victims, pointed to him as a man whose eternal sufferings had begun.

Still more grotesque is the tradition of the " Cleppie Bells ":—A constable, who was held to have carried out his orders unfeelingly, as he fastened the women to the stakes, was asked how the poor creatures behaved when the cold wave roared and foamed about their heads. "Oh," he replied jocularly, "they just clepped roun' the stobs like partons, and prayed." Soon after, Bell's wife was brought to child-bed, when the midwife exclaimed in horror, " The bairn is clepped!" (i.e., the fingers grew firmly together). Another child was born, and yet another, and as each in turn was seen to be "clepped," the most incredulous were convinced it was a judgment of Providence.

SINGULAR DREAM OF MARGARET LAUCHLANE'S DAUGHTER.

The Rev. William Campbell, minister of Kirkinner, in response to a request by Wodrow, inquired into the story of a dream of the martyr's daughter, and replied under date 11th April, 1718, as follows:—

" Rev. Dear Brother,—In compliance with your desire anent Elizabeth Millikin's dream, know that I went and discoursed her this day, in order to give you the genuine account of it. The said Elizabeth dreamed, some weeks or months before the quarter sessions that met in November, 1708, that her mother Margaret M'Lauchlison, came to her, at the cross of Wigtown, with garb, gesture, and countenance that she had five minutes before she was drowned in Blednoch, and said to her, ' Elizabeth, go and warn Provost Cultrain that he must shortly appear before the tribunal of the great God to answer for his ways;' and immediately her sleep was broken, and it made such an impression upon her, that she resolved, for her own exoneration, and the Provost's edification, prudently and meekly to communicate the said dream to the said William Cultrain of Drummorral, with the first convenience; but not finding or expecting that, she told the dream to Bailie Lafries, Drummorral's friend, being married to Lady Drummorral's sister, a man of age, gravity, and experience, and an elder in Wigtown; and solemnly desired and engaged him to signify the said dream to the said Drummorral; and she doubted not but the said Bailie Lafries did tell the said Drummorral. And, accordingly,

· in the beginning of November, 1708, he rode from Wigton to the quarter session of the justices of the shire, that met that time at Stranraer, and there, on the Wednesday, at the court table, was suddenly struck with a lethargy, was carried to his quarters, and continued speechless till Saturday, the 8th of November, and then died."

Coltrain's participation in the persecution was too deep to escape being handed down to posterity. His name was so detested that many stories coupled with superstitious exaggerations were current. One was that when he died the windows of his house looked as if they were a blaze of fire, which was understood as conveying the fact that the Devil had then got possession of his own. It was also related that for long after his death to pass after nightfall the door of the house he had occupied was an undertaking requiring more than ordinary nerve.

Such are some of the stories that have come down to us about the Wigtown martyrs—stories strange and weird, but all going to show that among those on the spot and in the best position to know, the martyrdom never was doubted.

THE STIRLING MONUMENT.

In the New Cemetery at Stirling a magnificent monument has been erected to the memory of the martyrs. On a large pedestal, there is the figure of an angel standing beside two figures seated, representing the two Wigtown martyrs with the open Bible before them, and a lamb lying at their feet. This beautiful piece of sculpture is greatly admired. It is the work of Handyside Ritchie, Edinburgh. The figure representing an angel was cut in Rome. In the front of the pedestal on marble is the following inscription, with several emblematic designs:—

MARGARET

Virgin-martyr of the ocean wave with
her like-minded sister

AGNES

Love many waters cannot quench—God saves
His chaste impearled one in covenant true.
O, Scotia's daughters! earnest scan the page,
And prize this flower of grace, blood bought for you.

Psalm ix.-xix.

THE WIGTOWN MONUMENT.

On 24th September, 1848, a sermon was preached in Wigtown Parish Church by the Rev. Dr. William Symington of Glasgow, in aid of a fund for a monument to the memory of the martyrs, but it was not until ten years later that the present monument was erected on Windy Hill at a cost of £200. The foundation stone was laid in presence of a large attendance, by the late James Dodds, Solicitor, London, author of *The Fifty Years' Struggle of the*

Covenanters. The following are the inscriptions on the monument. On the north side:—

This Monument
has been erected
in memory of the noble army of Martyrs in
Galloway and other parts of Scotland, by
whom, during the age of persecution, our
Religion and Liberties, as now established,
were secured,
and
as a lesson to posterity never to
lose or abuse those glorious privileges
planted by their labours, rooted in their
Sufferings, and watered with their blood.

On the west tablet we read:—

A general desire having been manifested to
commemorate by some suitable Monument the
Piety, Constancy and Courage
of the Scottish Martyrs,
especially those whose ashes repose
in the churchyard of Wigtown,
a Committee of Gentlemen of the district
was appointed to carry out this object;
and a considerable fund being raised
by public subscription and otherwise,
the present Monument was erected in the year
1858.

The south side repeats the inscription on the tombstone of Margaret Wilson in the churchyard.

The inscription on the east side is:—

> Margaret Wilson, aged 18, daughter
> of a farmer in Glenvernock,
> and
> Margaret M'Lauchlan, aged 63, tenant in
> the farm of Drumjargon, both in this County,
> were drowned by sentence of the public authorities
> in the waters of Bladnoch, near this place,
> on the 11th of May, 1685,
> because they refused to forsake the principles
> of the Scottish Reformation, and to take the
> Government oath abjuring the right of the
> people to resist the tyranny of their rulers;
> also
> William Johnstone, gardener; and John Milroy,
> chapman in Fintilloch; and Gilbert Walker,*
> servant in Kirkala; all in this County, were
> summarily executed in the town of Wigtown in
> the same year and for the same cause.

In 1885, the bi-centenary of the martyrdom was commemorated at Wigtown by an immense concourse of people.

MARGARET MAXWELL.

The Court which condemned the two women to death on 13th April, 1685, had also before it Margaret Maxwell, servant at Barwhannie, in Kirkinner parish, charged with non-conformity. She was sentenced to be flogged through Wigtown streets and to be put in

---

* As will be seen from the inscription on the tombstone, the name should be " George " Walker.

the jougs for three days. This sentence was carried out by the Wigtown hangman, but he evidently had no liking for the work, as may be seen from the following Minute:—

"WIGTOUNE, Apryle 15th, 1685.

"*Councell Extraordinar.*

"The qlk Day, the bailzie and Councelors having convened John Malroy, hangman, befoir them, and examined him, what was his reason to absent himself at this tym, when ther was employment for him, he acknowledged he was in the wrong, and was seduced yrto; but now acknowledged himself the tounes ssrt (servant), and promised to byd be his service; but aleged that he had noe benefit or cellarie for his service, and craved to have some allowance for tyme coming; Which he refered to the toun councell at ane frequent mciting efter the provest's retourne from Edr.; and in the meintym the bailzie, with advyce and consent of the councell, appoynts the thessrer to furnish four shilling Scots ilk day to the sd. John Malroy dureing his abod in prissone, which shall be alowed to the thessrer in his compts; as also appoynts the thessrer to furnish him one beddine of Close, for ye which he shall be satisfied dureing his imprisonment."

Margaret Maxwell was one of those who afterwards gave Patrick Walker an account of the martyrdom, as referred to in his *Six Saints.*

CHAPTER XLIV.

OTHER WIGTOWN MARTYRS.

William Johnstone—John Milroy—George Walker—Peden's prophecy—The Milroys of Kirkcalla, captured and tortured, mutilated and banished—Gilbert Milroy survives the Revolution and returns to Kirkcowan.

THERE is another martyrs' tombstone in Wigtown churchyard. It is a little larger than Margaret M'Lauchlan's, and, like hers, has a waving top with the words ME MENTO MORI. The inscription is as follows:—

N
HERE LYSE WILLIAM JOHNSTO
JOHN MILROY GEORGE WALKER
WHO WAS WITHOUT SENTE
NCE OF LAW HANGED BY MA
JOR WINRAM FOR THEIR ADHER
ENCE TO SCOTLAND'S REFOR
MATION COVENANTS NATIO
NAL AND SOLAM LEAGWE
1685.

Johnstone was gardener to the Laird of Fintilloch. George Walker was servant at Kirkcalla, and John Milroy was a chapman living in Fintilloch. Johnstone had so far conformed as to take the test, but changed his views and refused to hear the curate, with

the result that the latter informed against him and
he was forced to take to the moors and mountains, and
in this way threw in his lot with the other two.
Tradition narrates that they had many narrow escapes,
and at last they were captured by a party sent out
by Major Winram, and were brought to Wigtown.
Winram questioned them, and, not being satisfied, had
them hanged the next day without even the form of
a trial.

Among the remarkable sayings ascribed to Peden
the prophet, is one referring to the execution of these
men. When he was praying at Craigmyre, many
miles distant, he suddenly cried out, " There is a
bloody sacrifice put up this day at Wigtown. These
are the lads of Kirkcalla." Those who lived near knew
nothing about it till afterwards, and then they realised
what Peden was referring to.

THE MILROYS OF KIRKCALLA.

In 1684, William Milroy of Kirkcalla took the test,
but his brother Gilbert got off by paying £12. Next
year these two, with a younger brother—Patrick—
rather than take the oath, left their home and hid
among the moors and mountains. In June or July,
the Earl of Hume sent his militia to quarter on them.
The soldiers pillaged their house, drove away all the
cattle they could find, and practically demolished
everything. They took away eighty black cattle,
many young beasts, about five hundred sheep, and
eight horses, some of them of great value. When the
women wanted to retain their clothes, saying men had

no use for them, some of them were seized and lighted
matches were placed between their fingers. William
and Gilbert were captured and taken before the Earl
of Hume at Minnigaff, and, refusing to disclose who
had sheltered them in their wanderings, lighted
matches were placed between their fingers also, but
without drawing any information. They were tortured, and threatened with immediate death if they
did not tell, but still they refused. Gilbert Milroy's
wife came to Minnigaff to wait upon her husband.
She had gone out to the fields to pray, and one of the
soldiers over-hearing her, came up to her and, drawing
a sword, threatened to kill her, but he was restrained,
and carried her prisoner to the Captain of the Guard,
who saw good to dismiss her. Her husband and his
brother, with several others, were carried under the
guard to the church of Barr, tied together two and
two like beasts of slaughter. They were ultimately
carried to Edinburgh and imprisoned at Holyrood
House, all the jails being filled. Mr. James Colquhoun, Episcopal minister at Penninghame, had no
small share in their being thus treated. Gilbert
Milroy found means to treat with him when he was
apprehended, and sent him a good wedder upon his
promise to speak for him. Gilbert's wife afterwards
went to Mr. Colquhoun and asked a line in her
husband's favour. He wrote a letter and sealed it,
giving it to herself to carry to Edinburgh. In this,
instead of writing in the prisoner's favour, he informed
the judges that he was a disloyal person of rebellious

principles. This, together with their refusing to comply and take the oaths required, brought on their sentence, which was to have their ears cut off, and to be banished for ten years. Their ears were accordingly cut off, with the exception of Gilbert Milroy's, who was so weak that he was thought to be dying. About five or six days afterwards, Gilbert Milroy and the rest of the sentenced prisoners were taken out, and six and six of them tied together, and such of them as were not able to walk, as was the case with several, were carried in carts to Newhaven, put into a ship lying there, and thrust under deck to the number of one hundred and ninety. They endured terrible privations, and when they landed at Port Royal in Jamaica, they were put in an open prison. They had, however, much friendship shown them from several people in the island. After ten days in prison, they were sold as slaves. Gilbert Milroy refused to work to his master on the Sabbath, and one day, after the master had ordered him several times, he drew his sword and had well nigh killed him, but afterwards, finding him faithful, conscientious, and diligent, he altered his way, and made him overseer of all his negroes. The blacks hated him for his fidelity to his master, and made various attempts to murder him. One of them struck him on the head with a long pole, whereby he was stunned for some time, and lost a great deal of blood, and was ever afterwards a little paralytic. At another time he was poisoned by some of the negroes, but was saved by the timeous application of antidotes. Many of the prisoners died in their bondage, but Gilbert lived till the Revolution, and came safe home to his wife and relatives, and was a useful member of the Session of Kirkcowan.

CHAPTER XLV.

THE SUFFERINGS IN PENNINGHAME.

The sufferings in Penninghame—The sufferings in Kirkinner—
William Graham, the Crossmichael Martyr—Grierson of
Balmaclellan—The M'Cartneys of Blaikit—John Gordon,
Viscount Kenmure, and Lady Kenmure—Gabriel Semple—
John Livingstone, minister of Stranraer—Knox in Galloway
—The Coves of Barholm—The Galloway Covenants of 1638
—Borgue Covenant and signatures—Minnigaff Covenants and
signatures.

FROM Penninghame Session Records we learn that the
Parish suffered severely after Bothwell. The dragoons
and foot soldiers spoiled the houses and took away the
cattle of those who had been implicated. John Martin,
Glenvogie, James Martin, Glenhapple, and Alexander
M'Clingan, Baltersan, had their goods and cattle
seized, and their wives were apprehended and cast into
prison. The cattle of John Hannay in Penninghame
were driven away, and his house was demolished.
James Gordon of Craighlaw, who was living in
Glasnick had his house spoiled, and his estate was
gifted to Major Main. He bought back his estate at
great expense, pledging it in security, and while others
at the Revolution recovered their estates, there was
none from whom he could claim, and ultimately the
creditor got possession. John MacTaggart, Hazel-
green, and Alexander Murray, taken at Bothwell, were

shipped to the West Indies. The ship was lost, and with it MacTaggart, but Murray was saved, and returned home. John M'Caul in Corsbie, taken at Bothwell, was afterwards liberated, but was again seized and imprisoned in Dumfries, while the soldiers helped themselves to his goods. He was liberated on Bond for a thousand merks. Alexander M'Clelland, Baltersan, taken at Bothwell, and afterwards liberated, had his whole stock and crop seized and sold by Sheriff Graham. Gilbert Douglas, Glenrassie, for being at Bothwell, suffered great loss, estimated at about a thousand merks. William Kennedy, Barnkirk, and John Ferguson, Garwachie, were also at Bothwell, and became marked men afterwards, and suffered accordingly. John M'Caw, cottar, Kirkcalla, had all he possessed taken from him, and was forced to flee for his life. John Stewart, Glenlochoch, suffered to the extent of over a thousand merks, and fled to Ireland. Patrick M'Clelland, Baltersan, was imprisoned for six months in Wigtown, and was fined five hundred merks, and his stock and crop were seized by Sheriff Graham. Thomas M'Keand in Balsalloch, and Gilbert Heron in Carsenestock, were imprisoned and only liberated on payment of considerable sums.

THE SUFFERINGS IN KIRKINNER.

The husband of Margaret Lauchlisone, John Milliken, suffered much at the hands of the persecutors. The soldiers were frequently quartered on him, and he was obliged to pay six of them eight shillings Scots each per day for a considerable time. He was taken prisoner to Dumfries, and fined. Andrew M'Cubbin and his wife, Elizabeth Milliken, daughter of the above John Milliken, were stripped of all their goods, their furniture burned to ashes, and themselves and their children turned out of their house. Alexander Vaux of Barwhanny, brother of John Vaux of Barnbarroch, and Margaret Maxwell, his wife, were harassed, processed, and fined merely for nonconformity and receiving outed ministers. William Sproat, Clutag, to avoid persecution, went to Portpatrick, intending to cross to Ireland, but was apprehended and brought back on foot between two dragoons past his own door to Wigtown prison. He was put in irons, his ears cut off, and his fingers burned with matches. He was sentenced to be banished to America, and died on the way. William Kerr, Boreland, was imprisoned at the same time as Margaret Lauchlisone, but managed to escape. John Stewart, Kirkbien, was stripped of all his goods. John Dunn, Stewarton, was imprisoned and banished, and died on the voyage. Janet Dunn, his daughter, had her fingers burned with matches, and was carried prisoner to Glasgow. Margaret Middinel, Meikle Airies, was imprisoned. John M'Reikie, Newton, and Agnes M'Culloch, Stewarton, wife of Anthony Hawthorn, were fined. Andrew Martin, Little Airies, being at Bothwell, was declared rebel, and his house was frequently plundered, and the crop seized by the dragoons. His wife, Margaret Kennedy, suffered severely, and was forced to flee with her children. She was taken prisoner, but managed to escape. "The search after these was so accurate that many hundreds of Oaths were taken anent the said Andrew and his spouse, so that they were obliged to more close hiding until King James' toleration."

WILLIAM GRAHAM, THE CROSSMICHAEL MARTYR.

In Crossmichael churchyard there is a martyr's stone, about three feet high by two feet broad, with the following inscription:—

HERE LYES
WILLIAM GRAHAM
WHO MAKEING HIS
ESCAPE FROM HIS
MOTHERS HOUSE
WAS PURSUED AND
TAKEN AND INSTANT-
LY SHOT DEAD BY
A PARTY OF CLAVER-
HOUSES TROOP FOR

On other side a skull and crossbones, and

MEMENTO MORI

HIS ADHERENCE
TO SCOTLANDS
REFORMATION CO
VENANTS NATION
AL AND SOLEMN
LEAGUE 1682.

Defoe includes William Graham among those whom Claverhouse murdered at his own hands. "Claver-house rode after him and over-took him, and although the young man offered to surrender, and begged him to save his life, he shot him dead with his pistol." He was brother to James Graham referred to at p. 237.

GRIERSON OF BALMACLELLAN.

Many of the Covenanters found for years a safe
retreat in a cave near Ingleston, but in April, 1685,
it was betrayed by "knavish Watson," who had
deserted the Covenanters and become a bitter persecutor. This was the Andrew Watson who is mentioned
with the Covenanters implicated in the tragedy at
Carsphairn Manse. Early in the morning of 28th
April, 1685, acting on Watson's information, Colonel
James Douglas and Lieutenant Livingstone stealthily
came to the cave and captured five fugitives. These
were John Gibson, brother to the Laird of Ingleston;
James Bennoch from Glencairn; Robert Edgar from
Balmaclellan; Robert Mitchell from Cumnock; and
Robert Grierson, also from Balmaclellan. When the
dragoons came up, they fired into the cave, wounding
one of the fugitives, and then rushed in and seized the
five. They were dragged out and ordered to be shot.
Gibson's mother and sister, hearing of the capture,
came upon the scene and interceded for him, but in
vain. The soldiers, however, allowed him an interview, and Gibson asked them not to grieve for him.
He was allowed to pray, which he did in a way that
impressed even the soldiers. He read part of Psalm 17,
and John 16, and, after praying again, was shot dead.
The other four were not allowed to pray, and were
immediately shot. One of them not dead was thrust
through with a sword, and, as he died, he cried,
"Though every hair of my head were a man, I am
willing to die all these deaths for Christ and His
cause." Gibson, Edgar, Bennoch, and Mitchell were

buried in Glencairn, where stones were erected to their memory. Grierson's body was carried to Balmaclellan and buried there, and a stone over his grave has the following inscription:—

AT INGLESTOUN IN THE PAROCH OF GLENCARN ANNO 16

THIS MONUMENT TO PASSENGERS SHALL CRY
THAT GOODLY GRIERSON UNDER IT DOTH LY
BETRAY'D BY KNAVISH WATSON TO HIS FOES
WHICH MADE THIS MARTYRS DAYS BY MURTHER CLOSE
IF YE WOULD KNOW THE NATURE OF HIS CRIME
THEN READ THE STORY OF THAT KILLING TIME
WHEN BABEL'S BRATS WITH HELLISH PLOTS CONCEALD
DESIGN'D TO MAKE OUR SOUTH THEIR HUNTING FIELD
HERE'S ONE OF FIVE AT ONCE WERE LAID IN DUST
TO GRATIFY ROME'S EXECRABLE LUST
IF CARABINES WITH MOLTEN BULLETS COULD
HAVE REACHED THEIR SOULS THESE MIGHTY NIMRODS WOULD
THEM HAVE CUT OFF; FOR THERE COULD NO REQUEST
THREE MINUTES GET TO PRAY FOR FUTURE REST.

COLONEL JAMES DOUGLAS,

GRIERSON WHO WAS SHOT TO DEATH BY COMMAND OF

Balmaclellan churchyard also has a stone in memory of Robert Paterson, stone engraver, well known as Old Mortality, who died at Bankhead of Caerlaverock, 14th February, 1801, aged 88.

THE M'CARTNEYS OF BLAIKIT.

The M'Cartneys of Blaikit, in the Parish of Urr, were zealous supporters of the Covenanters, and suffered accordingly. John M'Cartney, who was an

elder in the Parish Church in 1647, was in 1662 fined
£600 merely for adherence to the Presbyterian
Church. Other fines were subsequently imposed and
he was thrown into Kirkcudbright prison, where he
died.

He was succeeded by his son, George M'Cartney.
He was suspected of favouring the Dalry Rising, and,
merely because of this, Maxwell of Milton seized his
horses to the value of £160, spoiled his house,
and carried away his crop. Bannatyne next forced a
Bond from him for five hundred merks. In 1668, a
party of dragoons again plundered the house and took
away horse, and then shortly afterwards Major Cockburn arrived from Dumfries garrison with eighty
horse, waited two or three days, eating and destroying
everything about the place. In 1671, Sir Charles
Erskine, Lord Lyon, got a commission from the Lords
of the Treasury to uplift the Estates, goods, and gear
of those in Wigtownshire, Kirkcudbright, and Dumfriesshire, forfeited for the Rebellion of 1666 for the
crop of 1670. By some means M'Cartney's name was
got into this Commission though he appears to have
been neither forfeited nor an excepted person. The
Lord Lyon wished him to buy back his own estate,
and when he refused, he was carried prisoner to Dumfries, and then to Edinburgh. After several petitions,
he at last got his case considered, and it was clearly
shown that his name should not have been in the
Commission at all, and his liberation was ordered on
Bond of one thousand merks to appear when called
upon. Meantime he was taken back to prison. After

an interval, he made inquiries, and discovered to his dismay that the clerk had omitted to minute his liberation. Altogether he remained in prison over six years, and during this time his estate was laid waste and everything carried away by the Lord Lyon. After he was liberated and settled down again, David Graham came with a party of soldiers and kept garrison in his house for some weeks, seized his horse, and helped himself to corn and everything else he wanted. Wodrow says that the total of his losses, besides being impaired in health, was £9,827 16s.

He afterwards supported the famous John Hepburn, and was one of those who appeared before the Presbytery and asked help to get the Privy Council to give the stipend of Urr to Mr. Hepburn, "whose preaching they allow." In 1699, he appears in opposition to the former Episcopalian curate of the Parish, John Lyon, who had applied to the General Assembly to be admitted a Presbyterian minister. M'Cartney died in 1704, and was buried in Urr churchyard.

JOHN GORDON, VISCOUNT KENMURE, AND LADY KENMURE.

Sir John Gordon of Lochinvar was born about the year 1599, and in his student years had the privilege of living with John Welsh when the latter was an exile in France. Kenmure's early life was not remarkable for either good or evil, his chief desire being for worldly honours. Years afterwards he said to one of his kinsmen, " I would not have you drown yourself so much in the concerns of the world as I did."

About the year 1626, he married Lady Jane Campbell, third daughter of Archibald, seventh Earl of Argyle, by his first wife, Ann, who was a daughter of William, sixth Earl of Morton. Sir John was hopeful that the honours of the house of Gowrie, attainted for high treason in 1600, would be revived in his person as his mother was Lady Isabel Ruthven, daughter of William, first Earl of Gowrie. It is said that he sold the lands of Stitchill, the ancient inheritance of the family, and gave the price to the Duke of Buckingham the evening before his assassination by Felton as a bribe to support his claims. His hopes in this were doomed to disappointment. In 1633, Charles created him Viscount Kenmure and Lord Gordon of Lochinvar. He attended the Parliament of 1633, but when Charles wished to pass laws ratifying the Acts of Perth Assembly and for advancing the state of bishops, which he could not support, he feigned illness, and returned home. In 1634, he was back in Edinburgh still endeavouring to be elevated to the earldom of Gowrie. He took ill, returned home, and died on 12th September, at the early age of thirty-five. On his death-bed he exhorted Lamb, the bishop of Galloway, not to molest or remove the Lord's servants, or enthrall their consciences to receive the Five Articles of Perth, or do anything against their consciences as he would wish to have mercy from God. He added, "Since I did lie down on this bed, the sin that lay heaviest on my soul and hath burdened my conscience most was my withdrawing of myself from Parliament and not giving my voice for the truth, for in so doing

I have denied the Lord my God." To Rutherfurd
he said, " I did it with fearful wrestling of conscience,
my light paying me home within, when I seemed to
be glad and joyful before men." Rutherfurd continued with him in his illness. A few minutes before
the end, Rutherfurd engaged in prayer, and his
Lordship was observed smiling, his visage became
beautified, and we are told that the expiry of his breath
and the ceasing of his pulse (which the physician was
still holding) corresponded exactly with the close of
the prayer. Rutherfurd has immortalised his fame
in *The Last and Heavenly Speeches of Lord Kenmure*.

Lady Gordon in her early years was of a delicate
constitution, and Rutherfurd seems to refer to her
sufferings in his letter to her of November 15th, 1633.
" I knew and saw Him (Christ) with you in the
furnace of affliction, for there He wooed you to Himself, and chose you to be His." All her children died
young. Her only son, born after Lord Kenmure's
death, died when little more than four years old.
Nearly fifty of Rutherfurd's letters are addressed to
Lady Kenmure, and to her he dedicated *The Trial
and Triumph of Faith*. When Rutherfurd died, she
extended her beneficence to his widow and daughter,
and the suffering Presbyterian ministers received substantial tokens of her good-will, for she was warmly
attached to the cause for which they suffered. About a
year after her son's death, Lady Kenmure married
the Honourable Sir Henry Montgomery of Giffen,
second son of Alexander, sixth Earl of Eglinton, but
she was soon left a widow again. The exact date of

her own death is not known, but she was alive in 1672, for John Livingstone then spoke of her as "the oldest Christian acquaintance I have now alive." She was, however, in a very weak state of health, and her end was believed to be near.

GABRIEL SEMPLE.

Gabriel Semple was second son of Sir Bryce Semple of Cathcart, Sheriff of Renfrew, and was a great-great-grandson of John, first Lord Semple. At the age of twenty-five, he was unanimously called to Kirkpatrick-durham, as the Records of Dumfries Presbytery show:—

> "At Dumfries, 23 December, 1656, James Gordon of Bar, William Gordon of MacCartney with some others of the elders of the Parish of. Kirkpatrick of the Moore, compeiring did present ane unanimous supplication subscryved by the heritours, elders, and tennents of that parish earnestly desyring the Presbytry to present Mr. Gabriell Semple to his tryalls in order to his settling amongst them conforme to ane cleir and unanimous call subscryved by them and delivered to the said Mr. Gabriell Semple."

He was ordained on the 26th May following, when, "after sermon had by Mr. Walter Gledstaines, Moderator, the said Mr. Gabriell Semple was solemnly admitted into the ministry thereof by Invocation of God's name and Imposition of hands according to the custom of this Church, and was heartily received by the gentlemen, elders and people of the parish, who gave unto him the right hand of fellowship in corroboration of their former call and invitation which they had formerly and unanimously given."

He was thus the choice of the people, but he was driven out by the Act of 1662, and with Welsh of Irongray, took up his abode at Corsock. He joined the Dalry Rising, and preached to the Covenanters at Ochiltree and Lanark. Afterwards he left the country, but, venturing back to Scotland, proclamations were issued against him. He was captured in 1681, and, after three months' imprisonment in Canongate Jail, he was liberated on Bond for ten thousand merks. He withdrew to England and was afterwards appointed to Jedburgh, where he remained till his death in 1706, at the age of seventy-four. He was married to a daughter of Sir Walter Riddel of Riddel, and left several children.

JOHN LIVINGSTONE, MINISTER OF STRANRAER.

John Livingstone was born at Kilsyth in January, 1603. His father and grandfather had been ministers of the parish, and he himself preached his first sermon there. In 1626, he visited Galloway on the invitation of Lord Kenmure, who had in view to present him to the parish of Anwoth, but unforeseen delay occurred in getting it disjoined, and Livingstone accepted another call. "At that time in Galloway," he says, "I got acquaintance with my Lord Kenmure and his religious Lady and several worthy and experienced Christians, as Alexander Gordon, Earlston; Alexander

Gordon, Knockgray; Robert Gordon, Knockbrex;
John, his brother, and Alexander of Gairleuch,
Fullerton, laird of Carleton, John M'Adam and
Christina M'Adam of Waterhead, Marion M'Naught,
Kirkcudbright, and several others, for I preached at
a communion at Borgue where many good people came
out of Kirkcudbright, and I was present at private
meetings with the some of the fore-mentioned at Gairleuch, and in the Airds, where Earlston then dwelt."
He was invited to Cumbernauld, the seat of the Earl
of Wigtown, where he preached at intervals till 1630,
when he accepted a charge in the North of Ireland.
There were other Presbyterian congregations in the
neighbourhood, and among his near ministerial
brethren were Josiah Welsh, son of Welsh, the former
minister of Kirkcudbright, Robert Blair and John
M'Clelland, afterwards minister of Kirkcudbright.
These were deposed by the bishop of Down, and had
to flee for their lives. When on a visit to the Earl of
Cassillis, Livingstone accepted a call to Stranraer, and
was inducted in July, 1638. The more serious of
his flock assembled daily, and, after singing a few
verses of a Psalm, and reading a portion of Scripture,
he spoke to them for half an hour. He tells that the
neighbouring ministers with whom he kept most
society, by whose counsel and company he profited
most, were John M'Clelland, Kirkcudbright (married
to Mrs. Livingstone's sister); Robert Hamilton, Ballantrae; and George Hutchison, Colmonell; and in the
Presbytery of Stranraer, Alexander Turnbull, Kirkmaiden; George Dick, Inch; and John Dick, Glen-

luce; and in the Presbytery of Wigtown, Andrew Lauther, Whithorn; and John Park, Mochrum, who was afterwards appointed to Stranraer. He had been present at communions with most of these ministers, and they had been at his communions at Stranraer. He attended the Glasgow Assembly of 1638, and in 1640 was appointed chaplain to the Earl of Cassillis's regiment, and was present at Newburn. In 1648, he was translated to Ancrum. Refusing to take the Oath of Allegiance in the way desired, he was banished, and went to Rotterdam, where he died in August, 1672, in the seventieth year of his age.

KNOX IN GALLOWAY.
THE COVES OF BARHOLM.

When Knox found the times too dangerous for him in Edinburgh after the murder of Rizzio, he fled to Ayrshire, but it is not generally known that, instead of remaining there, he came to Galloway about 1566, and sought safety in Barholm Castle, between Gatehouse and Creetown. His signature was for many years to be seen on the wall of one of the rooms. The M'Cullochs of Barholm were zealous supporters of the principles of the Reformation, and this accounts for Knox coming here. After Queen Mary's escape from Lochleven Castle, Knox fled to the Continent, but, before leaving Scotland, he had his wife and family removed to Rusco Castle, near Gatehouse, where he left them in charge of Robert Campbell of Kingancleuch, Ayrshire. Rusco at this time belonged to

Gordon of Lochinvar, and Campbell was probably only a guest at the castle as Knox was at Barholm.

The caves or coves of Barholm often afforded a safe retreat to the persecuted Covenanters. Barbour speaks of three of these caves in his *Unique Traditions*—the Cove of Barholm, the Caa's Cave, and the Whig's Hole. They are in the rocks on the shore opposite Garlieston, in a line with Barholm Castle. The Whig's Hole extended inwards for some thirty yards and at a little distance from the mouth it became contracted and at this point could easily be closed by a stone. This, indeed, was frequently done when the persecutors sent out by Lagg were searching in the vicinity. Traditions are current in the neighbourhood of a woman who lived in a cottage at the Warld's End watching for favourable opportunities to lower provisions to the Covenanters hiding in the caves. In Welsh's *Life of Dr. Brown*, it is said that his grandfather, the minister of Kirkmabreck, was wont to send food to some of the persecuted, and that "the cave is still shown where such people were thus supplied."

THE GALLOWAY COVENANTS OF 1638.

BORGUE COVENANT.

The 1638 Covenant was received with enthusiasm in Galloway, and widely signed. Every parish in the province had its copy, but very few of them have been traced. The Borgue Covenant is preserved in the Register House, Edinburgh. It is dated 22nd April, 1638, and measures twenty-five by twenty-seven inches. It is in the usual terms and has the Glasgow Determination on the back. The following are the signatures:—

" Thomas Fullartone, James Drew, Jon. Drew, Thomas Tagart, Robert Gordone, Robert Bryce, James Tagart, Thomas M'Crobert, James Thomsone, David Thomsone, James Pauling, James Tagart, James M'Crobat, Jon. Mertein, Wm. Thomsone, James M'Kittrick, John Kirkpatrick, Jon. Tagart, James Carsane, Andro Carsane, Thomas M'Kinnay, Jon. Hendrie, Ninane M'Ilnae, John Hendrie, Wm. Bryce, James Tagart, Jon. Tagart, Thomas Sproyt, Alexr. Campbell, Andro Sproyt, Jon. Newall, Jon. Heuchell, Wm. Clyltane, Alexr. M'Qn. Thomas Kingane, Thomas Kennie, Thomas Keine, elder James Kenne, Patrick Tagart, Thomas Johnstone, Jon. Herreis, George Bryce, Andro Kenne, Jon. Herreis, Wm. M'Crobat, Adame Haffie, Jon. M'Quhatrok, Wm. M'Cyffie, Jon. Corbie, Jon. Sproyt, James M'Mine, Jon. Sproyt, Robt. Thomsone, James Bryce, Symone Clark, Jon. Gordone, Alexr. Muirhead, Jon. M'Quhitrok, Jon. Gordone, Mertene Callane, Jon. M'Kittrik, George M'Naught, Thomas Clark, Andro Sproyt, James Gordone, Jon. Cairnes, Jon. M'Kie, Jon. Comblenie, Robert M'Robat, Jon. Clyltane, Edward Pauling, Alexr. Clark, James M'Cuffie, Wm. Cuffie, Jon. Diksone, George Goune, Wm. M'Mine, Andro Cuffie, Thomas Broun, Jon.

Tagart, John Symsone, Jon. Sproyt, Jon.
M'Goune, George Warnok, Thomas Carsane,
James Bell, James Cliltane, Andro Bell, Wm.
M'Ghie, Thomas Robsone, Alexr. Bryce, Gilbert
Clark, James M'Mine, Thomas Combline, Jon.
Bryce, Jon. Broune, Jon. WmSone, Wm.
M'Callell, Jon. Robisone, John M'Kittrick, Jon.
Tagart, Jon. M'Goune, Jon. Law, Robt. Sproyt,
Jon. M'Alleill, Alexr. M'Murrie, Jon. Bryce,
James Thomsone, Thomas Raen, Wm. Shaw,
Gilbert M'Ghie, Thomas M'Gympsie, Jon.
M'Ghie, Jon. M'Cullreoch, Alexr. WmSone, Jon.
M'Mollane, David M'Quhae, Jon. Porter, Jon.
Kingane, Jon. Sproyt, Jon. Herreis, Andro
Ketrik, Merteine Halline, Symon Killigane, Jon.
Jonstone, James Jonstone, James Cultane, Wm.
Broune, Jon. Gordone, Jon. Hunter, Thomas
Gordone, James Jellie, Thomas Tagart, Patrick
Bryce, Jon. M'Couchtrie, Thomas Robsone, Jon.
Edgar, Jon. Douglas, Andro. M'Kie, Edward
Robinsone, Andro Suord, Andro Goune, James
Goune, Thomas Gone, George Muirheid, Wm.
M'Murrie, Jon. M'Cornok, James Corrie, James
Car, Jon. M'Knische, James Dungallheid, James
M'Goune.

"With our hand at the pen by the Notar
following at our commands because we cannot
wrycht ourselves.

".Ita est Robert M'Henchane Noric pube de
mandato darum. personarum scribere nescien ut

assruerunt manu mea propria Johne Makcachernie, James Reid, Robert Dalzell, Williame and James Henries, John Dalzell, Thomas Layng, William Newall, Gilbert Grier, Robert Makgoun, Johne Makmartine, Andro Corsane, Andro Kairnoquhen, James Carsane, John Makinsche, John Jolie, Andro Schaw, William Welsch, Andro Makcuffie, Johne Carsane, John Cambell, Niniane Cawdzell, John Cuffeis, Thomas Kinzean, Andro Carsane, Johne Dowglas, Johne Stewart, John Thomsone, Thomas Gibson, Robert Hunter? John Makcurrie, James M'Tagert, Robert Makquhen, Johne Makhallorn, James Makillnae, John Carsane, John Sproyt.

———— ———— ———— ?
———— ———— ———— ?

Thomas Lennox of
Plunton.
John Lennox.
Andro Lennox.
A. Cairnis.
Johne Robisoune.
Johne M'Quhene.
Robert Heuchane Notar.
John M'Tagart.
Samuell Arnot.
Thomas Arnot.
Johne Hutcheon..
Georg Gordon.
Andro Sprot.

M. Gaw. Maxwell,
Minister at Borge.
John Fullartoun of
Carletoun.
James M'Lellane in
Balmagane.
Robert M'Lellane.
James Kirk.
William Arnot.
Roberto Gordoun of
Knokbrex.
Thomas Sproit.
John Pailling.
Robert M'Garmarie.
Thomas Robesone.
James Robisonne.
Johne Sprot.
Robert Makcuffe."

The following signatures appear to the Ratification of the Articles of the Glasgow Assembly of December, 1638, endorsed thereon:—

Thomas Lennox.
of Plunton
—? M'Clellane
of Barmagachein
Walter Hamiltoune
Andro Sproit
Johne Sprot
James Robisone
William Tat

M. Gaw Maxwell.
Minister at Borge
John Follarton
of Carletoun
Robert Gordoun
of Robertoun
Robert M'Lellane
Johne Robisone
(James Robi)sone
Thomas Sproit
(Thomas) Arnot

John Gordon.
Johne M'Quheine.
John Pauling.
A. Cairnes.

Robert (M') Garmarie
John Gordoun
James Kirk
John Lennox
Robert Lennox
John M'Lellane
Robert Cuffe
Georg Gordon.

UNIQUE COVENANT AT CARDONESS.
MINNIGAFF COVENANT.

Until recently it was not thought that the Covenant had been printed contemporaneously, except in pamphlet form, but Mr. G. W. Shirley, Dumfries, has brought to light a printed copy which we have had the privilege of examining through the favour of Sir William and Lady Maxwell of Cardoness. It has been in the Cardoness Charter Chest for generations, and was exhibited recently at a meeting of the Antiquarian Society at Dumfries. We cannot do better than adopt Mr. Shirley's description of it:—

" The Covenant is of vellum, in three portions, which have become separated. The three parts are in an excellent state of preservation, a small portion of the margin only having been torn away. The upper portion measures $19\frac{3}{5}$ inches by $14\frac{2}{5}$ inches; the middle part is the longest, $21\frac{1}{5}$ inches, and of the same width as the upper part. The third part is the smallest, $5\frac{2}{5}$ inches deep, slightly narrower, and it is of a different and thicker skin.

" The first two parts bear the text. This is beautifully printed in double columns, the heading being tastefully set out, and the whole surrounded by a floreated border, which is of double breadth at the top and bottom. The text is continuous on both sheets, running down the left column to the foot of the second sheet before passing to the right column, but, though specially examined, there is nothing to show whether the sheets were joined before printing or were printed separately. From border to border the printing is $11\frac{1}{2}$ inches broad throughout and $17\frac{3}{5}$ inches long on the upper sheet and $16\frac{1}{2}$ inches long on the second."

It was probably printed and signed prior to the Glasgow Assembly of November, 1638, as it does not bear the Glasgow Determination. There is neither the name of the printer nor the place of printing on it. It may have been printed abroad, as many of the Covenanters' works were. It is scarcely conceivable that only one copy of the print was pulled. What has become of the others?

The holograph signatures leave no doubt that the printing is contemporaneous. On the left hand margin of the printing on the first sheet are the signatures:— Rothess; Montrose; Eglintoun; Cassellis; Lennox; Wemyss; Lothian; Lindesay; Dalhousie; Yester; Elcho; Johnstoun; Kirkcudbright.

There are no signatures on the right hand margin, and there are no signatures on the margins of the second page, but, joining the two sheets, is the signature "J. Coupar," and at the foot of the second sheet are the signatures:—Garthland; Dundas off thatt ilk; Cunnynghamheid; Erskine off Duns; W. Rig of Setherney (?); Williame Grahame of Hiltoun; W. Riddell; J (?) Murray; W. Moore, appearand of Rowallane; J. Cokburne, Clerkintyne, yr; William Welche, M.A. (?); Sr. J. (?) Murray; Robert Hamylton of Binning; Sr. W. (?) Foulis feer of Colintoun; Sr. W. (?) Rowallane; Alexr. M'dowall off Logane; W. Cochrane of Cowtoun (?); J. R. off Merland; Sr. J. (?) Fowstoun (?); Patrick Lissweis (?); James Hamelton belstene Alexander Mackie; ——M'Kie off Larg; Alexander Gordoune of erlistowne; M. Gibsone durie; R. Naper of Culcreuche; J. Grier (?) off Monzie; Hew M'dowall of Knokglas; Patrik M'dowell of Creichane; Sr. B. (?) Samingtoune (?) Mirhurig; Johnne Ker; Johne ——; ——

Lethun of etheringholm; T. Shaw of Cavers; W. dowglas of Redheide, Craigdarroughe; G. Douglas of penzery, Lyon; Sr. E. B. Sempill beltreis J. Dowglais Scheref of roxburghe.

The third sheet is all signatures. The parchment appears to have been cut off some other document, parts of the long letters of some signatures being visible at the top of this sheet. It has the following signatures:— —— Ogilvy (?) of Inchmartrie; James Ross of balneill; Johne Ramsay of Edingtoune; —— Hamilton; —— J. Broune off Carseleuthe; Fergus Kennedy; Gilbert Kennedie; Johnne Gordoun of Cardynes; David Kennedy; Jon Gordone; J. Turnbull of Mynto; William Menteath of Randifurd; —— Rutheris (?); Sr. D. Campbell; Sr. J. (?) Grier; Jo. Pringill of Stittchell; W. Menzies; Arthur A. Ersken; Sr. J. Drummond of Machaine; —— Braco; —— Burnett of Leyes; Sr. G. Ramsay ballmeine; Robert Ker; Ja. Creichtoune; W. Gordoun of Shirmers; harie Elphinstoune off Caderhall; Killmaher, —— Wmphra Colquhoune of Ballbey; W. Sandelandes; Patrik hepburne of Wauchtune; Johne M'Kie of glassoche; Jas. Stewart of corsuall; —— of Craig caffie (?); —— Bancharay; Johne Vansz; Robert hamiltone; J. Gordoun of Auchlane; M. H. (?); Charteris; Alexr. Scott; Daniell hay, finlamont; J. Knox, wrytter; Alexander M'Kie; R. Scott of Woll; Duncan craford off Drumphi (?).

There are other two Covenants preserved in the Cardoness Charter Chest, one of which is of the usual vellum type, written locally and signed by the

parishioners of Minnigaff. It measures about 27 by
26 inches, and has altogether 355 signatures. The
first is that of Mr. William Maxwell, minister of
Minnigaff, who, with the other Galloway ministers,
was turned out in 1662. His son was the gallant
Colonel William Maxwell, a Covenanter of the
Covenanters, who boldly stood by Argyle on the
scaffold, and followed his body to Magdelene Chapel.
He went abroad and returned with William of Orange,
who held him in great esteem and presented him with
a ring containing his hair and with portraits by
Kneller of himself and his Queen, which are still to
be seen at Cardoness. He was Governor of Glasgow
during the Rebellion of 1715, having " left his own
family and countrey, above seventy miles distant from
this place, at the desire of the Magistrates and Chiefs
of the inhabitants." The Town Council presented him
with a service of plate " as a mark of the town's favour
and respect towards him." He married Nicholas
Stewart, grand-daughter of the Earl of Galloway, and
heiress of Cardoness.*

After the minister's signature are the signatures
of the local lairds. These have evidently not been
adhibited at one time.

Then follow the parishioners' names written by
Notaries. There is a considerable space between the
lairds' signatures and those of the parishioners,
showing that it was intended to get other signatures.

---

* For Memoir of Colonel William Maxwell, see *One of King
William's Men*, by Professor Reid.

The parishioners' signatures overflow to the back, and the Glasgow Determination is also given on the back, being signed by twelve individuals.

The other Covenant at Cardoness is a long roll of paper formed of four sheets, each measuring about 14 inches by 12 inches. There has been at least one other sheet which is, unfortunately, amissing. The parishioners' signatures on the paper copy almost duplicate those on the vellum copy, and they are more distinct. The following are the signatures on the vellum copy:—

Mr. William Maxwell, minister at Minigoff; Arthore Dunbar off machermior; J. Dunbar; Alexr. Stewart; Patrik M'Kie, baillzie of Monygof; James Stewart, belze of Mongyf; Alexander Roxburghe; Johne Mcquharg; W. Hunter, notar; Johne Murdoch; Johne Sloane; Johne Stewart; Thomas Mcquharg; Thomas ——; Johne Mcquecheine; Johne M'Naght; Johne Mc co ——; M. H. Charteris; Andro Heroune in Kirouchtrie; Johne Maxwell; James M'Millane; James Stewart; Patrick Douglas; John Mc illoch; Johne Mcquhonnell; robert M'Kie; John M'Millane; William Mcgowne, ——; Johne Hamiltone; Thomas Mcquhonel; —— Stewart of ffisgill; Alexr. Stewart; Johne Stewart; Johne Mcquharg; Patrik Herroon; George Bell; Johne M'Millane; John Cunynghame; John Mcclymount; Thomas M'Kean; Archibald Makclanie; Patrig Thomsonne; Patrik

M'Cauell; James Muir; Johne Mccoid; Alexander Gray; James Gray.

Signatures on paper copy.—"Wryttene be Patrick Garroch, wryter in Wigtoune."

Mr. William Maxwell, minister at Minigoff; Sr. P. M'Kie off Larg; Alexr. Stewart; Andro Gray; J. Dunbar; Alexr. Steuart; Arthore Dunbar off Machermuir; Patrik Heron of Kirróuchrie; Johne Stewart; Pe Mcquharg; Johne Cunyghame; Patrik M'Kie, baelzie of Monygoff; William Dunbar; Andro heroune in Kirouchtrie; Williame Mcgowne; Johne Finlaystune; James M'Millne; Alexander Roxburgh; John M'Millane; Thomas M'Kean; David Mcculloch; Johne Mcgauchein; Patrik M'Kie; James Steuart; John Murdoch; Johne Maxwell; Johne M'Millane; Robert M'Kie; Johne M'Knocht; Patrik Douglas; Archibald M'Clauie; Johne M'Millane; John Sloane; John M'Coid; John M'Coid; James Muire; Patrick M'Cawell; Robert M'Cawell; Johne hamiltoun; W. Hunter; Johne M'Quharg; Johne Mcquharg; Johne M'Millane; John Mcquhonnell; John Steuart; Johne Roxburght; Johne M'Cornock; George Bell; Thomas Reid; Patrik Thomsoune; Gilbert Mc clliver; Alexr. gray; James Gray.

Paper and vellum.—

We, Jon. Mcclymount and Jon. Gordoune in Kirrireoche, Johne Mcgowne in Kirrimore;

George Gordoune in Kirrikenene; Johne Mcclymont ther; Thomas Mccully and Jon. Mctaggirt in Polgoune; Jon. Mcquhardg in Kirricastell; Mairteine Mcilroy and Patrick Thomson in Killkerow; Doncane, Andro and John Mcquhardges in Strone; Andro M'Millane in arshkonchene; Thomas, Jon Wm. and Adam gordounes in Inchbuchaine; Andro and Quinteine findlaysounes in Kiriachtrie; Gilbert, Alex. and Anchonie M'Caads in Trostane; Alexr. and findlay Mcquhardges in Auruch; Jon. aird ther; George M'Millane; Jon. M'Kie; John Mcquhennell in Clechmallock; Thomas Mcilroy and Alexr. Mcquhennell in Glencaird; Patrik M'Kie; Andro Mcquhennell; Patrik Mctaggirt in Largforag; Jon Mcgill and Andro Mcgowne in merkcove; Gilbert and Thos. Cairdes and James Herroune in Drumjohane; Jon. M'Millane, and Jon M'Teir in Lansboy; Jon and george Mcclurges in Carndirrie; Alexr. Douglas in Dalnaw; Jon Mcdowell in glenrubock; Archibald Heirreane and Jon Mccanise ther; Jon and patrick M'Kies in bargrenane; patrick and James Mc coires ther; James Campbell in Drummell-wantie; Jon M'Taggirt in Drumrichloche; Andro douglas ther, and Jon M'Kie ther; David Shaw and Andro M'Kie in Monewik; Alexr. Thomsonne in Brigtoune; Anthone M'Millane in Firrochbae; Patrik M'Kie in Meikle Caldounes; Quinteinne findlaysoune in littell caldounes; Johne and Gilbert M'Kies; Gilbert Mcgowne, Jon Hendrysonne

and Patrick Mctaggirt in holme; Rot. Tait and
Patrick tait in Borgane; Alexr. Jon. Thomas
Patrik Stewarts and Patrik Mcquhroyters, elder
and younger, in Larg; James Mcquhardge and
Alexr. Thomsoune in cammer, Archibald
Douglas, Walter Mctaggirt in Lagbaes; James
Willsone, Rot. Stewart, and Jon Mcquozd in Car-
dorkane; Jon. M'Millan in clonts, peiter Douglas
ther; John Mcquhroyter; thomas Mccoyd, Don-
cane Mcquhroyter; Jon. M'Millane in Toch-
regane; Jon Stewart elder and Jon Stewart
younger; Andro meines; Thomas Mcclellane in
Drongandow; Jon Mccrakane in Barclay; Jon
Watloun and george tait in Barclay; Alexr.
Mcclellane in Dirrigal; Jon. Mcgill in Dirrigal;
Rot. Mccord; Andro Mcgowne; Jon Mcchlauch-
line; Jon Murdoche; Alexr. Stewart; Rot.
Mcgowne; John Davidsonne, elder, in Borland;
Jon Davidsonne ,younger, in Borland; Mungo
herroune in Kirkland; Jon Simpsone; Jon
cunigame; Jon Stewart and Alexr. Stewart in
clauchrie; Jon Mcquhenill, elder, in Glenmalloch;
Jon Sk —— herne and thomas Mccaa in Glen-
malloch; Donnie M'Kie and Jon Mcclurg in
Knockbrex; William Stewart; Jon Campbell in
Glenshalloch; Barnard, thomas, Jon. Alexr.
M'Kies; Jon and Alexr. morrazes and patrick
Stewart in Garlarge; Jon mcchrachire, elder and
younger, in Lomoquhen; Andro finlaysonne and
Alexr. Simpsoun in Laggane; Jon and ninean
Mcmillanes; Jon Gordoune and Jon Mccornock

in Craigginkalzie; Jon Patrick and quinteine Mcmillanes in Craignell; Thomas mcquhroyter in firroch; Jon and James Mcmillanes in Polbrekburg; Mathew and Jon reids in craigde; Wm. M'Millane in Tonergie; Alexr. and James M'Millanes in Tonotrie; Jon M'Millane in Dickitrik; Jon and William M'Millanes; Thomas and michaell Mcclellanes in corwar; Walter M'Millane and Andro Mcgauchane in overdalashe; Jon Reid and Jon Steinsonne in Dalashecairnes; Jon M'Kinnell and patrik maxwell in Barhose; Rot. and Jon cunighame and patrik heuchane in Bargallie; Jon and Wm. culbertsonnes in ardwell; Michaell, Rot., and Jon M'Clellanes and Jon campbell in Gredock; Rot. and Alexr. Mccoskries; Jon and thomas heuchanes; Jon Mcgill; patrik mccleave; Jon Ramsay; Jon marteine; Rot. M'Millane; Jon Mccheitchie; Jon Doncane in Bardrochwood; Jon Walter and Jon M'Chessnyes in Little-park; Jon Mcgimpsies, elder and younger, and Jon murdoche in Little-park; Quinteine mccleane in Stron; Donald, Jon and James M'Kies in Blackcraig; Jon mcdowall in ——outane; Alexr. conchie; Thomas Steinsonne; Johne heuchane; thomas heuchane; Andro maillige; patrick edgeare in cawgell; James mcquhardy in Glennamore; Patrick Stewart in Craignine; Jon murrayes, elder and younger, in Barncauchall; Jon herroune in Drumneucht; Jon mcdowall in Corquhinock; Jon and gilbert mcdowells and alexr craik in

Lesons; andro mcgauchie in Drakmorne; Jon murray ther; Patrick murrayes, elder and younger, and peiter murray in Stronbay; Alexr M'Caa; Jon herroune; Patrick M'Millane; Jon Mcchessny in auchenlack; adam gordoune; Thomas Douglas in Risk; Jon ghrame; James and andro Mccornockes; george findlaysone in Drumnaquhinzie; Alexr. M'Brydes, younger and elder, in Glenhoise; Jon and Wm. M'Brydes; Patrick and Wm. M'Cawelles; Walter M'Millane and Rot. murdoche in Glenhoise; Andro M'Cornock in Kirtrochwod; Donald Thomsone in Kirochtrie; Jon M'Kie; George herroune; Jon Roxburghe in Kirochtrie; Johne ——

Paper copy ends here. Vellum copy proceeds:—

(fourth line from foot, right side)

—— mcquoyd in Machrimore; Jon Sloane; Alexr. mcdowalle in machirmore; Alexr. mcchuchie in Carsnaw; Alexr. Mcclurg in Carsnaw; Jon Dowane in Carsnaw; William Mccleave in carsmaneiche; Alexr. Mcclowane in Meiklecarse; Gilbert and Thomas herrounes in meiklecarse; George M'Millane; Robert Roxburght; Andro M'Millane; Alexr. M'Kie; niuean Bodden; hew menzies; david chalmers; James M'Millane and Jon Mccoskrie; Rot. good; Jo. M'Millane; patrick M'Kie; Jon M'Coskie; Jon Bodden; Alexr. M'Clachie; patrick Wilsone; William M'Kie; Jon M'Cord; Wm. Mcchachie;

Wm. Roxburgh; James Murdoche; Andro Bannoch; Jon Mure; Wm. Sloane; Culbert Simpsone; Jon Bodden; Patrick Stewart; thomas Mcilroy; Alexr. Herroune in the toune of monegoffe, with our hands at the pen led be the notars underwritten at or commands becaus we canot wryt or selffs. Ita est Andreas gray notarius publicus de mandatur dictarum personarum Subscriptorum scriben nescen asseruit ut premissis requisitus.

Ita est guillielmus Hunter not. p.

Back.—

Alexander Mccleave in bardrochwood; Robert M'Coskrie ther, and Alexander Heuchane ther; Alexander heuchane in reddock; Alexr. Mcchessny in Bargallie; Andro muligane in Dalaschcairnes; Thomas mcquhreyter in firroch; William thomsonne in Larg; Robert Stewart and Johne Mccoyde in Cardorkane; James M'Millane in firrochbae; Gilbert M'Kie, younger, in heliae; Williame Mezwale in Risk; Docane M'Kie in Markcove; Patrick M'Millane and John M'Ilwayane in Barlarge; William Mcdowall in Carsdoncane; Robert Mcchouchtie in Culgow; James Mccaddam in Laggane; Patrick Mcquhardge in nather Stronbae; John Mcclardge in glenhoyse; Jon Mcindric (?); Rot. M'Bryde in glenhoise; Jon. Mcquhardge in crouchlie; Jon. M'Millane in dricknaw; Andro. coutart in holme;

Jon and Patrick Stewarts in Caruuer; John tait in Drongaher; Thomas Simpson in Tochreline; Alexr. Stewart in Garlies; Andro findlay, younger, in laggane; James Allane Taylor in Carsnaw; John Mcclurdge in maggramore; Johne M'Dowall in Corsuall; Alexander M'Crakane in Caillgow; John M'Caa in drongandow; Alexr. Mcmulzerdoch and patrick taite in barony; Jon Dunell ther; Jon M'Jorrie, elder and younger, ther; Jon Mcrewa ther. Ita est Laurence gray notarius publicus.

Glasgow Determination on back signed by—

John Mcquharg; Mr. William Maxwell; Hew Stewart; J. Dunbar; —— Stewart; Patrick M'Kie; Alexr. Stewart; James Steuart; Alexr. Mcquharg; Andro Herron; Alexr. Roxburgh; Johne Keillie.*

The question in the early part of this article as to what has become of other printed copies of the Covenant similar to the one at Cardoness suggests a like question about the Covenants signed in the Parishes of Galloway, for there were undoubtedly other

---

* In endeavouring to decipher the signatures to the Covenants at Cardoness, the writer had before him the result of the labours to the same end of Mr. G. W. Shirley, Dumfries, than whom none is better fitted for such a task. As will be readily understood this proved of inestimable value, and the opportunity is gladly embraced to cordially thank Mr. Shirley for his hearty co-operation in the matter.

Covenants signed in Galloway besides those at Borgue and Minnigaff. What has become of them? Probably some of them were deliberately destroyed by both sides during the persecution; others may have been carried abroad by the Covenanters and lost; and there is just the possibility that one or two may yet be found in the Charter Chests of the local lairds.

INDEX.

Adair, Andrew, of Genoch, 219
—— Robert, of Kilhilt, 71, 76, 78, 80, 82, 83
Agnew, Alexander, 71, 92
—— Andrew, 70, 77, 78, 82, 86, 91, 128, 147, 162, 189, 215, 244, 258, 259
—— James, 71, 77, 215
—— Patrick, 45, 78, 82, 83
Aitken, Bishop, 176, 254
Alison, Adam, of Balmaghie, 97, 99, 100
Anna, Countess of Wigton, 144
Anwoth, 300
Apologetical Declaration, 236
Archibald, John, Stranraer, 201
Arnot, Captain, 81, 266, 277
—— David, of Barcaple, 61, 93, 355
—— Samuel, 97, 99, 108, 114, 124, 126, 153, 157, 158, 166, 274, 391
—— William, of Little-park, 103, 104
Arrol, John, 154
Auchencloy, 242, 314
Auchenleck, William, shot, 237
Ayr Covenant, 33
Ayrsmoss, 184

Bannatyne, Sir William, 121, 122, 128, 132
Barholm Coves, 459
Barscobe (M'Clelland), 142, 203, 285
Beeth Hill, 142
Bell of Whiteside, 174, 187, 301, 303, 382
Bennock, John, shot, 246
Blackaddar, John, 97, 108, 114, 142, 143, 146, 390, 396
Blair, John, of Dunskey, 153
Borgue Covenant, 460
Bothwell Bridge, 162
Brown, Abbot, 30

Brown of Priesthill, 324
Buglass, John, Crossmichael, 97, 99, 108

Caldwell of Caldwell, 124, 126,
Caldons, 351, 400
Cameron, Michael, 179
—— Richard, 179, 184
Cannon, of Mardrochwood, 124, 125, 136, 144, 166, 175, 1
Cant, John, 97, 99, 100, 108, 145, 222
Cardoness, Covenants at, 464, 4
Cardyness, Lady, 356
Cargill, Donald, 162
Carson, John, of Borgue, 87, 104, 140, 240
Carstairs, John, 124, 126, 274
Cassillis, Earl of, 27, 35, 45, 58, 75, 78, 79, 80, 82, 86, 110, 259
Clachan of Penninghame, Court 212
Clanochan, John, Stranraer, 20
Clark, John, of Carsphairn, 366
—— Samuel, of New Luce, 367
Claverhouse, 162, 166, 184, 1 196, 213, 304
Clement, James, shot, 303, 306
Clement, John, 371
Cochranes, of Waterside and Oc tree, 210, 222, 223, 228, 249
Coltraine, Provost of Wigtown, 2 259
Conventicle at Glenvogie, 110
Corsan, John, 240
Cowper, Bishop of Galloway, 60
Craighlaw, 249
Craigmoddie, 386

Dalry Rising, 116, 262
Dalrymple, Sir James, 71, 86, 18 207, 243, 245
—— Sir John, 193, 206, 259, 260

Dempster, John, tailor, 372
Douglas, Colonel, at Caldons, 402
Drumclog, 162
Dun, James, 400
—— Robert, 400
—— Roger, 403, 405
Dunbar, Archbishop, 27
—— David, Baldoon, 78, 86, 209, 237, 246
—— May, Baldoon, 402
—— of Machermore, 157, 174, 187, 224, 344, 359
—— of Mochrum, 78, 79, 86
Durie, Bishop of Galloway, 28

Earlston Castle, 38, 121, 122, 335
—— estate, 249
—— (see Gordon), 356
Edgar, Robert, 246
Ewart, John, Provost of Kirkcudbright, 102, 104, 259
—— William, Provost of Kirkcudbright, 102

Ferguson, David, drowned, 380, 381
—— John, of Weewoodhead, 365
—— Robert, shot, 315
—— of Hallhill, 322
Fines in Galloway, 91
Five Articles of Perth, 60
Fleming, Robert, 203
Forsyth, Andrew, 361
—— William, 124, 126, 274
Fraser, John, 185, 366, 369
Freugh, garrison, 177, 187
—— House, 83, 151
Fugitive Roll for Galloway, 223
Fullerton of Carlton, 93, 354, 356, 360

Galloway, Earl of, 62, 71, 75, 77, 82, 83, 86, 87, 88, 106, 127, 128, 147, 189, 259, 354
—— flail, 382
—— horse at Bothwell, 162
Garlies, Lord (see Stewart), 61, 76, 78, 86, 87
Garthland, Laird of, 75, 76, 79, 82, 141, 259
Gibson, John, shot, 246

Glendinning, George, Mochru 355-7
—— Robert, Kirkcudbright, 63
—— William, Kirkcudbright, 72, 78
Gordon, Alexander, of Airds, 75, 87, 93, 155
Gordons of Airds and Earlst 70, 164, 165, 174, 187, 249, 3 336, 344, 354
Gordon of Cardoness, 354
Gordons of Craighlaw, 76, 78, 157, 174, 215, 249, 344
—— of Culvennan, 157, 174, 34
—— of Dundeugh, 111, 144, 1 188, 231
Gordons of Garrary, 123, 125, 1 188, 229, 273
—— of Holm, 111, 121, 125, 1 144, 154, 175, 188, 273
Gordon of Kenmure (see Kenmu 453
Gordons of Knockbrex, 70, 72, 122, 144, 145, 175, 267, 277, 35
—— of Knockgray, 81, 93, 1 355, 357
—— of Largmore, 375
Gordon of Shirmers, 87, 94, 1 357
—— Edward, hanged, 331
—— John, Stranraer, 92, 106
—— —— shot, 329
Graham (see Claverhouse)
—— David, brother to Clav house, 185, 200, 215, 221, 2 246
—— James, Crossmichael, mart 237
—— William, Crossmichael, m tyr, 237, 449
—— John, Dalry, executed, 28
Grier of Balmaclellan, 123, 125,
—— John, shot, 315
—— (son) of Lagg, 75, 186, 2 246, 257
—— the spy, 282
—— (son) John, executed, 278
Grierson, Robert, Lochenkit, 3
—— of Balmaclellan, 246, 450
—— Bargattan, 78, 87, 89, 94, 3 356

INDEX.

Hallam, John, executed, 243
Halliday, David, Glengap, martyr, 228, 248, 304
—— David, Mayfield, martyr, 303
Hannay, Michael, 219
Harlow, William, 27
Hays of Ariolland, 79, 145, 175, 224, 225
—— of Park, 76, 78, 153, 155, 157, 232, 234, 259
Heron, Barglass, 425
—— Grange of Cree, 429, 433
—— of Kirroughtree, 87, 94, 204-7
—— of Littlepark, 157, 175, 188
—— William, martyr, 329
Highland Host, 147, 148
Houston, Cutreoch, 79
Hunter, Colquhassan, 175, 224
—— William, martyr, 318

Indemnity, 81, 91
Indulgence, 139
Inglis, John, Kirkcudbright, 157
Ingleston martyrs, 246, 450
Irongray Communion, 389
—— rioting, 101

Johnstone, Stranraer, 92, 157
Johnstone, William, Wigtown martyr, 441

Kay, Adam, minister, Borgue, 81, 97, 99, 100
Kenmure Castle burned, 38, 83
—— garrison, 177, 222
—— Lady, 453
—— Viscount, 62, 75, 77, 82, 87, 128, 189, 237, 246, 257, 259, 287, 354, 453
Kennedy, Quintin, 34
—— Barnkirk, 224
Kirk's martyrdom, 282
Kirkandrews martyr, 384
Kirkconnel moor, 303
Kirkcudbright Burgh Records, 383
—— Lord, 62, 71, 72, 75, 76, 77, 81, 82, 87, 89, 102
—— Presbytery, 89
—— rioting, 101
Kirkinner sufferings, 447
Kirkwood, curate of Sanquhar, 311

Knox, 25, 33, 459
Kyan, Edward, martyr, 245
Kyle, William, captured, 161

Lagg, Laird of, 61, 237, 257, 30
Laing, Patrick, of Blagannoch,
Learmont, Major, 123, 124, 1 203, 266, 273
Lennox of Cally, 354, 356
—— Robert, of Irelandton, mar 174, 188, 303
Lex Rex, 85, 295
Lidderdale, St. Mary's Isle, 186, 203, 212, 221
Linn, Alexander, martyr, 3?6
Listoun in Calder, 123, 124, 1 273
Livingston of Quintenspie, 95, 9 356, 357
—— minister, Stranraer, 68, 81, 83, 457
Lochenkit, 325
Lochinvar, Lord of, 62
Lochnaw, Laird of, 189, 257
—— and Highland Host, 151
Lorne, Lord, favours Rutherf 291
Luce Abbey, 31
Lyon, curate of Urr, 141

Machermore garrison, 222, 249
Malcolm, John, executed, 185,
Martin, Andrew, Little Airies, 425
—— of Dullarg, 94, 208, 234, 9 356
Mary, Queen, in Galloway, 32,
Maxwell, Gabriel, 124, 126, 274
—— Lord, 47, 77, 146
—— Margaret, Barwhannie, 43
—— of Cavens, 354, 355, 358
—— Milton, 93, 235
—— Monreith, 97, 123, 124, 9 273, 275, 277
—— of Munches, 87, 106, 126
—— William, Monygaff, 97
Milroys of Kirkcalla, 441, 442,
Minnigaff Covenant, 464
—— garrison, 222
Mitchell, Robert, martyr, 246, 3
Mowatt, martyr, 386

Muir of Cassincarrie, 355, 360
—— Henry, Kirkcudbright, 153
Muirhead, Bailie, 374
—— James, executed, 282
Murray of Broughton, 76, 78, 86, 87, 145, 161

Macadam, Gilbert, Waterhead, 111, 133, 141, 142
Macartney of Blackit, 93, 144, 155, 175, 188, 451
M'Briar, John, Cannon, 28
—— David, Irongray, 374
M'Bryde, Anthony, Stranraer, 201
M'Call, John, executed, 282
—— Andrew, martyr, 400
M'Clelland, Balmagaichan, 123, 124, 125, 144, 145, 174, 188, 273
—— Barscobe, 123, 124, 125, 144, 165, 175, 188, 203, 264
M'Clive, James, Glentrool martyr, 400
M'Culloch of Ardwell, 78, 86, 91, 94, 175, 188, 226
—— of Barholm, 93, 144, 145, 164, 277
—— of Myreton, 45, 78, 210, 215, 237, 246
M'Clurg, the Minnigaff smith, 197, 224
—— shoots a spy, 382
M'Dowalls of Freugh, 76, 78, 86, 147, 153, 154, 157, 165, 173, 174, 187, 344
M'Dowall of Garthland, 48, 62, 76, 153, 215
M'Dowal of Logan, 76, 86, 256
M'Ewmont, William, banished, 212
M'Ghie, Anthony, Glencaird, 205
—— of Larg (see M'Kie)
M'Gill, David, Dalry, 121
M'Kie of Larg, 72, 92, 174, 198, 246, 334, 354
M'Kechnie, John, shot, 314
M'Lauchlane, Margaret, Wigtown martyr, 410
Macleanochan, John, imprisoned, 201
M'Meekan, Miltonise, 153, 154
M'Michael, James, 383
—— James, 312, 313, 314

M'Michan, John, Dalry, 97, 100, 138, 145, 222, 338
M'Millan, William, Caldow, 9 347, 351, 374
M'Millans, 347-353
M'Naught, Cumnock, 125, 273
—— Dalry, 123, 125, 273
M'Quhan, Adam, shot, 247
M'Robert, Andrew, martyr, 3 305, 382
M'Roy, Half Mark, shot, 375
M'Whae, Robert, martyr, 384

Naismith, minister, Stranraer,
Napier, Sheriff, on Wigtown r tyrs, 416
Nelson of Corsock, 144, 154, 188, 225, 265, 278
Newburn, 72
New Galloway, Court at, 178
Nithsdale, Lord, 61, 87, 128, 162
Nonconformist ministers in G way, 96

Ochiltree estate annexed to Crown, 249
Osborne, John, Keir, 114, 115
Outed ministers, 100, 121

Park, John, Stranraer, 88, 98, 139, 146
Patriarch, The, 336
Peden, 98, 99, 114, 115, 124, 126, 253, 270, 274, 319, 442
Penninghame, 57, 212
—— sufferings, 446
Pentland (see Dalry rising)
Perth, Articles of, 60
Philiphaugh, 77
Pierson, curate of Carsphairn, 312, 313
Poe, David, Pokelly, 124, 126,
Porterfield, John, Duchal, 249
—— Quarrelton, 123, 124, 223, 274
Presbyteries and Synods fixed
Printed Covenant, 466
Privy Council and Galloway r ters, 98
Proclamation against rebels,
Protestors, 81

INDEX.

Queensberry, Earl of, 62, 72, 176, 189

Ramsay of Boghouse, 92, 157
Ravenston, Laird of, 147, 166
Reddick, John, Dalbeattie, 355, 359
Register of Synod of Galloway, 107
Renwick, 254, 344, 362, 378
Resolutioners, 81
Roan, Stroanpatrick, 313
Ross, minister, Kirkcowan, 97, 98, 253
Row, curate, Balmaclellan, 140, 154
Rullion Green, chapter xxx., 271
Rutherfurd, George, 299
—— Samuel, 63, 70, 81, 286, 287, 290

Sanquhar Declarations, 179, 247
Scaur, 144, 394
Scott, David, Irongray, 123, 125, 273
Semple, Gabriel, 97, 100, 114, 124, 145, 153, 157, 158, 166, 274, 340, 456
—— John, Carsphairn, 81, 85, 97, 124, 126, 145, 146, 274
Short, George, martyr, 248
—— John, Dalry, executed, 282
Smith, James, executed, 282
—— Robert, martyr, 318
Societies, The, 178
Spanish Blanks, 50
Stevenson, Glentrool, martyr, 400
Stewart of Castle-Stewart, 86, 244
—— of Garlies (see Garlies), 26, 27, 40, 48, 83
—— of Tonderghie, 79, 106
—— Robert, Ardoch, 111, 315, 316
—— William, martyr, 329
Stewartry War Committee, 354
Sword, Andrew, 167, 188
Sydeserf, Bishop, 64, 65, 69
Synod of Galloway, 88, 261 ; Register of, 107

Thomson, Thomas, minister, 97, 99, 145, 340

Thorburn (Torbran), Stranraer, 210, 225
Threave Castle, 341
Turner, Sir James, 115, 128, 136, 263
Twynholm, 213, 238

Urr parishioners fined, 140
Urquhart's dream and death, 1
Ussher, Archbishop, 288

Vans, Vaus, Barnbarroch, 48, 78
Vans, Patrick, Sorbie, 113
—— Robert, Drumblair, 145
Vaus, Patrick, Mochrum, 224

Walker, George, 441
Wallace, Colonel James, 123, 125, 264, 266, 273
—— John, New-Luce, 201, 25
—— John, martyr, 329
Warner, Patrick, 254
—— (Vernor), Thomas, 97, 98, 145, 156, 228
Welsh of Cornlee, 123, 125, 175, 188, 273
—— of Scar, 123, 125, 226, 394
—— John, Irongray, 97, 114, 124, 126, 145, 146, 153, 157, 274
—— John, Kirkcudbright, 57
—— William, martyr, 278, 281
Whitehead, Millhouse, 93, 175
Wigtown, Countess of, 144
—— Earl of, 58, 59, 60, 61, 66, 74, 75, 79, 144, 157
—— martyrs, 406, 445
Wigtownshire Lairds refuse Test, 215
—— War Committee, 78
Wilkie, John, 97, 99, 100, 108,
Wilson, Agnes, 409
—— Margaret, 407
Wilsons of Glenvernoch, 408
Wylie, Thomas, Kirkcudbright, 91, 97
Wynram, Major, at Wigtown,

WS - #0036 - 190221 - C0 - 229/152/26 - PB - 9781332343614